LITTLE DID YOU KNOW

The Confessions of
David McGillivray

An Autobiography

*For Harriet
You'll never speak
to me again

David
McGillivray
x*

FAB
PRESS

LITTLE DID YOU KNOW
THE CONFESSIONS OF DAVID MCGILLIVRAY

First edition published by FAB Press, May 2019

FAB Press Ltd., 2 Farleigh, Ramsden Road
Godalming, Surrey, GU7 1QE, England, U.K.

www.fabpress.com

Text copyright © 2019 David McGillivray.
The moral rights of the author have been asserted.

Layout and Design by Harvey Fenton.

World Rights Reserved by FAB Press Ltd.

A CIP catalogue record for this book is available from the British Library.

ISBN 978 1 913051 00 6

Printed and bound in Great Britain by Bell & Bain Ltd, Glasgow

For Pip Madgwick,
who has tried to keep me out of trouble.

*"Everything's got a moral,
if only you can find it."*
~ Lewis Carroll ~

CONTENTS

DISCLAIMER

The inclusion of a person's name or likeness in this book does not imply that the person has at any time bought, traded or accepted as a gift an illegal drug from the author or has used an illegal drug from any source. Some names and identifying features have been changed.

PART 1

OVERVIEW
(1947-2015)

I

"A lie has a short life."
~ Brazilian proverb ~

If I had watched myself growing up, I would have been in no doubt how I was going to turn out. According to my mother, I could read and write before I went to school. Some of my earliest memories are of the excitement I got from a fantastic story, and the pleasure of stringing words together myself. When my class at Hazelwood Primary School in Palmers Green, north London, was badly behaved, composition was given out as a punishment. But it wasn't a punishment to me.

At the age of four and a half, I was taken to see the film *Singin' in the Rain*. I decided afterwards that I didn't want to be a shopkeeper when I grew up; I wanted to be a film star. But while I was writing to Doris Day and Rosemary Clooney for their autographs, and playing the role of David McGillivray, his life filmed by secret cameras, I maintained the shopkeeper mentality that, presumably, was what Napoleon so despised in the English. I wanted absolute control of my little street-corner empire, I liked everything in nice neat piles, and I counted every penny.

Puberty played an unoriginal but none the less impressive joke on my hormones. As one who has spent most of his professional life writing comedy, I can now appreciate it: the boy who wanted Doris Day as his girlfriend was turned, almost overnight, into the teenager who didn't want a girlfriend at all. As I saw it, this metamorphosis occurred just as every other boy at Winchmore Secondary Modern had been blessed with the desire to spend playtime with his hand down some girl's knickers. We were all sex mad at fourteen, but I thought I was the only one not getting any sex.

It was sexual frustration that sent me into a world of my own. As much time as possible was spent watching other people have sex in cinemas. Before you ask, yes, on the screen and in the auditorium. At school, fuelled by the rebellious behaviour I saw in the 'X' certificate films I wasn't supposed to be watching, I stopped wearing school uniform, and wrote rude things about the teachers in a magazine I edited and duplicated myself.

My classmates in forms X and Y, the so-called 'grammar stream' at Winchmore, were intrigued by me, but most of them were too bright to be manipulated by me. The power I craved was wielded over the rough boys in the A, B, C and D forms, many of whom could barely read or write, and some of whom, refugees from the conflict in Cyprus, could barely speak English. Nobody else from the grammar stream mixed with this hybrid underclass, so my leadership was unopposed. The rough boys got up to very rough things indeed.

I began taking drugs when I was sixteen.

Today I wonder whether anyone else who knew me as a child predicted that I would end up a bossy, anally retentive, gay drug dealer with a penchant for pornography. And then write about it. If anyone knew my destiny, they didn't tell me. The man who came closest to defining my true character was Mr Phillips, my form teacher when I was eleven. He wrote in my report, 'David is a complete individualist and is reluctant to conform with the rest of the class.'

'He's got you in one,' sneered my father when he read this assessment. I was incensed. 'I am *not* an individualist!' I screamed at him. Well, naturally I did. I was eleven years old and I saw no appeal in being different. I wanted to be like everyone else. That's what we are rewarded for. I lost marks for refusing to conform. And I made myself miserable into the bargain. Now, as an old codger, when it's far too late, I could not be prouder that I was singled out as different at such a young age.

There was never the slightest chance of my hormonal imbalance being recognised by teachers and channelled into something creative, like the National Youth Theatre or an amateur ciné club. Harry Shepherd, martinet headmaster at Winchmore, was a scientist with no interest in the arts, only a determination to achieve more GCE exam passes than rival grammar schools.

I was not much help to him here. Because nothing I was being taught was going to be of any use when I became a film star, I didn't listen. Consequently I managed only four 'O' level passes and wouldn't have got these if I hadn't cheated. I never took another exam because Shepherd expelled me for persistently ridiculing Mr Brown, the Australian maths master, in my magazine.

I have always been a great believer in the realistic approach to life demonstrated in *The Wizard of Oz*. (You don't need a brain; you need a diploma to make people think you have a brain.) Therefore, when I was pushed out of school into the real world with insufficient qualifications, I decided to give myself some better ones. First of all I awarded myself six 'O' levels and two 'A' levels, which seemed reasonable. As you may know, I never became a film star but, through writing connections, I gave a few performances of sorts, mostly in Fringe theatre, and became embarrassed by being the only actor in the company who had never been to drama school. Consequently I invented a post-graduate course at London's Guildhall School of Music and Drama, followed by an apprenticeship at the Intimate Theatre, Palmers Green.

Finally, because influential people at parties never questioned anything I told them, I began dropping into conversations the lie that I had an M.A. Cantab. (I was mixing with more and more graduates and I liked to make them feel comfortable that I was one of them.) All in all, I have had the benefit of a very fine education, and sometimes I have to stop and remind myself that none of it exists.

The life to which I have hitherto lent my name has been a tissue of lies because lies brought me everything I wanted. I still tell acolytes, 'When in doubt, bluff,' because a silly little truth, told without regard for the consequences, can cause so much pain. Not only have I lied about academic qualifications, I also have lied about what I do in bed. Prior to this memoir, something like the truth has been given on a need-to-know basis. Originally it was my goddamned virginity that was the big secret; later, and especially while I was writing heterosexual pornography, it was my homosexuality. No way was I going to make myself the subject of the kind of ridicule I was all too keen to dish out to others.

Ah, but there comes a time when the need to confess is compounded by the fear that someone else will spill the beans first, or get it all wrong after my death. I regret that the truth will hurt the remains of my family and most of the friends with whom I grew up and a few nice old ladies in Southwold and King's Lynn. After all, I seemed like a nice boy and a lot of what I have written has been such gentle and affectionate comedy; in fact those were the very words used by *The Guardian* about one of my plays. Perhaps at this point I should stress that I haven't changed. I'm just telling the truth. And also bear in mind that, if all this could happen to me, and I was a nice boy, it could happen to you. If you have a taste for adventure.

Ian Dury summarised my life so succinctly when he wrote the song 'Sex and Drugs and Rock 'n' Roll.' He even got the elements in the right order. Sorry, Southwold, but I've got sex on the brain. I present the acceptable face of the sex maniac. Everything I do, every decision I make, every thought I have, every waking hour, there is only one driving force, and one goal: sex. This is not an exaggeration. I used to shop at Marks and Spencer because the checkout staff was better looking. I still look at the crotches of cartoon characters.

The first 35 years of my life were spent in pursuit of unattainable sex objects and, since I wised up, my entire career has been inextricably linked with those I have had sex with or sold drugs to. I became a drug dealer because the man with whom I was living suggested we go into business together. Although I implied (mainly to dissuade an undesirable element) that there was no sex at the cocaine parties, which raged at my house for five years, in fact a new, desperate, drug-crazed relationship developed every few weeks. And sometimes, when I presented a client, perhaps at Broadcasting House, perhaps at the Houses of Parliament, with a beautifully wrapped packet of 80% pure Charlie, he was so pleased he dropped his trousers.

Rock 'n' roll – well, actually, music of every type, with the exception of country and western – has been the soundtrack to the whole jamboree. My favourite form of music is the dirge. I like musical phrases to be repeated again and again, as in, inevitably, Ravel's 'Bolero.' 'It's got no tune!' my parents would moan. House music was invented specifically with me in mind.

I'm a dark horse; there's probably no dispute about that among my intimate friends. But the people who lived next door, and the cousins in Whitley Bay, and the other members of Trent Players, must have known I wasn't snogging in front of the telly every night with Miss Right. So what did they think I was doing instead? I dropped clues, mostly unintentionally, from childhood. And now they appear to me to be pretty easy to interpret.

II

"I think she [Stevie Smith] went to Palmers Green
before she flew off to death."
~ Kay Dick ~

I am the product of a mixed marriage. My father came from the north of England and my mother came from Essex. I think they loved each other originally, but probably what kept them together during the first few years of marriage in London was a shared desire to be middle-class. My mother had almost achieved it because her father was in insurance. But my father told stories about going to school with no shoes, and of other boys shitting on the floor of the cinema during the film, and life up north sounded grim. I surrendered to middle-class affluence without a second thought but, throughout my life, a force has continued to pull me back to the gutter where I belong.

If what I suffer from is an identity crisis – Who am I? Where do I belong? – this is because I was never sure of my relatives' names. My father claimed not to know whether he was registered at birth as 'Donald' or 'Don,' but I rarely heard him referred to as anything but 'Mac.' My mother didn't like her given name, Winifred, and called herself 'Wynne,' but my father called her 'Pete' because her maiden name was Peterson. After my father died, she gave herself yet another name, Pat (and a new personality to match). Not to be outdone, her sister Gladys decided to call herself Catherine. ('Whenever there's a really thick, common girl on TV,' she explained, 'she's always called Gladys.')

I was born in one of two rented rooms at 217, Gipsy Road, which is actually in the south London suburb of West Norwood, although subsequently, to give myself street cred, I downgraded my birthplace to nearby Brixton. The photographs, kept in a biscuit tin, of Egypt, where my parents met during World War II, kept me occupied for hours. Before the war, my father had worked in a shop, the Maypole Dairy, inspiring my early ambition, and my mother had been a secretary. After joining the RAF, they were posted to Alexandria, where they had a great war pen-pushing, and never heard a shot fired. I couldn't understand why the attractive couple in the pictures was so much happier posing under the sun in a strange land than living with me in London.

It wasn't as if anything I suffered while living at home could now be dignified with the word 'abuse.' But my parents rowed constantly, and the threat of physical violence hung in the air like a storm cloud. I was terrified of my father when he shouted and swore, threw his plate of roast beef and two veg across the room, threatened to leave us and go back up north, and periodically did. I only saw him embrace my mother once, and I felt discomfort. 'That looked just like a film,' I told them. I didn't know that romance existed outside the cinema.

Because I had come along after the Egyptian photographs, I decided that I was the cause of all the trouble. 'Your father worships the ground you walk on,' my mother tried to assure me, but I was not convinced. If he loved me, he had a funny way of showing it. I found it difficult to sleep at night because I thought my father would know as soon as I closed my eyes and take this opportunity to come into my room and kill me. Later, I revealed this to my mother. 'That's not right,' she said glumly. On the whole I got on with her. After I decided not to follow in my father's footsteps, I picked up her love of the arts. She had done some amateur acting in her youth, and sometimes we went to the pictures together.

The local state schools were too rough, my mother decided, and so I was enrolled, aged five, at Fidelis, a Catholic girls' school, which also accepted young boys. 'We're not Catholic,' my mother warned the nuns. We weren't anything much, as far as religion was concerned, and something happened at Fidelis to turn me against all religion for life. I don't know what occurred, and now I don't think I ever want to find out. But, to this day, a vague image – something to do with nuns, a dark corridor, coat-hooks and shoe-bags – occasionally insinuates itself fleetingly between more familiar sex fantasies, and shocks me into a state of intense loneliness. Whatever I experienced in the bowels of Fidelis, it had its purpose: I can now indulge my baser instincts without fear of divine retribution.

When I was six, my parents grabbed their chance to jump several rungs up the social ladder. My maternal grandmother's sister, Auntie Blanche, lived in a room in a house in Palmers Green and told us that the top two floors were available to rent. We left West Norwood, where there were too many poor people, and escaped north of the Thames to the heart of suburbia, where there weren't enough. Palmers Green in the 1950s was quaite naice, the place where Stevie Smith wasn't waving but drowning, while Winchmore Hill, the next suburb up the road, where I went to secondary school, was basically posh. The comedian Ted Ray lived there, in an avenue dubbed 'Millionaires' Row.' We were out of our league, and I was mortified to have schoolfriends richer than I was.

I don't know how my father managed to support our new lifestyle on the pittance he received as a sales clerk for the British Iron and Steel Corporation. My mother had given up work. Then along came my brother, Paul. I hated him as soon as I saw him, blue and shrivelled, minutes out of the womb. I suspected he was a rival for my position as the family's (literally) blue-eyed boy. So when he smiled up at me from his cot, I slapped him round the face and made him cry, and later I tried to push him down the stairs.

I was struck down for my wickedness by measles so severe that I carried physical and psychological damage well into my twenties and perhaps beyond. As I understand it, I took to my bed a stocky little fella and arose six weeks later a pigeon-chested, spindle-shanked streak of piss. It was clear to me that I would never be able to take off my clothes in public again, and I didn't for many, many years, thus giving my father another reason to berate me. 'Roll your sleeves up!' he ordered each spring. 'Get some sun on your body!' What lay ahead was decades of tedious physical exercise until finally I was ready for sun, sand and sex.

Something told me very early on that I was not going to make it as a film star. Consequently I shifted my attention from Doris Day and Hollywood to the small part players in British comedy films, the drones who appeared in one shot to say things like 'Mr Smith will see you now, sir' and 'No one goes up to the castle after dark.' I thought this job was more in keeping with my limited ability and deformed appearance. I tracked two of these actors, Michael Ward and Marianne Stone, through dozens of minor films, little realising that I would meet them forty years later and that they would have a profound effect on my life.

I cannot remember a thing I learned at Hazelwood Primary because I spent each week nervously anticipating the last period on Friday afternoon, when we did 'drama.' This consisted of kids getting up in front of the class to perform improvised sketches usually planned a few hours earlier during the lunch break. I was normally first on my feet with my tomboy friend Anne Jacklin and – wouldn't you know it? – she played the boy and I played the girl. One afternoon Mrs Young asked us why we did that. 'David's very good at playing girls,' piped up Anne. There's no answer to that when you're eight.

I decided that the afternoon would benefit from a professional-style production. I wrote a sketch, set in a film studio, gave myself the lead (a director named Pompous Fatilia, probably because I so wanted to be fat), cast friends in other roles, and rehearsed them for weeks in the playground. After the performance Mrs Pates, who was a frustrated actress herself, didn't believe that I had written a real script or that we had actually learned lines and moves. She got us to go through the piece again. When she saw that it was indeed word-for-word as before, she was very impressed. I glowed. I was about nine.

Among those in my class who later made careers in the arts were Mervyn Stutter, who became a stand-up comedian, and Christopher Beale, Channel 4's press officer until his sudden death in 1998. But at the time I was at Hazelwood, the only other boy who wanted to act was Philip Sandell, and so he was my kindred spirit. Like me, he was something of an extrovert;

unlike me, he loved getting his willy out. We played proto-sexual games at the back of the class, round at his place, and in his garden shed, and the main consequence was that I learned how to masturbate, not that I recognised what I was doing by that word.

Philip and I didn't desire each other in the slightest, but there were other boys, not to mention a few grown men (Ty Hardin, who played a TV cowboy called Bronco Layne, springs to mind) that I was beginning to take a fancy to. The reward for enduring detested swimming lessons was watching Max Chandler, who had come to Hazelwood from romantic-sounding Canada, taking his trunks off. Somewhat predictably, I failed my 11 Plus exam, and went to Winchmore Secondary Modern a fully-fledged outsider.

Philip Sandell never became an actor. Max Chandler was killed in a road accident when he was thirteen. He was the first person I knew who died.

III

"I was fuelled by strange desires, revenge being only one of them."
~ Holly Johnson ~

Most of the male teachers at Winchmore were sadists the like of which I had never encountered. The slightest infringement of the rules was met with an old-fashioned clip round the ear, a dull thud that left your head spinning and would today, quite rightly, land the perpetrator in court. The worst of these Nazi swine was Mr Driver, the history master, with a granite face as severe as his name. Inevitably he was known as Slave Driver. I saw only one brave child stand up to this monster, and that was my new friend, Dirinda Pierotti.

Dirinda was a bright, wild child with a shockingly dirty mind and mouth. One afternoon, she grabbed hold of my bollocks in the Barrowell Green swimming pool. Winsome she was not, nor sexy, and so the strutting young bucks on the school football team steered well clear of her. I stood in as her boyfriend. Driver was always keeping us in after school. At the end of one such detention, he ordered, 'Put the chairs on the desks, Pierotti,' and she retorted, 'Do it yourself, Driver.' The earth stood still, and then Driver slapped Dirinda round the face, hard. She just returned his glare, and didn't cry.

If I could live my life again, the only thing I would change would be my cowardly neutrality at that moment. Instead of cringing in horror, I should have leaped to my feet and floored the repugnant little tyrant with one blow. I was already taller than he was, and at the very least I could have given him something he would remember with a shudder for the rest of his life. Plus I was due to be expelled anyway, and the punishment should have been for something worthwhile.

I think I told Dirinda years later that I fought for her in spirit. She became a prominent member of my gang, mostly comprising the dimwits in the 'A' and 'B' streams, except that they weren't dimwits by my standards. David Bubb was a brilliantly witty comedian, and he and his crazier sidekick, David José, made a great double act. Roger O'Gorman was whimsically funny. Dirinda was outrageous. These comics needed an audience, and that was Christine Lemon, who was in love with me, Christine's friend Janice Millard, and Janice's boyfriend Jeffrey Heap. I brought these complementary personalities together and I organised most of our exploits. There was tacit acceptance, therefore, that I was the leader. This was the first of many gangs I formed throughout my life, the most recent of which consisted of more than three hundred dope fiends who came to me for drugs and entertainment at my house in London's King's Cross.

Because we were in different classes, the Winchmore gang existed only in the evenings, at weekends, and during school holidays. In the language of earlier generations, 'We made our own entertainment,' in this case a combination of loitering, parties and minor vandalism. I remember breaking into a derelict house and taking photographs of each other 'ghost hunting,' and I recall we found an empty garage and threw a party in it. We were always throwing parties. The youth culture that had died when Elvis went into the army in 1958 had exploded again, this time on our side of the Atlantic, with the birth of the Beatles in 1963, and we were bonded by the clothes we wore and the records we took to parties.

None of the Winchmore gang was a mod or a rocker, but the mod influence was very strong. I was captivated in particular by the battles, between snappily-attired mods on Vespas and old-style ton-up boys on Harley-Davidsons, which wrecked seaside resorts each bank holiday. This pointless conflict widened the generation gap to an unbreachable gulf for the rest of the Sixties.

As kids, we felt privileged and smug that we knew weeks in advance which coastal town was going to be the next target, whereas our parents didn't. When I saw the press reports, written by old men who wondered why they'd fought in two world wars to save England for thugs like us, I desperately wanted to stake my personal claim against authority by kicking a policeman's helmet along the promenade. But I was too frightened of getting hurt. Violence, like sex, was something to be observed from a distance.

I listened enthralled to the tales told by kids who did fight on the front. I can remember exactly where I was standing in the playground when a boy told me he'd seen another boy in Margate selling purple hearts and black bombers. It doesn't matter that I am now almost certain, because those were the names of the amphetamines most often quoted in the press, that he was lying. This was a defining moment in my life.

The press had been getting very agitated about these awful mods selling each other uppers in dance halls and discotheques. I was intrigued. Wasn't every sixteen-year-old at the time? The stories – about London's most fashionable teenagers and the happy pills with names borrowed from the confectionery industry – sounded as though they had been concocted by an advertising agency. The drug trade had never seemed so glamorous.

But although I imagined being part of a trendy, wicked nightlife, cultural light years from prim and proper Palmers Green, I never once considered trying to break into it. I think that, by this time, most of the gang were smoking and drinking, but I don't remember the subject of anything stronger even coming up in conversation. Winchmore Secondary Modern was a drug-free zone.

Until the arrival of Randolph Cozens.

Randolph had trouble written all over him. He came from another town, he wore mod shirts with the points of the collars fastened by tabs, and he had long hair. He joined David Bubb's class, and David told me about this new kid, and the rumours about his sudden departure from his previous school. It was something to do with drugs and, what's more, he was still using them. To my delight, Randolph began to hang out with us.

I was very taken by the contrasting messages he sent out. He had a little elfin face and a slight speech defect, but also looked dangerous because of the hair down to his collar. No other boy at Winchmore had long hair. As soon as your hair began curling over your ears, you got a tap on the shoulder from the likes of Driver and the order to go to the barber. Grown-ups' fear of long hair in 1963 cannot be overestimated. When Randolph returned to school, day after day, with his locks unshorn, you can imagine how I admired him.

I showed him off to the rest of the school by casting him in a small role in the end of term concert, which I directed at Christmas, 1963. He was in a commercial for VO5 Holding Hair Spray. Having fully ingratiated myself, I then spent the Christmas holidays prowling Palmers Green, hoping to find him alone. One evening I spotted him in the Wimpy bar and went in and asked if I could buy a purple heart or a black bomber. To my mounting excitement he produced his stash in a Kensitas packet and sold me a pill that was neither purple nor heart-shaped for the exorbitant sum of two shillings and sixpence (12½p), half a week's pocket money. I offered not a word of complaint for fear of appearing unhip.

With naïveté that only Palmers Green could breed, I decided to use it almost immediately at the St Paul's Youth Club disco, but some incident prevented me from attending. Destiny, a force in which, in the absence of religion, I was to place increasing faith, had already planned a far better showcase for drug-induced frenzy, although she rather mischievously altered the course of my life in order to stage it. On 20th July, 1964, I was expelled from Winchmore Secondary Modern.

I can see now how I subconsciously collaborated with the mystic force in my own downfall. Mr Brown, the Australian maths master, already had warned me that, if there was any further mention of him in my magazine, there would be trouble. I responded to this challenge by filling what was to be the magazine's last edition with column upon column of the stupid remarks, e.g. 'Wright! What's your name?', Brown had made in class.

On the same morning that copies of my magazine were seen being read around the school, I was ordered into headmaster Shepherd's office for a very brief interview indeed. 'Get out of this school and don't come back!' he roared. I did get out, there and then, but my literary tidy-mindedness would not allow me to close an important chapter of my life so abruptly, without a satisfying conclusion. I knew I had to come back.

While my anguished parents argued with the headmaster, the deputy headmaster, and the Education Office, all to no avail, I secretly plotted to return to Winchmore for the summer dance. I reasoned that the male teachers, whose knowledge of popular music stopped at 'A Scottish Soldier' by Andy Stewart, would all be back home in Hertford and Bletchley before the dance began. But, as I walked towards the school gates, Randolph's pill producing my first surge of euphoria, I regretted that Shepherd himself wouldn't be on guard duty, because right now I wanted to tell him how *fabulous* it felt to be expelled!

There wasn't a sign of the male teachers, as my all-seeing eye had predicted. Two of the female teachers, however, greeted me quite cordially. My rising awareness of the truth of all things past and present told me why: they had a soft spot for me, because they viewed my difference as something positive.

I glided into the assembly hall, my skin and hair alive, knowing that my classmates would treat me like the celebrity I was, and of course they did. But I became irritated by their questions and, elsewhere, the arguments over which record was going to be played next, because I wanted to *dance!* I wanted to *show off!* And as soon as I heard something I liked, 'Needles and Pins' by the Searchers, I broke away and went into the hitch-hiker, a dance I saw Patrick Kerr and Theresa Confrey demonstrate on TV's *Ready, Steady, Go!* I danced like a well-oiled machine and I thought that sooner or later somebody was bound to ask me how I'd learned so well. What was I going to reply? I wanted to tell everyone I'd taken a purple heart, but I knew I couldn't.

My sense of self-preservation was so concrete-hard that even amphetamine could not chip at it. I knew exactly what I could and couldn't say and do. There was not the slightest chance of me flinging my arms around my first real inamorato, Kristofas Panayiotou, the most sullenly beautiful of the Greek Cypriots. But what I found in me was to become the heterosexual I'd been impersonating since puberty. I went up to Penny Davis and danced with her. There was no possibility of rejection since she was in love with me as well as Christine Lemon, and indeed, as I now realised, most of the girls in the hall.

It was time for the miming contest, something else inspired by *Ready, Steady, Go!,* and I clapped and cheered the girls who got up on stage to mime to Cilla Black's 'You're My World.' Then boys were asked to volunteer to mime to P.J. Proby's 'Hold Me.' I rushed forward, confident I would wipe the floor with the competition, but found there wasn't any. The boys didn't want to do anything so nancy. Finally a rather jolly prefect called Roger Buse came up to challenge me, and we launched into the raucous number, me word-perfect and giving an exact impersonation of the American singer's snake-hipped, constipated style. But Roger won the prize because the judges were his fellow prefects.

The dance was probably over by nine or ten, but for me it was just a prelude to a night on the town starring me as the life and soul of the party. I couldn't understand why my friends were faffing around, trying to decide where to move on to, and eventually I wandered off again, out of the school and into the high street, where I became intensely interested in the contents of the electricity showroom.

The next time I looked at my watch, I realised I had missed the last bus, and stuck my thumb out for a lift because I had seen this done in films. After a while a young, black businessman in a comfortable car picked me up. 'I didn't think anyone was going to stop,' I told him. 'I saw you about five minutes ago,' the man replied, 'but I drove round the block and came back to make sure you weren't a villain.'

'But I *am* a villain!' I protested. 'I've just been expelled from school!' He laughed and put his hand on my leg, which I thought was very friendly. By this time we were in Palmers Green and I asked the man to let me out, thereby thwarting my first gay sexual encounter. My mother was waiting up for me, which she had never done before. I thought, 'She knows everything,' and tried to act natural. She gave no sign of knowing anything. 'But it's one o'clock and she's not in bed!' my brain insisted. I didn't sleep a wink that night.

I saw Randolph Cozens several times after I left school, but he was always with mates I didn't know, and so my experience on his 'doob' was never discussed. I next saw his name on the front page of the *Palmers Green and Southgate Gazette*. He had appeared in court after being arrested for trying to throw himself in front of cars on the North Circular Road. According to reports, he had a history of mental illness. I so wanted to know everything. But I never got the opportunity to ask. The rumour circulated that he killed himself in 1969 at the age of 22. The invaluable BMD site has no record of this death, only that a Randolph Cozens of the right age died in London in 2003.

Whatever the case, I learned years after our momentous encounter in the Wimpy bar that the street value of a purple heart in 1964 was no more than a shilling (5p).

IV

"The only love that lasts forever is unrequited."
~ Woody Allen ~

Freed from my genius tutelary, I scanned the pages of the theatrical newspaper, *The Stage*, and answered an advertisement headed, 'Teenagers wanted to train for the stage.' At her house in Fulham, a nicely-spoken auntie named Vivienne Guignard made it clear she charged for her services. I didn't have any money, so that was the end of that. 'You have a nice, direct eye so you may have some drama in you,' she added magnanimously.

While I was waiting to be spotted, I thought I would keep my hand in with an amateur dramatic society and chose the Trent Players, a well-established group with something of a reputation in Palmers Green. For my audition I was required to read a piece of my choice, but I *learned* the whole of one of Joyce Grenfell's *Nursery School* sketches. This feat so astounded the committee that they snapped me up without considering what they were going to do with a seventeen-year-old female impersonator.

After they realised their mistake, I was given backstage work, and walk-ons as policemen and servants. I didn't mind at all, because my ambition was now to be a bit-player, and I loved being for the first time a child in an adult world. Trent Players was the epitome of English am dram, a group of outwardly straight-laced pillars of the local community, who behaved like prima donnas on stage and beasts of the field at the after-show party.

The leading roles were always played by John and Dorothy, who were having an affair although they were both married to other people. There was a gay couple, Brian and Tony; a silly old queen called Bill; several plain women past marriageable age; still older matrons with names like Maureen and Ivy; and, unusually, quite a few young people, including Stuart, swarthy like a gypsy, who became my latest infatuation. I think Stuart was suspicious of my puppy-eyed devotion because, when we shared a bed together during Trent Players' visit to Bremen, my first trip abroad, he wore pyjamas *and* a vest and pants underneath.

Even in the swinging Sixties, when it seemed that every school-leaver could choose between half a dozen job offers, a would-be bit-player with neither training nor talent was not likely to get work. Since there was no shortage of menial work in the film industry, it made sense to accept this in the hope that I would make 'contacts,' whatever they might be. My first paid job was in the despatch department of Gateway Films, a Palmers Green outfit that made educational and training films so stiff and amateurish that they were laughed out of the classroom even in 1965. My screen debut was in one of these, *Grooming for a Career*, about how to dress for a job interview. Today this kind of stuff is drooled over by the terminally hip, those jaded by proper movies made by people who know what they're doing.

I parcelled up these films and sent them to schools and colleges, sometimes assisted by a jack-the-lad also called David, who got me very excited by telling me how he'd shagged his girlfriend the previous evening. Because I never capped his anecdote with one of my own, as lads are wont to do, he asked me one day, 'Have you had sex?' 'No,' I replied, thinking, 'Well, you can't hold this against me. I've only just left school.' But David stared at me, aghast, as if I'd told him I'd got an incurable disease. He became embarrassed and changed the subject. 'Right,' I decided. 'That's the last time I'm telling anyone *that*.'

I soon got bored with the routine at Gateway and began messing about. When my boss, Mr Webb, came into the despatch department and found David trying to stuff me into a dustbin, he decided to let me go. Gateway was the first of a string of jobs from which I was fired. I was next employed as a slave in the film repair department of Contemporary Films, an art-house distributor. This job brought me to my beloved Soho, London's celebrated 'dirty square mile.' Forget the bright lights; it was the red lights that attracted me.

It was while I was at Contemporary that I began to make useful contacts. The most important was actor Michael Billington, who used to slip me a couple of quid, much less than the going rate, to borrow a W.C. Fields movie over the weekend. The whole repair department made pocket money out of private rentals and sometimes, if a film had been sitting around forgotten, we'd sell it. Contemporary's grumpy Harry Brown knew what we were doing, but never caught us red-handed. Later I made Michael one of the guest stars of my film, *Losing Track*, about a sports day. It was ostensibly in the style of British silent comedies like *A Home of Your Own* and *The Plank*. Actually it was inspired by my desire to see boys running around in shorts. Not surprisingly, considering its wretched motivation, it was agonisingly bad.

Sacked from Contemporary, I moved to a soul-destroying office job at Data Film Distributors, whose sole product was a newsreel called *Mining Review*, dutifully sent each week to cinemas, most of which, I was told, never took it out of its transit case. At Data I met John Lawrence, a tortured genius, whose brain could have changed the world if only he'd been able to get it into gear. But he changed my life, for which I am profoundly grateful.

On a superficial level, John and I shared a love of movie trivia and erotica. After I left Palmers Green in 1967, we also shared a flat in Hampstead until he couldn't stand any more of me. Destiny had decreed, however, that we should meet again, decades later, in order that he could guide me, unwittingly, to the house in King's Cross where I would ply the devil's dandruff.

While my youth and looks were slipping away in dead-end employment, I was all too aware that London was swinging right past me, just out of reach. I can remember the Sixties, and I *was* there, but I just didn't know any flower children or American draft-dodgers, and therefore I was never offered any lysergic acid. My friends – office juniors, trainee chefs and car mechanics – smoked pot, dedicatedly yet strangely solemnly. Five years earlier, we hadn't even known the meaning of the word 'cannabis,' and now I smelled it at every party. Where had it all come from so suddenly? Come to that, when did we stop being teenage tearaways and become young adults?

I have a distinct recollection of unconsciously aping adult behaviour by working hard all week and going to the pub at the weekend. The mimicry altered at chucking-out time, when we went back to somebody's flat. Usually within seconds of arrival, out came the Rizlas and then there was the ritualistic business of heating and scraping a small, black lump into a strip of tobacco. I was never party to the preparation but, when the joint reached me, I always took a casual drag because it was still worse than death to be square.

Marijuana did nothing for me and didn't seem to do much for anyone else. I wanted everything to seem hysterically funny, as it did to Jack Nicholson in *Easy Rider*, but thousands of miles from the American mid-west, in utilitarian digs in the crescents and groves of north London, people just fell silent and stared at the wallpaper. I lost all interest in dope, preferring to fantasise about the new mind-expanding drugs. I followed their trail to the *14 Hour Technicolor Dream*, a now legendary 'happening' at the Alexandra Palace, where I saw people trying to get high on the pith of banana skins. I also put regular references to LSD in the column I wrote for Trent Players' monthly newsletter. What Maureen and Ivy made of all that, I cannot imagine.

Given my notice by Data Film Distributors, I applied to audition for RADA, but couldn't face the prospect of returning to school for three years and thus condemned myself to a lifetime as an actor unable to act. I drifted into my years as an aimless drifter. I alternated skivvying for a Carnaby Street agency called Clean-a-Flat with crowd work for films and television series. That's me in *Cromwell* as the soldier who closes the gate after Alec Guinness walks into the Mansion House to be executed.

Most of the clients on Clean-a-Flat's books were housewives in Golders Green, who already had cleaned the house before I arrived, and required me only to polish the bath and wash the coal. A decadent couple who lived in a mansion block near Baker Street provided the exception to this routine. He was a burned-out case and she was his sultry moll. They got up to all kinds of tricks and left the evidence for me to clear up. A jar of Vaseline on the bedside table, full on Tuesday, was empty on Friday.

One Friday I arrived at their flat to find them in the hall with packed suitcases. 'We won't need you for a while,' she told me. 'We're getting out of the country until things quieten down.' While things were still noisy, the reprobates featured in an exposé in the back pages of *Private Eye*. I can no longer remember the details, but King Freddie of Buganda was involved. I had met the cheerful little monarch leaving the Baker Street flat and said hello and goodbye. Weeks later he was found dead under highly suspicious circumstances.

I detested cleaning and most of my vulgar, haughty clients, and took outrageous liberties in their homes, usually stealing something that wouldn't be missed. I was so poor that I would remove light bulbs and replace them with blown ones I'd brought from my flat. But the Baker Street couple was good fun, and the only thing I took from their flat was a cloth-wrapped phial marked 'amyl nitrate.' I suspected it was a new drug and I wanted to try it. But on the bus home, my mind flashed back to my days at Contemporary Films, where nitrate celluloid was stored in a dank vault under the pavement because it was combustible. I was convinced I'd stolen an explosive and that I would be blown up at any minute. As soon as I got home, I submerged it in a bucket of water.

The terraces and squares of the north London suburb of Islington have now regained much of their late Georgian grandeur thanks to an invasion of rich pseuds who became known as the chattering classes. But in the late Sixties, many of these buildings were virtual slums, and polite society ventured into Islington only for the antique market in Camden Passage.

Late in 1968, I went to Camden Passage to try and sell two photo-montages I had pasted together in my spare time. I got talking to a stall-holder whose name was David, but who called himself De (and that's how he spelled it.) De was a hippie businessman. Due to monumental conflict of interest, few of these half-breeds succeeded, and De most certainly wasn't one of them. He didn't like my art, but he liked me, and invited me to help him open a shop further down the passage. It was to be a community venture that would sell anything that craftspeople brought in.

I filled holes in the walls, arranged the stock (mostly, needless to say, beads, bells and tie-dyed T-shirts), and painted the name 'Youre Shop' (De's spelling again) above the door. De had little interest in finishing anything he started and sometimes didn't roll up to open the shop until three in the afternoon, particularly galling for me if I'd been waiting outside since nine in the morning. 'Don't get uptight, man,' he advised me without a trace of guilt.

Youre Shop was discovered by a raggle-taggle band of drifters and drop-outs (musicians, designers, and a one-legged Hell's Angel) who, as the fancy took them, hung around to serve, steal and get 'stoned,' a new American word that rapidly had replaced the British 'blocked.' (When Bob Dylan sang 'Everybody must get stoned' in 1966, the BBC thought he meant 'hit by a stone' and didn't ban his record.)

An almost continuous chain of reefers was passed around to staff and customers alike (where *was* it all coming from?) and I still took my turn because everybody was so cool and I didn't want to appear more uptight than I already was. One evening, much to my surprise, I turned on for the first time.

It was a Tuesday, the shop had closed, and four of us were upstairs, smoking in the flat into which De and his American wife, Julie, had moved. My companions were more catatonic than usual. I became aware of a peculiar sensation in the nape of my neck, but wasn't unduly bothered. Then I felt a tingling spreading down my back, and began to feel faint. Now I was worried, but I couldn't say, 'I feel ill,' because everyone would think, 'What an amateur.' I decided I needed fresh air.

I tried to stroll casually out of the shop, into Camden Passage, and thence to Islington's shopping centre, Upper Street, but I was barely in control, and my mind was wandering as much as my feet. I still thought I was ill and didn't relate my sudden bad turn to the drug I'd just smoked. I walked along, trying to use mind over matter, but my mind was being continually re-wired and plugged into the wrong sockets. Suddenly I found myself in Sainsbury's, without knowing how I'd got there and, in another instant, the full force of the demon weed with its roots in Hell hit me like J. Arthur Rank's gong, and I realised I was being made privy to secrets normally kept from ordinary people such as me, like the true meaning of the bell that alerts shoppers to this week's special offer. I knew I had to share this vital information.

Back at the shop, nothing had changed. I may have been away minutes or hours. But everyone was slumped in the same positions and my last shred of common sense told me they didn't want to know about this week's special offer at Sainsbury's. So I kept it buttoned up. But then somebody asked De how he felt. He replied, 'Not too good – stoned,' and suddenly I relaxed because it wasn't just me feeling like a character in my own dream, it was everyone, and I could share the experience with them! Well, maybe not the one-legged Hell's Angel.

As soon as De and I were alone, I shot the scrambled thoughts out of my head at him, my words taking on yet more meanings as I uttered them. But I didn't care and, as I rambled, all anxiety passed. Old pot-head that he was, De told me to keep talking, and that instruction unshackled my last inhibition, and I told him with the greatest delight that I thought he was a wanker, and that he sounded really stupid when he said, 'Do your thing, man' and that furthermore Youre Shop was a catastrophe. De said he was glad I'd said all that because he really liked me. And then he went to attend to something downstairs and I was distraught because I wanted to keep talking because I loved De and everything about Youre Shop.

There was more of this nonsense for the next hour or so, during which my mind reassembled itself, leaving me with a profound sense of peace and the wistful regret ('Why can't it always be like this?') that inspired many a hippie of my generation to keep turning on and dropping out. I left Youre Shop that Tuesday a new man, but within hours I was back to suburban reality at the New Southgate Conservative Club, where Trent Players was auditioning for its next production, *Goodnight, Mrs Puffin*.

While we were sitting on the sidelines, waiting to read, Sonia, one of the young crowd, turned to me and whispered, 'Have you been taking drugs?' My heart skipped a beat. 'How can you tell?' I ventured. Apparently it was my eyes. I was still determined to keep everything about my private life private, but now my body was betraying me. Paranoia was to become a prime factor in my drug exploits.

Following my conversion on the road to Sainsbury's, my brain chose to subordinate the memory of the way in which it had exploded to the nicer one of the state of ultimate bliss that evolved from the chaos. I tried to recapture this bliss by smoking pot at every available opportunity. But return trips to Shangri-La were dogged by preconceptions and I never again arrived at the place I remembered.

Youre Shop went bankrupt in 1970, two years after it had opened.

V

"Fame is a powerful aphrodisiac."
~ Graham Greene ~

A high-powered young siren called Trudi-Joy Caron was passing through Trent Players in search of a husband. She cast an eye over me and swiftly thought better of it, but was sufficiently impressed by my thespian talent to recommend me to another group to which she belonged, Cameo Players. They were Jewish, I wasn't, but they couldn't find a Jewish juve to play the title role in *Trevor*, a very funny comedy about a lesbian couple forced to hire a 'boyfriend' for the evening.

I played the part, and then stayed with Cameo Players for several years. I loved being the token gentile, the focal point of the company, and moved effortlessly from leading actor to director. The entire company hung on my every word, and there was often a rush to claim the seat next to mine at rehearsals. Little did they know, however, that I had eyes only for Herschel, puckish and darkly brooding, a devastating combination for me. I thought I could win over this tempestuous creature by becoming his mentor. Later I wangled him an Equity card, and he did a couple of professional stage jobs. But – surprise, surprise – he did not express his gratitude by turning gay.

I very nearly pined away for love of Herschel, and when I could take no more of his heartless heterosexuality, I took refuge, for the first time, on the psychiatrist's couch. I wanted the doctor to dredge something out of my subconscious, possibly the hidden horrors of Fidelis, the knowledge of which would make me straight. When he kept searching down other avenues, I accused him, 'You're trying to turn me into a happy homosexual, and I won't have it!' Because, ultimately, he wore down my resistance and turned me into a happy homosexual, I am bound to say that psychiatry works.

When I was not lost in Herschel's eyes, I was forging a bond with another member of Cameo Players, Walter Zerlin Jnr., a law student, who behaved like an overgrown, camp schoolboy. His sense of humour was not everybody's, but I thought he was a potential star, the funniest man I had met since David Bubb at Winchmore. It turned out that his main ambition lay in raising a family, but we worked together professionally for more than twenty years, forming a touring theatre company, Entertainment Machine, and writing fifteen comedy plays, many of which are still produced throughout the world. Both the company and the plays were more me than Zerlin because, as always, I had to be the boss; but none of this would have existed without him.

In 1971 I moved from Hampstead to nearby Kilburn, where I was to spend the next 24 years. At first I rented one room in a flat belonging to Jean Salter, the accountant at Contemporary Films. Later I raised £5,500 to buy the uninhabitable basement of the same building. Also in 1971 I began my last regular, nine-to-five job, assistant editor of the British Film Institute's *Monthly Film Bulletin*, an academic journal which reviewed every new film released in the United Kingdom.

I thought I could do the job because I knew a bit about films, but I was hopelessly ill-equipped and gradually the BFI found out. I could not pretend to be interested in the Hungarian masterpieces my colleagues eulogised, and I grabbed all the sex films to review. There was a lot in those days, with titles like *Passion Pill Swingers* and *Housewives on the Job*. I was in my element, like Charlie in the chocolate factory. Today I get a mischievous thrill when I see a student in the BFI reading room xeroxing reviews of sex films written by a man who hadn't had sex.

When, a few months after my appointment, I wrote something very sordid about porn for a gay magazine, *Films and Filming*, the head of my department (a fearsome old bluestocking called Penelope Houston) decided I had gone too far and gave me the boot. I walked out of the BFI, meaning to get another job, and I still wonder how I have survived since then without finding one.

For most of the Seventies I wrote screenplays. Michael Billington, the actor I met at Contemporary Films, recommended me to a director who needed a script in a hurry, and then one project led to another. All the films were part of a genre then called 'exploitation.' They were independently produced on low budgets (rarely above £60,000) and they exploited, rather than merely included, sex, violence and horror.

I honestly thought I was just writing to order, giving the directors the exploitable ingredients they demanded. But today, bright sparks who have studied these movies and written books about them contend that we revealed in them rather more about ourselves than we were aware. My films, it transpires, are about strong women and emasculated men terrorising girls who behave like boys. I'm no psychologist, but I gather that film-makers who are contented husbands and fathers tend not to exhibit this kind of angst. The biggest give-away was my sex comedy, *I'm Not Feeling Myself Tonight!*, the only film which went out with my original title. You do not need Sigmund Freud to interpret this statement as 'Tonight, for a change, I'm not going to masturbate.'

While I was writing films, I was still doing crowd work. During several days on a *Carry On* film, I was relentlessly wooed by another extra called Tom. I said to my shrink, 'He's invited me to his place for dinner, but I know he wants to have sex with me.' My shrink replied, 'I don't think you're ready.'

Ready? I was champing the bit, pawing the earth, and abusing myself to insanity. Consequently I let Tom seduce me. We did everything because I didn't know what I didn't like. I discovered I did not like being fucked up the arse like a jackhammer. I came home and had a bath.

When I got bored writing the same film over and over again, I allowed myself to be headhunted by Mike Sparrow, a producer and presenter on BBC Radio London. He was putting together a live, daily arts programme, called *Look, Stop, Listen*, and he wanted me to join the team. When I had first met Mike, at a party in 1972, he was living with his girlfriend, but in the intervening four years, he had met and fallen in love with television director Nigel Finch. Mike was now pretty much full-time gay, and he brought an atmosphere of camp degeneracy to the *Look, Stop, Listen* office. It's fair to say I became a practising homosexual *and* a practising heterosexual at the BBC. And then there were the drugs. But this was mostly extra-curricular.

Mike's co-producer was Chris de Souza, a sweet little classical music buff, who could not operate the machinery. You had your heart in your mouth every time he was running the programme. I did film and play reviews. There was another David in the office, David Sweetman, who did a poetry spot, so he was known as Sweetman and I became McG, the nickname I've retained to this day. Sarah Dunant, now a distinguished novelist, came in to cover arty stuff that nobody else had heard of.

Nigel did art gallery reviews. I think he was probably the sexiest man I ever met, looking as macho as Kris Kristofferson, but oozing not testosterone, but a cheeky ambivalence. He was also arrogantly extrovert, and caused consternation among the secretaries by taking off his clothes, sometimes all of them, and doing handstands against the filing cabinets.

Mike was a highly intelligent pretty boy with pop star hair who had been in radio since he left university. He presented all kinds of programmes on Radio London. He thought he was the bee's knees, and to many he was. But as *Look, Stop Listen* dragged on, year after year, he became complacent, leaving us to put the whole programme together, and then strolling into the studio, sometimes literally seconds to air time, to read out with consummate calm and professionalism whatever script we'd given him.

Although this maddening behaviour caused much grumbling among the ranks, it meant that we could do whatever we liked, plug whatever show we fancied, and propagate the most personal ideology, all unchecked and unedited. I sensed that never again would we have such carte blanche, and told the others that we would look back on our days on local radio as the happiest of our lives. For me, until I became a drug baron, this was indeed the case.

The freedom that was the very essence of the arts office of Radio London had a concomitantly liberating effect on my libido. I went to bed with Mike,

Nigel, and the office temp's boyfriend, but not all at the same time. Denise, the editor of a magazine called *Psychology Today*, wanted to make absolutely sure I wasn't gay, and as Denise had the face and body of a hand-maiden in the temple of Eros, I thought I would help her out.

Although I got through the night, I was pretty dreadful. Strangely, although I never had trouble being the man with a man, I had to learn how to be the man with a woman. I'm sorry to say I practised dispassionately on the actresses with whom I toured in my theatre company. Another tour; another hit and run. Word must have got around that, after years of unavailability, I was suddenly free (in both senses of the word.) Out of the blue I got a call from Christine, abandoned wife of Trent Players' leading man, John, and I was taken away for a dirty weekend in Bath. It is inexcusable, but inescapable, that I was making up lost time.

Even in the Seventies, drug abuse at the BBC was rife. I had more new drug experiences during my time with the Corporation than anywhere else. Amyl nitrate by this time was no longer in a phial, but a bottle, a 'popper,' sniffed not only in the bedroom, but also on the dance floor. At a party, Mike passed me a cigarette dipped in the pungent liquid, which produced an intense thirty seconds of heart-pounding exhilaration.

Nigel, damn his eyes, gave me, without telling me, grass laced with opium, which precipitated an earth-shattering 24-hour trip, every hour of which was torment. At its most potent, at midnight or thereabouts, I staggered from my flat and knocked up the neighbours, convinced I was in Hell. Poor Jean Salter bore the brunt of my mania and spent hours talking me down, while I tried to persuade her to hide the kitchen knives in case I stabbed her. Jean was my surrogate mother and didn't deserve this kind of treatment. The next day, when I had to interview the playwright Robert Patrick, I was still high, and convinced that every question I asked revealed my addled state of mind.

And as for cocaine!

Before I went to the BBC, I had no experience of the top people's drug, and not much knowledge of the rituals associated with it. I heard it was something used in the fashion and music industries, and I had no idea it had already crept into the media. In those pre-digital days, audiotape was edited manually with a razor. I remember going into the edit suite and asking a reporter named Sue, still a good friend today, if she had a blade I could borrow. 'Ooh, I'll have a line, please, McG!' she responded. 'A line of what?' I replied.

It turned out that, while I was banging away at my typewriter, some of my colleagues were in and out of the toilets like the manikins on a Swiss clock. I just thought it was wonderful how they were always so energetic. Eventually Mike chopped out a line for me on his desk, but it had no effect. I expect it was rubbish. I never had any Charlie as good as mine.

Look, Stop, Listen survived until 1980, when it was one of several programmes cancelled during the panic that followed the publication of shockingly low listening figures for Radio London. Apparently only 1.9% of London's population knew we were broadcasting. We suspected things were bad when we held a phone-in competition and nobody rang. The re-scheduling achieved nothing. Radio London is itself long gone.

Throughout the Eighties I was an ageing starlet of stage, screen and radio. For several months every year, I toured with my theatre company, Entertainment Machine, eventually covering virtually the whole country, from the Orkneys to the Channel Islands. I prided myself on being able to do everything, from directing, through poster design and prop-making, to sweeping the stage before taking a leading role.

In retrospect, I think my sole gift lay in sweeping the stage. I was a hilariously bad director and actors still torment me today with things I said in 1983. But I did make lasting friendships, usually at least one from every production. Actors could rarely afford to work for us more than once, and so a new batch, fresh from drama school and willing to suffer any hardship, was recruited for each show. I was aware that my situation was *The Picture of Dorian Gray* in reverse. I got older and the cast remained aged 23.

Rather too many of our actors for my liking never worked again after leaving us. We finished a lot of careers before they got started. The one who broke the mould, and survived Entertainment Machine to become a star, was Julian Clary. Rather like very old people who say, 'I knew Doris Day before she was a virgin,' I say, 'I knew Julian Clary when he was straight.' He had a girlfriend when he toured with us in 1982. He was vividly unimpressed with the way I organised the dates, and I will never live down the nightmare journey required to give performances in the Isle of Wight and Scotland. On consecutive evenings.

The drug of choice for young actors on the road in the early Eighties was amphetamine sulphate, 'speed,' poor man's cocaine. Unfortunately it was a poor substitute for the amphetamine tablets of the Sixties and Seventies, which had become very hard to get now that chemist's shops were so difficult to break into and the chemists themselves had learned how to identify forged prescriptions. Speed was wrapped in a Rizla and swallowed in the dressing room. It made for some very lively performances, but plenty of aggression and screaming matches the next morning.

Whenever we were in Scotland, we toured the Campsie Hills in search of magic mushrooms, my first hallucinogenic drug, and very nice too, although I once infuriated the stage manager with whom I was sharing a room by keeping him awake with my descriptions of the changing patterns in the wallpaper. It's something else I shall never be allowed to forget.

Although our comedies were not Molière (critic Nicholas de Jongh once told a London theatre never to book us again because we were so amateurish), they were very popular in the sticks, and Entertainment Machine might still be touring if the VAT people hadn't caught up with us in 1987. Rather than pay the bill, we closed the company.

A new agent then found me a job presenting a programme on Premiere, Britain's first cable movie channel. I suppose that in 1988 there were about as many people who had cable as those who had television in 1936. (Not a lot.) Although I appeared twice a week for over two years, I was able to walk the streets without the inconvenience of being recognised. There was, however, the consolation of, by my standards, big money, £20,000 a year. I had never earned anything like it.

I began to get itchy feet. I used to maintain that I moved on because I was tired of Kilburn. But really I was tired of the man with whom I had shared a flat for fifteen years. There has been no mention of him until now because the memory is too painful. J.P. was a carpenter with theatrical ambitions. When he walked through the door in 1979, to audition as my new stage manager, I think it was as near as damn it (on my part) love at first sight. He was a coffee-coloured Scouser, whose rare smile, demolishing his well-rehearsed mean and troubled look, was to tantalise me for many nights to come.

We had nothing in common. I had such difficulty talking to him that I prepared notes in advance. He didn't make me laugh. And he was straight. Here was one working-class hero I should have admired from afar, not rented a room to. I think I probably wrecked his life. I decided that, if I couldn't have him, I would destroy him. He was inspired by me to write, but I ridiculed his attempts. When he had success, I sulked. I cold-shouldered his girlfriends. Periodically I was crushed by remorse and bought him expensive presents. As late as 1992 I went public in my desire to make amends and dedicated my first book to him.

By that time J.P. was so utterly confused and demoralised by my mercurial behaviour that he was driven to commit an elaborate but hare-brained fraud, which required me to give fabricated evidence at a Housing Benefit tribunal. It nearly got him arrested. I decided divorce would be best for both of us.

John Lawrence had forgiven me for my failings as a flat-mate in 1970 and, after a chance encounter at BAFTA in 1991, we had resumed our friendship. He now lived in a flat in King's Cross, which I thought an eccentric choice. The grimy ghetto, just north of central London, was known only for its three mainline railway stations and the drug abuse and prostitution they attracted. 'We have no shops here,' John used to tell me, and this was not far from the truth. Reputable traders had been driven out by the vice, and rows of boarded-up buildings remained. There were rumours that most of the area was to be razed to make way for a new Channel Tunnel terminus.

But one day John, knowing my love of architecture, took me behind King's Cross station and showed me Keystone Crescent, a secluded haven of early Victorian elegance. It looked like a set from *Oliver!* (and in fact it has since been used as a set for much Dickensian drama.) Enchanting was not the word.

When number sixteen came on the market, I made an appointment to view it. It was a doll's house, with three floors of tiny rooms, plus a basement from which walls had been removed to create a substantial living space. From the moment the estate agent unlocked the front door of the house I knew that I would buy it. The basement was to prove the nerve-centre of my new business.

I sold the Kilburn flat to J.P. and moved to King's Cross on a beautiful summer evening, June 5th, 1995, while he was out. I never said goodbye to him, and never saw him again. I hope he never thinks about me.

VI

"King's Cross is full of surprising and enjoyable gems.
Many are little known."
~ Local map ~

Many King's Cross residents know that, until the middle of the nineteenth century, people came to our district to dump their rubbish. In 1846 the huge dust heap at the bottom of what is now Gray's Inn Road was removed. But one hundred and fifty years later the wheel turned full circle. Now human rubbish came from around the globe and descended on the blighted backwater.

Just before I moved to King's Cross, the police instigated another purge (called Operation Welwyn), which succeeded in ridding Grimaldi Park and the forecourts of nearby housing estates of discarded needles, generally regarded as the most abhorrent evidence of inner city decay. But for many years the perpetrators remained, continuing to imbue King's Cross with its dubious character.

During the warm summer evenings, the street corners of Caledonian Road were occupied by prostitutes who looked like Irma la Douce from a distance and Edna the Inebriate Woman in close-up. They guided their clients down the steps leading to my basement and administered a five-minute knee-trembler in a trough almost hidden from the road. In the morning I donned rubber gloves and removed the used condoms, soiled tissues, and crumpled fag packets.

Far less covert was the posse of black drug dealers that congregated, night and day, at the junction of Caledonian and Pentonville Roads. There they stood, blatantly trading in God knows what under the apparently unflinching gaze of the closed circuit TV camera. And yet any notion that they may have enjoyed some kind of official protection faded when they dispersed and vanished into thin air seconds before a police car cruised past. This was street theatre, King's Cross-style.

The environment I chose for my home may sound too sleazy even for an old sleazebag like me; but everything was not as it appeared. Although they looked mean, the street people had no interest in you unless you wanted to buy something. And their presence deflected police attention away from the gentility of Keystone Crescent and the large number of visitors to number sixteen. It was all meant to be.

I am in no doubt that all that happened to me in King's Cross was predestined, that the house lured me in, that I was perfect for the house and vice versa, and that that irresistible force drew others, an extraordinary cross-section of people from all walks of life, who generally did not come and go, but came and stayed, for hours and hours, even when the drugs had run out.

What to the psychically aware were good vibrations, and to others was a congenial atmosphere, coalesced little by little like ectoplasm. Shortly after I moved in, I left my actress friend Beth Porter in the living room and, when I returned, I found she had moved the sofa and the armchairs into a circle. I wasn't planning any parties, but I liked the arrangement and it stayed. An unusual number of guests left behind hats and handbags for which they were 'forced' to return. For the first time in my life I developed what I thought was a sixth sense and made pronouncements, like 'You're pregnant' and 'You're engaged,' always correctly. Cynics said I was just reading body language, but my new powers worked even on the telephone.

The house was demanding that I share it, but I resisted. I adored being the king of my four-storey castle, and luxuriating in its nine rooms. This was selfishness for which I had to pay in a big way. Unbeknown to me, I already had been introduced to the person who would move in, and then bring more people to the house than visited the Chinese take-away on the corner.

I first met Ricky in the BFI reading room in 1994. A librarian told me that a nice young man wanted to meet me. Ricky was a very nice young man, a neatly presented little college boy who hadn't been to college. I didn't notice, until somebody else told me, that he plucked his eyebrows. Ricky had come down from Yorkshire and didn't intend going back. He loved London's party circuit. A little too much, as it turned out.

Because Ricky didn't look like a Sicilian bandit, he wasn't my type. But friendship was instantaneous. I was greatly flattered that he liked my films. Although he was only 23, he knew more about British comedy than I did. And he was terribly funny, constantly throwing into the conversation lines that sounded as though they had come from *Carry On* scripts, but which he may have invented himself. Ricky became the latest in a long succession of court jesters that only I found amusing.

Ricky laboured in some tedious office job, but had interesting part-time work looking after a former bit-part actor named Michael Ward. Michael was one of the idols of my schooldays. He always played fey, supercilious types (queers, actually), often as a stooge to my favourite clown, Norman Wisdom. Now Michael was over eighty, ill and in a nursing home. I very much wanted to pay homage, and so Ricky and I kept in touch.

Ricky went clubbing a lot and could always score ecstasy. I'd had it a few times and thought it was great. Everything they say about early ecstasy, the stuff circulating during the first half of the Nineties, is true. It made you dance all night and hug complete strangers, who wanted to hug you back. It didn't matter in the slightest that I was now in my mid-forties and bald. I was hugged by all and sundry, from disco bunnies to bouncers. Why couldn't it always be like this?

Two pals from my radio days, now respectable wives and mothers, wanted to see what ecstasy was like, and so Ricky and I took them to the Fridge, a heaving gay club in a former picture palace in Brixton. We had a stimulating evening. Zena, who's quite upfront even without artificial stimulants, asked Ricky, 'Are you gay?' He didn't think twice before answering, 'No,' just like I used to.

After that night, Ricky disappeared, leaving behind only an unobtainable phone number. I suspected something was wrong, but I had no address to investigate. Ricky always had been cagey about where he lived. (It turned out that sometimes he lived with Michael Ward.) Then he telephoned me, just like that. My instinct about his absence was, as I had come to accept, reliable. He had become involved with a wild, high-flying gay set, and had been ill, landing up in hospital after a drug overdose.

We went to visit Michael Ward, now in a hospital, close to death, but occasionally lucid. He thought I was 'charming.' He loathed being in a ward with patients 'not out of the top drawer.' He made me cry. It meant more to me to meet this queen than the Queen, and Michael made me realise that however unimportant one may be to one's peers, one is almost always very important to someone younger.

Driving away from the hospital for what turned out to be the last time (Michael died in 1997), Ricky and I were feeling quite emotional. He asked me if I'd like a flat-mate (him) in my lovely new house in King's Cross, and I said 'yes.' I feared, frankly, that he had a date with a body bag, and I thought I could delay it. (I think actually that I did avert it.)

Ricky was a perfect flat-mate. There was no sexual tension and he never used the kitchen. Every so often we went out together. One Friday, around midnight, he persuaded me away from my word processor to Central Station, our local gay bar, which caters for all tastes. Upstairs, businessmen watched strippers and drag acts, and downstairs, guys in rubber pissed into each other's waders. We went upstairs.

We got into conversation with a man and a woman. 'I'm straight and so is my girlfriend,' the man told Ricky, and then asked him, 'What are you?', and I was almost sure I heard Ricky reply, 'I'm bi.' Back at home, on the sofa, I raised the issue with Ricky, only as a matter of interest, and he told me all about his sexual confusion, and how he'd always fancied me and, the next thing I knew, he had his tongue down my throat. My strange psychic powers had not prepared me for that development.

It may seem like a giant leap from snogging to drug dealing, but in fact it was a small step, accomplished soon afterwards. Ricky and I had a lot of common interests, drugs being a prominent one, and we had talked about going into business together. Cocaine required no business plan, no major investment, basically £1,300 for the first ounce, and a set of electronic scales. Cocaine was suddenly the drug everybody was doing. Ricky could get hold of it. And by this time I had the contacts.

Thanks to Julian Clary, I was now working in television. I had given Julian jokes (the first, although he denies it, was 'Who does your hair? The council?') since his earliest drag incarnation, Gillian Pie-Face, an agony aunt, who did the cabaret circuit. Then he said, on live television, that he'd fisted Chancellor of the Exchequer Norman Lamont (it was a joke, but not mine), and basically that was the end of the first stage of Julian's TV career. He returned to live shows and I began writing larger sections of them.

Then, in 1995, a very keen young BBC television producer called Claudia Lloyd decided she was going to put Julian back on top. He brought me in to help formulate his comeback, *All Rise for Julian Clary*, a series in which he passed judgment on 'real' disputes. Many of the disputes weren't real; the participants tended to put on performances; and Julian hated the way the programmes were edited. The reviews were lukewarm, and the series was trounced in the ratings by Reeves and Mortimer in *Shooting Stars*. But we got a second series and I was also passed on to programmes on the other four channels.

I was astonished to see how comprehensively cocaine had infiltrated television and to what extent it dictated the manic programmes being made. One day at the BBC, a comedian interrupted our script conference by declaring, 'I can't be funny without a line *now*.' We simply could not continue until I'd gone into the studio next door and scored a gram from an actor I'd seen hoovering it up at an after-show party the previous week. Although I felt I was back to skivvying, the rewards were greater. Cocaine is made for sharing, and the quality certainly had improved since the Radio London days. And half an hour of happy buzz often provided mad inspiration if not wit.

When Ricky brought some home, and after we had spent three quarters of an hour feeling the blood coursing round our bodies, we agreed it was the best stuff either of us had tried. There was clearly going to be a market for it. Ricky had got it from a friend's brother, a professional dealer for ten years, who sold cocaine, grass, cannabis resin and ecstasy from his flat in north London. We went round to see him. What can I tell you about Casey? Nothing. Until relatively recently he was still in business; and he introduced me to a relative who greatly advanced my legitimate career. A pity that I can't reveal anything now. His story is far more interesting than mine, and one day I shall put in a tender for his biography.

Ricky and I found Casey very morose, an occupational hazard for the long-time, big-time dealer with kilos of powder and weed burning holes in his fridge. He trusted no one for the first year. Every week I went round to see him, I found him sitting in the same chair, watching TV. He didn't go out. Dealing was his life. He had another job, but he worked less and less at it. The money he made from drugs gave him no incentive to persevere at anything else. 'He's just a dealer,' a mutual friend said with disdain. Those words cut deep and were a crucial factor in my eventual decision to stop. I didn't want anyone to say that about me.

Casey had to teach us everything about the business, every little detail. Neither Ricky nor I even knew how to fold a wrap, the traditional envelope that then held one gram of Charlie. First of all, Casey told us, we had to go to Hatton Garden, London's jewellery district, and buy the scales. Stationers in Hatton Garden also sell the plastic ziplock bags intended for gems but used for pills and dope. ('These are very popular at the moment,' a stationer said to me one day, then added with a knowing look, 'I wonder why?')

We could, we discovered, grind up the cocaine rock with a mortar and pestle, and this is what we did until the task became so boring that I invested in a 'herb grinder,' sold next to the silver-plated razor blades in a head shop in Soho. (The product was still too lumpy for clients struggling to cut lines swiftly on the toilet seats of London clubs, and we began sieving it through a tea strainer until it was like Homepride flour.)

The raw material was then cut with glucose, bought in boxes from Boots the chemist, to soften the blow. (Most clients began with this cheaper, adulterated version, which became known as 'Charlie Lite,' then graduated to the more expensive 'full fat,' the 80% pure, when they went up in the world.) The final stage of the operation I called 'origami,' the cutting and folding of hundreds of pages of leaflets, used for the wraps.

'Always use pretty wraps,' Casey advised, and we did. I went to great trouble to choose only the most attractive coming events brochures from the Wigmore Hall and the London Coliseum. This process also allowed us to have seasonal wraps, yellow for Easter, and red and green at Christmas. The effort was much appreciated. The ultimate accolade came when *The Guardian* did a piece on Colombian coca fields, and used a McG wrap for the accompanying photo. I got a lot of phone calls that day: 'It's one of yours!'

We didn't follow all Casey's advice. He was as unscrupulous as the next dealer and told us always to make the grams light, point one under, because nobody weighs them, and to overload the mix with glucose to make it go farther. Early on in the operation we not only vowed to give clients the full measure, but also to return money when, as frequently happened, coked-up crazies gave us too much. This was not exactly altruism, rather the logic that dissatisfied clients don't come back. I did want to keep people happy.

I had no idea just how happy people would be. Slow to take off, the business took an extraordinary turn within six months. At first, nervous people I didn't know would turn up at the house, do the transaction, and then bolt like guilty schoolboys with their first copy of *Playboy*. Gradually a pattern took shape. People I now knew slightly better came regularly on Fridays because cocaine had become the dinner-party drug, something for the weekend, used in much the same way that I had used alcohol in my youth.

Sometimes my guests stayed for a drink. Then they stayed longer. Then, quite without any planning, Friday night was party night in Keystone Crescent, the night when my new friends – doctors and lawyers, writers and artists, male and female, young and old, black and white, gay and straight – got together to use the product here, because there was no better party to move on to.

My life had changed forever. The rollercoaster had plunged over the first drop and would gather speed, with all of us screaming and waving our hands, to the end of the millennium.

PART 2

OVERTURE
(1947-1964)

I

"Only good girls keep diaries.
Bad girls don't have the time."
~ Tallulah Bankhead ~

I feel ambivalent about diarists because I should like to be mentioned in the same breath as Samuel Pepys (fat chance), but not Kenneth Williams (every chance). Nevertheless the fact remains that I have kept a diary, without missing a day, since I was twelve. The first forty years are the hardest. After that it becomes force of habit, like brushing your teeth. Normally I write about a page of A4 every night, unless I'm too drunk to focus, in which case I catch up the next morning. I would have thought that this is good practice and good therapy. What is more important, not that I want to subvert existentialism, is that there is more of me in my diaries than me myself. 'You can't change your character!' my father used to inform me. But he was wrong. I disown the young man who wrote, while working as an extra on the film *The Magic Christian* in 1969, 'The big hang-up was the number of pouves at the studio. I think Twickenham must be a rest home for homosexuals.' The only evidence I have of this homophobe's existence is these words. Fascinating. I should imagine that many people on their death beds say, 'I wish I'd kept a diary.' I'm very glad I won't be one of them.

Because my diary is the only proof that David McGillivray has existed in different forms from the hack who is writing this today, I am particularly disconcerted by the first eleven years of my life, which went unrecorded. This period of the past is indeed another country. I have only vague recollections of visiting it, although I have photographs and a few documents to prove I was there. I have even less knowledge of my ancestry. Until recently I had no interest in it. It seemed to me that I was related to the dullest people on Earth – there were no great achievers, no celebrities, no villains. But this isn't strictly true, certainly not on my father's side anyway. In the last years of her life, my mother, whatever her name was, became intrigued by her late husband's ancestors. She travelled to Scotland to pay homage to clan chief Alasdair (or Alexander) MacGillivray, who was killed in 1746 fighting the

English commanded by the wicked Duke of Cumberland at Culloden, in the last battle fought on British soil. The photo she took of his grave hung on my wall at King's Cross for many years.

After my mother died in 2004, my brother, Paul, and I decided that she would have liked her ashes to be scattered at Culloden, and so we made the trip to the blasted heath. I learned a lot. Brave Alasdair broke through the English lines before dying, and another relative, Robert Mor MacGillivray, killed seven English with the shaft of a peat cart, before he too was slain. But the raggle-taggle Highlanders generally were no match for the superior English army, who won the battle in less than an hour, then celebrated by slaughtering women and children in the area. I thought my Culloden experience might stir dormant Scottish pride; but I'm dyed-in-the-wool English, and ancient Scottish heroics didn't make bagpipes more appealing. Nevertheless, when I caught the glimpse of Alasdair's grave in Claude Friese-Greene's pioneer 1926 colour film, *The Open Road*, I flew to the telephone to tell my friends.

I understand that it was my great-grandfather, Dan MacGillivray, who changed the spelling of our name. He is also my most immediate Scottish ancestor. Born in Nairn, he crossed the border and settled in Northumberland. His first-born, also named Dan, was my grandfather. He married Lily Metcalfe and they raised their five children, including my father, Don (?), in South Shields. Dan died before I was born, but I remember Lily, who was known to Paul and me as North Nana. From the 1950s, she and my aunties, Joan and Pat, lived in what seemed to me to be some comfort in the seaside resort of Whitley Bay. My parents took Paul and me to visit them every summer. By the mid-50s, my father knew I was show biz barmy; and yet he never told me, until decades after she died in 1961, that North Nana had been an acrobat called Joan Kent.

She and her sisters, Tillie and Annie, were perhaps The Three Metcalfes or The Desmond Trio or both (the truth is lost in the mists of time), a troupe that toured the Northern music-hall circuit before the Great War. North Nana retired from the stage when she married my grandfather; and it seems that her former career was rarely mentioned again. Certainly it would not have been respectable, and my family's desire for respectability was very deep-rooted. But how I would have loved to talk about theatre to someone in my own family who had trod the boards. None of my other relatives on my father's side had any interest in the business. Auntie Joan married a cobbler, Wally Holdsworth, and they lived above his shop. Auntie Pat married a merchant seaman, Geoffrey Pollard, who died young. There were two other brothers, Billy and Jack. None of them seemed particularly interested in my father's life in London and, by association, me. After North Nana's death, we pretty much lost touch.

On my mother's side, the only professional performer was a distant relative, who sang light opera on the radio. The rest of the family were office workers determined to better themselves. In 1914, my grandfather, James Peterson, married Maud Clark, a publisher's secretary, who had grown up with her sister, Blanche, and brother, Bert, in an East London home run by their widowed housekeeper mother Lucy. James and Maud brought up three daughters – Winifred (my mother), Gladys alias Catherine, and Thelma – in salubrious Highams Park in Essex, which is why Maud was known to Paul and me as Essex Nana.

The story goes that Grandad spoiled his youngest child, Thelma, and was a stern Victorian papa to the other two. They were afraid of him and his towering rages. He wouldn't allow them to wear make-up or high-heeled shoes. My mother told me proudly that she left the house for work each morning fresh-faced, put on make-up in a public toilet, and then removed it before she came home. I think I remember this story best because it appealed to my rebellious spirit.

In 1942, after studying shorthand and typing and having a bit of slap-and-tickle in the local amateur dramatic society, my mother volunteered for the RAF and was posted to Egypt, where she became secretary to a wing-commander. She loved the excitement of being abroad. She was a good-looking young woman, very aware of her appearance. She dyed her hair blonde. One day in Heliopolis, a suburb of Cairo, she was accosted by a handsome little chap with nice, wavy hair and a James Cagney look about him. 'Hello, blondie,' he said. He was to become my father.

He'd been in Egypt since 1940. He'd volunteered to be a tail gunner, but was rejected because he had a perforated eardrum. My mother maintained that, if he'd been accepted, I wouldn't have been born because he would have been killed. As it turned out, he had an easy life in the post room. My mother was very well educated without being academic. My father was, frankly, not up to her standards. But Mum was interested in good breeding stock and Dad was that. He was courteous and well-spoken, without a trace of a Geordie accent, and he had good legs. They became engaged at Christmas, 1944, and at the end of the War in 1945, they returned to the UK. Dad, whose acquired Southern accent became even posher on the telephone, grasped his opportunity to move South. He found a job with British Iron and Steel. He and Mum were married on 19th October, 1946. He was a virgin and she wasn't.

Because of bomb damage, there was a severe housing shortage after World War II, and Dad had no option but to lodge with the in-laws. By his account, the months spent in Highams Park were purgatory. Dad's family in Whitley Bay was not gregarious (North Nana didn't like visitors coming to the house), but they were very affectionate with each other. The Petersons were the exact opposite. They had social lives (Grandad was a Mason and Nana liked whist), but they were 'cold', as Dad complained constantly for the rest of his life. Grandad didn't like him, didn't speak to him, and ended up leaving him notes on the mantelpiece. Dad detested this more than anything.

Fortunately Auntie Tillie, she of The Three Metcalfes, was also by now down South, and knew of cheap rooms to rent in West Norwood. I was born there on 7th September, 1947. Definitely. (In the 1970s I became so irritated by one of my employers, the film director Pete Walker, who removed up to ten years from his true age, that I began adding five years to mine. Subsequently I regularly forgot how old I really was and sometimes had to work it out on paper.) Anyway, this is where the story really starts.

II

"The schoolboy, with his satchel in his hand,
Whistling aloud to bear his courage up."
~ Robert Blair ~

West Norwood and adjacent areas, such as Upper Norwood and Crystal Palace, are becoming quite desirable, which is only proper. This is how they started out. In the early years of the 20th century, this South London vantage point was promoted as 'the fresh air suburb.' Well-off Londoners escaped to Norwood's elegant heights to get away from the filthy fogs that blighted the districts at sea level. There are some quite substantial properties in the fresh air suburb. For years I thought I used to live in one of them. Then I returned to my birthplace and discovered that it's in a nondescript terrace. The garden I remembered as huge is a pocket handkerchief.

Gardens feature in two of my earliest experiences, only one of which I remember. I think I was playing with the girl next door in her garden. Or perhaps it was a patch of waste land, strewn with rubble, a piece of which she threw at me. It hit me on the head and I burst into tears. 'Cry baby,' she mocked. I've chosen to blank the incident that makes me appear even more of a cissy. Mum heard me screaming in panic and rushed into the garden to find me with a ladybird on my arm. That gave her a good laugh.

On the whole, however, I think Mum and I had a good relationship at West Norwood. She was very proud of the blond, blue-eyed son she'd always wanted, and thrilled when I turned out so beautiful that the local photographic studio put my picture in the middle of its shop window. I know we played games on the floor of our living room and that I was kept blissfully unaware of our relative poverty. Most of the money Dad made was spent on me. I received expensive Christmas presents including a train set. I'm told that Grandad also made a fuss of me because I was 'the son he never had.' By the time I was born, he was quite ill. He'd lost an eye to glaucoma. I think I remember him treading on me at London Zoo because I'd been walking on his blind side. He died in 1952.

Only one incident now smacks of post-war austerity. The mice got into the larder and ate our chocolate. Mum had to throw it away. This was a big deal. Confectionery was still rationed and we had to wait another week until we could buy more. (Chocolate became a treat for me, then an obsession and, much later, my livelihood. I talked about chocolate on the radio and spent four years writing about it for the magazine *What's On in London*. I really missed the freebies when that job ended.)

Bafflingly one wasp must have got into the honey of these carefree years. I have no recollection of this incident, but it happened. Both my parents were very disturbed by it and referred to it periodically as I was growing up. Apparently I left the house and went to the top of the road to await Dad's return from work. When he arrived, he greeted me. But I ignored him. I'm not sure what happened next. He may have left me there and gone home alone. What's more, this may have happened more than once.

What on Earth was I thinking of? Clearly I wanted to show my father, at the age of four or five, that I was rejecting him. Was it because of something he'd done? Or did I feel that Mum and I had a perfect relationship and I just resented his presence? I've no idea. I don't really want to think about it. I don't want to have been such a weird kid. Fortunately there's no record of my behaviour, and there is now nobody else alive who witnessed it, so I can pretend it wasn't me. If only I hadn't mentioned it, you wouldn't have known.

My halcyon days ended at the age of five with my sojourn at Fidelis, which probably was unadulterated trauma from the day I was hauled through its gates. Mum remembered my first day at school as one of the most agonising of her life because she abandoned me to a strange woman in black and white robes, who dragged me shrieking into a basement. 'Don't worry,' the nun told Mum. 'He'll be all right.' Well, perhaps I was and perhaps I wasn't. All I know is that I can recall only my desperate alienation and confusion as well as the possibility that the boy next to me in class may have been in a worse state than me. He sat under rather than at his desk.

What did we learn? I don't know, but I think it involved slates and chalks. Or maybe I saw slates and chalks in British films made in the early 1950s. I look at these films, with men in wing collars lighting gas lamps and dipping pens in ink wells, and it looks as though these scenes were captured in the time of Dickens. It seems incredible that this era was part of my own lifetime. Do people younger than me now look at *Love Thy Neighbour* and think, 'I can't believe I was alive when it was considered funny to call a black man a wog?' Possibly.

Unlike today, when I have the social diary an 'it' girl would envy, I could not make friends at Fidelis. I stood in the playground quite alone. I said to Mum, 'Nobody will play with me,' and she replied, 'You must ask someone.' I'd had my eye on one particular girl and so the next day I asked her if she wanted to play with me and she said, 'No,' and walked off. I wasn't having much luck with girls. I think the final straw, one that may have contributed to my departure from Fidelis, was my complaint to Dad about the amount of praying we had to do. We always seemed to be kneeling down and getting up again. I didn't like this at all. Dad didn't like the sound of it either. 'We're not having that,' he snapped. The only time Dad went to church was for a funeral.

In 1953, thanks to Auntie Blanche, we moved to 20, Park Avenue, in Palmers Green, where I was to spend my formative years and Mum and Dad were to spend the rest of their lives. (The rent was so cheap, right to the end, that the flat wasn't worth buying.) It was in another shared, terraced house, with an ancient crone, Mrs Looseley, on the ground floor, and Auntie Blanche in the first floor back. But compared to the hovel in rough old South London, it was grand. We had a big lounge, with a superb marble fireplace, and I had my own bedroom.

Partly because it was miles from a tube station, around which more vibrant civilisation tends to develop, Palmers Green was almost stuck in an Edwardian time warp, rather like Southwold today. It was a little bit of Middle England in North London. It was very, very Conservative. People just went about their own affairs and had little or no desire to achieve anything. The town attracted people who liked going shopping and playing bowls. If you didn't live there, you wouldn't have heard of it, and not many people have heard of it even today. It boasts absolutely nothing of interest and nothing has ever happened there.

The sole exception to this ridiculous generalisation is Broomfield House, a 16th century farmhouse with many later additions up to and including a mock Tudor make-over in 1932. It only gained a measure of fame when three fires virtually gutted it in the 1980s and 90s, and all subsequent attempts to raise millions to restore it failed. But when I lived in Palmers Green, it still stood and housed what was to this head-in-the-clouds child a crashingly down-to-earth museum, full of stuffed birds and butterflies in cases. (In 1963, as part of an exhibition of arts and crafts at Winchmore School, I found 'a pretty awful picture of me!')

Palmers Green only succeeded in inspiring my fantasies because, for a little while at least, it managed to support two cinemas and a theatre. The first film I was taken to see was probably *An American in Paris* in 1951. But it was undoubtedly *Singin' in the Rain* that changed my life in 1952. It was a film about the film industry itself. I couldn't have had a clue what the film industry was but, whatever it was, it looked like the most exciting thing in the world, so much more exciting than Grouts the haberdasher, my previous goal. As I said in an earlier memoir[1], 'That Technicolor swirl of glamour and gaiety set my head a-spinning.' I was absolutely convinced that, when I grew up, I would be part of it. And thus it came to pass. Except that I was in a hardcore porn film called *Hot Girls*.

---

1   *Spawn of Tarantula!* in *Shock Xpress 1* (London: Titan Books, 1991)

III

"Alas! That such affected tricks
Should flourish in a child of six!"
~ Hilaire Belloc ~

I can't tell you what a boon it is to have your entire career mapped out at the age of four and a half. From then onwards I could ignore everything unrelated to movies – like algebra and rugby football – and instead put all my energies into daydreaming, dressing up and showing off. The daydreaming – which included endless 'scribbling' as my parents dismissed it – came in particularly useful when I lost interest in starring in Hollywood musicals and contented myself with writing buggery jokes for Julian Clary. It's all worked out rather well. *Je ne regrette rien.*

Like 1952, when I saw *Singin' in the Rain*, 1953 was also crucial. I have a feeling this was the year I was taken to the theatre for the first time. I saw the ventriloquist Peter Brough in panto at the nearby Wood Green Empire. Significantly I can't remember anything about the show, but I can still re-live the excitement I felt as I scrambled for my seat in a sea of red plush. That makes it sound as if I were trying to get back into the womb. What I mean is that I have always loved theatres, but it took me a long time to love plays. I became used to the cinema's often fantastic spectacle. Plays usually consisted of people just standing there talking, and I found this boring.

Television was marvellous because it was like having a cinema in your own home. But Mum and Dad weren't impressed. They saw TV demonstrated in the Bon Marché department store in Brixton, but said that the picture was terrible. Then, in June, 1953, the BBC pulled out all the stops in order to make a fitting record of Queen Elizabeth's coronation. By this time Essex Nana had a television set and so Mum and Dad took me to Highams Park to watch the programme. It was very impressive indeed, and the demand for TV sets soared. Dad bought one of them, a twelve inch Bush.

This was our one and only luxury. We had no refrigerator, no telephone and no car. We had electric fires in the living rooms, but nowhere else in the flat because the wiring was too old. In the winter we woke up with ice on the insides of the windows, and washed in a tin bath in front of the fire in the dining room. TV was a godsend. I have nothing much in common with kids today, but we are one in that we grew up mesmerised by the box in the corner, which showed us fantasies which seemed real and other kids having different experiences to our own. Later TV taught me almost everything I know. I love it.

TV also made me understand the concept of acting. One day, while reading the *Radio Times,* I said to Mum, 'Why have people on TV got two names?' I was referring to a cast list, e.g.:

Mr Jones .... John Smith

Mum explained the difference between the two names and then added, 'You don't think it's real, do you?' I remember those words because they were such a shock. Up until that moment, yes, I had assumed that everything I watched on the screen *was* real. It didn't matter at all to discover that it wasn't. The subterfuge was even more exciting. Children like me were paid to pretend they were different children! That's when I decided I was going to be an actor.

Rapidly immersed in the subterfuge of acting, I became obsessed with the actors themselves. I loved the names that rolled off the tongue, like Sheila Shand Gibbs and Wensley Pithey. I learned that sometimes these names were made up, and so I decided to give myself a new name. I liked Melvyn Hayes and Alaric Cotter, who played bad boys in *Billy Bunter of Greyfriars School.* I told my parents that my name was now Melvyn Leighton. They accepted this with equanimity. They could hardly do otherwise, having several pseudonyms themselves.

When I was not watching TV, I was lost in many other solitary pursuits. We had a gramophone and a collection of Uncle Billy's 78rpm records that he no longer wanted. He'd kept them very well in cardboard covers stamped 'Saville Bros., 37, King Street, South Shields.' I gave them an equally good home and hated it when they got scratched or broken. My favourite tunes were the ones with insistent rhythm, like 'Tico Tico' by Mickey Katz and His Kosher Jammers, and 'Music! Music! Music!' by Teresa Brewer. Then I saw *Calamity Jane* and fell in love with tomboyish Doris Day. I played my copy of 'The Deadwood Stage' until it wore out. I didn't like classical music apart from Bach's 'Jesu, Joy of Man's Desiring.' Essex Nana, who went to church, delightedly bought it for me. There was no point in telling her that I only liked it because it consisted of the same phrase repeated over and over again. About twenty years later, I wrote the melody into my script for Pete Walker's rabidly anti-clerical *House of Mortal Sin.*

I was also a member of the last generation to grow up listening to the radio. In the 1950s radio was still extremely popular, and kids planned their evenings around the latest episode of the sci-fi serial *Journey Into Space.* Although I was fascinated and sometimes repelled by scary stuff (more about this later, at regular intervals), it was comedy that first inspired me to write. There were dozens of comedy shows on the BBC Light Programme every week. I enjoyed them all, even rubbish like *Educating Archie,* starring Peter

Brough, and *Life with the Lyons*. But I recognised quality. Ray Galton and Alan Simpson's scripts for *Hancock's Half Hour* brought out the richness of English sarcasm. The stupidity of *The Goon Show* sometimes had me weeping with laughter. I used to think that all the Goons were wonderful, but gradually I realised that writer Spike Milligan was their genius. He became my one and only idol. The sketches I wrote at home and the compositions I wrote at school became more surreal.

I constructed quite elaborate fantasy worlds. One was inspired by the new phenomenon of Disneyland. Because I had no concept of copyright, I used Disney characters in a lot of my stories. I was very jealous of Donald Duck's nephews, who had thrilling adventures in *Mickey Mouse Weekly*. Later I told my psychiatrist that, when I was a lad, I wanted to be Huey, Dewey or Louie. ('Didn't they all look the same?' he enquired. Hmmm.) I also amassed a sizeable collection of toy farmyard animals, which I moved around the dining table in enactments of tales I invented. I provided them with their voices. 'What's he saying?' asked a friend of Mum's, who overheard me muttering. 'He just talks to himself,' Mum replied. Oh, I thought, perhaps this isn't normal?

Far too late for him to be any use as a mate, my parents had another child. They couldn't decide what to call him and eventually agreed to my suggestion, Paul. (It was a name that, almost uniquely in my family, he kept.) Days before his arrival, on 25th September, 1954, the weird kid in me reappeared. I had a temper tantrum, screamed and yelled from inside the toilet and repeatedly kicked its door. Mum had to drag herself from her obstetric bed and down the stairs in order to give me a good hiding. My ridiculous prejudice against my brother lasted a lifetime, during which we rarely met. Then, after Mum died, we became quite close. He sounds like me and we share the same interests (apart from the illegal ones). For a while we enjoyed going to museums and galleries together. It's almost never too late. Telephone your estranged relative this very minute.

Every so often, I tore myself away from escapism and tried the real world, or at least that which existed within a square mile of our flat. Unlike the nameless terrors of West Norwood and Fidelis, Palmers Green and Hazelwood Infants' School were safe havens. A few doors away in Park Avenue there lived a girl of my own age, Susan Cordell, with whom I played regularly. Sometimes we pretended that the divan in our lounge was a boat and that the floor was the sea. Since the games didn't end with her throwing bricks at me, I was fairly sure that, when I grew up, I would marry Susan Cordell.

Further down the road, there was a Jewish family. I think the boy of my age was another Melvyn. When Mum found out that I was playing with him, she told me, 'Don't go in that house.' Because she gave me no reason,

I disobeyed her. My family's anti-Semitism, which reared its head regularly, made absolutely no sense to me. Auntie Thelma took me on a day trip and we passed two men shouting at each other. 'Two Jew boys arguing,' she observed with contempt. Why is their race significant, I wondered? On occasion, my parents' attitude really irked me. Every time an obviously Jewish man appeared on TV, Mum would cry, 'Vot you tink!!!,' and Dad would laugh, or vice versa. Dad liked singer Alma Cogan until he found out she was Jewish. He also found effeminate men hilarious. The first time David Bowie appeared on TV, he yelled to Mum, 'Pete! Come and look at this!'

My parents were staunchly Conservative, but I honestly believe that they were only casually racist and homophobic and not even that by the standards of the 1950s. Remember that, another twenty years later, it was still funny to call a black man a wog. Homosexuals were queers and poofs even in the press. By that time, the mid-1970s, I was mostly in the company of Jews, Communists and Jewish Communists. I then proceeded to add Afro-Caribbeans, Asians, homosexuals, illegal immigrants and whatever other minority was in vogue to my circle. And I married a Pole. All in order to get back at my parents. To their credit, they moved with the times. Mum adored Julian Clary and became almost girlish when I introduced them. One day, she came round to my flat in Kilburn and found me in the company of a black bodybuilder named Jason. We all spent a pleasant afternoon together; and when Jason flattered her, she preened.

The two years I spent at Hazelwood Infants are an almost complete void. I don't know why. I don't have any negative feelings about the school. Mum liked the headmistress, Miss Hughes, a sprightly little woman. My sole memory, almost inevitably, is my public stage debut. I was in the Nativity play, probably in December, 1954. Even aged seven, I was a mean-spirited actor. I resented being fobbed off with the nothing role of a Wise Man, while my friend, Philip Sandell, had the only memorable part. As Herod, he stamped his way through the auditorium before ordering the murder of the male infants. I looked at the parents, including my own bloody mother, smiling at him appreciatively. I was disenchanted with theatre already. I didn't appear in public again for another seven years.

IV

*"I can't remember a single thing I studied in ninth grade French or science,
but I can still recall how much it cost to fly chilli from Chasen's in
Beverly Hills to the "Cleopatra" set in Rome."*
~ Paul Monette ~

According to my first report, I moved up to Hazelwood Junior School in September, 1955. My class teachers were unanimous in their assessment of me. They thought I could write. By 1959 I was scoring a somewhat fulsome A+ for composition. 'David has excellent ideas and originality,' wrote Mrs Pates. But I couldn't do anything else, especially maths. 'He will not exert the effort required to improve his arithmetic,' Mr Phillips complained, 'and does not pay sufficient attention.' Consequently I was judged a relative dunce. In end-of-term exams, I was always near the bottom of the class, on one occasion 35th out of 40. I wasn't the slightest bit bothered. School was a chore that had to be endured while I was learning about life from other sources.

Even in sedate Palmers Green, where running for a number 29 bus was practically a breach of the peace, word filtered through that, following a few years of peace, Britain was now threatened by a worse menace to society than the Third Reich – teenagers. Nobody had yet seen a teenager in Britain. But apparently it was only a matter of time before these drunken young hoodlums, already terrorising the United States, rode into Market Harborough on their motorbikes and smashed up the soda fountain, whatever that was.

To me, a teenager was the sort of adult I wanted to grow up to be. Teenagers screamed and shouted, wore jeans, said 'No!' to their parents and teachers, and had their own music, the most thrilling I had ever heard. It was much better than Doris Day and Rosemary Clooney, who, as soon as rock 'n' roll arrived, were instantly forgotten. 'Shall I buy it?' Dad asked me, after we heard Bill Haley's 'Rock Around the Clock' on the radio. 'Yes!' I exclaimed. It was the last time that my musical taste was the same as my father's. Rock 'n' roll was the first wedge that opened up the generation gap. Very quickly the new music became intolerable to adults. In 1958 Dad pleaded with me to take 'At the Hop' by Danny and the Juniors back to the shop and swap it for Perry Como. From then onwards all I got was 'Turn it down!' and 'It sounds like cats on the roof!'

British teenagers did go on the rampage, but not until the 1960s. In the 1950s they were too scared to step out of line. British law and order, in that it included birching and execution, was Sharia-like. British teenagers lived with their parents and preferred coffee bars to pubs. One of the few places where they could go a bit mad was the cinema. It helped that it was dark. When they weren't jiving in the aisles to *Don't Knock the Rock*, they were snogging or screaming at a new genre of youth-oriented horror films. By the mid-1950s, many were convinced that it was only a matter of time before the Russians and the Americans blew up the Earth. This paranoia was sublimated into a succession of ridiculous monster movies in which mad scientists created new life forms, often via radio activity. A new one opened every other week and I cut out the newspaper adverts and pasted them in a scrapbook. Naturally I was too young to see the films themselves.

One of my life's journeys has been in search of the film, book, fairground ride or other entertainment that will scare me almost to death. There must be a reason for this, and as I was unaware of the Cold War when I was in short pants, there is a possibility that I came to prefer make-believe chills to the very real terror of my murderous father. At the back of my mind, I am sitting on my mother's lap and she's reading to me from a *Noddy* book. In one story, set in the Dark Wood, a gang of golliwogs attacks poor Noddy and strips him naked! It's so deliciously scary that I won't let her read it to me again. (Its subliminal message about black thugs also was so disturbing that later the story was withdrawn.)

The prospect of unimaginable horror became an irresistible temptation. When Dad took me for a day out in London's West End, I would guide him away from places of interest towards the London Pavilion cinema in Piccadilly Circus, where there was always something ghastly playing. The film I remember best is *Tarantula!*, whose story somehow managed to include a giant spider and hideously misshapen men. There were big photos of John Agar and Mara Corday looking understandably concerned, and for months afterwards I worried for them.

Then suddenly unimaginable horror seemed to be within my grasp. Just after my eighth birthday, Nigel Kneale's serial, *Quatermass II*, was screened on television. Kneale was already famous because he had written Britain's first science-fiction drama for television, *The Quatermass Experiment*, about a man who turns into a vegetable. Now, for the sequel, he promised a full-scale alien invasion. I begged my parents to allow me to watch it and was then stupid enough to admit to nightmares. Despite my protests that Quatermass was not to blame, I was forbidden to watch any more. By 1958, I was eleven and more than ready for Kneale's masterpiece, *Quatermass and the Pit*. Decades later I met him in Cardiff. (I've been lucky enough to meet almost all my childhood heroes, even Ty Hardin.) I told Kneale that I'd struggled and failed to be as good a writer as he, someone with fantastic ideas, brilliantly developed. Unfortunately I also failed on that occasion to be intelligible. The poor old bloke didn't know what I was talking about.

In the 1950s British people didn't travel much, but the McGillivrays travelled even less. This suited me fine as I didn't like to be torn away from scribbling and the telly. There were regular Sunday visits to Essex Nana. I didn't enjoy these trips because they necessitated a long walk to catch the bus to Highams Park, another long walk at the other end, around the back of the Walthamstow dog track, and nothing much to do when we arrived at Nana's house in Selwyn Avenue. A loose railing at the bottom of her back garden was the secret entrance to her allotment. But the novelty of that wore off pretty quickly. There was a piano in the front room and I liked to thump the keys. One Sunday, after she could stand no more, Auntie Thelma closed the lid and locked it. I went right off her after that.

I could be a moody and sullen kid. Dad was always warning me not to bear malice. But I delighted in it. When Auntie Gladys told me off, I sent her to Coventry for months and got great pleasure from the distress this caused her. Mum and Dad's opinion was that my temperament was inherited from spoiled Auntie Thelma. Every time I did something unlikeable, I was reproached with, 'Too much of Thelma in him!', which really irritated me because I knew she wasn't nice. She got less nice as she got older. She hated the London rat race and in 1960 immigrated to New Zealand under the famous 'assisted passage' scheme designed to attract Brits to the sparsely populated country. That was the last we saw of her. Then in 1962 she stopped writing letters and sending money home. She hadn't been abducted or murdered; she just didn't want anything more to do with her family. Essex Nana died heartbroken. In her dotage she was wont to say, 'I used to have three daughters. But I've only got two now.'

My most delinquent behaviour occurred during one of our annual summer holidays in Whitley Bay. I very nearly blinded Dad. As with all my childhood weirdness, I have no idea what came over me. My memory is that, once I got to Whitley Bay, I quite enjoyed myself. There were Auntie Pat's sons, Roger and Timothy, kids of my own age, to play with, and we loved messing about in Uncle Bill's Sunbeam Talbot, the first car I was ever inside. There was soft ice cream at a parlour called the Venetian. Also, best of all, there was a funfair, Spanish City, with excitingly clattering rides, called the whip and the waltzer, and excitingly dark-haired youths, who spun the cars to make the girls scream. (I became obsessed with funfairs. I set the prologue of Pete Walker's *Frightmare* in the fair of London's Battersea Park.)

Perhaps it was just over-excitement that made me, one morning on North Nana's front lawn, fling an electrical adaptor at Dad's head. It caught him above the eye and there was a lot of blood. North Nana screamed furiously at me and the holiday was ruined. I had no feelings whatever. I just accepted that this was the way things had to be. Nowadays I read newspaper reports of the trials of young people who have committed senseless, brutal murders. As often as not they show 'no reaction' as they are sentenced to life imprisonment; and I think, for want of a better expression, 'There but for the grace of God go I.' I committed my one and only violent act when I was about eight or nine. I didn't do it again because it didn't give me a buzz.

At Hazelwood Junior School in the mid-1950s we became aware that we were part of 'the Bulge', the generation of children that resulted from men and women either getting back together again, or getting married, after World War II. The school wasn't big enough for all of us, and we were taken daily by coach to prefab buildings somewhere in the middle of a field. Even here the classes were huge. Sometimes there were nearly 50 of us. But there were no discipline problems. We all sat there learning docilely. But, as before, I can't tell you what. Because I took nothing in, I eventually left school pig-ignorant. I thought the London suburb of Hampstead was on the south coast of England, and I didn't know that a Hasselblad was a camera. (Photographer: 'I've just bought a Hasselblad.' Me: 'I bet that eats up the petrol.')

Although I can't remember what I was taught, I can remember what I absorbed, probably not from school, but from a combination of parental and environmental influence, the same influence that more than likely makes us decide whether we're going to opt for an easy life and be straight or opt out and be gay. (I don't believe in the theoretical gay gene, which in my view would be as much use as a chocolate fireguard.) Naturally I should like to give prominence to the intelligence that makes it appear as though I was some kind of liberal prodigy. Because of my parents' conservatism I was attracted not only to Jews but to blacks (although this was then a term of abuse and we used the politer 'negroes').

I didn't know any negroes. This is because, in the 1950s, there were only two negroes in the whole of the U.K., Winifred Atwell and Cy Grant. To this white child, these popular entertainers looked interestingly sun-burned. I said to Mum, 'After they've been here a while, does it wear off?' In 1956 Mrs Young, our teacher in the first year of junior school, told us that in the old days some white people wouldn't eat their food if a negro's shadow passed over it. 'That's daft,' I thought.

Definitely by 1958 I had sussed that religion was superfluous to my needs. I enjoyed reading one book of short stories, but not their last paragraphs. These consisted of morals. Thus a story about the electric eye that opens the door as you approach it reminded us of the all-seeing eye of God. I skipped the last paragraphs of the remaining stories. The following year we were old enough to be told about the campaign to replace capital punishment in the UK with life imprisonment. 'That's a much better idea,' I whispered to Anne Jacklin, who nodded sagely.

But enough of this self-complacency. I was not a prodigy, I was euphemistically described as 'slow' and sometimes I was even stood in the corner. I was also a nasty piece of work. I scribbled over Susan Gilmore's exercise book, and then denied I'd done it. Worse still, Philip Sandell and I, together with two other bullies, Stanton Matthew and Ian Gardner, ganged up on the aforementioned Christopher Beale, for no reason that I can recall other than that he was a loner. We wanted to make him cry and we giggled in triumph when he ran shrieking from one end of the playground to the other. Later he retaliated by hitting me in the face with his satchel. It really gets my goat when columnists pontificate about the innocence of childhood. Children are rarely innocent. They can be downright evil, worse than adults because they have no conscience. I should know.

School bullying will never be stamped out because it is such delicious fun for the bully. If you believe in karma, as I do, then bullies tend to get their come-uppance. You can't tell kids this. But, for the record, I got mine. Beale and I ended up working in the same business. As Chris Griffin-Beale, he was Channel 4's press officer from the station's inception in 1982. In 1992 we had a reunion. Yes, of course he remembered the way I victimised him. What he couldn't understand was that we used to be friends. Then I turned against him. Why? Er…we were kids, Chris. I meant to talk more about this to him. But I never saw him again. Six years later he was dead. 'This is a real piece of unfinished business and I may have to write something to get it out of my system,' I wrote after I read his obit in *The Guardian*.[2] Will this do, Chris?

Almost throughout the 1950s I was lost in my fantasy world inspired by Hollywood, Pinewood, Disneyland and the BBC's television studio Lime Grove. I pretended to friends that I'd been cast in Norman Wisdom's next film. They weren't the slightest bit interested and forgot all about it, thus saving me the trouble of making up more stories about what had become of the film. *Up in the World* was the Norman Wisdom comedy I felt I should have been in. I saw myself in the part of the boy millionaire played by Michael Caridia, a child actor slightly older than me. He had a great name, too. (Nearly fifty years later I engineered a meeting with him.)

Bursting with creativity, but unable to express it except in Friday afternoon playlets, I wrote my own newspaper, also my own version of the *Radio Times*, and sketches comprising jokes lifted from comedy shows. I didn't like writing by hand because it didn't seem professional to me. Dad couldn't afford to buy a typewriter and so he liberated an ancient, lead-weight Royal from British Steel. Mum expressed reservations. In the

---

2   27th May, 1998

50s boys didn't type. But I thought it was the best present ever, the means to escape from unsatisfying childhood into a grown-up world.

Locked in my bedroom, banging away on my typewriter with one finger, I amused myself no end. Sometimes I was left helpless with laughter at my own jokes. But nobody else shared my high opinion of my ability. I entered a short story competition and I don't think I even received an acknowledgment. But failure is like falling down on the ice. When you're a kid, you just get up again and carry on. When you're an adult, you've got farther to fall and it hurts.

The violent intrusions into my private world of hilarity and horror now appear to be nigh-on devastating and at the very least character-forming. But at the time they were nothing more than part of the daily routine: get up, have a row, go to school, come home, have a row, go to bed. Once I got over my fear of being murdered in my sleep, I accepted that Dad shouted, Mum cried, and that I was probably the cause of their arguments. I was, after all, a delinquent. (Years later I found that my co-writer, Walter Zerlin Jnr., had a similar upbringing. 'I thought I was the naughtiest boy in the world!' he told me. Many more years later, just before she died, Mum told me the real reason she used to argue with Dad, and a light bulb was switched on over my head.)

Without question Dad directed a lot of his anger at me. He hit me quite regularly. I learned that, when an argument started and he called me a fucking bastard, I had to get out of the way. I did this by flying downstairs and pretending to burst into Mrs Looseley's flat. He never followed me. After a few minutes it was safe to return upstairs because Dad would have calmed down. This became something of a game. Mum also hit me, but not as often. Once she slapped me round the face for screaming, which made me scream, so she slapped me again, and so on. It was such an absurd situation that my screams turned to laughter until I couldn't breathe and then the assault stopped. Domestic violence of this type enlivened everyday life in Palmers Green; and when sex and violence became part of the cinema experience a few years later, I became a glutton for punishment. Later still, I became swept up in the 'video nasty' furore and risked arrest to hunt down the sickest tapes in existence.

During 1959, my last year at Hazelwood, puberty struck and I became an 11-year-old sex fiend. My last report from Mr Phillips was my worst ever, but this was because I had developed an equally manic dislike of authority (another character defect I failed to channel usefully). Because there was no longer drama in the last period on Friday, there was nothing on the curriculum that interested me. Swimming struck terror into me. I was ashamed of my skinny body and hated taking my clothes off.

Curiously, every other boy in my class was perfectly proportioned and thought nothing of stripping off, while quite a few enjoyed showing me their cocks. I didn't mind looking at them. I wanted to reciprocate, but something held me back. It seemed rude. (It's no accident that my history of British sex films was called *Doing Rude Things*.)

In the 1950s there was no sex education in British state schools, and at Hazelwood we didn't even learn biology. Mum and Dad were far from prudish. Mum liked saucy humour and I found Dad's stash of girlie mags at the bottom of his wardrobe. But by the time he sat on the edge of my bed and asked me if I knew the facts of life, I'd learned just about everything from Philip Sandell. It's difficult to remember how I felt about this information apart from confused. I found other boys' exhibitionism exciting, but as soon as the flat was empty I rushed to pore over Dad's copies of *Spick* and *Span*. I must have decided then or soon afterwards that the best bet for me was voyeurism. It was out of the question to have actual sex, with boys or girls, because that would involve taking my clothes off.

I was about to lose almost all the friends I'd made. The split came about because of my refusal to study. This is why I failed the 11 Plus examination. Most of my friends, however, were swots. They went on to grammar school and then to university. My education, on the other hand, ended at Winchmore Secondary Modern, where I spent most of my time masturbating, but also took drugs. This is where the story really starts.

V

*"I have talked to a number of my gay friends, who all report
that they were aware of their different nature very early in life…
Many friends report a life lived internally; a world where fantasy,
theatre and the imagination predominated."*
~ Jeremy Norman ~

Let's talk about puberty. Not so long ago I listened to an interesting radio programme in which my friend, Dr Mark Lythgoe, explained why a child finds it easier to learn a foreign language than an adult. It may have something to do with the child's lack of inhibition. Because he's more open-minded, he's able to accept new ideas more readily. For some reason this facility is lost at puberty. I can relate to this.

Up until the age of 11, I was a very uninhibited child. At the least pretext I sang, danced, recited and did impressions. I was also not afraid to show my feminine side (so much so that in my late teens I went through the family photograph album and removed all evidence of me looking like a pansy). It would appear that, very early in life, I also revealed my gay side. The only evidence I've got for this theory is a 1967 diary entry in which I record throwing away my infant school art book because it was 'painfully revealing'. As to what I drew my mind boggles.

Puberty made me clam up. It was not so much a dam bursting, more a dam. Of course much of this inhibition was to do with awareness of sex. I was in no doubt that nobody in my new school except me was attracted to my own gender. I was also painfully shy about my body, its weediness and the way it was developing. Because of the way my birthday fell, a day before the new term started, I was up to a year older than other boys in my class. Although it should have filled me with manly pride, I was stigmatised when I grew pubic hair before anyone else. (I shaved it off until Howard Woollard caught up.) Believe it or not, I also hated having the biggest penis. After John Franklin said, 'You've got a big one, haven't you?' I used every excuse possible to avoid showers.

Acting the part of a normal, happy-go-lucky schoolboy was such intensive work that it left me unable to express myself naturally on stage. At Hazelwood I had been the star of tomorrow. But at Winchmore, and for years subsequently, I was a dull actor with stiff delivery and movements, unable to colour my performances with accents, business or any of the other actors' tricks. Consequently I was relegated to walk-ons. I was middle-aged before I even began to learn my craft. Let that be a lesson to any gay would-be actor. Come out before you go to college.

Even as I write this I realise that the puberty theory may be nonsense. Not only was every other post-pubescent boy at Winchmore heterosexual, they were also superbly well-adjusted, poised on the brink of becoming respected breadwinners. The school revolved around its handsome, well-built sportsmen, who took their pick of its most attractive girls. Oddly, they behaved completely differently in the changing room, which resembled the set of a gay porn movie. Parents who are worried about what their children get up to when they're out of sight must come to terms with the reality that as often as not they're playing with each other's sex organs. For gay boys there can be no environment more terrifying and alluring than the changing room.

At Winchmore regular physical exercise was obligatory. Some of this was extremely scary. There was now no way I was going to be seen in public wearing only trunks. I simply stopped going swimming. I don't know quite how I managed this, but I know I had a lot of verrucas. PT, which I couldn't avoid, was an hour of pure torment. I was expected to do things, like jumping on a springboard and vaulting over a horse, which I thought were going to cause me serious injury. I was utterly incompetent and my school report cruelly reflected this. 'Slow and ungainly. Seems to lack vital energy,' wrote Mr Stirling in 1960.

Compared to these terrors, track and field sports were merely tedious wastes of time. Cricket was acceptable only because it was played in the summer. Since I could neither bat nor bowl, I was always positioned long off, where I simply lay down in the long grass and went to sleep. Every so often I heard 'McGillivray!' and knew I had to jump up and retrieve the bloody ball.

Football, however, was utter misery. Each match began with the captains picking teams and, as every wimp before me has recalled, I was always the last chosen: 'Oh, all right, we'll have McGillivray.' There was nothing like this process to destroy a boy's confidence. The match was then played as often as not in mud and rain; and in the 60s the winters were much colder. Because I couldn't kick, I didn't like to tackle, and so I just stood there and froze, counting the minutes. Sometimes I passed the time by talking to the goalie; and once, while I was leaning on the goal-post, the approaching ball bounced off my elbow, and Peter Gray missed a shot. 'I wouldn't mind if you were playing!' he moaned.

Nowadays, after I've done a gruelling acting job and I'm in the dressing room taking off an uncomfortable costume, the years fall away and I'm back in the Winchmore changing room, peeling off my sodden football kit with the same kind of relief. The changing room was like the Chamber of Horrors. I didn't want to go in because I didn't know if I could endure it. But once I was in, the excitement could be unspeakable, unforgettable.

The knack for me was getting one set of clothes off and another on without the teacher in charge noticing that I hadn't had a shower in between.

On occasion, the teacher was Mr D. Clarke. His name distinguished him from that of Mr C. Clarke. Mr D. Clarke was known as 'Dirty Clarke' and I'm sure you can guess why. He liked what is now known as inappropriate touching. Unusually he liked both girls and boys. What he especially liked was feeling girls' backs to see if they'd started wearing bras. But he would also hang around the male showers and tell boys how to get undressed. Some of the comments the lesbian wardress makes to the pretty prisoner, Ann-Marie, in my film *House of Whipcord* are Mr D. Clarke's.

When there was no teacher around, Peter Gray and his pals would get erections and wank each other. Peter lived next door to Chris, an older pupil at Winchmore. Chris was basically my god, a sex-mad Adonis with a bad boy aura. I've used many of my friends' names in my scripts, but only Chris gets his in one of the titles. Chris was such hot stuff that girls let him finger them in the playground. He and Peter had sleep-overs in each other's houses; and one morning Peter described to me their wanking session: 'This spunk was pouring out!'

And there was I pretending that this information was of only marginal interest.

Although Winchmore boys were proud of masturbating both themselves and others, I knew instinctively that it would not go down well if I said what I wanted to say, namely, 'Next time you do it, can I come and watch?' So I kept shtum. There was no alternative. Peter and Chris were straight. And come to think of it so was I. I may have played my version of their homo-erotic horseplay in my head a hundred times. But I was still straight. I was still going to get married. Homosexuals were nancy-boys and I certainly wasn't one of them.

Gay men of the generation after mine complained that in their youth they had no role models, only poofs like John Inman and Larry Grayson. But in the 50s we had nothing. Homosexuality was banned from films, radio and TV until the 60s. Queers led a literally subterranean existence in basement bars unknown to the general public. Occasionally one of these exotic creatures would be glimpsed out of the corner of your eye. On holiday with my family in Hastings, I boarded a bus with a mincing, bleached conductor. The passengers looked at him in wonderment and sniggered to each other. 'Some people are like that,' Mum whispered to me, as though talking about the mentally ill. Which of course is what queers were.

I thought, 'Well, I don't want people staring at me like I'm some kind of freak.' Accordingly never once, throughout Winchmore, did I give any intimation that I liked looking at Ty Hardin with his shirt off. But of course people knew. More advice: you can't hide it. A documentary, *Rock Hudson's Home Movies*, demonstrates how the red-blooded, eligible bachelor, the last guy you would have suspected, gave the game away in film after film. Somehow I gave the game away in the school dinner queue, where a tough guy told me not to push in, 'you lanky queer.' Later David José stunned me by observing, 'You're quite effeminate.' All that hard work for nothing.

What do you know? There were people at Winchmore far more screwed up than me. One girl had a nervous breakdown at the age of 15. One of my gang was put on probation at least twice, once for pulling a knife on a policeman. Later people drank themselves to death, committed suicide, and even got murdered. And I wasn't the only queer. Did I really need to add this paragraph?

VI

"[Mr Hill] says my latest script is too saucy and he'll have to censor
a couple of lines. Can I help it if I'm too controversial a writer?"
~ Diary entry, 1ˢᵗ June, 1962, aged 14 ~

From 1ˢᵗ January, 1960, I know exactly how I struggled out of my childhood built on make-believe, because on that day I began keeping a diary. (The entry for 2ⁿᵈ January, 1960, reads, 'Had row.') From the earliest days entries were sometimes in code. This is because I knew people read what I wrote. Mum once admitted it. In the 1970s Mike Sparrow let slip something he could have known only by sneaking a peek. This was embarrassing enough. But if I'd been completely candid, my life may have been ruined. (If the police had read what really went on in my house in the late 90s, no further evidence would have been required to ensure a substantial custodial sentence.)

Today I don't give a monkey's about privacy. I leave the current volume of my diary lying around for anyone to open. I think that probably this is something most people do only once. In 1987 'C.B.' wrote to an agony aunt to confess that 'While [my friend] was out of the room, I read her diary from 1985, and it said the most horrible things…She has really hurt me mentally, and I'm so depressed.' Somewhat predictably the reply was, 'You should never have read her diary – it was private and you know it!' All I can add is that, if you knew how therapeutic it is to write down what you really feel about someone, having told them the exact opposite, you'd never read someone else's diary.

If you have reached this point in my memoir, you'll find it easy to decipher my childish codes. For example, on 8ᵗʰ January we find, 'Managed to skip P.T. by leaving my things at home as I wasn't too keen on it today.' (In other words I'd forgotten to shave my pubes.) On 8ᵗʰ July there's the even more obvious, 'Didn't go to school again all today. Felt "sick" again. (Ho-ho!) School sports was today.' The constant references to rows probably would be enough today for Social Services to be called in. ('Terrible Whit Monday. Row after row. Nearly all TV shows switched off,' 'Terrible Day. One long row. Dad was going mad,' 'Had steaming row. No dinner. Furious onslaught on David by Dad,' and even 'Christmas Day spoilt mostly by rows and bad feeling all round. Not much TV seen.'

Even though it had only one channel (until we got ITV in December, 1960), the loss of TV seems to have been a very big issue indeed. Radio appears not to have been banned. I had a set in my room and often listened until very late at night, picking up ideas. 'Alley-oop' by the Hollywood Argyles, which DJ Jack Jackson used to play a lot, became my all-time favourite pop record. I want it played at my funeral. Throughout 1960 I wrote a collection of short stories called

Some People Like It. The title is typical McG. 'It' probably refers to some form of sexual activity, while the whole title, implying that most people wouldn't like the book, is an early example of my self-deprecation, later to get out of control. My first proper literary effort was turned down by the two publishers to which I sent it. Subsequently I destroyed all but one story. To judge from the title of another, *The Launching of Westminster Abbey*, I was plagiarising *The Goon Show*.

As soon as I got to Winchmore, I joined the Drama Club. I must still have had some vestige of spirit because I was immediately cast in the title role of *St George and the Dragon*. I have no record of this production, but it was almost certainly performed in 1959 as part of the school's annual Christmas concert. I considered the Drama Club shows childish and I wanted to liven this one up. While I was running around in circles, pretending I was climbing a tower to rescue a beautiful princess, I felt my tights slipping down. I thought that, if I stopped to hitch them up, I might get a titter. I was wrong. I got an enormous roar of laughter. Music to my ears. Unfortunately I was unable to mess about with the show the following Christmas, which was another Nativity play, this time called *A Small Angel*. I had a supporting role as a shepherd. 'A boy', actually the lead as I recall, was played by Keith Hasemore. Later in the 60s Keith began turning up on TV and I got back in touch with him. For a while we exchanged Christmas cards. I believe he still does bits and pieces as neighbours and magistrates.

My best friend at Winchmore was Geoffrey Ring, a rich boy, from one of the classiest parts of Winchmore Hill. I used to visit his beautiful, detached house with its own tennis court. Once, Geoffrey's father gave me a lift home to our humble flat in Palmers Green. I was so ashamed of the state of the building in which we lived that I pretended I lived in the slightly more attractive house next door. Geoffrey was a member of my first gang, which was founded by the rebellious Dirinda Pierotti and called the S.S. (It stood for Sexy Social.) Originally it met during the lunch break. I took charge when I became the school celebrity.

My fame, which soon developed into notoriety, came about because of 'Kookie' talk, a now forgotten trend of the early 60s. It was a form of beatnik slang popularised by actor Edward Byrnes, who played a character named Kookie in TV's *77 Sunset Strip*. He also made a record called 'Kookie Kookie (Lend Me Your Comb)', which I thought was great. The things Kookie said, like 'I've got smog in my noggin ever since you made the scene', I translated in a series of dictionaries I compiled and passed around the class. (The lingo derived from American black slang first catalogued in 1944 by bandleader Cab Calloway. But I couldn't possibly have known about this.)[3] I then decided to include Kookie talk in a magazine called *Dave*, which promised on its front cover 'DRAMATIC REVELATIONS!' and 'SCANDAL AT ITS HEIGHT!'

---

3   *The Hepster's Dictionary* (New York: C. Calloway Inc., 1944)

These photo galleries are roughly in chronological order and arranged under four headings: Childhood, Youth, Maturity and Decrepitude. See if you can detect any sense of progression. Aside from the page numbering, I'm not sure I can.

right:
A Scottish soldier.
The memorial to my ancestor at Culloden.

below:
Relative peace.
My maternal grandparents with my Auntie Thelma on Essex Nana's lap, my mother and my Auntie Gladys front. Back garden of Selwyn Avenue, 1928.

above: Blondie. Mum as she looked when she met Dad in Egypt, 1944.

right: The object of her desire. Dad was put on a charge for wearing his RAF cap at this jaunty angle.

opposite top: Madonna and child. Me aged 8 months 10 days. Front garden of Gipsy Road, Whit Sunday, 1948.

opposite bottom: A star in my own mind. Aged 5 with Dad, 1952.

below: Love & marriage. My parents' wedding, 1946. Front, L to R: Auntie Thelma, Essex Nana, Auntie Pat, Auntie Blanche.

Harry Corbett *I.B.M.*

and

SOOTY

TEDDY BEAR MAGICIAN OF TELEVISION FAME

TELEPHONE · GUISELEY 846

1 PARK GATE CRESCENT
GUISELEY · LEEDS

20th January, 1959.

Dear David,

Thankyou for your very nice letter. Sooty says he hopes you like his photograph. He has lots of pictures in his bedroom, and Mrs. Corbett gets quite cross with him when she has to lift them all up to dust round them ! Sooty sometimes does his own dusting, then the trouble really begins - he just sweeps everything to the ground!

I expect you have great fun with your Sooty. Is he mischievous, too ?

Well, David, I must dash off. I left Sooty washing the car, and I shouldn't wonder if he isn't hosing it down INSIDE as well as outside.

Lots of Love,

Harry

above: A bear behind. 1957 at London Zoo with my brother Paul, and Brumas, who was born in the zoo.

opposite main and inset: Harry Corbett wrote me this letter in 1955. The same year I pretended I was Harry.

opposite lower right: Butter wouldn't melt, etc. Studio portrait, 1957.

below: Could do better. My report card, 1959.

NAME David McGillivray DATE December 1958 DATE July 1959

SUBJECTS.	OBT	MAX	MARK.		MAX	OBT	MARK.
SCRIPTURE				Writing	10	8	B
ENGLISH :—READING	10	10		Reading	10	10	A
COMPOSITION	19	20		Comprehension	20	18½	B+
HANDWRITING	6	10		Composition	20	19	A+
READING COMPREHENSION				Spelling	20	19	A
GEN. ENG.	37	50		English	30	26	A
SPELLING	38	40		Interpretation	10	8	
LIT.							
ARITHMETIC	32	50		Arithmetic	50	25	C-
MENTAL ARITH	22	50		Mental Arith	50	28	C-
HANDWORK							
DRAWING				History	25	14½	C+
NEEDLEWORK				Geography	25	20	B+
				Nature Study	25	18½	B
OTHER SUBJECTS:—				Religious Inst	25	17	C-
GEN. KNOW	21	30			320	231½	
NATURE							
HIST	135	200		Art	—	—	A
GEOG				Handwork	—	—	B+
CONDUCT	Fairly Good			Good			
PROGRESS	Slow			Still very slow			
ATTENDANCE AND PUNCTUALITY	Absent - 10 out of 128			Absent - 9 out of 227			
CLASS AND POSITION	Class 4A Pos 32/61			Class 4A Pos 35/40			

Class Teacher's Signature W. A. Phillips
Parent's Signature
E. M. Bellefontaine Head Teacher.

above: Wild child Dirinda Pierotti, pictured in 1981. When I told her I was writing this book, she said, "Publish and be damned." She died in 2012.

left: Leader of the gang. At Selwyn Avenue, 1962.

opposite: Me at Winchmore School, May, 1964, two months away from expulsion.

below: Two more of the gang.
David Bubb and David José, pictured in 1973.

photo credit: Dirinda Pierotti

above: Thrust into the world, 1965.
The offices of Gateway Films. Long gone.

right: In the lighting gantry of the Intimate
Theatre with Patricia Phipps.

below: All eyes on me, you'll notice. As a
sheriff in *The Remarkable Mr Pennypacker*.

photo credit: Kenneth Prater

I still have the solitary, handwritten copy of the first issue of *Dave*, a schoolboy tabloid with gossip columns written by Geoffrey, Dirinda and Anne Jacklin. We were quite precocious 14-year-olds in 1961. Under the headline, 'Brenda Whitham's scandalous affair with Rodney Wilkinson,' Brenda stated, 'He reeked of beer and I shan't go out with him again.' This was nothing compared to the savage rudeness of later editions, which finally were to bring about my expulsion.

After *Dave* most people at Winchmore knew me. Teacher Mrs Gayler asked me to play the king in her panto *Forty Winks Beauty*, performed as part of the 1961 Christmas concert. Unlike the earlier 'childish' shows, this was a romp involving many of the school's personalities. The school's best actor, Keith Morris, was the narrator. (He too went professional and in 1974 I went to see him in *Pyjama Tops* in London's West End.) Anne Jacklin was my queen and Dirinda was a witch. Toughs from the 'D' stream were fairies. Best of all, hunky head boy Mick Cook was Sleeping Beauty. In the last scene I had to kiss him on the cheek. 'You can just kiss the air,' Mrs Gayler assured me. As if! I gave him a big smacker. Howls of laughter.

Getting a bit of attention was all that concerned me in 1961. This is remarkable in retrospect because the US invasion of the Bay of Pigs, and the Cuban missile crisis that followed it, threatened the destruction of the world. We kids were certainly aware of the problem, but I don't remember any alarm. I do remember being quite excited about the idea of men in space. (Yuri Gagarin was the first on 12th April.) This was science-fiction come true. But the only news report that got us talking was 'TEACHER TELLS OF MY CLASS OF DEVILS' in the *Daily Mail* on 29th November. The teacher was Lois Kronberg and her class was at Winchmore. She'd taught us very briefly earlier in the year. She claimed, among other outrages, that she had been 'set upon by a group of girls and thrown against a playground wall.' Sadly for headmaster, Mr Shepherd, who dreamed of academic glory (our motto was 'Ad maiorem gloriam'), this probably was the only time that Winchmore appeared in the national press during his term of office.

It wasn't only the kids who enjoyed *Dave*. In 1962 my form master, Mr Sell, suggested that in future we should duplicate issues on the deputy headmaster's Banda. Although cheap and unreliable, a poor man's Gestetner, this machine produced colour copies and so I was able to get creative with the design. For the cover of the second issue of *Dave* I drew Gorgo, a current movie monster. (*Gorgo* was the first 'X' film I saw on 2nd November 1961. I was more frightened of being asked for proof of my age than the film itself.) Inside there was an interview with Ian Taranto (eyes brown, hair black, born 8th August, 1947), a glamorous refugee from war-torn Beirut, for whom I had the hots.

The most mature article was a report of a 'court case' that we, the gang, had convened. It reveals surprising knowledge of the legal system for 13- and 14-year-olds. My guess is that we picked up most of the process from the TV show *Perry Mason*. (At one point Anne quotes one of its catch-phrases, 'This is incompetent, irrelevant and immaterial.') The background to this event was Anne's claim, in the first *Dave*, that Dirinda had been seen 'dancing cheek to cheek' with yet another exotic foreigner, this time from Pakistan, Abdul Aziz Reshamwala, known as 'Resh.' Dirinda claimed that this allegation was untrue and sued Anne for 2/6d (12½p).

The case was heard before 'Justice' Geoffrey Ring. Dirinda chose as her counsel Suzette Alli (eyes brown, hair black, born 31st October, 1947) from Trinidad. She was one of Winchmore's first black pupils, which is why I also interviewed her. She seems to have had the makings of a fine barrister:

'[Suzette's questions] revealed that Resh wanted to teach Dirinda the quickstep.
Suzette: "If Resh was teaching you the quickstep you would not have been dancing cheek to cheek."'

I wonder if Suzette ever went into law? She won her case on this occasion. Justice Ring found in the plaintiff's favour (although subsequently Anne appealed).

By chance the second issue of *Dave* was distributed at the same time as the second issue of the official school yearbook. A dry publication, stuffed with exam results, poems and essays, *The Winchmore Magazine* was largely ignored while the playground separated into knots of people – prefects, even – huddled around copies of *Dave*. Overnight I'd become Winchmore's Rupert Murdoch. I knew what my readers wanted and I gave it to them. This was the beginning of my first smug period.

There were two more issues of *Dave* in 1962, which were the magazine's halcyon days. Previously, according to teachers, I was slow, talkative, 'intent on showing off.' But now I was regarded as a bright spark. Two teachers began contributing to *Dave*. I heard that one, Mrs Phair, considered me 'a borderline genius.' (I'm not, incidentally. My IQ is 92, strictly average.)

The first harbinger of doom was in the Christmas issue. (I loved topping the *Dave* logo with snow.) David Bubb did a drawing of 'Brown's boomerang' and captioned it 'Guaranteed not to work.' Australian maths master, Mr Brown, was a figure of fun, who carried a string shopping bag. As soon as we realised he couldn't instil discipline, we played havoc. There were times during his lessons when he went beetroot with impotent fury and I laughed so much that my sides ached. Mr Brown did not think I was a bright spark.

Somehow I still found the time to make personal appearances. I had about six lines as a police inspector in Arnold Ridley's old potboiler *The Ghost Train* and received my first notice. ('David McGillivray played a police inspector' – *Palmers Green & Southgate Gazette*.)[4] The stars were Keith Morris and John Sherlock. The latter became a BBC cameraman and we worked together regularly until the 1990s.

The most important acquisition since my typewriter was a reel-to-reel tape recorder. This meant I could preserve performances of my sketches. The first was *The Alma Crutt Murder Mystery*, which the gang and I recorded in October and later performed in the Winchmore Christmas concert. Somehow both the tape and the script have survived. There is not one original joke from beginning to end:

Det-Insp. Jim Crint:	My first port of call was an hotel called the Dirty Fiddle, so called because it was a vile inn.
Crint:	Firstly, is there a woman named Ruth here?
Lady Twinge:	No, why?
Crint:	Just as I thought. Another ruthless murder.
Crint:	Miss Twinge, where were you last night?
Letitia:	I was on the second floor of a flat in Chiswick.
Crint:	Did you ever go up to the third floor?
Letitia:	Yes, but that's another storey.

The sketch doesn't get any better than this. I seem to have been born to write panto, and it's a mystery to me why I didn't work on my first, *Dick Whittington*, in Northampton, until 2006.

Although sex in my sketches is cheekiness copied from comic writers of the day, sex in my day-to-day life caused turmoil I tried to confront in my diary. The Hastings holiday was spent at the Coombe Haven Caravan Park. ('Pity about the rows.') On our last night I went to the clubhouse. ('Had a twist, watched the one-arm bandits and enjoyed myself. Wish I'd gone before. Afterwards I watched teenagers jumping fully-clothed into the swimming pool, then chucking all the chairs and tables in after them.') Whereas I could report the fun I derived from this rebellion, I couldn't write down the real reason I hung around the swimming pool until midnight: I was transfixed as the teenage boys emerged from the water and stripped off their soaking clothes, even their underpants.

Back in London, the gang began organising party after party. At Dirinda's on Christmas Eve, there was a 'good deal of snogging going on at 11-ish.'

---

4   6th April, 1962

Christine Lemon was inspired to make a move on me, and I gave her the brush-off. She sulked and I felt bad. But this wasn't because I was queer. As I wrote later that night, 'Chris won't take the hint that I haven't got time for that sort of thing at the moment and want to leave it till I leave school.'

All that's true about that statement is that I was busy – so busy that I wonder how I managed to produce a magazine single-handedly and rehearse shows while studying for GCE exams. But occupying my time was essential because work provided subterfuge. In *House of Whipcord*, when villain Mark E. Dessart spurns the lovely Ann-Marie with 'No, not tonight. I must do some writing,' that's me talking.

It now appears to me that I invented *Dave* to fill a gap that wasn't going to be filled with sport or girlfriends. Prior to 1961 there are too many diary entries that read 'Usual day,' 'Got bored,' or 'Watched TV.' There was no social life at Park Avenue. Mum had a couple of friends, but otherwise people rarely came to the flat. (When I visited Geoffrey, I was intrigued to find his parents having a party. Grown-ups have parties? I didn't know that.)

After *Dave*, I never really had a 'usual day' again.

VII

"Come, worthy Greek! Ulysses come;
Possess these shores with me!"
~ Samuel Daniel ~

In the depths of the interminable winter of 1963, the coldest in London since 1947, pipes froze and the temperature was sometimes below zero *inside* our flat. I donned duffel coat and gloves to carry on typing. The snow, which was on the ground for more than two months, didn't melt until March. Just as it does today, abnormal weather inspired gloomy predictions of climate change. 'Scientists say that winters like these,' I reported, 'will continue for 30 years.' I was now, finally, taking an interest in the news, and was sometimes affected by it. I professed myself 'terribly shocked' by President Kennedy's assassination on 22nd November and, a few days later, confessed that 'Every time I find myself laughing or enjoying something I tend to think I shouldn't.'

I was cock of the walk throughout 1963. My conceit was reinforced by the new edition of *The Winchmore Magazine*. The anonymous editor wrote, 'It has even been suggested that we emulate the slick raciness of *Dave*, but much though we admire our enterprising rival, we wonder whether that would quite fit the bill? Is a School Magazine merely for our own private amusement or should it have a wider, more lasting appeal?'

The question was answered by the readers themselves. David Royce, 5Y, grumbled, 'I should like to level a criticism at our school magazine. In my opinion it…becomes bogged in far too many essays and poems. I should think as it is a magazine for young people, it should deal with young people's interests.' Ian Wakefield, 5Z, suggested, 'I think we should get away from the conventional type of magazine, introduce jokes, anagrams and doodles and a light-hearted approach. Poems are all very proper, but as it is our magazine I think we, its readers, should have what we want in it.'[5] On 29th April, I confided, 'Hope it doesn't all go to my head!'

I like to imagine that there was a staff meeting at which the suppression of this rebellion was on the agenda. Certainly I sensed a concerted effort to bring the ringleader into line. It began in January when Mrs Phair, who thought I might be a genius, noticed that I hadn't worn school uniform for three and a half years. She marched me to headmaster Shepherd, who announced, 'I am writing to your parents.' This was a threat I was to

---

[5]   No. 3, 1963

hear regularly. Unfortunately Phair also drew Shepherd's attention to *Dave*. He wasn't impressed.

Two issues of the magazine appeared in 1963 and both caused trouble. In May almost every page featured something amusing that Mr Brown had said in class ('Don't imitate my eccentricities, children!') Geoffrey, who had conducted a poll to discover Winchmore's most popular teacher, included Eric Lewis' vote for Mr Baxenden because 'he's got a fat stomach.' Because of that remark, deputy head Chalmers insisted that in future he must check everything before it went to press. In November he censored a two-page exposé on the Upper Sixth.

Shepherd too began exerting his authority. When I agreed to chair a meeting of the Debating Society, the announcement was put on the poster. Shepherd refused to approve it unless my name was excised. Then, after a row with Brown, I was back in Shepherd's study. He warned me that, unless my maths improved, he'd remove me from the grammar stream. (Around this time I got nil for a geometry exam because I even got the date wrong.)

Possibly I said something facetious to Shepherd because he lost his temper. 'You're full of your own superiority,' he barked, 'because of a rag that goes round the school.' How he got from this to sex I can't remember, but his next major observation was, 'Whenever I see you you're messing about with a crowd of females around you. I suppose you think you're a regular Don Juan.' That night I added five exclamation marks to the great lover's name and added with complete honesty, 'The thought couldn't be farthest from my mind.'

True, I was likely to be found gossiping with the girls, but my dream date was not among them. With sex god Chris expelled, and Ian Taranto back in Beirut, never to return, I focused my attention on the influx of Greek Cypriot boys, in particular Kristofas Panayiotou from Limassol, with lustrous hair swept around the back of his head in a duck's arse of the most fascinating intricacy. I made lovelorn attempts to communicate. When he first arrived at Winchmore, he didn't speak English. I learned the Greek for 'good morning' but he wasn't impressed. ('Did I get any change? Not a word.')

Gradually I wore him down. ('Kris gave me a Rowntree's Fruit Pastille today. I gave him a Maynard's Peppermint Cream.') But no sooner had we exchanged these love tokens than Kris left Palmers Green for the Greek Cypriot ghetto of Holloway. For me this was 'definitely the saddest event of the year' and I would have cried myself to sleep had it not been for the next best Cypriot thing, Steven Georgiou. This happens to be Yusuf Islam's real name, but I am not referring to him.

Steve spoke quite good English and we swapped swear words. I can still say, 'I fuck your whole family,' in Greek. We interviewed him for *Dave* and, although he thought that 'All English are mad,' he began going out with us in the evenings. Geoffrey and others, who may have suspected that I was a bad influence, slowly drifted off, and I spent more time in the company of Steve and others in the 'A' and 'B' streams. At one party I noted with amazement that 'I was the only grammar stream person there.' Parties like this were wilder than those I'd known. There was another with 'most of the food thrown at each other, champagne all over the piano, sausages on sticks and gorgonzola trodden into the carpet.' At a séance at David José's house I made sure I sat next to Steve so that we could hold hands.

The year ended with what was to be my last appearance in the Christmas concert. Mrs Gayler allowed me to punctuate the show with parodies, mainly written by David Bubb and me, of TV commercials. The content was suitably anarchic, with plenty of custard pies and a guest appearance by my latest protégé, long-haired Randolph Cozens, who brandished a can of hair lacquer. On the same day I received my school report. My new PT teacher, Mr Letton, noted my 'complete lack of aptitude for this type of work.' I thought my report could not get any worse. But I was wrong.

VIII

"'Dave' has been my downfall."
~ Diary entry, 20th July, 1964, aged 16 ~

Although we were supposed to be devoting all our time to imminent, all-important GCE exams, the partying continued into 1964. By this time I felt confident enough to throw a party of my own. Naturally it couldn't be held at my parents' flat. Dad was now obsessive about privacy; and if friends had the temerity to call without an appointment, he hid upstairs, or locked himself in the toilet, until they'd gone. For some reason, Essex Nana allowed me to use her new house in nearby New Southgate, a suburb so bleak and ugly that I couldn't wait to get back to Palmers Green. (Nana's former home in Highams Park had been compulsorily purchased for demolition. She moved to New Southgate with Auntie Gladys and her new beau, Dennis Sawyer, who married on 4th April. Their wedding breakfast – cold soup, salad and ice cream – was pathetically frugal: 'Rolls and butter were the best.')

At the party at Nana's my gang and I behaved like the typical young teenagers we were. Wild child Dirinda Pierotti 'brought most of the fags and booze and consumed most of it.' Janice Millard tried to get off with Peter Meekings. Apparently 'the fun began when the lights went out.' I was thrilled I was finally making headway as a heterosexual. 'I had my first arm-in-arm dance with a girl,' I wrote excitedly. But in the next line my diary tells another story. It seems I was also hanging out of the window, 'shouting at handsome sailors.' Later I heard that another gang member, Penny Davis, had tried to make a play for me and was disappointed that I treated her like a friend.

Penny wasn't unrealistic in her expectation for me to put out. Although I seem deliberately to have associated myself with a small group of kids whose prime interest was having old-fashioned japes, the rest of our school year, mostly prefects and sub-prefects, seemed intent on pairing up in readiness for marriage. Although they were only 15 or 16, they had been breaking the law for some time. It was common knowledge that several girls 'spent their spare evenings with rockers in mobile brothels in Alexandra Park Fields' and a party at Delia's had developed into an orgy during which my sporty hero Peter Gray had been among those who took girls upstairs. I know what you're thinking: young boys tend to boast of non-existent sexual conquests. But decades later I met Peter Gray again and asked him, 'Were you really having sex at school?' and he replied, bluntly, 'Yes.'

While many of its pupils were enjoying the new Permissive Society, Winchmore School was still being run like Dotheboys Hall. Canings were commonplace and on 24th March there was a mass flogging of boys who had played truant rather than participate in the hated cross-country run. 'Michael Halsey forged a note from his mum, but it didn't work,' I noted. 'He still got belted.' Because I was now not only a good writer but a good calligrapher to boot, I developed a reputation for forging convincing excuse notes from parents.

Being a born rebel I also had no qualms about cheating in exams. Nor, as I discovered, did anyone else. Our mock GCE exams were a travesty in which most of us had dictionaries and reference books under the desks and passed notes to each other throughout. For the German exam, Giles Sholl guessed which earlier paper we'd be tested on and bought it at a University shop. He was the only one of us to finish it. I would not have gained the four 'O' level passes I managed if I hadn't cheated. I took into the exam room crib notes hidden all over my body ('two in handkerchiefs, one in my spectacle case, two in the inside of my waistcoat.') I was aggrieved, after all this pre-planning, to see that 'Ross Bowden and several others had books on their laps.'

After sitting our exams there was a brief period before the summer holidays during which we were required to come to school even though there were no lessons. One day I turned up with my hair back-combed into a bouffant as worn by David Bowie on *Ready, Steady, Go!* I was called a cissy. I didn't have the courage to repeat the experiment. To fill our time some liberal in the staff room decided that the girls should be taught woodwork and metalwork and the boys cooking and typing. I learned to touch type, just about the only school-learned skill I still practice.

Much of my time was spent preparing what was to be the last issue of *Dave*. For weeks Deputy Head Mr Chalmers had been checking every word and censoring practically everything. At one point he refused to allow me to use the word 'ruddy' because 'everyone knows what that word really means.' Finally he demanded that every reference to a teacher must be shown to him or her and signed off by them before it was printed. It appeared that so much would have to be cut that there would barely be enough left to fill the magazine. On 2nd July, with only eleven pages printed, I made the decision to scrap the whole issue and went round the school refunding money. Then I decided to leave school at the end of term.

On 20th July, as a parting shot, I stapled together about ten copies of the unfinished magazine and gave them away to classmates as souvenirs. When Chalmers saw someone reading one of the copies in a corridor, he had a fit. I was expelled the same morning and cleared out my desk in a daze. My parents took my side but were powerless. I, however, wasn't.

Secretly I sent letters to the press suggesting that they investigate the matter. A few days later I arrived home to find Mr Godfrey from the *Evening News* waiting on the doorstep. I was thrilled to bits and invited him in to tell him the whole story. He told me he thought the school should be exposed. When Mum and Dad came home they were less thrilled. Dad telephoned the *News* to stop the story. 'I don't want our name in the papers,' he grumbled. I was furious. But soon I had something else to excite me. I was going to become a pirate radio disc jockey.

PART 3

OVERAWED
(1964-1972)

I

"People in Palmers Green liked a good Agatha Christie
– not the sound of a lavatory flushing."
~ Palmers Green & Southgate Gazette, 1973 ~

I was fortunate that my first national press exposure taught me a lesson every writer should learn very early on: no matter how good you may think you are, you will be re-written by somebody who thinks he's better. As has often been pointed out, this does not happen in other areas of the arts. Nobody looks at an artist's painting and then re-paints bits of it. But everyone thinks he can write. My mother repeated to me a story she'd heard. It had a great punch line. I sent it to the *Sunday Mirror*, which printed it on 16th February, 1964. I was shocked, not just because my story had been completely re-written from beginning to end, but because the punch line had been removed. But my name had been spelled correctly. That's all that mattered to me. I've been re-written regularly ever since and I've almost never complained. That's the way it goes. But if there ever has been the merest hint that I might not get a credit, I've raised my voice. Credits have been the be-all and end-all for me ever since, as a child, I read every name in the *Radio Times* and later stayed, sometimes alone, in the cinema to see the dregs of the cast list. 'Come on, let's go!' insisted Joan Byrne, the only girl I ever took to the pictures. '2nd Man in Street? You want to know who the 2nd Man in the Street was?' Well, yes. I was interested in all these people. I knew I was not going to leave children behind after my death. I wanted my name up there on the screen, with everyone else's, to prove that I'd been here.

For some time before I was expelled from school I'd been going to the cinema with a classmate called Jim Giddens. He was one of the football team and so we had nothing in common. Except films. He didn't seem to be anywhere near as obsessed with them as I was. But he was interested. Shortly before the end of my last term, when we were going to school and doing nothing in particular, he suggested we play truant and visit Soho. I had known for years that this small area of London was the heart of the British film industry and I had begged my father to take me. But we would go as far as Piccadilly Circus and no further. He wouldn't take me into the dirty back streets behind the London Pavilion because of the prostitutes that patrolled them.

Jim and I went to Piccadilly Circus and saw a gimmick film there called *Circlorama Cavalcade*. It was shown in a special cinema in which the audience stood inside a 360° screen. (The film was co-directed by soft porn mogul Stanley Long for whom I later worked.) Afterwards Jim and I explored Soho. In Wardour Street we saw a delivery boy carrying a pile of 35mm film cans. We looked at each other almost in awe.

In 1964 the idea of me, an inexperienced 16-year-old, getting anywhere nearer to the film industry than walking down Wardour Street was out of the question. Why I thought that breaking into radio would be a more realistic goal I have no idea. But that's what I attempted. I set my heart on joining the UK's first pirate station, Radio Caroline. It's often claimed that, prior to the 1960s, there was no pop music on BBC radio apart from David Jacobs' rundown of the Top 20 on Sunday afternoons. This isn't true. There were also several record request programmes and by the mid-60s they mostly played pop, even quite outlandish tracks like 'Surfin' Bird' by The Trashmen. I would sit for hours with my reel-to-reel tape recorder waiting for my favourites.

Certainly, however, there was no pop station in the UK while I was growing up. All we had was Radio Luxembourg. The signal from the Grand Duchy was weak, but it was worth persevering in order to hear all the new music every evening. Then in 1964 Radio Caroline began broadcasting pop all day, seven days a week, from a ship moored outside British territorial waters. The operation wasn't illegal because there was no British legislation in place to prevent it. Nevertheless the new station had an insubordinate image and so naturally I identified with it. During school holidays I listened to Radio Caroline and little else. 'We can't have this on *all* the time,' my mother protested. This cry probably was heard in many homes. But the so-called pirate stations (the UK was encircled by radio ships until the Marine Offences Act was passed in 1967) were what most young people wanted. BBC listening figures began to slump.

In the early days of Radio Caroline the disc jockeys were amateurs and they sounded amateurish. Some of them seemed never to have heard of the artists they were playing. I thought I could do better. Even Caroline thought its listeners might be able to do better. 'Enter for our DJ contest,' the station announced. 'Send a tape of yourself introducing five records.' I thought I'd go one better. I'd go down to the coast and board the ship. Like a pirate. I didn't tell anyone.

Two days after my expulsion I took a coach to Felixstowe on the Suffolk coast. There was by now a lot of press interest in Caroline and reports always mentioned the location its ship, the 'Mi Amigo', had dropped anchor. I had everything planned. I would spot the ship with the aid of the binoculars I'd brought, hire a boat and sail up alongside. The crew would be so taken aback by my daring that they'd take me aboard. Unfortunately the ship was nowhere to be found.

I traipsed up and down the Felixstowe front for hours, asking passers-by for help. Opinions differed. Sometimes the ship was off Harwich, sometimes off Walton-on-the-Naze, and sometimes still here in Felixstowe but obscured by mist. All I found was a Caroline coffee bar. But even the staff couldn't agree. The general consensus was Harwich and so I took a ferry to the port, the next town up the coast. Here I wandered about for half an hour until I met a man who seemed to know everything and pointed at the horizon. 'How far is that?' I asked. 'Sixteen miles,' he replied. I gave up. I had to catch the last coach back to London. Back at Felixstowe I just had enough time to go to a funfair. I went on the waltzer and nearly made myself sick.

Subsequently I plagued Caroline with begging letters and even visited their smart office in Mayfair. (Business was booming.) Eventually I received a nice, one-and-a-half page reply, which in effect said 'no.' The time wasn't right for me to make my radio debut. (Only eight years later, even though I'd still had no training, the time was right. After my eight hundredth broadcast I gave up counting and I'm still writing for and about radio today. It's often a lot easier working for radio than it is for television. Pictures complicate things in so many ways.)

Everyone who left school shortly before or after me walked straight into a job. They were mostly, by my standards, crap jobs – local government, retail management – but there were plenty of them. My next port of call was our local repertory theatre, the Intimate. While I was waiting for a reply I tried a radio and TV shop called R. Wright. Mr Wright gave me a piece of paper and told me to write down six reasons why I wanted to become a salesman. I didn't have one genuine reason; but Mr Wright was delighted with the lies I wrote and gave me an immediate trial.

I reported for duty at nine o'clock one Saturday morning and was told to do the dusting. Then I went out in a van with head salesman Robert to deliver a washing machine. When we returned, there were more appliances to load in and out of the van. Robert told me of the sense of achievement he felt after he'd finished polishing the shop's floor. I left at lunchtime and never went back.

The Intimate Theatre was largely unknown outside of Palmers Green. Probably this was because it was antiquated and did really unadventurous work. But it had an illustrious history. It had been opened in 1935 in a former church hall by up-and-coming young actor John Clements. He'd been in London's West End and had done a couple of movies. But his ambition was to run his own theatre. He made a modest success of the Intimate and continued to run it even after he was given a contract by London Films in 1939 and starred in *The Four Feathers*. Well-known actors began to make the trek to my home suburb and Richard Attenborough and Roger Moore were among the many that made their stage debuts there.

In 1942 a RADA graduate named Mary Stone began work backstage at the Intimate. I only mention this because Mary Stone became Marianne Stone, who went on to appear in more films than any other British actress and to become my surrogate mother. It was only then I discovered that I had been following her around for most of my life without knowing it.

I was shown the Intimate Theatre by its avuncular manager, Billy Budd. It looked as though it was much as it was when it opened nearly thirty years earlier. There were gas mantles on the walls. The stage, never intended for professional productions, was tiny. Sometimes an actor would exit stage left and then enter stage right panting and soaking wet. This was because the only way to get from one side of the stage to the other was to go out of a door, run around the exterior of the building, and come in another door. Lighting was controlled from a narrow gantry above the stage. Each lighting cue required a huge iron wheel to be turned. The whole place stank. The smell emanated from under the stage, where canvas flats were coated in size. The theatre, the last in London still doing weekly rep, wasn't to survive much longer. By the end of the decade it was pretty much dark and then the amateur companies took over.

Mr Budd told me I could start immediately as a dogsbody, helping out on the shows. Although I proudly claimed in a book[6] that I was paid, I wasn't. (Nor was Bob Hoskins before me.) My first job was as a call boy on *Dear Charles* starring an Intimate regular, Miki Iveria, who otherwise played bit parts on TV. I knocked on the door of the number one dressing room and said, 'Five minutes, please, Miss Iveria', and she replied, '*How* many?' This was the first conversation I had with a professional actor, albeit through a door.

While working at the Intimate I learned that I'd had a successful interview at Gateway Films, local producers of educational and industrial documentaries. I was engaged as an assistant film librarian (dogsbody) at a wage of £6 10s (£6.50) a week. Somehow or other, and only a little over six weeks after I had left school, I had realised my dream and got into the film industry. Today I'm still making films. Sometimes for about the same amount of money.

---

6 *Intimate Memories* by Geoff Bowden (Westbury, Wilts.: Badger Press, 2006)

II

"It is beginning to be hinted that we are a nation of amateurs."
~ Earl of Rosebery ~

I began my menial job – wrapping 16mm films in corrugated cardboard and brown paper and taking them to the post office – on my 17th birthday. I loved my first job, not really because of the work (although I learned useful new skills like tying knots and changing plugs) but because I was able to run riot in a teenage manner I should now as an adult find shameful but don't. Teenagers behave badly. That's what they're known for. 'School?' I wrote after my first day. 'You can stick it.' I was led astray by two lads a year older than me. One was David Budd, tough guy son of the Intimate Theatre's manager, Billy, and the other was David Rowley, an imperious posh boy, who I grew to admire because he seemed so clever. Budd plodded through the film business in lowly occupations for decades. Rowley was obviously destined for the BBC and that's where he ended up. But he fell in with a heavy-drinking crowd (that also included the comedy director Bob Spiers) and a promising career went down the toilet. Booze killed the pair of them.

On my first day at Gateway the lads showed off to the new boy by taking an axe to the worktable. On a recent 'We hate Gateway' week, they told me, they'd smashed a glass-fronted cabinet and some French windows. They were thinking of having another session shortly. We did as little work as possible and filled in the time by playing 'ice hockey' with two mops and a cake of soap on the newly-washed floor. On one occasion we stuffed lighted newspapers under the door of the toilet while secretary Joan Byrne was inside.

Budd also introduced me to pornography. One day he brought in a set of photographs taken at an orgy. 'I could hardly believe my eyes!' I wrote. I knew so little about sex that I described what I saw as 'sick-making perverted acts.' I daresay this makes the pictures sound a lot hotter than they were. I'd heard about filthy postcards and knew that you could be fined if you were caught in possession of them. But here was Budd bragging that he was going to blow them up and sell them for £5 a print. Somehow I doubt he ever did.

Despite my sexual inexperience and latent homosexuality I seriously considered having my first relationship with a woman. David Budd, Joan Byrne and I had a lot of play fights in the Gateway office. We would soak each other with water and on one occasion Budd held me down while Joan stamped 'SOLE AGENTS: GATEWAY EDUCATIONAL FILMS LTD' on my forehead. She was flirting with me but I was oblivious to this and indeed most things except movies, pop music and men in bathing trunks.

After a few months she began calling me on the new telephone we'd had installed at home then writing me twelve-page love letters. I was excited, not sexually, but by the prospect of being seen in public with an attractive, sophisticated, older woman. (Joan was 22.) She was also vivacious. There were some putative dates. I'd seen enough teen movies to know that, at the cinema, the boy *has* to put his arm around the girl's shoulder. I found this very uncomfortable and, when I got pins and needles, I couldn't concentrate on the film. Then Joan got up to leave before the end credits had finished. This relationship was doomed.

While messing around at Gateway, I began pursuing loftier ambitions. I sent articles to newspapers and magazines and stories to film companies, but everything was rejected. I spent a year compiling what would now be called a 'found footage' film, consisting of off-cuts from cutting room bins spliced between squiggles drawn directly onto celluloid by another Gateway librarian named Michael Austin. The film, *Swingin' Gateway 1964*, was the first production from Pathétique Films, a company I still own. Only ever shown to workmates, it's now lost. I lent the sole copy to film editor Jim Elderton, who casually informed me years later that he'd thrown it away. Probably it was my only masterpiece.

Having been introduced to the smell of the size I was also determined to get back on the boards. This was swiftly accomplished by joining Trent Players, North London's most prestigious amateur dramatic society. David Rowley, from Gateway, had been there since boyhood. The society trained several actors who later turned professional, the most celebrated of whom was Valerie Holmes, who said a couple of lines in an episode of *Hawaii Five-O* and then married one of composer Nelson Riddle's sons. Another famous member was bank robber James Hurley, who was rehearsing Trent's production of *Not Now, Darling* when he was arrested. His part was taken over by David Rowley. Hurley escaped from jail in 1994 and was one of the UK's Most Wanted until his recapture in 2007.

Trent Players was a hive of activity and always had several productions on the go. From the time I made my debut as a sheriff in *The Remarkable Mr Pennypacker* on 5th February, 1965, I spent many of my evenings playing walk-ons, collecting props and operating sound effects, sometimes back at the Intimate Theatre, which was one of the spaces Trent hired. The society also ran an Experimental Theatre Group, which attempted more offbeat work. This may have been Palmers Green but even Trent Players was aware of an exciting new movement called Fringe Theatre.

Then, only eight months after I joined, I was carried off to West Germany to play a policeman in Trent's production of *Gaslight*. I believe this was the UK's contribution to the one thousandth anniversary of the foundation of the city of Bremen. But I may have got this wrong. Memorably, however, the trip opened my eyes to the way adults behave when they are abroad.

Before the first performance of the play at Bremen's Niederdeutsches Theater, the British Consul invited our company of fifteen to a party in somebody's hotel room. Within minutes, it seemed, we were all falling-about drunk. Dizzy after one gin and tonic, I observed Cyril, the husband of leading lady Dorothy, pawing Sheila, and Dorothy herself draped around her leading man, John. The *grande dame* of the society, Eve, had left her husband back in London and come to Bremen with her lover, Bert, who bawled at the director, Norman, that his lighting was *horrible*. Meanwhile boorish old queen Bill screamed about how much he *adored* women.

In the early hours of the morning, other hotel residents began complaining about the noise. The party ended with John and Dorothy staggering to Sonia's room to rescue her from the British Consul. Now aged 18, but feeling 'very young and left out of everything', I went to bed to await the arrival of my room-mate, stage manager Stuart. But by 6.30am he still hadn't appeared. I wasn't the only one smitten by him and Anne the prompter had made the first move. After returning to London I got my photos back from the chemist. There was Anne, hovering somewhere around Stuart in every adoring picture I'd taken of him.

The novelty of wrapping films in brown paper at Gateway had worn off for me and everybody else at the firm knew it. After about a year on the job, I'd fallen out with most of the rest of the staff, but particularly the officious office manager, Mrs Bedell, and her prissy assistant, Penny, who'd both decided that I was a bad lot. On 21st October, 1965, Mr Webb called me in for a chat about what I wanted to do with the rest of my career. It took me at least fifteen minutes to realise I was being sacked.

Gateway Films was a lark of no significance on the rest of my life. But it set a pattern. I would also be fired from every nine-to-five job I attempted until 1972, when I realised that full-time employment was not for me. I've been freelance ever since. It could also be said that, while I was at Gateway, I first became a big influence on others. Two people whose lives went in a different direction because of me were my school pal, Jim Giddens, and his friend, Godfrey Kirby.

Jim had been following me on the road to perdition for some time. At the Winchmore School speech day I was forbidden to attend Jim had slouched up on to the stage, chewing gum, to collect his GCE certificates. For this misdemeanour he too was expelled. (For headmaster Shepherd expulsion was the last resort of an impotent megalomaniac. Months later he expelled Anne Jacklin's brother, Christopher, for refusing to be caned.)

Jim had been labouring in some soulless office, as was Godfrey. But when I told them about the fun I was having at Gateway, they both chucked in their jobs and went into the film business. Jim did a great deal better than me as I found out when I visited some of his lovely homes in California. Godfrey became a sound recordist and we've worked together to the present day.

III

*"There were hookers in all the doorways, porn shops, clip joints,
near-beer clubs and strip shows in every basement, and protection
gangs who were regularly exposed in the Sunday tabloids. Meanwhile,
Soho's regulars got on with the serious business of the day."*
~ Keith Waterhouse ~

Contemporary Films was one of several companies that exploited the popularity after World War II of foreign, subtitled films. The films were popular mainly with men who went to see them in the hope that they would include scenes in which naked women had sex. Contemporary, run by a group of idealistic Jewish Communists, aimed higher than some of its more exploitative rivals. But it was still very successful, so successful that, by the mid-1960s, it occupied the whole of one of the grand Georgian houses in London's Soho Square.

The company distributed its product to the UK's art houses. Every major city had at least one cinema that screened so-called 'Continental' films and London had around twenty. Contemporary also maintained a huge 16mm library consisting of films with what philistines called 'writing on the bottom' along with Hollywood classics, Ealing comedies and more. These were rented to film societies – clubs for what would now be known as film buffs. Before the video age these clubs offered one of the few opportunities to see old films.

The film trade called 16mm sub-standard in that it was inferior to the industry norm, 35mm, that was generally used for cinemas. But in the case of Contemporary, the 16mm prints were literally sub-standard. They were scratched to blazes and spliced to buggery as a result of being projected by amateurs. Less than a month after I was fired by Gateway, I was hired by Contemporary as one of the slaves who attempted to repair these tattered prints.

This job was sheer drudgery. But for a while I was again in my element. Here I was, not merely in Soho, heart of the British film industry, but Soho Square, heart of the heart. Next door to Contemporary was the animation studio of Richard Williams, a charming Canadian who showed me extracts from his masterpiece, *The Thief and the Cobbler*, destined never to be finished. Next door to Williams was the photographic studio of Jean Straker, always in trouble with the law because he distributed 'unretouched' pictures, in other words photos of naked women complete with their obscene pubic hair. Further round the Square were the Association of Cinematograph Television and Allied Technicians, the industry union which foiled my every attempt at membership, and the British Board of Film Censors, later to become the bane of my existence.

My compatriots in the repair department were another couple of Jack-the-lads. One was Ron Lloyd, a wiry Cockney geezer who loved movies. The other was Robert Hill, a good-looking, sexually ambiguous film fan, who, like David Budd, thrilled me with stories of his heterosexual love life, but also tried to kiss me in the film vaults and asked me, 'Do you love me?' If I'd had any sense, I would have bonded with Robert. But, because I was in denial, I told him I didn't answer stupid questions and chose to bond with Ron. Robert soon went off on a series of adventures that included digging the Victoria line and trekking around Europe. Decades later, to my huge surprise, he re-appeared as the star of a movie, *Down Terrace*. It's a funny old world.

Soho was as dirty and dangerous as my father had led me to believe. Prostitutes hung around in the doorways of St Anne's Court asking passers-by, 'Looking for a girl, darling?' When Robert took me to a coffee bar full of 'pill-pushing, street-walking, swearing, greasy types', I couldn't concentrate on a word he said to me because I was so scared. But where there's muck there's movies.

I excitedly recorded in my diary every celebrity I glimpsed, not just starlet Jill Mai Meredith in a restaurant and old ham Sir Donald Wolfit in Leicester Square, but semi-famous names in Contemporary itself, where the visiting cinéastes included character actors Victor Maddern and Martin Benson. One day I was required to project the first reel of *Shakespeare Wallah* for its director James Ivory. On another I saw a TV crew filming in Carnaby Street and made sure I walked behind the person being interviewed. Four days later I watched myself on the Saturday evening show *On the Braden Beat*. Thanks to Soho I was now a star of stage, screen *and* television.

After a couple of months I'd made such an enemy of my boss, Harry Brown, that I hated going into work and longed to escape. I still felt I had the ability to be a professional writer of some sort, any sort, and from 1966 I really began to put myself about. Godfrey Kirby lent me a copy of the script of the Hammer version of *The Phantom of the Opera*. Nowadays kids have to pay gurus to teach them how to write screenplays. But all I did was read screenplays until I knew enough to write my own. I also completed my first full-length play, *I'm Not Doing What You Think I'm Doing*, yet another McG title that implied masturbation. As before, all the jokes were stolen, but this time the entire plot was stolen, too (from *Murder on the Orient Express*). At one point, strange to relate, it was going to be directed by Nicholas Parsons at the Hampstead Theatre Club. Nothing happened. In 1983 I found a copy of the script and re-read it. It was so bad that I tore it up.

My first breakthrough was the magazine *Films and Filming*. I sent editor Peter Baker film reviews I'd written for *Dave* and he invited me to his luxurious flat near Baker Street. He gave me a glass of wine, we sat on his couch, and he told me he was 'a great torch-carrier for youth.' What he meant was that he liked boys. But I didn't pick up on this. *Films and Filming* was a gay magazine but everyone knew it except me. I remember telling fellow film critic Tony Rayns how I met Peter Baker and Tony remarking, 'Did he fuck you?'

I'm jumping the gun now but I ended up writing for *Films and Filming* for nearly 25 years; and, when it was about to fold, I was asked to write a potted history of the magazine for the final issue.[7] Rather boldly I outed the magazine for the first time, observing that it was known in the business as *Queers and Queering*. I even recounted the story about sitting on Peter Baker's casting couch but added, quite honestly, that 'I wasn't 100% sure what a homosexual was.'

Years later, when I was fairly sure what a homosexual was, I wrote regularly for the London gay magazine *QX* and in one issue[8] I exposed even more about *Films and Filming*. I revealed that, until homosexuality was partially decriminalised in England and Wales in 1967, men contacted each other via coded messages in the magazine's personal column ('Active young man, 20s, with gay disposition, required to accompany London bachelor, 42.') Frequently these messages disappeared, presumably because of police intervention. Then, after a few months, they would creep back.

In 1966, however, I was unaware of all this. No, Peter Baker didn't fuck me. He began giving me films to review (at £1 a go). I became acquainted with a previously secret institution, the preview theatre. This was a cinema where press shows were held. Every other basement in Wardour Street had one. Some of them had more seats than the small screens in Leicester Square have today. At one, called the Anglo, I saw the first film I was paid to review, *Spy in Your Eye,* an Italian second-feature. When it was published in the October, 1966, issue of *Films & Filming,* I ran all the way from the newsagent to Contemporary to show it to everyone. For a while I was Britain's youngest film critic.

By the end of the year I was in print again, this time in *Film,* the magazine of the Federation of Film Societies.[9] Somehow I'd managed to persuade the editor to let me write about the first blue movie I'd seen. I described how I'd been walking down the road in Palmers Green when John Vilton ran up to me and invited me to Jim Giddens' house. An 8mm projector had been set up and a bed sheet had been nailed to the wall. Godfrey Kirby had got hold of a stag film.

I recounted its entire content in a crass, tongue-in-cheek style: 'The couple seat themselves on the divan and after a brief interlude, during which the stars are chided by the cameraman as to what comes next, the young

---

7   March, 1990
8   30th June, 2004
9   Winter 1966

gentleman suggests an idea which is obviously agreeable to both of them and the plot deteriorates rapidly.' After publication I was told by more than one person that I could be prosecuted for viewing a pornographic film. I wasn't. So I carried on writing about porn for the rest of my life.

Now that I was a professional writer I felt that Contemporary had nothing more to offer me. I was desperate to leave and Harry Brown obliged by firing me. I met John Dickie, the man who was going to take over my job. I found him a darned sight too cocky, dead lazy and pretty incompetent. 'He reminded me of me,' I wrote, 'which came as a shock.'

IV

"One road leads to London,
One road runs to Wales,
My road leads me seawards
To the white dipping sails."
~ John Masefield ~

Towards the end of my stint at Contemporary I was no longer merely ogling celebrities as they passed, I was hob-nobbing with them. My hoist up this next rung of the show biz ladder was provided by actor Michael Billington, who was now in the TV soap *United* and making a name for himself. He took Contemporary films to parties and sometimes invited Ron Lloyd and me to come along as well.

More than once we went to the Notting Hill flat of former child actor Andrew Ray, son of Winchmore Hill's Ted Ray. Andrew had a wife, Mike had a girlfriend, but Mike and Andrew used to fondle each other on the sofa when the lights were turned off, and most of the other guests seemed to be gay. Ron and I were a little concerned about this. We were both, after all, heterosexual. Just before I left Contemporary I went to the Food Fair and 'fell passionately in love with a girl at the Cow and Gate stand.'

A regular visitor to Contemporary was Sam Goodman, who ran Data Film Distributors from a room in a Victorian edifice in Newman Street, five minutes from Soho Square. Sam was a dapper little Jewish grafter, who made me laugh. He even made me laugh when he offered me a job. 'As long as you've finished your work, you can do what you like,' he promised. 'Bring a girl up. I don't care.'

I accepted his offer, but I regretted it almost immediately. For the next year I was trapped in the kind of desk job I'd always dreaded. I was typing despatch sheets and filing stupid pieces of paper alone in a room with my boss so I had to keep working. It turned out that comical Sam also had a bad temper. The arguments started when I asked for time off to go to press shows for *Films and Filming*. He gave me it but he didn't like it.

After about five months he sacked me. He'd found my replacement, an agitated spinster named Miriam Ritblatt, who he felt would be better suited to mind-numbing routine. He was wrong. She lasted three days before handing in her notice, and Sam was forced to bribe me with £5 to stay on. God knows what made me accept it. But it was all meant to be. Subsequently Sam spent more time out of the office and I was left to my own devices. One of my devices was to hang out in the room next door, where a smouldering Greek

Cypriot ran a handicraft company. He was grateful that I coached him on his upcoming English exam and I was grateful that I could look at his face.

Sometimes Sam's wife, Vi, would pop in. She was a pleasant enough old biddy. But she would ask me questions, out of the blue, like, 'Have you been to China?' and I thought she was a bit dotty. It turned out that she was a mystic. Her favourite method of psychic reading was psychometry. One day she asked to hold my watch and then predicted my future.

I have to confess that, until quite late in life, I was a sucker for the paranormal. For me it had all the nonsense of religion but none of the portentousness. I'd been playing with Ouija boards since I was at school and I was so convinced by my first séance, held by candlelight at Jennifer Battley's on Halloween, 1964, that afterwards I woke my parents in the early hours of the morning. 'The glass practically floated!' I gushed. 'It was *not* being pushed!' I was still taking part in séances until the mid-1970s. By this time I was on tour with my theatre company. At the digs after the show we would bring out the letter cards and the wine glass. On one occasion all the messages were for one actress, Jean Selfe. We asked her to close her eyes, after which the 'spirit' could spell out only gibberish.

Vi Goodman had me in her thrall from the moment she told me that she was in contact with my Auntie Annie. From where did Vi pluck that unusual name if not the ether? Annie told Vi that I had connections with Ireland and children – clearly this was a reference to Fidelis School – and that, although I would be successful later in life, my potential was being crushed by my family who didn't understand me. Oh, how true! Only now, reading my diary, am I reminded of the things Vi got completely wrong. Or perhaps the huge significance of Switzerland in my life has yet to manifest itself.

The supernatural – and Hammer films like *A Taste of Fear* and *Paranoiac* – fired my imagination. When Ron Lloyd told me he'd made a new contact who needed a script for a horror film set in a cotton mill, I immediately knocked out a treatment for *Screams from the Mill of Blood*. The contact turned out to be Tony Tenser, who'd co-produced one of my favourite films, Roman Polanski's *Repulsion*. The months went by and not a word was heard from him. I later incorporated one of the script's grislier deaths into Pete Walker's *Schizo*.

When Ron's own horror film also fell through, he told me to write a script for a film that we could make together. This was to be *Losing Track*, a gargantuan undertaking with dozens of locations and a cast of hundreds. Because I was involved in so many other assignments, all of which had to be written while Sam was out of the office on business, it took me more than six months to complete the shooting script. If you were to see the film – and I'm afraid this one hasn't been lost – I think you'd be surprised to learn there was any kind of script at all.

It was also during this period that I honed my brand of malicious sarcasm and Goon-like absurdity in a column I wrote for Trent Players' new monthly newsletter. In amidst the rehearsal schedules and social calendars there appeared something called *Looking at You* in which I poked fun at other members of the company. From the first issue I caused outrage, in which I basked. The editor refused demands for the column to be dropped but began censoring references to the society's senior citizens.

I regularly bunked off early from work because my evenings were now as full as my days. I was out almost every night, usually at a party. This was the era of the first large-scale 'happenings' and I was not only present at the *14 Hour Technicolor Dream* but also its lesser-known follow-up *The International Love-In*. Unfortunately it was also the era when the acts were so stoned that they lost all track of time and stayed on stage seemingly for hours.

Until it was discontinued by the executive committee, Trent Players' Experimental Theatre Group had degenerated into a piss-up. The same party animals would meet at each other's houses, get rat-arsed and play the Truth Game, devastating for me when Sheila asked me, 'What would you do if you found yourself in bed with a girl?' (I was able to reply honestly, 'She would have to make the first move.')

Sometimes I carried joints for those too lily-livered to transport them from one house to another. One evening, on the way to another shindig, I was stopped by a policeman on a so-called 'Noddy bike.' By this time I was earning £13.10s (£13.50) a week, much of which went on frilly shirts and kipper ties bought in Carnaby Street. On the night in question I was in loons and an op-art PVC shirt. The copper told me to turn out my pockets. When I asked him why, he replied, 'You look like the type that carries drugs around.' I wasn't carrying drugs so I complied. But I protested. The copper said, 'Well, if you will go around wearing those clothes, what can you expect?'

When they heard of my run-in with the law, my parents were incensed. Soon we were all at the police station and I was filling in a statement sheet, which was to be passed to Superintendent Stubbs. A few days later I came home to find the man himself explaining to Mum and Dad that stop and search was legal. I had the devil in me and wanted to make a formal complaint. I did. Probably Superintendent Stubbs filed it in the wastepaper basket.

Just before I completed a wasted year at Data I absconded twice to follow my secret love, Trent Players' stage manager, Stuart, to the Rhondda Valley. After breaking up with his girlfriend, Stuart had decided to save the world. He contacted the International Voluntary Service, which sent him to work on community projects in Wales. When he asked me if I'd like to come down there and do some manual labour, I said yes. I'd taken leave of my senses.

As befitting a good deed done for the wrong motivation, my Welsh sojourn caused me more heartbreak than anything I'd experienced to date in my young life. This had nothing to do with Stuart, who picked me up in Cardiff, dumped me in the village of Llwynypia and then disappeared out of my life forever. No sooner had he departed, however, than I fell for volunteer Peter from Nottingham.

'People are *not* going to believe I have done this,' I wrote after spending my first night in a derelict boys' club, where young people from all over Europe slept on the floor, six to a room. During the days we dug a pit, which was to be turned into a children's adventure playground. I loved every minute of this backbreaking work because Peter, a blond Adonis who could have been a Warhol superstar, latched on to me and began dropping hints. He talked about Edward Albee and left more and more of his shirt buttons undone.

In the evenings the international volunteers drank in the pubs that admitted foreigners (even the English were foreigners) and danced to a record player back at the boys' club. One evening everyone drifted off one by one until only Peter and I were left. What should have happened didn't. When Peter said, 'Do you want to go somewhere?' I knew what he meant and was suddenly petrified. 'I think I'd better go to bed,' I replied, stupidly. I think he was hurt. I say this because, when the time came for me to return to London, I said goodbye to a crowd of my new friends and noticed Peter saying nothing and then turning away to look at the floor.

In the back of somebody's van, returning to a job I loathed, I was in the depths of despair. At home I had a bath, which only served to wash away the last traces of Wales. I started crying and then couldn't stop. 'Little things kept reminding me of Wales,' I wrote. 'What made it so special?' I seem to have convinced myself that I missed the camaraderie of the international volunteers who all, regardless of the amount of English they spoke, knew the words of 'All You Need Is Love.' A romantic notion. The truth is I wanted to see Peter again.

When I told David Rowley about my adventures in Llwynypia, he surprised me by agreeing to drive me back there the following weekend. I received a tumultuous reception and before long I was ankle-deep in mud, digging a trench in a forest. Peter, however, was now somewhat distant. On my final day I joined a party that went down the local coal mine. We were given lamps and helmets; descended at 60 mph in a cage; crouched beneath sagging roofs waiting to be propped up; and visited stables where horses were kept in the pitch dark. This was 1967, not 1867, and yet horses were still being used to haul the coal, and canaries were still being used to detect gas. I know I experienced all of this because I wrote about it. And yet I cannot remember any of it.

What I remember as if it were yesterday is the communal shower we had when we returned to the surface. I can picture the layout of the showers and exactly where Peter was standing naked; and how I deliberately stood far away from him, next to a fat, plain boy; and how it was only his presence and his mundane chatter that stopped me getting an erection every time I glanced at Peter, silently soaping his perfect body. This was a vision of what might have been. It would have to suffice.

All I allowed myself to write about this *amour fou* was, 'I'd sincerely like to keep in touch with Peter.' I can now translate this as, 'I need to see Peter again so much that I can barely concentrate on anything else.' Subsequently, at various times, I tried to trace him. Although his surname is unusual, I never succeeded. Let this be a lesson to everyone reading this.

V

"I did one of my prima donna acts because everybody was saying that they
had to leave in five minutes and couldn't come back, and Rosamund,
our utterly useless continuity girl, walked out on us for good..."
~ Diary entry, 8th June, 1968, aged 20 ~

Sometimes, to alleviate the boredom at Data, I went through the trade press looking for films Sam Newman might be interested in distributing. He even went along with my suggestion of *No. 4*, Yoko Ono's film in which 365 naked bottoms walk away from the camera. It wasn't such a daft idea. Yoko was hot and the film was getting a lot of publicity. But when Sam went to meet the producer, Yoko's husband Anthony Cox, he didn't show up.

Godfrey Kirby, now working as an editor for a Soho production company called Cineform, told me that one of its bosses, Jim Elderton, had made a short called *The Bent Man*. 'A bit of a mess', it wasn't going to be Sam's cup of tea, and I took it no further. But I'd made another contact and, a few months later, I joined Cineform as an odd job boy. Jim ran Cineform from an office above a tailor's shop in Noel Street. He was beaming and owlish, a bit like a trainspotter, but he was different in that he was always searching for something indefinable. One of the things he found was a cult, EST, which sent him a bit doolally. Jim and I worked on a few projects down the years. But he was always trying to escape and he ended up in Canada. It seems to be working for him.

Jim's business partner was Michael Brandt, a dry old stick who may have lived in Swinging London but certainly wasn't part of it. He'd begun as a clapper boy on *Caesar and Cleopatra* in 1945 and to Godfrey and me he still seemed to date from that era. But he was probably in his late 30s. A shareholder in the firm was Nicholas Parsons.

Cineform made documentary films perhaps one notch up from Gateway, but I don't think I ever saw any of them. All I was required to do was build shelves and answer the phone if nobody else was in the office. But, as before, I was distracted from my work by more interesting people next door. Cineform rented a cutting room to a sleazy producer named Bachoo Sen and, as I've described elsewhere,[10] I was fascinated by the film that was being edited there. It was *Her Private Hell*, a pioneer British soft porn drama, and I'd never heard of it.

It was the first feature film directed by 25-year-old Norman J. Warren, who told me he was looking for scripts. I inundated him with my rubbish,

---

10   Notes for *Her Private Hell* (BFI Flipside DVD/Blu-ray, 2012)

Screams from the Mill of Blood et al. He wasn't interested in any of it. But in the 1970s, when the time was right, he shot two of my screenplays and we've worked together on bits and pieces ever since. Norman is one of the nicest people in the business. I expect this is why he hasn't worked much lately.

It was around this time that I left home.

Things had improved at Park Avenue because I was hardly ever there. But when I was, it was business as before. On one terrible evening, Dad threatened once again to leave for Whitley Bay and Mum tried to commit suicide by stuffing pills in her mouth. Then, after another row, Dad crushed a metal cigarette box in his hand, cutting it so badly that he had to go to hospital to be stitched up. They both had been telling me to *get out of this house* for years and I would have been quite happy to comply if I'd had enough money for rent. Later an opportunity presented itself. Auntie Gladys and Uncle Dennis moved from Essex Nana's house in New Southgate to their own flat in Palmers Green and now Nana was willing to have me as a lodger.

I moved to 86, Warwick Road, on 8th October, 1967, just after my 20th birthday. It was another of my bad decisions. After all, Nana's three daughters and two sons-in-law couldn't live with her, and Dad couldn't even bear having her to stay with us for Christmas. Maud Peterson was an intelligent and relatively emancipated woman. But, as I discovered, she was now very set in her ways, and as it transpired marking her time until death. She wasn't the most generous of my relatives. When I was in bed with 'flu, she brought me a light snack. After I'd recovered, I received a bill:

1 soup	1s 6d
1 egg	3d
1 slice toast	1d
1 cup tea	5d
Total	2s 3d (11p)

Out on my own at last, I had to learn more new skills, like ironing and shopping. It was tough. I astonished Jim Elderton when I asked him, 'How do you buy tomatoes?' He didn't know what I meant. 'Well,' I said, 'do you buy them one at a time?' I really hadn't got a clue. Boys of my era, who generally went straight from being looked after by their mothers to being looked after by their wives, didn't need to know this information.

Looking back at 1968 the biggest mystery is how I got through the year. I did the occasional day at Cineform and other cutting rooms. But I wasn't able to accept much professional work because I was too busy being an amateur. I wrote *Dead on his Feet,* a ghost play for Trent Players, and with Jim Giddens I completed my first feature-length screenplay, *The Small World of Edward*

Type, a James Bond-style espionage adventure with a cast of children playing adults. It pre-dated *Bugsy Malone* by eight years.

David Rowley, by now a regular collaborator, recommended me for the juve lead in a play, *Citizens Are Soldiers,* a translation of Lope de Vega which Ruth Fainlight and Alan Sillitoe had done for a youth theatre called 1520 CT. I liked its work but I also liked the idea of being in close proximity for a few weeks to a Byronic actor with an unromantic name, Martyn Benge. The play was done at Oval House, one of London's earliest Fringe theatres. I was to return there regularly.

But for most of the time – often seven days a week, day and night – I was preparing and directing the calamity that was to become *Losing Track,* a comedy film as funny as the unfunniest film you've ever seen in your life. It was doomed before the camera started rolling. Jim Elderton read the script and said that it had no cohesion or progression. 'You could almost put the scenes in any order you liked,' he told me, 'and it wouldn't make the slightest difference.' The same could be said of the finished product.

Reading my account of the protracted shoot is agonising because I was in such misery from beginning to end. The feat of assembling unwilling participants every weekend is now incredible to me. It was achieved at a time when there were not only no mobile telephones but no answering machines either. Day after day, if people couldn't be reached, I walked to their homes and put messages through their letter boxes or waited for them to return. I was forever in public telephone boxes, making free calls by tapping out the numbers on the phone rest, a ruse I'd learned from delinquent mates. This crime had to be carried out in the knowledge that at any moment the fuzz could descend. The police had a lot more spare time in those days. In November the local paper reported that, after keeping watch on a Southgate telephone kiosk, police arrested a 14-year-old boy for 'fraudulently extracting electricity' from it. He was fined £4.

The slog of film production came as a complete surprise to me. I thought everybody would want to help make a movie. They didn't. They had to be begged, and, if they agreed, they regretted it because I didn't know what I was doing. After a month, our cameraman, David Percy, was so disappointed by my incompetence that he feigned a nervous breakdown in order to bail out. (The next I heard of him he was a conspiracy theorist, claiming that men never landed on the Moon.)

He was replaced *faute de mieux* by Derek Scott, who stuck with us to the end but never once turned up on time and was sometimes hours late. He wasn't the only one. Regularly actors didn't turn up at all. I moved heaven and earth to secure the services of TV newsreader Gordon Honeycombe. We waited for him, he didn't show, we telephoned him. He said he wasn't coming because it was raining. It rained a lot that summer, problematic for a film consisting entirely of exteriors. Scenes were re-scheduled again and again and then re-shot again and again because we couldn't get things right.

Matters came to a head one July weekend when I took a huge number of people in several cars to Southend-on-Sea for a scene on the beach. There was trouble all the way there and back. David Rowley and Bob Spiers, now working for the BBC, fell out with my schoolmates, David Bubb and David José. As a parting shot, José let down the tyres of Rowley's car. Rowley found out who the culprit was. 'Get rid of that kindergarten that follows you around!' he yelled at me down the phone.

Because the stock was processed secretly by lab technicians whenever they could spare the time, our rushes – which another of our guest artistes, Michael Billington, called crawls – sometimes didn't appear for weeks or months. Latterly they didn't look at all good. My co-producer, Ron Lloyd, called in a professional cameraman, Ray Selfe (his name will come up again), who confirmed that the film was fogged. Light had got into the camera. About 50% of the footage was unusable.

Ron wanted to re-shoot the following summer. I told him I'd rather have teeth pulled. I suggested salvaging the usable material and putting it into a documentary along the lines of *The Epic That Never Was,* a great BBC film about *I, Claudius,* left unfinished in 1937. I suppose that was a little unrealistic. Eventually I let Ron talk me into carrying on. All in all, *Losing Track* was in production for five years. I'm trying to think of a more colossal waste of time. But I've gone back as far as the days of Sisyphus and I still can't.

VI

"If I'd mastered a pen, I would have become a great writer."
~ John Lawrence ~

1968, the most joyless year of my life, appears now to have galvanised me into action. In November, while *Losing Track* was struggling to a standstill, I offered my services, at £1 per day, to Youre Shop, the Islington boutique where I later tuned in, turned on and freaked out. Whether this opened my mind to new horizons, who can say? But it's on record that the following year I was gainfully employed for the first time in major motion pictures and prime time TV. As an extra, granted, but this was the equivalent of an Academy Award to this star-struck kid from Palmers Green.

During 1969 I worked on my second screenplay, *In the Fast Lane,* with John Lawrence. John was a fellow screenwriter *manqué*, who had been following in my footsteps, first at Data Film Distributors then at Cineform. Back in the day *Reader's Digest* ran a regular feature called 'The Most Unforgettable Character I Ever Met.' I always said that, if the magazine asked me to contribute to this feature, I would nominate John.

He was, and is, that rarity, a charismatic, ebullient polymath who has chosen never to share his singular genius with the world. He fascinated me because he appeared never to have had a job that lasted more than a few minutes and, lacking any official documents, never to have existed. (He is now, libel lawyers please take note, completely legitimate.) As with my drug-dealing partner, Ricky, years later, John and I clicked immediately because we shared the same love of obscure British bit-players. Marianne Stone brought us together. But John knew more about everything than I and, for example, I was rendered speechless by his ability to reel off every British prime minister since Pitt the Younger. 'Well, everyone can do that,' was his typical response to my disbelief.

John had an idea for a movie. I liked it and began working on it with him. I can't remember what it was about and, because the script is almost certainly lost, it's unlikely we'll ever know. But, while it existed, it created interest. John sent it, with a fawning letter, to director Lindsay Anderson, who sent an equally fulsome reply, but regretted that it was not for him. Jim Giddens' flatmate, TV commercial director Misha Norland, on the other hand, wanted to direct it. It never happened. Misha became a homeopath. But while the script was doing the rounds, it fell into the hands of Michael Billington, and basically, because of this twist of fate, I'm now writing this book.

After John had followed in my footsteps to the extent of being fired by Data and Cineform, he took a succession of lowly jobs. He ran a bookstall at London's grandest new alternative arts venue, The Round House, during the run of *Hamlet* with manic Nicol Williamson as the Dane and hippy chick Marianne Faithfull as Ophelia. When the cast came to buy books, I shmoozed them. Roger (*Colonel Blimp*) Livesey was particularly chatty and I was all a-flutter. Meanwhile John rummaged in the wastepaper baskets and came up with a letter from Kenneth Anger asking Miss Faithfull to be in his film *Lucifer Rising*. Eventually she was.

I also accompanied John when he drove around the Home Counties selling second-hand 45 rpm pop records to corner shops. His boss, Johnny Franks, was a blue comedian, who needed material for TV. John and I went to see his act in a working men's club in Deal, Kent. I thought he was abysmal. But John loved him. We wrote him some new gags, which he turned down. In 1970 he made it to TV. He was on *Opportunity Knocks*. He told the same gags he told in Deal. He got the lowest score of the evening. But he was still playing care homes up until his death in 2013 at the age of 86.

I thought I'd discovered a nice little earner when Godfrey Kirby showed me a piece in the *Sunday Express* about Britt Ekland paying a company $35 a week to take her dog for a walk. I advertised my services – 'YOUR DOG WALKED TWICE DAILY' – in *The Times*. I got no response apart from a heavy-breather who asked, 'Is it a lady offering the service?' Weeks later, two young men advertised an identical service in *The Times*, got nationwide publicity in other papers, and in all probability made enough for their planned 'trip to Spain.' I hope the paella choked them, the gay bastards.

I doubled my Youre Shop daily rate to £2 when I signed on at a cleaning agency called Clean-a-Flat, run by Marvin D. Brown, a whiz kid who boasted to me that his agency and various other enterprises brought him in £1,000 per week. He may have shouted his mouth off a little too much because one day, while I was out working for him, he was robbed by the self-styled Black Power leader Michael X, who told Brown that, if he wanted his record books back, he'd have to bring more cash to a notorious commune in Holloway Road called the Black House.

When Brown did as instructed, he was tortured by Michael X and at least seven other men. All eight went on trial in April, 1970, and two were sent to jail for assault. Within months Michael X was again charged with extortion, but skipped bail posted by John Lennon and returned to his native Trinidad, where in 1975 he was hanged for the barbaric murder of Gale Benson. I mention this only because of what was going on in the real world while I was intent on self-promotion.

I was Brown's lackey for about 18 months, on and off, and although most of the work was soul-destroying, the people I met made it almost worthwhile. If there was a big job, like an hotel room wrecked by an Arab playboy, I got to know some of Clean-a-Flat's other operatives. Most of them were musicians. 'If they all got together, they'd be a supergroup,' I wrote. One of them was Richard Denton, who told me he'd written the score of the film *Loot*. He wasn't lying. I met him again by chance and interviewed him.[11] He's now a TV director.

My clients included a survivor of the Titanic; a teen heart-throb of the 1950s (Jerry Wayne); an American monologist in London to appear in a Marty Feldman movie (Shelley Berman); and a crazy American film director (Fred Marshall), who did one pop musical, *Popdown,* and then vanished along with his film, now highly sought-after by cultists. My most illustrious client was Lady Charteris, wife of HM The Queen's Secretary, who lived at St James's Palace. To my surprise their rooms were quite shabby, 'well below the Golders Green standard I've become used to.'

Brown told me shortly after I began at his agency that, as a kind of rite of passage, all his cleaners had to work at least one day for Mrs Gubbins, who he claimed was as mad as a hatter. She was indeed. She would tell me to do something and then yell at me to stop doing it this instant! The most disturbing moment came during my break, when I put sugar in her coffee. 'She stormed around the kitchen for some minutes, crying, "How dare you come to my house and put sugar in my coffee? Thousands of people in this country don't take sugar!"' I got a tiny insight into her troubled state of mind when she mumbled, 'I can't seem to make people understand me.'

That night I wrote, 'There's a mountain of material for a script here.' The script came to pass, a mere 36 years later. In my film, *Wednesday,* a young woman named Lilli (Rebecca Santos) comes to clean for mad Mrs Furnival (Anna Wing). Almost everything Lilli observes – even the arrival of Mrs Furnival's gentleman friend, Mr Pomeroy (Victor Spinetti) – happened to me. I named Lilli's agency Clean-a-Flat. I felt that these two lunatics were quite capable of killing me and that's what they end up doing to Lilli. It's such a cliché, but nevertheless true that, if you're a writer, even your worst sufferings need not be wasted.

I needed this dreadful cleaning work during the times when I was resting from my proper job as a professional actor. I'd joined the Film Artistes Association, the union which controlled all crowd work in British films and television and also ran the famous agency Central Casting. I'd missed out on the last golden age of the film extra during which it was possible to work for

---

11   *Films Illustrated*, May 1973

months on end in epics financed from Hollywood. But I caught the tail end of it and can still be glimpsed in quite a few major movies.

The first was Michael Winner's *The Games,* about the Olympics, shot in the White City stadium, which had been built for the 1908 Olympics, but was now a white elephant awaiting demolition. There was no longer enough investment in British films to fill it with spectators. Instead it was filled with dummies plus groups of human beings into which the camera zoomed. One of the real people was me, clearly visible for a couple of seconds behind a starlet named Elaine Taylor.

Most of the extras were elderly eccentrics, who'd been human cattle for years. On my first day as one of their number, I was befriended by Rita Tobin, who reeled off all her pictures going back to the silent days. I found the work only slightly less degrading than cleaning. 'The tea breaks remind me of the workhouse in *Oliver Twist,*' I complained, 'and at the end of the day 500 stampeding animals fight each other up the stairs for £4.10 [£4.50].' But for many years the thrill of going to the cinema and waiting to spot myself on the big screen made my heart pound.

Don't worry, I'm not going to list all the films in which I'm a face in the crowd, only the significant ones. In *The Magic Christian* I'm standing bottom right of the screen when the passengers disembark from what they think is a ship and realise that they're in a film studio. The film was directed by Joe McGrath, whose career reached rock bottom when he later directed my script for *I'm Not Feeling Myself Tonight.* I'm also in the theatre audience watching Orson Welles in *12 + 1,* a film remembered only, if at all, for being Sharon Tate's last.

Also largely forgotten is the Charlton Heston version of *Julius Caesar* in which I'm one of 350 plebs listening to speeches outside the Senate. One is the opening speech of the play, where Marullus upbraids the fickle rabble for transferring its allegiance from Pompey to Caesar. The scene took all day and around 30 takes to complete because the actor playing Marullus kept fluffing his lines. (He was a TV actor; this was his first big film and also his last.) By late afternoon we all knew his speech, but he never did and the scene was patched together from the bits he remembered. I still know the speech ('Wherefore rejoice? What conquest brings he home?') and I can recite it at the drop of a hat.

While I was on *Cromwell* the extras' stop steward asked me if I wanted to do TV work and of course I said yes. I was taken on by a Poverty Row agent, Jeff Shane, who told me to get some photos taken. The photographer I chose, Dugald, had a family that would have inspired Tennessee Williams. Dugald's father drank two bottles of spirits a day and regularly went missing. Sometimes he had to be tied to his bed with washing line. An attempt was made to dry him out at 'a nursing home for rich lunatics' that turned out to be The Priory. Its fees, I recorded in astonishment, were as much as £9 per day. Dugald's father wore spectacles with one blacked-out lens, which made him look very sinister. When I was writing *House of Mortal Sin* for Pete Walker, I gave the weird housekeeper, Miss Brabazon, the same specs.

When I wasn't flitting from studio to studio and from sink to dustbin, I was either stoned or plodding on with my godforsaken film *Losing Track*. Another year of shooting required me to go cap in hand to Enfield Council for the continued use of the Broomfield Park running track, our main location. We got it, but the grumpy park superintendent, Mr Marsh, was openly hostile and instructed his park keepers not to co-operate with us. We borrowed equipment then returned it when they weren't looking.

By the end of 1969 I'd asked almost everyone I'd ever known to step in front of the camera – school friends, family, Trent Players, Clean-a-Flat clients (after a morning's shooting Mrs Madden wandered off and was never seen again) and Nicholas Parsons. We began editing at weekends at Cineform, but in June the company shut up shop. At Ron Lloyd's we ran hours of unedited rushes for friends. Michael Billington said, 'There isn't one memorable shot there.' Another three years of this ordeal stretched ahead.

Just before Christmas I became a temporary postman, helping with the Christmas rush. Another temp was Greek Cypriot medical student Alexis Tsianides; and when I sat next to him in the mail van, gazing at his profile in silent admiration, all my troubles were forgotten. On our last day together I was distraught. But you would never have guessed this from the single, vague reference I made to him in my diary: 'I will keep forming attachments for people. Breaking up is hard to do.'

For some months I'd been desperate to get out of the house I shared with Essex Nana or, as I now called her, Crabface. By early 1970 we hated each other. She left me a letter informing me that in future I should keep to my room and not trespass in the rest of her home. Fortunately John Lawrence had come up with a solution. We'd been looking for a flat to share together and now he'd found one, the basement of a house in the Vale of Health, a 19th century encroachment on to Hampstead Heath. The Vale was a charming enclave that had long attracted artists, thinkers and pseuds. While I lived there, my neighbours included the actors Alan Bates and George Coulouris. The house was owned by Ivan Seruya, another old Commie with connections to Contemporary Films. More recently, however, he'd been working for Johnny Franks.

At first glance, the basement at 1, The Gables, appeared to be my dream home. It was only after we moved in, on 1st March, 1970, that I noticed the plaster peeling off the walls and the fungus in the bathroom. But squalor isn't very important when you're 22. Eagerly I got down to work. Trent Players produced my play, *Dead on his Feet,* at the Intimate Theatre as part of the Southgate Drama Festival, and in the bar afterwards I got my first taste of adulation. The play did even better at the Maidenhead Drama Festival, where adjudicator Bernard Prentice declared, 'It's difficult to understand why it hasn't been published.' Accordingly he gave it an award, Best Unpublished Play, and that certificate is still on my wall. I became a professional playwright in 1971, when *Dead on his Feet* toured schools in Surrey.

Godfrey Kirby tipped me off that documentary film producer Joe Mendoza needed some help. Joe was a jolly old soul but a bit garrulous. Every topic of conversation reminded him of a film he'd once made. His most successful, *Yeats Country,* had been nominated for an Oscar. Joe wasn't feeling well and needed somebody to do his shopping and cook his lunch. He took an instant shine to me. I suppose sex was at the back of his mind because one day I went round to see him and found him in the shower with the bathroom door open. After he died in 2011, his daughter told me somewhat ambiguously that he liked to help young men. I didn't press her.

Joe was very good to me. He recommended me for two jobs he didn't want, writing the narrations of an advertising film for Pontins holiday camps and a travelogue. These became my first films as a professional writer. Joe and I also worked together for a long time on a screen adaptation of the Robert Louis Stevenson short story *The Bottle Imp.* I came to look on Joe as a father confessor. He was the first man I ever told that I was 'confused.' I didn't go into too many details, but the exact nature of my confusion must have been obvious. Joe didn't take advantage and instead asked me if I thought psychiatry might help.

My sexual confusion was caused by self-denial of such magnitude that surely the only person hidden deeper in the closet was Liberace. I longed for a man but had a very real horror of homosexual sex. When I was first seriously propositioned, just before Christmas, 1967, at the ABC cinema, Turnpike Lane, I recorded the incident as 'a very frightening experience.' A queer sat next to me and put his hand on my arm. I glared at him and he said, 'Sorry.' Then he put his foot against my leg and I moved to another seat. That night I wrote, 'When I got over the horror of it all, I could only look back on the event with disgust and sincerely hope that it doesn't happen again.'

It did happen again in 1970. This time it happened because I'd gone to see the uncensored version of the film *Flesh* at the Open Space, a private club that, because of a loophole in the law, was able to show films rejected by the BBFC. I kidded myself that I was there only to see the first screening in London of an Andy Warhol film. I expressed dismay that almost all the people coming out of an earlier screening were male. I was nervous as I took my seat.

No sooner had the lights gone down than I felt a clutching hand. I was so petrified that, when Joe Dallesandro stripped off, I pretended to go to sleep. My hysterical diary entry, a whole page of it, needs no further comment from me other than my plea for every openly gay man's forgiveness:

> 'My legs literally [sic] turned to jelly. One of the worst experiences of my life. The combination of ghastly sex on the screen and ditto in the audience was thoroughly revolting and has affected me very badly. I'm angry, too. How dare people make advances to me? Why didn't I make him regret it? Why didn't I shout out loud, "Fuck off, you queer! Sit somewhere else!"? Why? Because I haven't got the guts. Suppose the rest of the audience were queers, too (quite likely), and told me to shut up? Horrible. I'm in a state of shock.'

I was in such shock that almost immediately afterwards I went to see Andy Warhol's *Lonesome Cowboys* at the Arts Lab.

I find it astounding that, another four months on, this homophobic basket case was working for the British Film Institute. It shouldn't have happened. One day I was a sexually mixed-up cleaner and almost the next I was helping to edit one of the world's most respected film magazines. But it happened. And this is where the story really starts.

VII

*"When I came to the NFT to be interviewed, the fact that you take film so
seriously there made me feel proud to be an artist."*
~ Liv Ullmann ~

The British Film Institute is not what it was. It was once an elitist organisation consisting entirely of stuffy intellectuals who had little idea what was playing at the Essoldo, Neasden, in other words the commercial films that normal people wanted to watch. The only members of the public who were aware of the BFI's work were a handful of sandal-wearing beardies who went to Bergman screenings at the BFI's National Film Theatre.

Nowadays of course the situation is completely different. The BFI's London Film Festival promotes Hollywood blockbusters that open in Leicester Square with red carpet events that attract screaming teenagers. The National Film Theatre, now called BFI Southbank, is thronged with young people who spill out of its bars and restaurants on to the fashionable South Bank of the Thames and may have no idea that, in addition to being a party venue and pick-up joint, the NFT is also a government-sponsored art house.

Let me take you back, however, to the mid-1960s, when I discovered the BFI's *Monthly Film Bulletin,* which synopsised and reviewed every film released in the UK and listed all their credits, sometimes even including Marianne Stone as 4th waitress. You can imagine how much I appreciated this. I became a BFI member in 1966. By 1970 I reckoned I knew the *MFB's* house style well enough to apply for a job as a reviewer. Assistant editor Jan Dawson tried me out by sending me to a minor Western, *El Condor.* I passed the test. Jan described my synopsis as impeccable and gave me half a dozen more films to review.

Simultaneously I was writing the scripts of the two films for which Joe Mendoza recommended me. This work involved going to and from the offices of Drummer Films, which were in what remained of Alexander Korda's Denham Studios. Drummer was yet another company that produced dreary documentaries. I saw one of them, *The Buccaneers,* in 1968 and wrote, 'A lot of aeroplanes of the Fleet Air Arm take off and then all land again. Tough on those who don't like looking at aeroplanes.'

The publicity film for Pontins required me to visit several of the camps with a three man crew. Assistant cameraman Mike was a cool young buck and electrician Chic was a rough old navvy, and they both pulled birds every night. I heard them going at it hammer and tongs on the other sides of the thin chalet walls. The resulting film, which I called *Where Do We Go From Here?,* was shown to prospective campers at Pontins' Oxford Street offices and was also used as part of the company's Christmas Day TV commercial. This included drunken old Fred Pontin himself, reading his lines off cards. It was ludicrous.

The other film consisted originally of rushes brought back from Yugoslavia, the only Communist bloc country that encouraged tourism from the West. I looked blankly at this collection of unrelated shots of buildings and had not the slightest idea of what to do with them. I went to the library and borrowed a stack of travel books on Yugoslavia. These became the substance of my commentary (spoken by Bob Holness, the *Blockbusters* host). I asked John Lawrence for ideas for a title. He suggested *Slav Trade*.

Everyone involved in Drummer's post-production was a tired old hack who had not the slightest interest in what he was doing. All that mattered was that the films were the right length so that they could qualify for subsidy provided by a government fund. When the rough cut of this film, now called *Wonders Will Never Cease*, was run, it was too short. The editor simply pulled the off-cuts out of the bin and joined them on the end. 'But just before we leave Yugoslavia, let's remind ourselves of some of its sights...' To my amazement, the film was actually shown in cinemas, supporting *Tora! Tora! Tora!* I later found out that this happened only because the Yugoslav National Tourist Office had promised someone prominent on the Rank cinema circuit a free holiday.

Drummer's producer, Martin D. Harris, knew I was a beginner and had little faith in my ability. But he was also desperate and offered me another film, this time for the Navy. I had to go to sea. One morning I was in an hotel in Weymouth, waiting to be collected. I wasn't collected and the ship sailed without me. When the Ministry of Defence's PR man, Mervyn Ellis, found out about this, he was livid. On 2nd December, 1970, he wrote Martin a letter that I have kept to this day:

'Dear Martin,

Thank you for your letter of 25th November, 1970, about Mr McGillivray. I have deliberately left the matter for a day or two before replying to it so as to be certain that my actions were not governed by my outraged sense of courtesy, responsibility and enterprise.

'I do not think it profitable to pursue the question of blame or whether Mr McGillivray was given the correct instructions. What sticks out a mile, however, is the total lack of enterprise, responsibility and courtesy he possesses. Whether or not he can produce the sort of script we are looking for must clearly be in some doubt...'

Mr Ellis was right to be doubtful. I couldn't produce the script he was looking for and, to my huge relief, I was fired by Drummer Films. But I would just like to say to Mr Ellis that, three years later, I wrote *House of Whipcord*. So put that in your Navy Mixture and smoke it, you self-important cunt.

Although I was now officially a professional writer, I was still an amateur as well and I honestly don't believe I've ever stopped being one. In the autumn of 1970, Trent Players returned to West Germany, this time to Hamburg as guests of the Hamburg Players. I tagged along again. We performed *I Have Five Daughters*, a dramatisation of *Pride and Prejudice*, at the Theater an der Marschnerstrasse, and I played a servant. By 1970 the standard of living in Germany had soared even higher. I went shopping with the girls and we gazed in awe at the stylishness of the clothes. I remember April Reid holding something up and asking me, 'If you were a man, would you wear this?' People were beginning to suss me out. I ventured with the blokes into the Reeperbahn and peeked at the women sitting impassively in the windows, reading newspapers to pass the time.

David Rowley came along to play Darcy and to instigate most of the misbehaviour in the hotel rooms. The doors slammed and feet thundered up and down the stairs until 5am. Rowley was shagging at least two women in the cast and was drunk from lunchtime onwards. I've got a photo of him lying incapacitated on the floor of our ferry cabin. All the signs were there that he couldn't handle his drink, but not that one day it would kill him. (It also killed one more of the cast, Alan Clark, who was another of Rowley's drinking pals.)

Rowley was by now editing my film *Losing Track* after hours at the BBC. I was still shooting it. Periodically I would find myself back at my co-producer Ron Lloyd's house with a regular crowd of minor celebrities, hangers-on and dope fiends. We would watch rushes, then as often as not we would watch porn. Lots of people now seemed to be able to get hold of it. The air would grow heavy with dope smoke. Sometimes I lay there thinking that, if the police raided us now, the *News of the World* would get the mother of all front page stories.

Ron said that his new lodger had £18,000 to invest in something profitable. John Lawrence had an idea for 'Midnight Theatre', offbeat plays performed in the early hours of the morning. At a typical evening at Ron's, the Bacardi came out and John proceeded to drain the bottle. Another of the guests was Michael Billington, who loved our script, *In the Fast Lane*, and had recommended it to Gerry and Sylvia Anderson, the *Thunderbirds* people, who were now producing *UFO*, Michael's new TV series.

Michael was as drunk as John and I watched in horror as the evening disintegrated. A film of *In the Fast Lane*, produced by the Andersons, became less likely by the minute. John's description of Midnight Theatre became more incoherent and suddenly he was asking if Michael wore a toupee. (He did.) Suddenly Ron and John were fighting on the floor. Michael departed, saying, 'Why not open a midnight launderette?' Looking back at my escapades, I see that my career very easily could have ended around this time in intemperance and debauchery.

But I was pulled back from the brink by the British Film Institute.

While I was writing reviews for the *Monthly Film Bulletin,* I was also ingratiating myself with its management by finding hard-to-find information about films. When I was at Drummer I would pop next door to Rank Film Laboratories and copy credits off their prints. Suddenly the *MFB* was able to print reviews that had been on file for months. In November Jan Dawson told me she was being promoted to editor and asked me if I'd like to apply for the post of assistant editor before it was advertised. I said yes. At my interview I casually handed over to Jan a Peter Sellers checklist, verified as accurate by Sellers himself, for the *MFB*'s back page. The job was mine.

VIII

"If you hear a mysterious scraping sound on the South Bank...
there's no need to worry:
it's just a generation of snooty cinéastes turning in their graves."
~ Time Out ~

I've always said with great pride that I introduced the rot that destroyed the foundations of the British Film Institute. Prior to my engagement as the assistant editor of the *Monthly Film Bulletin,* established in 1934, the BFI never had employed anyone like me. By that I mean someone who actually preferred trash to masterpieces. Wikipedia, not that we should give it any credence, gives me a kind of official recognition for this achievement. ('David McGillivray and Paul Taylor took exploitation movies more seriously than had previously been considered acceptable.')[12]

I took up my appointment at the BFI's office at 81, Dean Street, right next to Soho's wicked St Anne's Court, on 18th January, 1971. My salary was £1,492 per annum, a colossal £28.69 per week. (Decimalisation arrived in 1971, causing delightful confusion.) I worked in a room with editor Jan Dawson, a little ball of erudite nervous energy with, as it turned out, massive insecurity. I discovered that she never could review a film before going to the BFI library and checking what other critics had written about it. She would only ever toe the party line. We were both under the aegis of the editorial department head, Penelope Houston, who worked further down the corridor editing *Sight and Sound,* an egghead quarterly nobody read.

For a while Jan and I got on famously. Even though she was intimidatingly bright and I had no education, I thought we were kindred spirits. 'The BFI is full of spinsters of both sexes,' she told me, absolutely true. If you'd come out of university with a bookish mentality and little ambition, you could work for the BFI until you retired. But, as soon as we'd discovered each other's little ways, Jan and I fell out. Everything I did irritated her. After I left the BFI, I believe she developed some kind of hopeless infatuation with a *Wunderkind* of the New German Cinema and she couldn't handle it. She first attempted suicide in 1975 and succeeded in 1980.

In 1971 the UK was in the eye of the softcore porn hurricane. Sex films had been growing in popularity throughout the 1960s. But in the 1970s they became a box office phenomenon, and *Adventures of a Taxi Driver* was one of the most successful British films of 1976. Almost as soon as I arrived at

---

12 *Monthly Film Bulletin* (Wikipedia)

the *MFB* I was sent to review *Alyse and Chloé* because nobody else could be persuaded to sit through it. A pattern soon developed and I saw a lot of soft porn. I didn't mind in the slightest. Normally I would have paid to see these films. In June I actually did pay to see Pete Walker's *Cool It, Carol!*, one of the most momentous films in my life. It was while I was working at the BFI that I began worming my way into Pete Walker's life.

I expressed astonishment that most of the *MFB*'s reviewers – David Robinson, John Russell Taylor, Tony Rayns, Tom Milne, Nigel Andrews – were gay as were many of the film makers that drifted in and out of our office. The classically beautiful Antony Balch had clocked me at the BFI's Christmas party and asked Jan if I was available. She said she didn't know and so he tried to pick me up in a preview theatre. Naturally I wasn't having any of that. But my irrational attitude to queers began at long last to mellow during this period. (This was partly because I was having my head examined.) I allowed Tony Rayns to take me to the Biograph in Victoria, Britain's oldest surviving cinema, opened in 1909. It was also London's best known gay hang-out and had been for decades. Quentin Crisp mentions it, though not by name, in his autobiography *The Naked Civil Servant*. He simply says that there is a cinema in London, where all kinds of films are shown, except those with snow scenes, because these reflect too much light back into the auditorium. I knew full well what went on in that auditorium. Here's how I described my first evening there. Note the difference in tone to my previous description of my experience in a gay cinema, which had occurred only the previous year:

'The whole place is a mass of activity, which never lulls. There are not the usual noises of a cinema. No one speaks and few people laugh because nobody watches the films. Instead there is a constant squeak of springs as men change their seats and keep up a steady traffic to and from the lavatory. At any one moment there are always two or three men on their feet.

'Initially I thought all the transactions must happen in the bogs. But no. In the row in front of us, one man started masturbating another and, when the act was completed, he casually wiped the sperm off his hand on to his trousers. Then two men sat down beside me and immediately unzipped each other's flies. An usher patrolled the aisles, checking that things didn't get out of hand. The lights never went up.

'We joked about it over coffee afterwards. The surprising thing is that nobody seems to go to the cinema to make a pick-up. The prime object seems to be to masturbate as many men as you can in one evening.

And that's all you do. No kissing, no communication. You just sit next to someone, toss them off, and then change your seat.

'I asked Tony, 'What would be the film that would stop them wanking?' He didn't think there was one. We saw Curtis Harrington's camply sinister *Games*. It was hard to concentrate on it.'

The Biograph suddenly was demolished in 1983, allegedly to forestall a preservation order as a building of outstanding interest, which it was for more reasons than one.

As with Gateway Films I loved my work at the BFI so much that I couldn't wait to get to the office each morning and sometimes stayed there until 9pm. But as always I became bored with the routine and distracted. I continued to work for Jeff Shane and regularly took time off to do TV bit parts. Apparently (we'll never know because the episode was wiped) I was prominent in *The Shattered Eye,* an episode of a cult horror series, *Out of the Unknown*.

On another shoot I met a New Zealand actor, Murray Noble. I was convinced he had star quality. We began hanging out together, regularly sampling a newish trend, lunchtime theatre. At a film preview I introduced Murray to one of the *MFB*'s few heterosexual reviewers, David Pirie. David had a room to rent in his house and Murray took it. I had begun putting people together, a skill I subsequently honed.

Because I was now in the thick of it, film journalism-wise, others asked me to pen movie-related pieces. I began writing for *Time Out* and was still doing this when I wrote Pete Walker's film *Frightmare*. This is why I mentioned the London listings magazine in my script. I also contributed to Gothic authority David Pirie's seminal book *A Heritage of Horror*.

Then *Films and Filming* began running my reader service column, which made me an extra £10 per month. (I was to continue answering readers' questions, for a succession of film journals, for the next 25 years, until, typically, I was fired.) It was through *Films and Filming* that I met another lifelong friend, Michael Armstrong, Like me, Michael was an actor who never really had acted and instead had been sidetracked into journalism. Unlike me, he'd managed to pass himself off as a film director and already had helmed a couple of morbid slashers, *The Haunted House of Horror* and *Mark of the Devil*. Michael fascinated me. He was a powerhouse, forever dreaming up grandiose projects, a handful of which came to fruition. Down the years I've participated in a couple of these.

This was also a period of major emotional upheaval. Things had soured between John Lawrence and me at 1, The Gables. John moved out and sub-let his room to a bohemian couple, Harry Scott Gibbons and Marion Chesney, both of whom subsequently became successful authors (although all I remember about them is that I lent them £25 and they never re-paid me). When landlord Ivan found out about the sub-let, he gave us notice to quit.

It wasn't hard to find alternative accommodation. Contemporary Films' accountant, Jean Salter, had bought a ground floor flat in nearby Kilburn and she offered me the front room. It was huge, and Kilburn High Road, with its bustling shops and four cinemas, was on the doorstep. (I didn't know it then, but Marianne Stone and her journalist husband, Peter Noble, lived around the corner in Abbey Road.) My rent was £4.50 per week. I moved to 22, Birchington Road, on 18th April and was to stay in Kilburn for the next 24 years. Jean, a sensible, middle-aged spinster, was the perfect landlady. We never had a cross word. Within a few years she set me up for life.

I also sorted myself out once and for all by undergoing psycho-analysis. I was writing *The Bottle Imp* with Joe Mendoza, who had by now discovered pot. We grew very close. When I told him I thought I needed help, he recommended the Brent Consultation Centre, where I poured out my heart. I was referred to the Portman Clinic, quite a well-known establishment, where treatment was free for young people. I told my shrink that I'd heard there was a cure for homosexuality and that's what I wanted. Fortunately the Portman didn't go in for that sort of thing. I was told to come back once a week and lie on the couch. I wasn't hopeful. 'It's just talk, that's all,' I wrote. 'How can it help?' When I told friends what I was doing, they were sympathetic. One woman, whose daughter suffered from depression, told me, 'As soon as you think you need help, get it.' Today that's what I tell other people.

I suffered the most terrible blow to my self-esteem around this time when I attempted to revive *Dave,* my school magazine. As the tenth anniversary of the first issue was approaching, I thought it would be fun to produce a special, anniversary issue. My former contributors didn't just think this would not be fun, they were astonishingly hostile to the idea. 'Are you overcome with nostalgic grief for the past?' John Franklin wrote. 'How nauseating.'

David Bubb, once my comrade-in-mischief, went even further. 'Dear Cunt,' he wrote, 'Bollocks to your letters of 19th July and 2nd August. Why do you try so hard to preserve your old friends? Probably because you haven't any new ones.' He enclosed a piece of toilet paper on which he'd written, 'This should wipe the slate clean.' I didn't know what I'd done to deserve that. I telephoned him. He claimed he'd been drunk when he wrote the letter and that I shouldn't take it to heart. I hung up on him and didn't speak to him again for several years. This was my last attempt to keep in touch with school friends.

Profoundly hurt, I decided to cheer myself up by going to New York. I'd wanted to go for years. An American student, Abby Moss, came into the *MFB* office. I asked if I could stay with her and she said yes. I left London on 21st January, 1972. I'd never been on an aeroplane before and was captivated by the push button that reclined my seat, and the painting on the wall that was reversed to become a movie screen. Take-off was euphoric, 'an almost exact equivalent of grass,' I wrote. (I'd tried grass, the new successor to cannabis resin, for the first time the previous year.)

Abby's mother was a theatrical angel and, no sooner had I landed, than I was whisked to a rehearsal of *Dylan*, starring an old movie star, Carleton Carpenter. 'It seemed largely to consist of people walking in and out.' Days later I was at the opening night of *The Sign in Sidney Brustein's Window*, also dull, but with a terrific 'new' actress called Frances Sternhagen. Then we all went to Sardi's to wait for the reviews. They weren't good and the play was taken off after five performances.

Abby and her mom soon tired of me. But Abby's stepfather was kind and drove me to every landmark and through deadly Harlem. Although it was broad daylight, I wasn't allowed to unlock the car door, let alone get out and take pictures. On my own, however, I was drawn again and again to Times Square and 42nd Street, forming an attachment to the area that lasted until it was gentrified in the 1990s. Probably you can imagine why I loved it so much. But for anyone who never knew it in its scuzzy prime, it was Soho higher, wider and dirtier.

The stretch of 42nd Street between 7th and 8th Avenues was lined on both sides with cavernous old theatres that had been turned into cinemas or, as they were then known, grindhouses. They ground out double and triple bills sometimes almost 24 hours a day. Here and there were the new porno cinemas. *Deep Throat* and porno chic hadn't quite arrived. But the earliest examples of hardcore porn were playing. *Screw* magazine, the obscene likes of which never would have been allowed in the UK, recommended the Park-Miller theatre, where I saw *Get That Sailor*. As with mainstream cinema, there was a full supporting programme – silent shorts ('loops') which were shown with strangely incongruous music, for example 'What Kind of Fool Am I?'

Back at the BFI, I realised my days were numbered. Everything I did was wrong. I spent weeks compiling a checklist of the work of Bessie Love, whose career went back to *Intolerance* in 1916. In 1972 she was doing a walk-on in a John Osborne play in London. She was my kind of actress and I had tea with her. Boring academic Colin MacArthur marched in to the *MFB* office. 'Who chooses the checklists?' he demanded. 'Bessie Love for fuck's sake! How does she fit into the culture of the cinema?' After he'd stormed out again, I had one of those *l'esprit de l'escalier* moments. 'She has quite a lot to do with the *history* of the cinema,' is what I should have said.

I thought about moving on again. I was bursting with new ideas and the demand for my services was growing. But work of any kind was difficult at this time. The miners were on strike and we were experiencing the first of the power cuts that eventually were to bring down the Conservative government.

Having never experienced the blackouts of World War II, it was eerie to walk down streets in pitch blackness. Not even traffic lights worked. At the BFI we kept working until the natural light failed and then we groped our way home.

I bumped into De, the Youre Shop man, and reluctantly agreed to go round to his Islington flat to discuss his idea for a revolutionary TV series. Youre Shop was no more. But in the flat upstairs everything was much as it was. Before she departed for a meeting of her women's liberation group, De's wife, Julie, told me that they'd got some amazing new grass that had left her with no self-control. De lit up a joint and I hardly need tell you that our business meeting didn't get very far.

De told me about his idea, but it didn't make any sense. Probably this was because it didn't. I didn't tell him this. But half an hour after I'd puffed the magic dragon, I heard a placatory comment I'd made echo back to me, mockingly, and then the atmosphere of the room folded in on itself and the room became Drugland, where the truth had to be told. I had no option but to tell De that I'd never been able to communicate with him and that his idea was shit. Just like before, De loved all this. 'Are you gay?' he asked me. We continued in this manner for some hours, becoming along the way confidants so close that I felt that De should divorce Julie and marry me. Then the drug wore off and I knew full well that I couldn't work with this crazy man if my life depended upon it. De's revolutionary TV series was never made.

Everything 'fell into place,' as I described it, when I went to collect some credits from the Wardour Street office of Miracle Films and found Ray Selfe there. Ray was a larger-than-life character who described himself as a journeyman film maker. He'd helped out with my film, *Losing Track*. As I wrote in *Shock Xpress 1*,[13] 'I wasn't quite sure what he actually did for a living, but it was something between mending projectors and running ITN.'

Ray was working on a 3D sex film, *The Four Dimensions of Greta*, directed by Pete Walker. By this time I'd seen not only Pete's *Cool It, Carol!* but its follow-up, *Die Screaming, Marianne*. I thought Pete had talent and I wanted to interview him. I asked Ray to put in a good word for me and he did. I got a call from Pete the same evening to say that he would be 'fascinated' to meet me.

By 1972 I'd seen an awful lot of skinflicks. The standard was low. Even Pete Walker's early work – the likes of *Strip Poker* and *Man of Violence* – was poor, but it had ambition. Suddenly, with *Cool It, Carol!*, it was almost as if Pete had grasped not just the rudiments of film making, but the trickier art of storytelling. He had a good script based on a true story about a silly country girl lured away to the bright lights of London; and, despite the opportunistic sex scenes, the moral tale seemed to reflect new attitudes as

---

13   London: Titan Books, 1991

the swinging Sixties gave way to the more cynical Seventies. I'm on record as saying[14] that *Cool It, Carol!* is 'probably the best British sex film ever made.'

Pete Walker had got into soft porn early enough to have made a fortune from it. He had an office in Mayfair, and a mansion in Esher, Surrey, and he travelled between the two in a Rolls Royce Corniche. He was urbane and witty and, like virtually all the smut merchants with whom I've worked, obsessed with Hollywood's Golden Age. He was also flattered by my attention and we got on extremely well. I wrote a long piece about him and sent it to *Films and Filming*. As with almost everything else I wrote for the magazine, it was filed away to be brought out months and, in this case, years later.

The one exception to this practice was something of mine that was rushed into the August, 1972, issue. In June the editor asked me to write an introduction to a feature he was running on the arrival of dirty movies in US cinemas. The editor was now Peter Baker's former assistant, Robin Bean, who could no more edit a magazine than give birth. But his salacious photo spreads kept generations of gay men entertained when there was little else of a similar nature to look at. Robin was a gay maverick, pretty much talentless, but none the less an important figure in the secretive annals of gay history. I was very upset when he died, aged 53, of an asthma attack in 1992.

When I opened the August, 1972, issue, I was appalled. 'The piece I wrote on exploitation has been attached to one of the most garish, homosexually-slanted articles the magazine has ever published,' I whinged. 'My 1,000 words have been stretched over several pages, filled out with lurid stills. I sincerely hope this won't get me a bad name.' Unfortunately it did. Penelope Houston gave me my notice shortly afterwards.

What I wrote in my diary about *Films and Filming* was shameful backsliding into self-loathing. It wasn't the lurid stills to which I objected, it was their homosexual slant. The article I prefaced was essentially a puff for Wakefield Poole's hardcore porno *Boys in the Sand,* and I didn't want to be associated with that either. This is despite the fact that I considered seeing *Boys in the Sand* when I was in New York, but had been put off by the bad review in *Screw* and chose *Get That Sailor* instead. What a fool I used to be. Quite apart from that, the dirty movie article, by Peter Buckley, was far better written than my own in *Film* in 1966. Looking at this embarrassing situation from another angle, however, it now seems as though I was making statements about my sexuality even while I was struggling to come to terms with it. Here I was, after all, attaching my real name to a piece about gay porn in a gay magazine. I was to take more baby steps of this nature in the months following my departure from the BFI. I never officially came out. I really must get round to this.

---

14   *Doing Rude Things: The History of the British Sex Film 1957-1981* (London: Sun Tavern Fields, 1992)

PART 4

OVERWORKED
(1972-1995)

I

"My mother groaned, my father wept,
Into the dangerous world I leapt."
~ William Blake ~

After I left the BFI I had every intention of finding another job. But I never did. I've described myself as unemployed ever since. Initially I continued to work morning, noon and night as an amateur. Throughout 1972 I toiled on the post-production of *Losing Track*. This was as arduous as the production itself. Editor David Rowley had given up trying to make a silk purse out of a sow's ear and had been replaced by Jim Elderton, who hacked and hacked until the running time was reduced to about 20 minutes.

The film had been shot silent and therefore required a commentary. There was no possibility of going to a professional recording studio. The session took place in Ron Lloyd's back room, soundproofed with quilts. The projector was in the garden pointing through the French windows. Indoors Godfrey Kirby taped the microphone to a broom handle. Ron's friend, Roger Moffatt, and I improvised the commentary while we watched the film projected on to the wall. There were no re-takes. That's how we did it in those days, kids.

Towards the end of the year there was technical stuff – sound dubbing, negative grading and the preparation of a finished print – that I had to pay for. Through Ron's connections we arranged to show the film to cast and crew in the New Year at the huge MGM preview theatre in Mayfair. At this time I still had faith in my comedy film. 'This will be the gala event of the decade,' I predicted.

I was also still a big cheese on the am dram scene. There had been an unfortunate incident at the party after a Trent Players production. After three glasses of wine, I'd asked John if he was really having an affair with Dorothy, and outed a new, female member of the society as a lesbian. Consequently it was necessary for me to move on to Cameo Players. This was a Jewish group and I became their gentile plaything.

I met Herschel when we were both in a one-act play called *Ritual for Dolls*. I was a golliwog, he was a monkey, and although the relationship was never going to go anywhere, I didn't care. I just wanted to be in his presence.

Because of the huge success of my improvisation classes, Cameo asked me if I wanted to direct a play, Ann Jellicoe's *The Rising Generation*. I didn't like the script. But Herschel was the stage manager. I said yes.

This was one of the most chaotic stage productions I ever worked on. The young cast was so undisciplined that they turned up late for every single rehearsal, and one of them turned up late for a performance. I saw him sneak on to the stage after the play had begun and casually take over his lines from his understudy. But another of the cast was Walter Zerlin Jnr. Within three years Walter and I would leave Cameo and set up our own company, Entertainment Machine, which created the Farndale Ladies, the only one of my comic achievements which will outlive me (because I want 'Floreat Farndale' on my gravestone).

Despite its socialist principles, *Time Out* sometimes didn't pay me. This was OK by me. But sometimes the magazine overstepped the mark. 'Furious that I was not given a credit this week,' I wrote in September. 'That's the only reason I'm doing it!' Apart from the *MFB*, for which I continued to write, my only paid work was for a new magazine, *Let It Rock*. This was partly the brainchild of John Pidgeon, who nearly got my *MFB* job, then stayed on as a reviewer.

John and I shared an interest in early British pop. Therefore I was able to sell him my idea of interviews with nonentities from the pre-Beatles era. The first interview I set up was with Heinz. He was the bass player with The Tornados and, because their producer, Joe Meek, fancied him, Heinz was launched as a solo artist. He was quite hopeless, but that didn't matter because he was sexy. I saw him in a film called *Live It Up!* in 1963 and he became my latest flame.

By the time I met Heinz, it was fairly common knowledge that he'd been Joe Meek's lover. I tried to get him to confess, but he skirted around the subject and finally took his 'secret' to the grave. I loved Heinz because he had absolutely no pretension. He also had no personality or ability, also plusses in my book. Read my interview with him[15] and marvel at my adoration. John Pidgeon and I went on to work together many times and, for a reason I can no longer remember, I named the hero of my film *I'm Not Feeling Myself Tonight!* after him.

Following my interview with him, Pete Walker began to court me. I was invited to the press show of his 3D sex film, *The Four Dimensions of Greta*, then to the shoot of his next picture, *The Flesh and Blood Show*, done in the theatre on Brighton's Palace Pier. I wrote a piece about my visit for Tony Rayns' short-lived *Cinema Rising* magazine. 'Jane Cardew, her toes curling up with the cold, glumly removes her knickers for the twelfth time that day. You can see the sea through cracks in the floorboards.'[16]

---

15   *Let It Rock*, December 1972
16   *Cinema Rising*, May 1972

Four months later (Pete Walker didn't mess around) I was invited to the cast and crew screening of *The Flesh and Blood Show,* an Old Dark House thriller with sex. I predicted that this would be Pete's crossroads picture. Would he continue with sex films or move to the mainstream? (I was to find out sooner than I expected.) Also at the screening, although I didn't discover it until I read his biography more than forty years later, was Pete's friend, Sal Mineo, who had his fifteen minutes of fame as the boy who idolised James Dean in *Rebel Without a Cause.* Mineo now wanted to direct a movie of Robin Maugham's scandalous novel *The Wrong People,* and was hoping Pete would put up some money. It didn't happen. Mineo and his partner, Courtney Burr, hated *The Flesh and Blood Show.* 'It was awful,' Burr claimed, 'And this was the guy we were trying to get to produce our film.'[17] (Decades after Mineo's murder in 1976, I began chasing the rights of *The Wrong People* myself.)

Because he felt indirectly responsible for the loss of my job at the BFI, Robin Bean rather touchingly offered me the post of advertising manager at *Films and Filming.* I declined because I had bigger fish to fry. By now I'd met Ray Selfe several times. He was a wonderful raconteur of the wind-him-up-and-leave-him variety and he'd entertained me enormously with his strife-torn stories about a sex film he'd produced called *Sweet and Sexy.* This was another story I wanted to tell the world.

Ray gave me a great interview, which stretched over several evenings.[18] At the end of the first session, he asked to read *In the Fast Lane,* which Michael Billington had recommended to him. Ray read half of it before offering me £100 to re-write the script of what was to be his first film as a director, *Albert's Follies.* Yes! I'd made it! I was 25, the age Vi Goodman (and Gordon Honeycombe, also psychic) told me I'd be when I made it. I hasten to add that, if you've seen *Albert's Follies,* or *White Cargo* as it was re-named before it went out on the bottom half of a double bill, you may question my definition of making it.

Ray's script was *The Secret Life of Walter Mitty* re-set in Soho, where a daydreaming civil servant finds himself caught up in a real adventure involving strippers being sold as white slaves. One legend about this film is that it was written originally for the comic team The Goodies, who turned it down. I knew nothing about this until I read it online. By the time I came on board, the title role had been earmarked for David Jason, a talented comic actor from TV, where he'd already established himself as Ronnie Barker's stooge.

It's also been reported that I re-wrote the script in three days. This is absolutely true. I worked on it from 27th to the 29th November and took it to

17   *Sal Mineo* by Michael Gregg Michaud (New York: Random House, 2010)
18   *Films Illustrated,* August 1973

David Jason the next day. He sniggered as he read it. Then he said he thought it needed some changes. This is where the trouble began. Later the distributor wanted nude scenes added. Later still the distributor cut the film to under an hour and David Jason disowned it. But we'll get to that later. As far as I was concerned I was in the movies. I applied for my first credit card.

On 1st January, 1973, the UK joined what was then called the Common Market. I didn't approve. In 1971 I'd even gone on a march to protest against it. That had been my first political statement. Of course I had no idea what I was doing. I was influenced by the Communists, who told me it was a bad thing. Today I am wholeheartedly a European. Be that as it may, the New Year seemed to promise a brave new world. On 2nd January I went round to a rich friend's house and found that he had a video recorder. It was the size of a fridge freezer. Inside were enormous reels of videotape, two inches wide. I would have sold my soul to possess one of these dream machines.

I came down to earth on 3rd January. That evening I showed *Losing Track* to its cast and crew. It was the most crushing night of my life. There was virtually no response. When the lights came up, almost the entire audience slipped away without a word. The few who stayed had a variety of opinions. Some disliked it, others hated it, and most people loathed it. Richard Combs, who had taken my job at the *MFB*, told me concisely what was wrong with the film: it wasn't a film. Ray Selfe and David Jason seemed unable to form words. 'Interesting,' grunted Jason before walking off. I went with a few old drunks to a pub. I then spent a sleepless night and at 6am I was violently sick.

The next day, Ray was ruthless in his criticism. He said the film was totally incompetent from beginning to end. He and David Jason had discussed it all the way back to the Garrick Theatre, where Jason was starring in the trouser-dropping farce, *No Sex Please – We're British*. Jason was so appalled by my film that he was actually upset. I was convinced my film career was over. But it was far from over. A few years later I directed another comedy film. It was even worse than *Losing Track*.

Being 25, I bounced back from my débâcle within hours. Far from holding anything against me, Ray Selfe became one of my most treasured friends, a huge part of my life for the next thirty years or thereabouts. He built up my bit part in *White Cargo*. He and his wife, Jean, ran a music-hall company and, within a month, I was one of its performers, performing the monologues 'Brown Boots' and 'The Night I Appeared as Macbeth.' The rest of the company was clinically insane, but none more so than Ruxton Hayward, a man mountain whose high-pitched voice and boy scout attire inspired Peter Sellers to create his character of Bluebottle. For a while, he, too, became part of my entourage.

Bob Spiers, the star of *Losing Track,* also didn't think the worst comedy ever written should be held against a comedy writer. Bob was working his way up the BBC ladder and meeting all kinds of influential people. We tried to develop several programmes. *Live Connections,* a new music show that combined *Top of the Pops* with *Ready, Steady, Go!* came to nothing. So did my first sitcom, *What a Liberty!,* a women's lib satire set in a world where women went to work and men stayed home and looked after the children. (In 1973 the BBC could not conceive of such a notion.)

It was through Bob, however, that I got to write for probably the most popular TV comedian of his day, Dave Allen, who got through material like nobody's business. On 26th March my sketch, £10 Note, was first broadcast. Its idea – a man finds a £10 note trapped underneath the wheel of a parked car and tries to retrieve it – had come to me on the top of a bus. My plan was that, after the success of *Losing Track,* I would make this film with newcomer Richard Beckinsale, with whom I'd struck up a friendship on one of my Jeff Shane jobs. In the end the BBC made a much better job of it than I would have done.

'*Dave Allen at Large* gave me pleasure bordering on ecstasy,' I wrote after seeing my sketch on TV. 'The anticipation was delicious, the realisation (all three minutes of it) was orgasmic, and my credit was the cherry on the cake. They played the sketch absolutely beautifully. O frabjous day!' £10 Note has been broadcast continually, all over the world, ever since. I still get paid for it (£709.50 last year).

Even though I'd made it, I continued to make time for am dram because I wanted to spend two or three evenings a week admiring Herschel's eyelashes. Despite the chaos of *The Rising Generation,* Cameo Players offered me another play to direct, David Perry's *As Good As New.* This one I liked very much. But I threw caution to the wind and declared that I'd only take it on if Herschel was involved. I got what I wanted: another five months of heartache.

Meanwhile Pete Walker had churned out yet another film and I received my invitation to the preview. *Tiffany Jones,* based on a comic strip, suggested to me that Pete was still moving in the right direction. This time the film was a slick espionage comedy. But the plot was silly. As always Pete seemed very interested in my opinion. I had no idea that I was being auditioned or that I'd passed the audition. A few weeks later I was invited to his office.

I found out that Pete's latest project was in jeopardy. *The Flesh and Blood Show* and *Tiffany Jones* both had been written by an old drudge, Alfred Shaughnessy, who'd been around since the 1950s. Now, however, he was involved in a TV series, *Upstairs, Downstairs,* that was becoming a big hit. He'd swanned off to devote more time to it, leaving his new Pete Walker screenplay unfinished. Pete showed me some pages. My memory is that they consisted of an opening scene and a synopsis of the rest of the plot.

I read it all and found to my delight that it was the script I'd always dreamed of writing. The story was about a young girl, who is picked up by a sinister stranger and taken to a private prison, where victims are stripped, starved and hanged. Will she escape? I thought that Pete's title, *House of Whipcord*, was tawdry and I told him so. 'It sounds like a sex film and I think you need to move away from exploitation,' I advised him. Pete wasn't having any of that. He loved the title and he'd already designed the poster, which he said would pack 'em in. A girl's face screaming through a hangman's noose.

I discovered within days that Pete would accept only a certain amount of criticism. He made his films with his own money. The early ones all had made a profit. He didn't want to try anything too different. All I was expected to do was to write the script, following Shaughnessy's story, and write it fast. Filming was due to start, he claimed, in eight weeks' time.

I kept my mouth shut. For now. I went away and wrote the script, as required, in exactly two weeks. This time I was paid £200. The lead characters already had names. But the supporting characters didn't. One character I gave Herschel's name (his real name, not this pseudonym). Then I decided to cover my tracks by using the names of everyone else in the cast of *As Good As New*.

OVERWORKED

II

"All actors are egotistical poofs and all actresses are pompous prostitutes."
~ Pete Walker ~

1973 was the first year I spent doing what I'd always assumed I'd end up doing – hanging around film sets, appearing in front of the cameras, and shmoozing with other actors. There were so many exploitation pictures in production in the 1970s that it was possible to move from one project to another, barely without a break. Sometimes I worked on several pictures simultaneously. I recorded my rising bank balance with incredulity. £500 in June. £600 in August. £800 in November. I had sex for the first time as well.

I wrote *House of Whipcord* while I was working as an actor on *White Cargo*. In another subconscious gesture of self-exposure, I'd written myself a part as a gay customer in a carpet shop. There's a toilet scene with me, David Jason, Hugh Lloyd and Tim Barrett, which ends with Barrett pinching my cheek and saying, 'Saucepot!' Lloyd and Barrett are bumbling Special Branch officers, roles offered to – and this is not apocryphal – Morecambe and Wise. Each day Lloyd and Barrett would come in with their dialogue re-written. I thought their re-writes were corny. I said nothing. But it was obvious, when we saw the rough cut, that the script wasn't funny. Jason was witheringly cruel. Even at this stage, he wanted his name removed from the credits.

Many of my evenings were spent accompanying *As Good As New* to drama festivals. (The adjudicator at Havering was Buster Merryfield, who switched years later to acting. He saw out his days as Uncle Albert in TV's *Only Fools and Horses,* starring David Jason.) *As Good As New* was a success, dragged around the country for months. All the women who worked on the play were lovelorn and, at the after show parties, they poured out their hearts to me while I watched Herschel out of the corner of my eye being unaware and unavailable. 'If only they knew,' I wrote in my sad bedsit in Kilburn. 'I must work as much as possible to get my mind on something else. But the weekends alone here are the worst.'

By now I wasn't doing a great deal of film extra work, but on a whim I telephoned Central Casting and was given two days at Pinewood on *Carry On Girls,* the episode that satirises women's lib. Feminist June Whitfield turns on the sprinklers at a beauty contest and the audience, including me, is drenched. I was fascinated to meet Jimmy Ray, a former child actor I used to watch in *Whack-o!,* a TV comedy set in a public school. Now Jimmy was down on his luck, just another face in the crowd. But another face in the crowd, Tom, was fascinated to meet me. He was quite forward. He invited me for dinner at his place the following Monday.

Tom was a well-turned-out, well-preserved man in his 40s, with a neat 'tache. I wasn't particularly interested in a father figure. He was simply the first man I met who wouldn't take no for an answer. I remember, however, that I deliberately stayed until the last tube had gone. 'You can sleep here,' he told me, indicating his double bed. I got into it, said, 'Good night,' and turned away from him. When he put his arm around me, I removed it, more than once. I'd decided that, because I was heterosexual, he would have to force me to have sex. The trouble is that he did. 'Take it easy, Tom,' I groaned. Years later I worked with Julian Clary on *Lord of the Mince*, the show in which he roller-bladed. 'The first time you wear roller-blades,' he told his audience, 'it's a bit like the first time you have anal sex. You're not sure you'll ever walk again.' I think we'll leave it there. All I confided to my diary was, 'Slept badly.'

Just before *House of Whipcord* started shooting, Pete Walker excited me with news of who was going to be in it. There were always parts in Pete Walker films for older actors, and Pete would throw out the names of stars of yesteryear willy-nilly. The staff at the prison, for example, was going to be played by Jean Kent, Peggy Cummins, Margaret Lockwood, Freda Jackson, Yvonne Mitchell – and the list went on. None of these ladies appeared in *Whipcord* and, while I was working for him over the next four years, Pete never got the stars he wanted. I don't believe he came anywhere near getting most of them. But fantasy casting was a ritual that had to be gone through before each new film.

One of the whiplash girls was played by someone who went on to become quite famous. *House of Whipcord* marked the big screen debut of Celia Imrie and she's never allowed me to forget it. She enjoys shocking fellow National Theatre thesps by including the film in her programme biogs and she inscribed her autobiography, *The Happy Hoofer*, "for David, who wrote my favourite film ever." I can show you if you don't believe me.

I gave myself the part of Cavan, a photographer, on *Whipcord,* partly so that I could observe Pete at work. I'd been impressed with what I'd seen of his skills on *The Flesh and Blood Show*. He knew what he was doing and time was never wasted. He didn't disappoint me on *Whipcord*. My first scene was completed by 10am. Pete Walker became the biggest influence on my own film-making career. When I became a producer, I would tell my crews, 'We're going to do this like Pete Walker. No messing about.'

After doing my bit as Cavan, with Ann Michelle and Ron Smerczak, I hung around the set. Over lunch Pete told me to think of an idea for his next film. This was a tall order. I was convinced at this time that I hadn't got an original idea in my head and that I could only spark off other people. Also, because I decided early on that I would never say no to any job offer (a policy that's done me more good than harm), I'd already said yes to an offer from another director. Norman J. Warren was back in my life. He'd heard I worked fast (all that mattered in the exploitation business) and wanted me to re-write his friend Tony Craze's script *The Naked Eye,* which was being fashioned as a vehicle for none other than Vincent Price. This was to be a tortuous affair that dragged on for three years before emerging as *Satan's Slave,* another film for which I'm unlikely ever to be forgiven.

I also said yes when I was asked to become a director of a new film distributor, Paladin. The brains behind this venture was Peter Jacobs, who stage managed Ray and Jean Selfe's music hall shows. He knew nothing about film distribution and proved it by buying up garbage you couldn't pay people to watch. In less than two years the company was £58,000 in debt. But, as I'll describe later, there was far worse to come.

My other main strategy – never refuse a party invitation – has been with me for life purely because, in September, I went to the Gordon Fraser Gallery, for the launch of David Pirie's book *A Heritage of Horror,* and met BBC Radio London producer Mike Sparrow. He liked my review of Michael Winner's latest film, *Scorpio,* in *Time Out* and asked me if I'd like to interview Winner for his weekly movie programme, *Close Up.* That's how I got into radio. It really was only a matter of meeting the right man at the right time. And having sex with him. But that came later.

Shortly after I received Pete's demand, an idea dropped from the sky. I was talking to Godfrey Kirby about a recent air crash in the Andes. Several passengers who had survived managed to stay alive for months by eating those who hadn't. Godfrey claimed that the survivors began on the corpses' brains because they were the most nutritious. I've told this story many times, but it's absolutely true: I telephoned Pete and said, 'Cannibalism.' He loved the idea. Within two days we'd worked out a story about a cannibal who's released from jail and immediately goes back to her old ways.

The stories about *White Cargo* were getting worse and worse. 'A disaster! A disaster!' producer Negus Fancey allegedly exploded to Peter Jacobs. 'I don't know what I'm going to do with it.' But there was no time to worry about this. The following week *House of Whipcord* had its cast and crew screening and nervously I took my seat.

I thought it was Pete Walker's best film to date.

In recent years claims have been made that Pete Walker's grubby films accurately reflect the grubby era in which they were made. Undoubtedly the UK was not living through its finest hours in the early 1970s. The strikes seemed almost continuous; and by the end of 1973 there were also power cuts, petrol rationing, and no TV after 10.30pm each night. The infamous 'three day week' was yet to come. The Conservative government had no intention of submitting to union demands; but to many of the public it seemed that both sides were united in their determination to bring the country to its knees. I have to say, however, that none of this made any difference to me. In the days before word processors, I could continue working on my manual typewriter by candlelight; and I did. Ingenuous as it may appear, I never considered for a moment that the horror films I was writing were allegories engendered by social unrest.

I don't deny, however, that there's more going on in these films that may have met the eye in the 1970s. I think that Jon Towlson gets closer to the truth than others, some of whom have read all kinds of hidden meanings into my scripts for Pete Walker. To Towlson, Pete Walker was 'the pre-eminent proponent of generation gap horror in the 1970s.' He believes that Walker's films 'provide a radical commentary on the conservative forces at play in Britain during the time which followed the suspension of capital punishment, the legalization of abortion, decriminalization of homosexuality and the relaxation of divorce laws.'[19] If Pete's films achieved this, then it was because Pete, a Conservative, really did think that Britain was going to the dogs, and because I had problems with authority.

I would now go even further. I'm prepared to admit that *Whipcord,* in particular, is quite plainly the work of sexually screwed-up men ('Speak for yourself, McGillivray!' I can hear Pete snorting). The chief victim is cute little Ann-Marie de Vernay (Penny Irving), who's persecuted because she's a nude model. This to my mind reflects Pete's true feelings about women. 'I hate tits. Horrible things,' he told me when I met him in 1972.[20] A lesbian wardress called Walker, played by lesbian actress Sheila Keith, secretly desires Ann-Marie, but punishes her because she won't stop being heterosexual. 'I'm going to make you ashamed of your body,' Walker tells Ann-Marie. 'I'm going to see to that personally.' It's later revealed that Ann-Marie's boyfriend, Mark E. Dessart (Robert Tayman), is a mummy's boy, who isn't interested in sex with women at all. Yes, it's a gay film. It could have been even gayer, but Pete lost his nerve.

I'd noticed that Pete liked to use gay actors and situations. He worked with Derek Aylward five times (Aylward and I were both at the screening of *Flesh* I mentioned earlier). 'He was this sort of guy you could lift out,

19 *Subversive Horror Cinema: Countercultural Messages of Films from Frankenstein to the Present* (Jefferson, North Carolina: McFarland & Co., 2014)
20 *Films and Filming,* December 1974

put him amongst girls and nobody would believe he was actually screwing them,' Pete laughed.[21] In *Cool It Carol!* there's an odd scene where the very gay actor Alec Bregonzi tries to seduce Robin Askwith. And Pete talked a lot about Sal Mineo, whom he'd met in Hollywood. 'He used to be straight, but now he's certainly not.' He also claimed to have seen Rock Hudson going down on another man. I didn't ask how he came to witness this. Anyway, hoping to curry favour, I put a gay waiter into the script of *Whipcord*. But Pete bristled. 'He shouldn't be queer,' he told me. He turned the waiter into a waitress and made the restaurant a transport café. I think I'd already gone too far by having Mark's mother stroke his face while Ann-Marie is being whipped. 'It's very strong,' he confided to me after he'd seen the rushes.

The only script I've written that was consciously inspired by current events was *Bomber!* The idea for this action adventure was Laurie Barnett's. Laurie was a boom swinger, who'd been working in soft porn since the turn of the 1970s. He and his business partner, John Lindsay, were to involve me in all manner of shady deals over the next few years. Laurie was amusingly Jewish, an attribute I've always found irresistible. One day I muscled in on a conversation he was having with Ray Selfe. Laurie wanted to make a film about a mystery man who tries to extort a million pounds from the British government by bombing London landmarks. It wasn't an original idea (there had been a similar film in 1950), but now it was a topical one. To add to the British people's woes, the IRA had begun its most indiscriminate bombing campaign. Nobody was safe. On Christmas Eve two bombs exploded near my Kilburn flat and several people were injured.

I told Laurie I wanted to write this film and that's what I did (in my customary fortnight). The production never got off the ground, but it came perilously close to lift-off on a couple of occasions. In 1980 the trade press announced that it had started shooting in London under Douglas Hickox's direction. It hadn't because a bunch of Swiss gnomes hadn't come up with the cash. Ten years after I wrote it, my battered old script was still doing the rounds. It wouldn't surprise me if it was still propping up a table leg somewhere in the world.

Before the end of the year I'd finished the scripts of *The Naked Eye* and Pete Walker's cannibalism movie, which was to become *Frightmare*, now regarded by some as his most frightening picture. It certainly was his most groundbreaking, coming as it did seven years before the cannibal holocaust of the early 1980s, which was partly responsible for a huge moral backlash and the enforcement of the Video Recordings Act. The story of *Frightmare* is complete rubbish. But I'd learned from superior rubbish like *Rosemary's Baby*

---

21   ibid

and *Night of the Living Dead* that an audience can be temporarily distracted from reality by the inclusion of convincing detail. I made a lot of exploratory phone calls while I was writing *Frightmare*. I discovered how brains can be extracted from a skull and whether cannibalism is a pathological condition. You may not believe me, but a lot of research goes into my screenplays.

The exception, of course, is *White Cargo*. While I was writing my third feature film, *Frightmare*, my first feature film opened as a support to a 3D sex comedy called *The Stewardesses*. Pete Walker and I went to the first showing at a grindhouse in the Charing Cross Road. I squirmed with embarrassment. I found it ironic that Ray Selfe, who knew exactly what was wrong with *Losing Track*, couldn't make a funny film himself. I didn't hold that against him. It's really hard to make good films. I appreciated Pete Walker even more.

Pete and I came out of the cinema. 'Much as I expected,' he muttered before he jumped into a taxi. He never referred to *White Cargo* again.

Because I couldn't say no, I accepted an invitation to sit on the Drama and Written Word sub-committee of the Westminster Arts Council. The other members fascinated me. They included a mad old bat called Miss Aherne; Lord Lucan's mother (I'm not making this up); and a gay couple, Robert Henderson and Peter Lindsay, who ran Studio '68, quite a prestigious drama school. Henderson was married for reasons best known to himself to actress Estelle Winwood, who was by then 90. Lindsay, who dyed his hair and reeked of alcohol at all hours of the day, tried and failed to get me into bed.

The chairman of the committee was Peter Lovell, a production assistant at the BBC. He was a cheery and likeable fellow with a shock of curly hair. Him I found very attractive. Within weeks he invited me for a drink and then back to his place. 'You can stay if you like,' he told me in the early hours. But I was still almost literally smarting from my deflowering, and I asked him to drive me home. I didn't know then that the role-playing in gay sex can be negotiable. Peter shrugged off my coquetry and we remained friends. Later he directed my panto *Hot Cinders*. But I needed to get laid and so I fucked Denise, who'd told me that cannibalism was not a pathological condition. (I wasn't having any of that and invented a psychosis called caribanthropy.)

III

"One cannot make any kind of firm line between high art and pornography. Even Michelangelo's Pieta, the supreme artefact of the Vatican, is a work of pornography – when you look at it up close."
~ Camille Paglia ~

Essex Nana died in the first week of 1974. She was 88. She had been put in an old people's home the previous summer. We hadn't seen much of each other since I left her house in New Southgate in 1970, and I hadn't seen the rest of my family since I'd blown my top at my parents' flat in 1972. I've got no memory of this incident. But there it is in my diary: 'I told them I didn't love them and that they'd wrecked my life and that I'd never forgive them.' I wonder what brought this on? Repressed homosexuality I expect. Nana's funeral brought us together again, briefly. Then we divided up her belongings like the ghouls around Scrooge's death bed.

While *Bomber!* was being touted to every A-list agent in Hollywood, its instigators, Laurie Barnett and John Lindsay, seem to have made the decision to fall back on what they knew best, low grade smut. They threw together some putative sex fantasies, which they expected me to expand into a screenplay. I did what they required. What I loved more than anything was that Laurie's backers felt that my sauna scene lowered the tone of the film. Eventually my efforts emerged as *Hot Girls,* a sex film which seemed to consist largely of crash zooms into girls' pubes. (There was an even hotter version, with unsimulated humping, for foreign markets.) When I saw the film, I was so appalled that later[22] I threatened that, if a print had survived, I'd break into the lab and destroy it. Now I'm immensely proud that I worked on something that's a strong candidate for representing the nadir of the British film industry.

Having worked myself to a frazzle, I decided to pop back to New York. Just before I left, Pete Walker invited me for tea at the Dorchester Hotel. This was one of only two social occasions I shared with Pete during the four years we worked together. Later he confirmed to his biographer[23] that we were never close. 'I could never befriend him,' he said of me. 'I could never socialise with him.' Pete preferred the company of my more flamboyant friend Michael Armstrong. 'Michael's very showbizy and I know where that

---

22 *Spawn of Tarantula! Part 2* in *Shock Xpress 2* (London: Titan Books, 1994)
23 *Making Mischief: The Cult Films of Pete Walker* by Steve Chibnall (Guildford, Surrey: FAB Press, 1998)

comes from and I respect it and I enjoy it,' he enthused. The argument I had with Pete at the Dorchester, which lasted until mid-evening, suggested to me that we were never going to be bosom buddies. He professed to hate art in all its forms. I protested that life without art is existence. He thought I was a pretentious fool.

Within days of arriving back in New York, I was caught up in a drug- and porn-fuelled whirlwind. On this occasion my hosts were Jeanne and Lewis, a couple who had been involved with 1520 CT, the London youth theatre with which I had flirted. I noted that since my last trip Stateside, the focus in the 'typical' upwardly mobile Manhattan living room had shifted from the TV to the coffee table containing hash, pipes and cigarette papers. I was soon catatonic on choice gear costing $60 an ounce.

I hooked up with Vincent Price's biographer, who told me that Price was just about to embark on a month's lecture tour. This was news to me because, as far as I was concerned, the horror star was due to fly to England within days to begin shooting my film *The Naked Eye*. The biographer's friend, Jim, another writer, took me to my first gay bar, but I was still experiencing post-penetration stress disorder and fended off all approaches. Secretly I stole back to 42nd Street to drool over such porn classics as *The Devil in Miss Jones* (straight) and *A Deep Compassion* (gay). 'At one point,' I wrote, 'I found myself unable to endure the sight of yet another cock being sucked.'

I was also supposed to be working as the representative of Paladin Films. I saw all kinds of eye-wideningly incompetent films, but none with quite the audacity of *Blood of Ghastly Horror*, a ludicrous, incoherent mess that subsequently attained cult status among bad movie collectors. Its distributor was Sam Sherman, an extremely engaging film buff, who knew full well how bad his films were. We became friends and later I interviewed him.[24]

As with Abby Moss two years earlier, Jeanne and Lewis regretted throwing open their apartment, which they thought I'd treated like an hotel. They told me this to my face. Another of my unpleasant traits had emerged. I am a very badly behaved guest. If I stay in your home for any length of time, our friendship will end. I still travel abroad regularly to visit friends. But I always use hotels.

A lot had happened in the UK during my absence. A new (Labour) government was in power and the miners' pay claim had been settled. This meant the end of the three day week and, in my words, 'those infuriating TV commercials, which kept telling us to switch everything off as if it was all our fault.' Also, as I suspected, production of *The Naked Eye* had been

---

24   *The Dark Side*, August-September, 1994

shut down. I expect Vincent Price didn't like my script. Director Norman J. Warren was at his lowest ebb. He told me that he was avoiding asking his doctor for sleeping pills in case he took a deliberate overdose.

Pete Walker, on the other hand, was in high spirits. *Frightmare* was due to start shooting in April and, days earlier, *House of Whipcord* was to premiere at the vast London Pavilion, where as a child I'd gazed in fear at the lurid pictures advertising *Tarantula!* The *Whipcord* display, with stern Sheila Keith and her eponymous weapon towering forty feet high over Piccadilly Circus, was just as eye-catching. But Tim Evans, Miracle Films' publicity man, felt that the film still needed a bit more push. A couple of days before the opening, Tim and I sat in his office telephoning moral reformers to complain about this disgustingly sadistic film. To our delight, a letter ('Surely it is time the law took steps to put an end to these repulsive and degrading public displays') appeared in the *Daily Mail* shortly afterwards.[25]

Two of the most favourable reviews of *House of Whipcord* were written by gay men, friends from my *Monthly Film Bulletin* days. In general the press ignored the film. When I asked the distinguished critic Dilys Powell why she hadn't written anything, she told me that she thought *Whipcord* was 'potentially dangerous.' The worst review, by Russell Davies, is still quoted to this day: 'What an exceptionally feeble fladge-fantasy like *House of Whipcord* is doing at the London Pavilion, I don't know, but it won't be there long.'[26] Davies was in fact quite wide of the mark. *Whipcord* packed them in. When Pete and I drove past the Pavilion in his Rolls, we noticed with interest that the queue stretching around the building consisted almost entirely of young people. I'd written a generation gap drama without intending to. I was down with the kids for the one and only time in my life. *House of Whipcord* was to be Pete Walker's last big box office hit.

My thrilling new show business career, however, had only just begun. Most days found me writing film reviews or radio scripts on the way to and from and sometimes during other script meetings and other film screenings. With another BFI mate, Paul Madden, I wrote *Tribute to a Writer*, a TV documentary about Lord Ted Willis, creator of *Dixon of Dock Green*. I had no idea what to write, but we were given a strict deadline, good training for so many other projects in which I had no real interest.

Ron Lloyd took me round to Michael Billington's to meet a bloke called Dave, who claimed that he could produce a no-budget film by stealing

---

25   8th April, 1974
26   *The Observer,* 31st March, 1974

everything from Visnews, where he worked. Billington wanted me to come up with a sex film script, which he would direct. I didn't like the sound of this at all and I wondered why Billington would even entertain such an idea. (Within a couple of years he was to become even more embroiled in movie skulduggery. Clearly 'borrowing' films from Contemporary had been a gateway crime.)

I made polite noises about Dave's project and then forgot all about it. I was about to start a more legitimate job, my third screenplay for Pete Walker. He'd found a pulp novel about a killer vicar and thought that we could change enough of it to avoid paying its author for the rights. The vicar became a priest and the film became *House of Mortal Sin*, the one in which mad Father Meldrum goes on a killing spree armed with rosary beads and a burning censer. (He's sexually frustrated of course.)

I did my best to make this melodrama plausible, even to the extent of spending time with Sister Edna of the National Catechetical Society, but I failed. Re-writes dragged on and on, and at one point Pete fired me. I was re-hired only, I believe, because he couldn't find anyone else to work for £500. (The Writers' Guild minimum at this time was £2,500.) By the end of the year I came up with a script with which he seemed happy. In all honesty I couldn't see much difference between this final draft and my first, which Pete had thrown back at me, saying it read like 'a *Play for Today* with murders.'

In between my trips to Mayfair and Esher, I slipped back into the murky Soho underworld of soft porn. I was fascinated by Ray Selfe's new venture. He had 'inherited' several premises from a criminal friend who was forbidden by the police from renewing his leases. Ray was turning these premises, one by one, into cinema clubs, where he showed sex films. As these grew more and more explicit, they attracted the attention of the Metropolitan Police's notoriously corrupt Clubs and Vice squad. I would listen in disbelief as Ray told me stories of how the cops would raid his cinemas, remove the films and projectors, and then sell them back to him so that he could re-open, normally later the same day. Despite these expensive inconveniences, which all Soho's club owners endured as par for the course, Ray was making money hand over fist. This attracted the attention of a film maker who called himself David Hamilton Grant. (His real name was Willis Holt.) He became Ray's business partner. Grant is without doubt the most disreputable and mysterious character in the entire history of British soft porn. Naturally I had several dealings with him. We'll hear about him regularly from now until his death. And then we'll hear about him coming back to life.

photo credit: Colin Brett

above: You're not fooling anyone, McG. Working alongside cameraman Derek Scott on the agonisingly bad film *Losing Track*, 1968.

above: Drug den. The shopfront I designed, Camden Passage, London, 1968.

right: I'm a real actor, honest.
From my first *Spotlight* photo session, 1970.

below: One of the main title cards I designed for *Losing Track*, finally completed in 1972.

photo credit: Dugald MacNeill

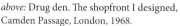

above: Things were different back then. As the golliwog, with Brian Rothfeder, "Herschel" and Anita Moore in *Ritual for Dolls*, tour, 1982.

below: Peter de Rome and me back to back in 1974. We weren't destined to meet for another 33 years.

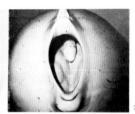

PETE WALKER FILM PRODUCTIONS
LIMITED

FLAT 9, 23 DOWN STREET, LONDON, W.1

Date 28th. Feb. 1975

To David McGillivray,
22, Birchington Road,
LONDON N.W.6.

A remittance against your account is enclosed, calculated as follows:

Few old words....

Balance as your statement/invoice(s):

£350. 00.

Adjustments:

apologies for my usual laxity....

above: Dirty money. My fee for writing *House of Mortal Sin*, 1975.

left: Men in need. Producer Les Young and director Norman J. Warren at my Kilburn flat to discuss nastiness, 1974.

below: Christmas treat. *Frightmare* at my beloved London Pavilion, 1974.

above and below: I played two different priests in scenes shot a year apart in *Satan's Slave*, released 1976.

SATAN'S SLAVE 'x'
Starring: Michael Gough ★ Martin Potter ★ Candace Glendenning
Directed by: Norman J. Warren   RELEASED BY BRENT WALKER FILM DISTRIBUTORS LTD.

This copyright advertising material is licensed and not sold and is the property of BRENT WALKER FILMS LTD. and upon completion of the exhibition for which it has been licensed it should be returned to Bovince Ltd. Printed in Great Britain

photo credit: Frank Manning

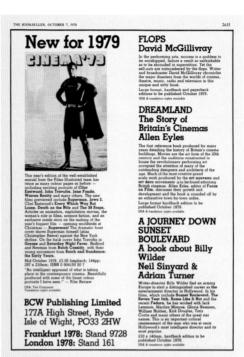

above: With Sandra Manning in the premiere of *The Farndale/Macbeth*, Edinburgh, 1976.

right: The book that never was.

below: Phwaaoor. Alan Jones (L), Walter Zerlin Jnr. (R) with teen starlets, one of whom, Cleo Rocos, made her screen debut in *Terror*, 1978.

above: Hero 1. Michael Ward.

right: Hero 2. Marianne Stone.

below: Hero 3. David Sweetman.

right: Hero 4.
Walter Zerlin Jnr. in *Deathwatch*,
London, 1975.

below: Hero 5.
Soo Drouet in *Robin Hood,
Prince of Thieves*, 1991.

photo credit: Gary Conway

144

Still on the subject of smut peddling, Laurie Barnett and John Lindsay were back in touch with me almost as soon as *Hot Girls* had finished its run. Like Walker, they'd found a paperback, which they expected me to plagiarise without making the story's origins too obvious. This I did and called the resulting farrago *I'm Not Feeling Myself Tonight!*, a title that was irrelevant to the tale of an odd job man at a sex research institute who develops a sound wave that turns people on. One of the doctors was played by Marianne Stone.

Pre-production was worryingly stalled when Lindsay was had up in Birmingham Crown Court for conspiring to publish obscene films. The press loved this story because Lindsay had shot *Juvenile Sex* and *Classroom Lover* in Birmingham's Aston Manor school and used the former *head boy* (quiet at the back) as their star. I went up to Birmingham to appear as a character witness, but I wasn't called. Lindsay was found not guilty. He was by this time well-known as a pornographer. But the UK obscenity laws were difficult to interpret, and juries tended to acquit. Double standards being what they are, however, the producers of *I'm Not Feeling Myself Tonight!* didn't want to associate themselves with a man who made dirty movies. They removed Lindsay's name from the credits. Lindsay wasn't pleased. But he went on to show his own porn films, and those of others, in cinema clubs. He did very nicely out of this for a while. But eventually the law caught up with him and he was imprisoned in 1983.

I agreed to write one more movie script in 1974. Determined not to be defeated, Norman J. Warren had re-worked *The Naked Eye* into a new story, *Satan's Slave,* about a wicked uncle who wants to use the body of his niece to resurrect an ancestral witch. I believed Norman when he said he was going to start shooting in a month, and consequently bashed out his script in nine days. It was no great shakes. But *Stan's Slave* (a genuine misprint that I found amusing and subsequently adopted) was an early example of what's now called guerrilla film making, and I had quite a lark doing bits and pieces on it for the next couple of years.

I went to the cast and crew screening of *Frightmare*. I was disappointed. I thought there was far too much boring chit-chat in flats and streets. Sheila Keith was terrific as the driller killer and I suppose this is the part for which she's now best-known. But I didn't like the other performances. It goes without saying that Pete didn't get Jack Palance or Peter Cushing to play the male lead. Instead he'd acquired Rupert Davies, who used to be *Maigret* on TV. It was to be his last film. Nor did we get Pamela Franklin to play the juve lead. Her replacement, Deborah Fairfax, looked bored to death to me. She never made another movie either.

Pete telephoned me the next morning to get my reaction. Because he'd always said that he valued my opinion, I told him roughly what I wrote in the previous paragraph. He was absolutely furious. He insisted that it was the best thing he'd done and that everyone else agreed. From that day to this, if I haven't liked someone's work, I have never told them the truth. In fact don't bother to ask my opinion. My answer will always be the same: 'I loved it.'

Frightmare opened, again at the London Pavilion, just before Christmas, 1974. I regret to report that I'd been a lot kinder about the film than the critics were. They were apoplectic with rage, calling it horrendous, nasty, morally repellent, disgusting and repulsive. Many critics blamed me. 'The script is truly dreadful,' is representative.[27] But this wasn't the half of it. *Films and Filming* had decided to publish, only two years late, my interview with Pete Walker. *The Sun* found it and used quotes from my article which, taken out of context, made Pete appear a stupid, talentless, hypocrite. Fergus Cashin's hatchet piece was headed, 'What are stars like these doing in trash like this?'[28]

Pete telephoned me at 8am on the morning *The Sun* appeared and whimpered with some justification, 'I don't deserve this treatment.' I tried to limit the damage by suggesting he take out advertisements in the evening papers that listed every pejorative comment made about *Frightmare*. This is what he did. But nothing could save the film. On 24th December the take at the 1,186 seat London Pavilion was £23.

Despite this setback, all animosity seemed to be forgotten at Pete's Christmas party, the second of the two social occasions at which we met. Everybody was there. I noted that Sheila Keith seemed to be getting on very well with her co-star Barbara Markham, and that Pete showed particular interest in young actor Eddie Kalinski. 'Betcha he's in the next film,' I predicted. He wasn't. But he was back in Pete's *The Comeback* and then I grabbed him myself for my film *The Errand*.

I faced 1975 with renewed optimism, not just because I had at least three films waiting to go before the cameras, but because it seemed I would also be able to buy my own flat. Jean Salter, my landlady at 22, Birchington Road, had seen an opportunity of getting rid of me. The basement of the building was for sale and she was quite insistent that I put in an offer for it. The basement previously had been occupied by an old lady, who recently had died. It was a hovel, now officially uninhabitable. The agent would accept £9,000.

Where was I going to find that kind of money? My only hope, I thought, was my parents. Firstly they had just sold Essex Nana's house. Secondly they were putting my brother, Paul, through university, and they'd never had to do that for me. But Mum and Dad didn't see my reasoning. They told me

---

27 *The Tablet,* 14th December, 1974
28 7th December, 1974

that they'd worked and saved all their lives and that this was the first time they'd had a bit of money for themselves. I told them what I thought of their decision in no uncertain terms. Voices were raised. I walked out of their flat and didn't speak to any of my family for the next five years.

Because the flat was unsaleable, the agent kept reducing the asking price. I held out. Finally I offered £5,000. The agent countered with £5,500 and I accepted. I raised this money by going cap-in-hand for eleven £500 loans. I found out who my real friends were. Pete Walker said no. Ray Selfe put a cheque in the post the next day. So much work needed to be done to my new home that it was more than a year before I could move in. By that time, I was such a successful writer that I'd paid everybody back. In full.

IV

"Look on my works, ye mighty, and despair!"
~ Shelley, *Ozymandias* ~

In 1975 a piece appeared in the *Sunday People* headed, 'Mr X turns to kids' stuff.'[29] It was a reference to the fact that sex and horror writer David McGillivray was now writing a children's television series. The story wasn't made up. For the whole of 1975 and much of 1976 I wrote eighteen episodes of *The Adventures of the Bengal Lancers* for producer Jacques de Lane Lea, who had been involved in *The Naked Eye*. The production was in trouble almost from the outset. Jacques was in partnership with an unstable scion of the Courtauld family. Jacques dumped him and travelled around the world trying and failing to do deals in India, Afghanistan, Pakistan and finally Spain. The series was shelved, but I got paid for it, which helped with the extensive renovations of 22a, Birchington Road.

I was also paid for writing all kinds of other films that never saw the light of a projector. Early in the year Pete Walker got it into his head that he was going to switch to directing pop musicals. The fact that he knew nothing about pop music seemed not to matter. While he was going through this phase I wrote him a version of *Svengali* in which the sinister hypnotist became a has-been rock 'n' roll star, a part Alvin Stardust wanted to play. The film was cancelled almost as soon as I'd finished typing the last page.

While *I'm Not Feeling Myself Tonight!* was in production, Laurie Barnett persuaded me to write him another sex comedy, this time one about a family of sex maniacs. I called it *Unzipper de Doo Dah*. I still love that title. Laurie planned to save costs by shooting on videotape, which would then be transferred to 35mm. This process was in its infancy. Laurie shot a test sequence starring Herschel surrounded by porn starlets. It didn't look too bad. But subsequently my script was deemed too parochial and the whole idea was scrapped.

I came perilously close to writing a film even worse than *Hot Girls* when a director called Georges Robin contacted me, claiming that he wanted to make the British *Emmanuelle,* but in one location for £25,000. I told him that all he was going to get for that kind of money was another crappy sex film, but that I was happy about this if he was. He was. The working title of this movie really was *Clitoris*. I still have Robin's hand-written contract as proof. I wrote the script in thirteen days, handed it over to Robin, and he absconded with it.

---

29   16th November, 1975

Because I never said no, I was by this time writing a new script every other week, and this industriousness brought me my first media attention. One of my biggest fans was Peter Noble, editor of the trade paper *CinemaTV Today*, for which I did film reviews. (My friendship with Peter meant I was now only one degree of separation from Peter's wife, Marianne Stone.) I wangled myself an entry in Peter's annual *British Film and TV Yearbook*, a directory of almost every actor, writer and director in the business. This was a dream come true. Philip Sandell and I used to pore over this book on Saturday mornings in the Palmers Green library. I imagined what it would be like to be in between Hugh McDermott and Cecil McGivern. When my time came I was between Henry McGee and Joe McGrath. Yes, Joe McGrath who was now directing my film *I'm Not Feeling Myself Tonight!*

My fifteen minutes or, to be more precise, fifty minutes of fame was brought about by *X-Ploitation*, a programme in BBC television's *Man Alive* series. The corporation could no longer ignore the fact that exploitation films had become big business and chose John Pitman to host an investigation. The participants were a motley crew that included Hazel Adair and Kent Walton, a soap opera writer and wrestling commentator respectively, who made soft porn under the collective pseudonym 'Elton Hawke'; John Hamill, a young muscleman, who appeared in gay loops and as Cowboy in the London production of the play *The Boys in the Band* before turning to heterosexual sex comedy; Bachoo Sen, producer of Norman J. Warren's *Her Private Hell*, who was still churning out filth; and his writer Jonathan Gershfield, who more than thirty years later made a comeback with the Burt Reynolds comedy *A Bunch of Amateurs*.

Laurie Barnett was to be involved, but the researcher didn't like him. Pete Walker, on the other hand, featured prominently, directing *House of Mortal Sin*. Unfortunately Jack Palance, Trevor Howard and Lee J. Cobb were all unavailable to play the lead and it was taken by Anthony Sharp, who normally played doctors and barristers. The director, James Kenelm Clarke, enjoyed contrasting Pete's high-flying lifestyle with mine in my Kilburn bedsit. While he was filming me there, I heard Clarke whisper to his cameraman, 'Pan off the sink on to David.'

The critics, who hated exploitation films, loved the programme that exploited exploitation films. *X-Ploitation* got unanimously good reviews. Several mentioned my story of the sauna scene that had been cut from *Hot Girls* because it lowered the tone of the film. But not everyone was happy. Producer Kevin Francis took a full page advertisement in *CinemaTV Today* to deplore the way the programme traduced the British film industry.[30] (Kevin was the industry's most optimistic champion; but unfortunately he also made very dull films.) After *X-Ploitation* was broadcast, on 24th April, 1975, I was recognised

---

30   3rd May, 1975

in the street for the first, and pretty much the last, time. Only months later, James Kenelm Clarke left the BBC and began making a series of soft porn films starring Fiona Richmond.

Flushed with success, I participated in the orgy scene of *I'm Not Feeling Myself Tonight!* Joe McGrath, who at his peak had guided the TV careers of Peter Cook and Dudley Moore, so hated what he was now required to do that he directed one bit of pretend copulation with his back to the set. He turned round once to mutter, 'Move your bum up and down a bit, Curtis.' The stupidity of the situation made such an impression on me that I adapted it for the porn sequence of *Terror,* my last major horror film. I even called the male character Curtis.

Months later *Stan's Slave* began its unplanned seven month shooting schedule. I'm in this film, in various guises, from beginning to end. The crew was tiny and everybody did everything. I arrived at a location one day to find one of the producers digging graves. My principle role is as a priest officiating at a funeral. There I am sharing a scene with horror star Michael Gough and Fellini discovery Martin Potter and I've got all the lines. On another ten-hour day I was even busier. 'I was supposed to drop spiders and snakes over a naked Gloria Walker. But the spider man never showed. I did some other things instead. First I played Michael Gough's hands fiddling at a black magic altar; then I was Martin Potter's right hand, stabbing Gloria; then I dragged Gloria across the floor; then Norman and I were robed, masked loonies; then I was Gough in a goat's head mask; and finally I even dubbed Gough's voice incanting something for the prologue. I found it all great fun.' There was even more fun in store.

The year ended with a succession of screaming matches and threats out of which came *Schizo,* my last film for Pete Walker. Pete and I had been bereft of ideas for many months and Pete kept returning to a script by his previous writer, Murray Smith, which he'd previously rejected. I could see why. It was a conventional whodunit far removed from the shockers that had made him Britain's leading exploitation director. But Pete saw it as his chance to be hailed as the new Hitchcock. Even the title was meant to evoke *Psycho.* Eventually I agreed to enliven Smith's idea with a succession of graphic murders. The inspiration for one of them came to me when I was going through Jean Selfe's props box. I found her knitting and thought, 'Couldn't a knitting needle be rammed into someone's ear?'

While I was labouring on the first of two drafts of the *Schizo* script, I saw *The Texas Chain Saw Massacre* at the London Film Festival and recognised the future of the horror film. Only two years earlier Pete had made *Frightmare,* one of the films that had paved the way for Tobe Hooper's terrifying story of a family of cannibal maniacs that slaughters young people. Now here I was writing Pete the kind of murder mystery that only could have thrilled the audience at the Intimate theatre, Palmers Green. I hated it. It was the beginning of the end.

I was still at work on *Schizo* when *House of Mortal Sin* opened after a long delay caused by Pete's regular distributor, Miracle, refusing to take it unless Pete paid the rental of the London Pavilion. Eventually it was released through a major distributor, Columbia-Warner, which spent little on promotion. The reviews didn't bring in the crowds either. Far from finding the sins of Father Meldrum sacrilegious, the critics were actually bored. 'A couple of sleeping pills should see you through it,' advised the *Daily Express*.[31] Even the *Financial Times'* Nigel Andrews, one of the few who'd liked *House of Whipcord*, turned against us. 'A load of old rubbish,' he sneered.[32] After struggling at the Warner cinema, *House of Mortal Sin* went around the country on the bottom half of a double bill.

I'm Not Feeling Myself Tonight!, which opened shortly after *House of Mortal Sin* closed, went on to become one of my most successful films. But there's as much chance of me watching it again as taking holy orders. At the first preview, I slunk lower and lower into my seat. Most of my dialogue had been ditched and replaced with jokes that sounded as though they'd come out of crackers. But I knew the film would do well. It was filled with dozens and dozens of naked women. Additional sex scenes had been shot. One sequence featured hardcore porn goddess Mary Millington, who previously had worked for John Lindsay. Her name meant little to me, but her fans went to see anything she was in. *I'm Not Feeling Myself Tonight!* grossed over £5,000 in its opening week, enough to send it straight into the London box office chart at number ten.

On 3rd March, 1976, I moved into 22a, Birchington Road, the first property I owned. I took the back room with a view of a mile-long garden. The front room was occupied by my flat-mate, Vernon, a colleague of Ron Lloyd's, whom I'd known since the 1960s. He was an easy-going charmer, who spoke mostly in clichés. If he saw me at the kitchen sink, he would say, 'A woman's work is never done!', and if we passed in the corridor, he would say, 'We must stop meeting like this!' This was a straight man's attempt at gay banter. He also dressed in form-fitting clothing; and when he bent over in front of me, his arse encased in blue denim, I didn't know where to look. Vernon chose his clothes to attract women, and after a few months he moved his latest girlfriend into his room. She was a screamer and I could hear them having sex from halfway down the street.

I'd given up my psychiatrist the previous year, but often wondered in the months that followed if I'd done the right thing. Crude sex was always available. I'd even gone back to Tom, my vile seducer. But I was still making myself ill by hankering after heterosexual men who, even if a magic wand turned them gay, I never actually would have liked. 'The strain of keeping up my public façade is killing me,' I wrote. Writing down my concerns was a help and sometimes I even

---

31   6th February, 1976
32   13th February, 1976

joked about them: 'My mind wanders on to personal matters. These matters still rule my life and, as you know, I don't like losing control like this. What am I to do? If I don't get a grip on myself, I'll become a neurotic. But what does getting a grip on myself mean? Is this the price of genius?'

Shortly after I moved, I became very ill indeed, doubled up with the most excruciating pain I'd ever experienced. It was as if part of my entrails were being squeezed by the Devil and there was no respite. I could barely crawl to the telephone to dial 999. At the hospital I was told I had kidney stones. Renal colic was to become another of my chronic illnesses. I had three in all and they crippled me with pain for four decades. The first was what I called indigestion, gas that bloated my stomach, which wouldn't deflate unless I lay down. I first suffered it throughout the car journey with Stuart across Europe to Bremen in 1965.

Far more debilitating and frequent were my migraines, which were the scourge of the gruelling years I spent touring with my theatre company, Entertainment Machine, in the 1970s and 1980s. Periodically I would have to retire to a darkened room with a damp flannel over my eyes, a procedure I later utilised as one of Julian Clary's running jokes. But all this was manageable compared to renal colic, which put me into hospital innumerable times. I would collapse at home, in the street, once in the theatre, once while interviewing the film director Frank Ripploh, and be rushed to whichever A&E was nearest, sometimes for days on end, until the stones passed in my urine.

But consider this: when I stopped agonising over work I found difficult, and love I could never have, the illnesses stopped as well. I've been right as rain for most of this century. Ask a doctor how much illness is caused by stress and I think you'll find I'm not imagining the reasons my mind and body revolted against me. Do you hate your work? Get another job. Do you have a secret? Tell it.

A succession of producers toyed with my affections during the long, hot summer of 1976. Laurie Barnett took me to Pinewood Studios to meet his new backer George Davis, whose name had appeared on a couple of unexceptional action pictures. George wanted a horror script and had written a lame synopsis. I didn't think this project was going anywhere and I was right. George never made another film. Nor did Laurie (although, in the 1980s, he re-appeared as a production manager on TV's *Challenge Anneka*). As I was leaving the studio I was hailed by the aforementioned Kevin Francis, who seemed to have forgotten about the part I played in the destruction of the British film industry and told me I must write him a screenplay. I pursued this for a while, but Kevin's days as a movie producer with his own parking space at Pinewood were also numbered.

Because his sex movie empire was getting him rich quick, David Hamilton Grant was able to indulge himself by making short films at weekends.

He showed me an unfinished compilation of them, which he intended to call *Pink Orgasm*. He kept telling me that he wanted me to write things for him, but never once made a down payment. With nothing firmed up for the months to come, I began seriously to consider the prospect of another screenplay for Pete Walker. By the way he courted me, you'd never have guessed that we had been at each other's throats only months before. Now he wanted me to write a film about underage sex. I didn't like his synopsis and I stalled him.

What happened next was completely unexpected. My theatre company, which had been messing about in London, getting nowhere fast, took a play to the Edinburgh Festival Fringe. It was a smash hit. When I got back to London, one of the first interviews I did was for BBC Radio London's new daily arts programme, *Look, Stop, Listen*. Mike Sparrow asked me to work on the show and I said yes. A few days later I said no to underage sex. Eventually this film was made. It became *Home Before Midnight*, written by Murray Smith, the man who wrote *Cool It, Carol!* and the original story for *Schizo*.

Schizo opened in November to even worse reviews than *House of Mortal Sin*. The condemnation of the contrived plot was almost unanimous. 'Quite awful,' protested *The Guardian*. 'God help the British film industry if this sort of farrago becomes its staple diet.'[33] Later TV's Barry Norman rubbed salt in Pete Walker's wounds by declaring that *Schizo* was 'after Hitchcock, but so far after that it couldn't catch up if it were on Concorde.' The box office takings were disastrous. At Bayswater the film managed only £500 in its first week, the cinema's lowest take of the year. *The Texas Chain Saw Massacre* opened the same day to sensational business.

Thus ended my formative years at the feet of the king of British exploitation. As far as I'm concerned, something I wrote about Pete Walker in 1996[34] still holds good: 'He has driven me up the wall virtually from the day we met and yet I still cannot believe my good fortune in being able to work for him. His meanness is infuriating and yet he has been unstintingly generous, never once allowing me to buy so much as a cup of coffee, let alone the slap-up meals of which there have been countless. The films we made together were terrible. The critics hated them and the public wouldn't go to see them. But they were cults even in the 1970s, and the reason they are back on video this year is that they're great. But enough of trying to prove that Pete Walker was a man of contrasts...'

---

33 18th November, 1976

34 *Shock* (London: Titan Books, 1996)

V

*"One of the most hilarious moments in the 1976 Fringe
came from the Entertainment Machine from London.
[The subject of their play] was ham acting and some said
that no more appropriate subject could be found on the Fringe."*
~ Alistair Moffat, *The Edinburgh Fringe* ~

I think that my theatre company, Entertainment Machine, was successful because my friends and I were able to exploit our weaknesses. Our main weakness is that we weren't very good. We exploited this by doing plays about actors who weren't very good. We started out, like the characters in Jonathan Gershfield's film, as a bunch of amateurs. In 1975 I was directing a rehearsed improvisation for Cameo Players when Walter Zerlin Jnr. suggested that we form our own theatre company. We set it up like an amateur dramatic society with a committee consisting of me, Walter, Walter's girlfriend Pat Lock, Herschel, and three other people. I'd been associated with all the other committee members since *The Rising Generation* in 1972.

For our first production I proposed my version of Jean Genet's *Deathwatch*. This dated back to my days on the Play Selection Committee of Trent Players. Among the scripts I read was Genet's play, translated by Bernard Frechtmann. I didn't understand the play at all and I thought the dialogue was unspeakable. But I had the idea of turning the drama into comedy by inventing business that mocked Frechtmann's lines. Accordingly my version of *Deathwatch*, about three men in a prison cell, is probably the only one to feature slapstick, a production number and the prison guard played by a woman, who entered to 'Nellie the Elephant.' Don't ask me anything more about what was going on in my head. Obviously the main reason I was drawn to *Deathwatch* was that it was queer.

Walter, who was a heterosexual queen, couldn't wait to get started. Herschel, who was a heterosexual, was much less keen. But he was developing serious thespian ambitions and became putty in my hands. Along with playing Maurice, the prison punk, he also designed the set, mostly out of cardboard. Cardboard and Sellotape were to become Entertainment Machine staples. Unlike *Losing Track,* on which I had had to do virtually everything myself, the *Deathwatch* committee worked very hard. Soon they had set up a mini-tour, opening at the Little Theatre in Upper St Martin's Lane, very near Leicester Square. My first West End engagement. When we weren't fund-raising, by holding house parties and selling old clothes in a street market, we were fly-posting.

The show drew big houses most nights. But it wasn't everyone's cup of tea. One evening, about fifteen minutes in, there was a scuffle and three people walked out. It transpired they were The Incredible Orlando and other members of Lindsay Kemp's company, to whom Genet was a god. I wonder what it was that made them decide this wasn't the production of *Deathwatch* for them. Possibly it was when Walter entered on roller skates, wearing a green wig and an ice cream tray, with a rose in his mouth.

Box office takings in the second week were boosted by a review by Colin Bennett in *Time Out* ten times worse than any of my screenplays ever received. Bennett wrote about 'the worst performances I have ever seen, and for which the word "amateur" hardly suffices.' He concluded by saying that 'this group made Brian Rix look like Dostoevsky, a comparison I am quite sure they will cherish.'[35] We did, and for several years from then on we sent Colin Bennett a Christmas card.

Feeling as the 20-year-old Orson Welles must have felt after his first revolutionary production, *Voodoo Macbeth,* opened in New York in 1936, I decided to flex my artistic muscles. I demoted Entertainment Machine's chairman and took the post, re-styled artistic director, myself. This was the first stage in booting out the entire committee, one by one, until by 1977 Walter, Herschel and I were in sole control. Early in 1976 we put another play, the old melodrama *The Bells,* into production, again at the Little Theatre, despite the fact that the manager was displeased with the response to *Deathwatch* and didn't want us back. She relented when I paid the rent upfront.

Herschel made his inauspicious debut as director; but even Peter Brook couldn't have got performances out of the oddball cast. The lead was played by Gabor Vernon, known only for a Vladivar vodka commercial. I roped in crazy Ruxton Hayward to play two bit parts. A judge was going to be played by Michael Armstrong until, after one look at the rest of the cast, he walked out. He was replaced by Norman J. Warren's friend, Andrzej Jasiewicz, a Polish director, who had persuaded me to write a movie called *Dead Centre,* yet another rip-off, this time of the best-seller *The Dice Man.* 'This script will not be filmed,' I wrote. And of course it wasn't.

The Bells ground on for three weeks to general indifference although, after he came to see it, Michael Armstrong expressed quite strong feelings about the shortcomings of the cast. I was cheered up by a call from Norman, who invited me to an old people's home in Cuffley, Herts., to torture some naked women. Apparently *Stan's Slave* needed some more production value. Norman asked if I knew anyone else who'd like to be a torturer and I recommended Walter and Andrzej. One of the best-known stills from *Stan's Slave* is of me as

---

35   10th-16th October, 1975

a witchfinder, who orders the branding and flogging of a naked starlet. It didn't seem to matter to anyone that I was already in the film, playing a completely different part. Exploitation films played by different rules.

After a hard day's flagellation, I went to meet my old friend Ron Lloyd, whom I hadn't seen in months. He had startling news about Paladin, the laughably inept film distributor for which I was briefly some kind of sales agent. It had been wound up the previous year and the man who had run it into the ground, Peter Jacobs, was now driving a minicab. But there was more. Jacobs' associates, including Dave, who had intended to make a film by stealing everything from his employers, had been arrested on suspicion of film piracy. Michael Billington, involved in some way, had fled abroad. He kept his head down until he was tempted back by a Bond film, *The Spy Who Loved Me*. Not the title role, promised him for years, but a Russian spy killed off before the main credits. (In 1978 the ringleader of the alleged piracy operation was given a conditional discharge.)

I still have the minutes of the Entertainment Machine committee meeting, dated 23rd June, 1975, which read, 'A then quite ludicrous suggestion was put forward that we should try and perform *Deathwatch* at the Edinburgh Festival.' The suggestion was mine and I drove it forward. We realised early on that a revival was not going to get us noticed and that we had to write something new. Walter suggested a play as performed by incompetent amateurs. Both of us had had long experience of am dram mishaps. But Walter was thinking in particular of the hilariously bad plays he'd seen performed by his mother's Townswomen's Guild drama group at the Onslow Village Hall in Guildford, Surrey, where he grew up. Early in 1976 Walter and I completed a rough outline of the first of many plays we were to write together – *The Farndale Avenue Housing Estate Townswomen's Guild Dramatic Society's Production of 'Macbeth'*. The play, like the nine other *Farndale* plays that followed, was set in Guildford. But Farndale Avenue is a road I often walked down on my way home from Winchmore School. Walter and I both were re-living our youth.

I took the night train to Edinburgh to look for a venue. At Newcastle a Geordie oil rigger called Toby got in to my compartment and struck up a suggestive conversation that lasted until I reached my destination at 7.30am. The Fringe Society administrator, Alistair Moffat, sent me to look at eight prospective spaces and I chose Tollcross Primary School, Sean Connery's alma mater, in Fountainbridge. It had been used the previous year by an experimental group, Forkbeard Fantasy, whose performance art had not been appreciated. I asked how many chairs the school had available for the audience. 'You won't need more than twenty,' the dour janitor informed me.

Walter and I went to see two one-act plays at the Onslow Village Hall for research purposes. We sat at the back, giggling and making notes, something we were to do regularly over the next eleven years. Things we saw go wrong in church halls throughout the Home Counties were incorporated into our plays. Our bad-tempered prima donna, Thelma, who storms out of every Farndale Avenue production, was inspired by Walter's mother, Mimi. She saw some of our plays and thought they were ridiculous. I don't think she ever recognised herself.

I finished the script in a fortnight in June. We had written parts for ourselves. I was the producer of *Macbeth* and Walter was the adjudicator of the drama festival for which it was entered. Walter wanted to play the role in drag. There was also a part for Herschel as the stage manager who has to drag up as Lady Macbeth. Other parts were taken by women from Jean Selfe's music hall company. But very late in the day we still had no one to play Mrs Reece, chairman of the Dramatic Society. We paid a rock singer, Seldiy Bate, to take it. She was a part-time witch. For years afterwards TV companies contacted her every Halloween and Friday 13th to talk about the dark arts. By 1985 she and her partner, Nigel Bourne, who had been one of our technicians, were appearing with their magically conceived child.

Even before rehearsals began, the monthly magazine *Plays and Players* picked *The Farndale/Macbeth* as one of the most promising of more than two hundred productions on the Fringe. There was then a snowball effect. During rehearsals I was contacted by an ITV arts programme, *Aquarius*, which wanted to film our premiere. By the time we arrived in Edinburgh I was feeling quietly confident. On opening night there was a queue to get in that stretched right across the school playground. The dour janitor was quite taken aback by having to put out not twenty but 150 chairs.

That night we were almost as incompetent as the actors we were portraying. The dress rehearsal had been a catalogue of accidents, forgotten lines and technical glitches, and the first performance was no better. But we could do no wrong. The audience laughed at everything. Never before had I been involved in anything that produced such gales of mirth. I'm reasonably sure no one had much idea which mistakes were planned and which weren't. When the curtain came down, the media pounced on me. 'You've got a hit,' said the man from Scottish Television, who seemed to know what he was talking about. 'After this the word will spread like wildfire.'

Within days Anthony Troon gave us a review in *The Scotsman* that made it sound as if we had re-invented comedy. 'One of the most original and hilarious of the year's ideas...a brilliant concept...an hour and twenty minutes of sustained satire and ribaldry...a barrage of explosive, multiform humour,' Troon gushed in the first paragraph of his review, which then got even better.[36] Days later we collected the newspaper's 'Fringe First' award from the distinguished thespian Andrew Cruickshank. After a week the entire two-week run was sold out. Four hundred people were crammed into the hall for every subsequent performance and some of them sat on the floor, on window sills, and radiators. Alistair asked us to transfer for the third week of the Fringe to a five hundred seat theatre. But we already had booked a London run and, even though this was only at a community centre, we had to decline.

The two weeks I spent in Edinburgh in 1976 were the happiest of my entire career. It was almost as if, having spent years fumbling with the combination lock to the show biz vault, I'd guessed the correct numbers and all the glitter and the magic had come spilling out. What I didn't realise was that success in Edinburgh can vanish when the Festival bubble pops. A producer called Hugh Wooldridge was determined to transfer us to London's West End. But in London his backers saw through our pretence immediately and backed off. Right to the very end of the nationwide tour of *The Farndale/Macbeth* the cast was still fluffing lines genuinely and making late entrances. We were, after all, amateurs. We shared a modicum of talent. Hugh tried to get Walter an audition as Herod in *Jesus Christ Superstar,* a part for which he was perfect. Herschel actually did get an audition at the Hampstead Theatre Club. But neither actor had an Equity card, a crime that in those days was the equivalent of a doctor practising without a medical licence.

For the remainder of the decade I nipped off periodically to supervise Entertainment Machine productions at provincial theatres while holding down my day job as a reporter for *Look, Stop, Listen,* BBC Radio London's arts programme. It was broadcast live, every weekday evening, for four years, despite the fact that its producer/presenter, Mike Sparrow, never once got his arse into gear. He was a charming dissolute who would have been unable to organise a piss-up in a brewery because he would have been pissed. The pile of unopened mail regularly threatened to topple over. But in the 1970s no one was fired from the BBC (not even for paedophilia). Mike wasn't rumbled until 1988, when he was drunk on air and had to be removed from the microphone.

For quite a while Mike's incompetence didn't matter to me. I was on the radio, where I'd wanted to be since *The Goon Show* fired my comic imagination, and I could do almost whatever I wanted. Within a few months I was presenting my own programmes and occasionally, when he was recovering from who knows what he did the night before, Mike left me to run *Look, Stop, Listen* on my own. I cued the discs and slid the faders and played the jingles just as I'd wanted to do on Radio Caroline. Everything comes to he who waits.

---

36   26th August, 1976

I was fascinated and not a little aroused by Mike's passionate affair with Nigel Finch. They made an attractive couple, the Marc Jacobs and Harry Louis of their day. Nigel was the bright young thing of BBC Television's Music and Arts department. He made documentaries about artists and eccentrics in an offbeat, informal style that became highly influential. (I didn't understand Nigel's films. I thought they were pretentious.) Nigel arrived every Thursday on his motorcycle at BBC Radio London to talk about art. Some of his broadcasts were little dramas in which I played a variety of roles. As Mike and Nigel drifted apart, Nigel and I grew closer. He made a TV documentary about me and I wrote and produced his first fiction film. And we had sex.

Although the exploitation craze had passed its peak, I was still considered to be one of its most egregious practitioners. In the *Hampstead and Highgate Express*[37] Adrian Turner stated that he objected to my editing the UK section of the 1977 *International Film Guide* because 'McGillivray has contributed more than most to the degeneration of British cinema with his screenplays for *Schizo* and *House of Whipcord*.' I was so proud of this acclamation that I began using it as part of my publicity. It's on the home page of my website.[38]

I was still being offered bizarre assignments right up until the time the British film industry suffered another of its collapses at the end of the 1970s. I had acquired a literary agent – rather excitingly Tony Hancock's brother, Roger – who put me on a plane to Amsterdam to write a hardcore porn portmanteau of four episodes entitled *The Rapist Rides Again*. Over many subsequent meetings, in London and Amsterdam, it transpired that the young Dutch director was *homoseksueel*. We began sleeping together. Because subsequently he married a woman in order to work in the US, where he still has a career, I'll call him Geert. Geert was head-turningly pretty as well as highly intelligent and motivated, an explosive combination. But I wasn't able to ignite it. *The Rapist Rides Again* was never made; and although one of its episodes was salvaged (I went to Amsterdam to watch it being filmed and again for its premiere), now I can find no trace of it.

One day Nigel handed me a copy of J.G. Ballard's novel *Crash*. He'd bought the film rights, he claimed, and wanted me to write the screenplay. Geert became interested in the project and, the next thing I knew, he was taking Nigel on a tour of Amsterdam's gay saunas. When I saw him again, Geert told me that Nigel hadn't got the rights to *Crash*. Nearly twenty years later the film was made by David Cronenberg. More than one critic called it 'depraved' and the *Daily Mail* led a campaign for it to be banned.

---

37   10th December, 1976

38   www.pathetiquefilms.com

I thought it was a masterpiece. Tragically, by the time the *Crash* scandal was filling the front pages, Nigel had been dead for a year.

For an equally brief period I was attached to a film so controversial it made *Crash* look like *Watership Down*. It was without doubt the most controversial film in the history of the cinema, the only one to have been condemned by the Pope, Queen Elizabeth II and the Archbishop of Canterbury as well as the woman who was more powerful than any of them, moral reformer Mary Whitehouse. One word from her was enough to convince the British government to ban the film's Danish director, Jens Jørgen Thorsen, not just from making his film on British soil but even from entering the UK. The title of his film was *The Sex Life of Jesus Christ*.

Up until 1977, when he became the wickedest man in Europe, Thorsen had had something of a reputation as an experimental artist. In 1970 I'd seen his earlier film, *Quiet Days in Clichy*, based on Henry Miller's novel, at the London Film Festival. I liked its innovation of having the characters' thoughts appear as captions, but I liked little else about it. In 1974 Thorsen contributed a short to a porn portmanteau called *Wet Dreams*. Bowdlerised as *Dreams of Thirteen*, this was distributed in the UK by none other than David Hamilton Grant. It was he who called me to ask if I'd be interested in writing an English novelisation of Thorsen's script, which would be published in the US to counteract the bad publicity in the UK.

I read the script, which had had its title page prudently removed. 'I was awestruck by its ambition and complexity,' I wrote. 'The controversial sex scenes are mere incidentals. The film is a political thriller.' As with *Life of Brian*, which was to follow only two years later, Thorsen's intention was to attack not Christ but Christianity. Despite this I was tormented by indecision. 'I could have stones thrown through my window at the very least,' I fretted. I contacted my agent, who refused to be associated with the property. 'It's my name on the notepaper!' he bleated. He then washed his hands of me.

After talking on the phone with Thorsen, who was holed up in Paris, I decided to throw caution to the wind. I began talking money and a contract with Grant. The last time Thorsen called me, he insisted in his funny, high-pitched voice that he wanted me to come to France as soon as possible to start work, but that he'd had no confirmation from Grant. After a while, as with all the projects Grant offered me, I forgot all about it. In 1992 Thorsen finally made his film, as *The Return of Jesus*, with money from the Danish Film Institute. It seems to have caused even less of a stir than *House of Mortal Sin*. Thorsen died in 2000. I still have his 'sacrilegious' script on my shelf. I bet the Queen never read it.

The Farndale/Macbeth was on the road sporadically for the first six months of 1977, finally playing fifty performances. The tour did well enough in the sticks, but my toes curled after the last night at the Round House, when the manager told me my cast was not of the standard required by such a prestigious London venue. I decided then and there that Entertainment Machine would stop using the amateurs that had worked so hard to get the company started. And we did. I felt bad, particularly when some of the amateurs continued to beaver away for us, doing unpaid clerical and backstage work. But, hey, that's show biz.

It was while we were in Norwich that all four of the films I wrote for Pete Walker were shown at a special all-nighter at the National Film Theatre. One of the amateurs drove like the wind to get me to London in time for the kick-off, but she got a puncture and I was absent from the most important night of my career to date. The films never would have been shown at the British Film Institute's flagship cinema if I hadn't known the programmer. But the fact remains that the event marked a turning point for Pete Walker (and to a lesser extent myself). Overnight Pete went from a shlock merchant to the cult director he remains to this day. (I remained a hack writer but one with official recognition.)

The Farndale Ladies were destined to reappear in a series of ten productions, seen around the world from Australia to Zambia. But it was only the failure of almost everything else Entertainment Machine produced that convinced me to stick to what we were best at, doing plays badly. The first of my bright ideas to go down the pan was *Creepy Crawlies*, a 1950s science fiction movie performed live on stage – in black and white – together with the full supporting programme I remembered from my youth. The evening began with a colour travelogue, *Glorious Guernsey,* and this was followed by a newsreel and trailers before the main feature. The undertaking required a complex music and effects soundtrack. I assumed correctly that this could all be done after hours at BBC Radio London.

Mike Sparrow and I spent an increasing amount of time together, sometimes from dusk until dawn, editing pieces of tape together. Like caged rats we ended up mating. As Sylvester Stallone once said[39] of his marriage to Brigitte Nielsen, 'The sex wasn't that interesting.' Mike and I didn't fancy each other. The ordeal of *Creepy Crawlies* brought an end to our mutual masturbation. I'd made the mistake of asking Mike to direct the show. He brought all his radio disorganisation to the play and, by the end of the run, most of the cast wanted to throttle him.

Among the dozens of young hopefuls that turned up to audition were Ruby Wax, Deborah Fairfax from *Frightmare,* and an actor who'd taken the train to London from Birmingham, gone straight back home when he learned that we weren't paying Equity minimum, and now wanted his fare refunded.

---

39   *Radio Times,* 21st December, 1996

My blood ran cold. Entertainment Machine was by now a member of the Independent Theatre Council, an alternative theatre organisation that was negotiating with Equity for the unionisation of the Fringe. Because Walter, Herschel and I wanted our Equity cards, we were pretending that we paid Equity minimum.

Mike set off on the wrong foot by refusing to allow Walter and Herschel to play the leads they assumed were theirs. During production week he was otherwise engaged while the company did all the donkey work. He arrived in Edinburgh moments before the start of the dress rehearsal to announce, 'I'm shattered, loves,' a *faux pas* that was to become a catchphrase whenever Mike's name was mentioned. It was evident from the first night, after which nobody rushed up to me begging for interviews, that we weren't going to repeat the success of *The Farndale/Macbeth*.

While we ground on to small audiences which didn't appear to understand the joke, our lunchtime show, in which Walter recreated his role as the *Macbeth* adjudicator, did even worse. Our former champion, Anthony Troon, described him as 'Edna very-below-Average.'[40] I discovered, while I was standing in the rain in Princes Street, offering damp handbills to uninterested passers-by, that Edinburgh is a wonderful place to have a hit and a terrible place to have a flop. To add to our misery, Michael Green, who had been inspired by the success of *The Farndale/Macbeth* to dramatise his book *The Art of Coarse Acting*, was enjoying a sold-out run. Our course was clear. As *Creepy Crawlies* gasped its last, Walter and I began preparing the comeback of the Farndale Ladies.

My last attempts to write another memorable horror movie are best forgotten. After more than a year in the provinces, *Stan's Slave* opened in London's West End on the bottom half of a double bill early in 1978. It wasn't shown to the national press, and so I shall always remember it in terms of *Time Out*'s malicious review, which began, 'Another absolute stinker from the withered pen of David McGillivray.'[41] Why director Norman J. Warren wanted me to try again, I can't imagine, but I wrote him *Terror* despite having no faith in the unfathomable plot outline, largely cribbed from an Italian masterpiece, *Suspiria*. When I saw it later in the year, I was stunned. 'It's the weirdest film I've ever written,' I decided. The American trade paper *Variety* took a different view. 'Scripter David McGillivray's dialog, and most of pic's thesping, are as medieval as the lingering curse,' it found.[42]

Most of my time was now spent on the wireless or with wireless people. *Look, Stop, Listen* was becoming very much a 24 hour party with Mike as the

40   27th August, 1977
41   10th-16th March, 1978
42   19th December, 1979

increasingly inebriated host. Few of us on the programme approved of his new boyfriend, Paul, generally regarded as a dopy substitute for Nigel Finch. Mike and Paul had little in common except alcohol, and Nigel predicted a violent end. (He was right.) There were too many temptations on a programme which revolved around its presenters being wined and dined by people who wanted publicity. Quite often the day would begin with a champagne reception; then the coke-fuelled afternoon would produce an adrenalin-charged live show; and then it was off to an opening or a premiere, and we would end the day with a party at David Sweetman's.

David Sweetman was a little older than the rest of the *Look, Stop, Listen* team and he had done everything – 'every variety of sexual kink and boozy self-indulgence'[43] – long before we had. He was the wittiest and most articulate of us all, so bitchy that he was too much for some, Mike especially, but not for me. I absolutely adored him. David had been working for the BBC World Service since 1970. He was a regular at the Sombrero, a gay bar popular with foreign students, and it was here in 1976 that he'd met the love of his life, the doll-like Thai student Vatcharin Bhumichitr. They shared a flat in Hampstead with a lawyer known somewhat callously as Mad David. He was indeed very troubled and died in 1983 when he threw himself under a tube train. In keeping with the conventions of the time, his stash of gay porn was destroyed shortly before his relatives came to collect his effects.

At David Sweetman's parties Vatch cooked exquisite Thai meals (Thai food was almost unknown in London at the time) and David behaved disgracefully. During a round of the Truth Game, he asked Sarah Dunant if she'd ever been fucked up the arse. I was thus emboldened to admit that Mike Sparrow and I used to toss each other off. It was all a very far cry, yet only seven years, from my 'revolting' confrontation with a queer at the Open Space theatre. Although David claimed already to have lived the life of Riley, his best years were ahead of him. He and Vatch ran a chain of Thai restaurants and wrote cookery books, and David made documentaries for BBC television. We enjoyed a succession of adventures together until 2002, when I was one of those involved in killing him.

My Kilburn flat became party central after my flatmate, Vernon, moved out and into the house next door. (Perhaps because my show biz lifestyle had rubbed off, he'd signed to a modelling agency and was just about recognisable in an Alfa Romeo advert. But he didn't have much ambition and I believe he spent the rest of his life driving a van.) Vernon was replaced in my front room by a stream of short-term lodgers including my school chum, David José, and my first heterosexual shag Denise's South African work colleague Steve.

---

43   *The Observer,* 23rd June, 1996

There was an evening of monumental and premonitory silliness, which began when Denise came round with a girl friend and a bottle because they wanted some of Steve's weed. But he'd left it at work. Although it was gone midnight, Denise began phoning other users. The only one willing to make the journey was Nigel, who turned up at some ungodly hour with Mike and Paul in tow. This would have been a volatile *ménage* even if played out on lemonade at a garden fête. But at dead of night in a basement heavy with the fumes from circulating joints, the sexual game-playing was magnified to Machiavellian proportions.

The seeds had been sown. Nigel took me for an Indian meal, told me he was aware that Mike was trying to make him jealous, and then became flirtatious. Things came to a head at another of my parties at which I was too busy serving food to eat anything myself. I was pissed by 8.30pm and my memories of the rest of the long night consist only of flash frames. At one point Nigel and I are wrestling on the floor and he is using an unnecessary amount of strength to pin me down. 'That looked rather homo-erotic,' observes Denise. Then Mike is trying to chat up Entertainment Machine's sexually equivocal lighting designer and Paul is sullenly watching the television. Then the flat is empty, and Nigel and I are both naked in my bed. To my dismay, because I'd seen but not touched his statuesque musculature on so many occasions, there is no foreplay. Rather there's a copulative version of the wrestling match in which I'm pinned down again and something is definitely going into my arse. But how this congress concludes I have no idea.

When I woke up I was alone in the flat.

The repercussions of this sex madness rumbled on for years. The first indication of Mike's displeasure was at his 30th birthday party weeks later. He'd hired the back room of a pub opposite the BBC Radio London offices. Seating was at a long table with Mike at its head. Guests were arranged on either side in descending order of importance. Nigel had been reinstated literally as Mike's right-hand man. Paul was on his left but one seat down. I was at the bottom of the table with the wives of sound engineers. At the very far end, even lower down the pecking order than me, there was David Sweetman being scathingly catty about the entire business.

I had embarked on my mindlessly promiscuous phase, for which I have no excuse. All I can say is that, in my mind, I had primly refused sex for far too long and now everything had to change. In answer to your next question – no, I didn't really enjoy it. Most of the time I was just showing off. I had sex with two actresses in *Creepy Crawlies* because that's what men did. Occasionally I sailed very close to the wind. Pretty, blonde Clare told me she loved me, then sent me letters from various world capitals threatening to commit suicide. Instead she married an Egyptian and taught English in Cairo. Sometimes, because alcohol and drugs were involved, I can't remember whether I had sex with people or not. For several weeks the 3rd assistant director on one of my films came round to my flat, ostensibly to work on a screenplay with me. But time and time again my diary reads, 'Leland stayed over.' The only memory I have is of us lying on my bed to make notes. We must make of this what we will.

My third trip to New York in July 1978 was my most unseemly to date. Officially I was there to research my book, *Flops,* a history of show biz failures. David Castell, the editor of *Films Illustrated,* one of dozens of movie magazines to which I contributed, liked the idea and paid me an advance. I spent some time at the Lincoln Center, looking at a file labelled 'Failure', and I visited Joe Allen's restaurant, whose walls are lined with posters for failed Broadway shows. (The qualification for this honour was that the show had to have lost at least $1 million.) A new friend, Alan Jones (then a schnorrer, who gatecrashed press shows, but later a horror authority of some repute) had put me in touch with Jay Reisberg, who had worked with Jobriath, a rock legend for the wrong reasons. His brief recording career in the early 1970s was a disaster. Jay and I went to Marie's Crisis Café, a gay bar, where Jobriath had been reduced to playing the piano as Cole Berlin. But he was no longer there. To many people's amusement, I failed to complete my book about failure. But, as we'll learn, Nigel Finch made capital out of this.

In the late 1970s New York was a Garden of Earthly Delights missing its left-hand panel. The third part of the triptych, Damnation, would be added within a few years. I was very easily tempted by the delights. There was Charles Ludlam's Ridiculous Theatrical Company with Ludlam himself as Camille. *Snuff,* a notorious slasher, which allegedly included a real murder, was playing the rat-infested Lyric theatre on 42nd Street. The whole place was in uproar. Black guys threw live fire crackers over the balcony, scattering dozens in the seats below. The cops led somebody away. Someone came and sat next to me, lit a joint, and passed it to me. When the woman was disembowelled on the screen, there was mayhem in the auditorium, with shrieking and yelling that I thought might develop into a riot. 'So very different from what I'm used to at the Odeon, Marble Arch,' I wrote.

Dirty movies, I also noted, were now half the price they were four years ago. At the Adonis I saw *Hot Truckin'* and then at the 55th Street Playhouse I saw *A Night at the Adonis,* shot in the very rotting picture palace where I had been the night before. There were also private cinema clubs, where gay men watched old Hollywood movies. In a basement called Joe's Place, Bob Santoni sat in the vacant seat next to me and we played with each other throughout *Second Wife* starring Conrad Nagel. Instead of watching the second half of the double bill, we went to a porn theatre and had more hanky-panky there before spending the night together at his apartment in Queens.

A fit, sassy Latino with come-to-the-back-room eyes, Bob could have been a poster boy for New York's gay club scene during the disco breakout years. He was my ideal, a sex-mad sex bomb, who bent over backwards to accommodate me throughout the night and, after a short respite, early the next morning. I eagerly anticipated more of the same. I wanted Bob to take me to the Mine Shaft, one of the heavy-duty 'fuck bars' that everyone in London was talking about. Bob said no, possibly because my paisley shirts weren't part of the Mine Shaft dress code, or possibly because a one-night stand in this hedonistic culture was considered a long-term relationship. I learned from others that sex with ten partners from Friday night to Saturday morning was not uncommon. Almost everyone with whom I had any connection in New York in the late 1970s died of AIDS. Jobriath was among the first to go in 1983.

The Farndale Follies, the musical that reintroduced the Farndale Ladies, was officially Entertainment Machine's most professional production to date. Just before we went to Edinburgh in 1978, Walter, Herschel and I became directors of The Entertainment Machine Theatre Company Ltd. Shortly afterwards, after lying through our teeth about what we were paying ourselves as actors, we received our Equity cards. Walter was reluctant to turn professional full-time and, to many people's disbelief, he continued to practise as a barrister while dragging up and tap dancing in our shows. But, for a while at least, Herschel gave up his day job to tour Scottish community centres and even to do a turn as a Judy Garland impersonator in a play in London. By 1979 he had an agent.

Within days of our arrival in Edinburgh with the show that gave the audience what they wanted, we were back in our old routine. People were turned away from almost every performance and after one show a policeman told us that he was going to report us to the Licensing Authority for overcrowding and blocking exits. He did, too. The next day we dutifully put out the regulation 250 chairs and told two inspectors that people had been standing only because they were at the back and couldn't see. As soon as the inspectors departed, Walter put out another fifty chairs until I told him to stop.

The show toured the UK almost until the end of 1979, but to nothing like the success it had enjoyed in Edinburgh. Our new set designer, who brought his family to our London engagement, told me that he was so embarrassed that he could barely keep his eyes on the stage. Elsewhere there was regular criticism that our satire was heavy-handed. It became the only Farndale Avenue show that was never revived, never published. Later, as even Gilbert and Sullivan had done, we cannibalised the script and used its serviceable material in other shows.

By the end of 1978 *Look, Stop, Listen* was in trouble. It appeared that no one was listening. One night we held a competition. All those who phoned in with the correct answer to a question would receive tickets to a concert. Later the secretary answering the phones reported that she had received one correct answer and one obscene call. There was a crisis meeting during which I told Mike that the running time of the programme should be cut from ninety minutes to an hour and that its drearier features should be axed. He took no notice. The fate of the daily arts show was sealed.

I continued on my merry way. Leaving the studio on a cold night just before Christmas, I was picked up in a Dormobile by two stoned Australians, who wanted to give me a lift home. We took the most roundabout route imaginable, while I puffed on their joint. By the time we reached Kilburn I was as incapacitated as my chauffeurs. I suppose this kind of behaviour would get us all arrested today. My expanded state of consciousness throughout the holiday season may have led me to make a remarkably frank New Year Resolution: 'Recently I have been reading two autobiographies, one by Frankie Howerd, in which he manages to tell his life story without mentioning once that he's gay, the other by Tennessee Williams, in which his homosexuality is proudly discussed in every chapter. After thirty years of hypocrisy, I know now which writer I would most like to emulate.'

VI

"Incompetence is what we are good at:
it is the quality that marks us off from animals
and we should learn to revere it."
~ Stephen Pile ~

The story of the man who failed to write a book about failure sounds like an urban myth. But I am here to tell you that I am that man. I began with good intentions and filled notebooks with recondite information about stage shows that were taken off after one performance and TV programmes that nobody watched. But of five planned sections, I only completed the first, on music. This included my interviews with all kinds of singers I admired because they had had little or no success. I talked to Keith West, who never completed the *Teenage Opera* from which he issued two excerpts in 1967; Doug Sheldon, the only one of a trio of flatmates in the 1950s never to make it (the others were Michael Caine and Terence Stamp); and Joyce Shock, a rock 'n' roller whose only claim to fame was that she was Frankie Vaughan's sister-in-law. Of course, when I met these people and quite a few others, I couldn't tell them I was writing a book about failure.

It's not clear from my diary why I stopped writing *Flops*. Midway through 1979, references to David Castell, who commissioned me, cease. This suggests he was no longer harassing me. I'm useless without a deadline. (Later I discovered that Castell had resigned from his publishing company to become the film critic of the *Sunday Telegraph*.) I'd also been pipped to the post by another *Sunday Telegraph* columnist, Stephen Pile, who'd published *The Book of Heroic Failures* earlier the same year. What with all this, as well as my *Farndale Avenue* plays, and *It'll Be All Right on the Night*, a new TV show, which exploited the humour of out-takes, there were the beginnings of a cult of incompetence. I was interviewed about this phenomenon several times, once in the *Daily Mail*.[44] This was read by Nigel Finch, who told me that the piece had inspired him to make a film about failure for the arts series *Arena*.

He introduced me to his producer, Alan Yentob, and the plan went ahead. I genuinely thought that Yentob had taken the decision to spell his 'real' surname, Botney, backwards. I mentioned my theory to Nigel. He thought this most amusing and began circulating the rumour. It's my contention that this is how Yentob became known as Botney, particularly in *Private Eye*. Despite/because of our sexual *contretemps*, Nigel and I were continuing to

---

44   19th May, 1979

collaborate. Already I'd appeared in a couple of his earlier *Arena* films, notably his dissection of the song 'My Way'. For this he wanted vox pops but didn't trust the public. He told me to turn up while he was shooting in the streets of Ealing, near the BBC TV studios. He then pretended that I was a passer-by. My rehearsed ad libs are in the finished documentary.

Because *The Farndale Follies* was still on tour, Entertainment Machine didn't go to Edinburgh in 1979. But I did go to Ndola, Zambia, to see an amateur production of *The Farndale/Macbeth*. This trip required that I be inoculated against typhoid and cholera. I was warned by the doctor who stuck in the needles that I would suffer delirious dreams. He was right. Mine consisted predominantly of a nightmare in which I was an injured soldier refused help by everyone I encountered. When I awoke, I knew it was the plot of a horror film. The next day I wrote it down. I showed it to Nigel and later it became his first fiction film, *The Errand*.

There was a general election in 1979. It pains me to say this but I voted for the first time in my life and I voted Conservative. On Planet McG this was the right thing to do because Margaret Thatcher was the Tory leader and I felt it was important to help facilitate the election of the first British female prime minister. I've never made a secret of what I did. But some of my friends have been rendered almost speechless by my action. I admit today that it's ridiculous to say that I was trying to ignore party politics and follow my heart. If I'd studied her policies, I never would have gone over to the dark side. A little learning is a dangerous thing.

I've been known to protest that, although she did fuck-all for women, Thatcher's election remains of symbolic importance. Can I submit that the jury is still out on this? Notwithstanding, idealists like myself in the soft porn industry realised pretty damn quickly that we had made a mistake. A year after the Conservative victory, the so-called Eady levy (a long-established government subsidy for British film production) had been withdrawn. In other words, the money that had helped finance the likes of *House of Whipcord* was gone.

I never left the film industry, but I had to adapt, a policy that has stood me in good stead. When I went to The Hague for the premiere of Geert's film, I saw another, *Absurd,* by an Israeli director, Zaev Nirnberg. I told him genuinely that I thought his film was a masterpiece and that's all it took for him to hire me to write his next, *The Lady and the Pedlar,* based on a story by S.Y. Agnon about a Jewish pedlar and his relationship with a Gentile lady, who may be a cannibal. I didn't understand what I was writing, but I went along with Zaev because I thought he might be a genius. If he was, he's still unrecognised. He never made another film.

I also laboured for months on Stanley Long's abortive sci-fi movie *Plasmid.* The inept but prolific soft porn director, responsible for a wide variety of tat including the money-spinner *Adventures of a Taxi Driver*, took me to lunch at the Angus Steak House to bad-mouth his rival, Pete Walker, and his former screenwriter, Michael Armstrong, but mainly to sweet-talk me into re-writing a cack-handed script by someone called Jo Gannon. I loved it. The story of genetically modified creatures living in the sewers put me in mind of Nigel Kneale, and furthermore the hero worked for a local radio station. I was convinced this was going to be my breakthrough movie. It was never made, but it lived again as a novelisation[45] that used my script, but gave me no credit. The phantom movie doesn't even get a mention in Long's autobiography.[46]

It was while *The Farndale Follies* was on tour that Jean Selfe introduced me to J.P., a stage-struck kid of 23, who wanted to do something, anything, in show biz, but had no experience. 'He's a rather attractive John Conteh colour,' is all I drooled on the day we met. But I was soon to be breathtakingly, heart-racingly, hand-tremblingly in love and to remain that way for the next fifteen years. Or perhaps I just went bonkers. J.P. was the last straight boy who drove me to distraction. I can't tell you how relieved I am that I broke this stupid habit. Pursuit of the unattainable is never going to be considered cool.

Because I was able to dole out Equity cards to young hopefuls, I easily could have abused my position of power by demanding favours in return. But I never laid a finger on J.P. Instead I gave him a job as a stand-in for our lighting man, who couldn't make our gig in Peterborough. J.P. managed quite well. In 1980 he became my new lodger and resident handyman. He could turn his hand to shelves, French windows and garden furniture. He also broke my heart. But without J.P. I may never have learned that you don't need to learn manual skills. You need to live with people who can do the jobs for you.

During the long period of adjustment that existed between the coded classified ads in *Films and Filming* and the sexual free-for-all that began with Gaydar, many gay men in London met through the 'Lonelyhearts' column in *Time Out*. Dozens of new 'personals' appeared every week. They were all discreet; the word 'sex' wasn't allowed and the customary euphemism was 'fun.' I began answering personals in 1978 and this got me into all kinds of scrapes. Then, as now, small ads gave you the opportunity to have sex with a stranger so desperate for companionship that he advertised for it. Before I realised that this was not the way to true happiness John from Maidenhead gave me hepatitis and Naim from East Ham sued me for almost every penny I had.

Quite unplanned, because we weren't what you might call close, I also had a one night stand with Mike Sparrow's boyfriend Paul. He had taken some blurred photographs of some of the singers I'd interviewed for *Flops* and came

---

45   *Plasmid* (London: Star Books, 1980)

46   *X-Rated: Adventures of an Exploitation Filmmaker* (Richmond, Surrey: Reynolds & Hearn, 2008)

round to my flat for payment. He asked for 'one fifty.' I honestly thought he meant £1.50 and protested that I must at least give him a tenner. But he meant £150. For that price I could have got Andy Warhol to knock me up some screen prints. Paul began drinking the jenever I'd brought back from The Hague and was soon weeping into his glass about the way Mike mistreated him. At 3am he took off his clothes and got into my bed, which was the last thing I expected.

The next morning Paul left 'still talking about his three-figure bill, which came as a bit of a downer after I'd spent the night servicing him.' The only benefit of doing business with drunks, however, is that they tend to forget little things like payments. The following day Mike announced that he and Paul had split. They hadn't. Mike later appeared at Radio London with his face lacerated by scratches and scabs, the trophies of a weekend of fighting. This was nothing compared with what was to come. In 1983 the word on the street was that Paul had attacked Mike with a knife. Mike later admitted to me that this was true and that his convalescence took a month. But as it was Paul who took Mike to hospital, they were still together.

My better pieces for *Look, Stop, Listen* had resulted in offers from other departments of the BBC. Since 1978 I'd been contributing to Radio 4. That year I bought my first answering machine and this inspired me to do something for *Woman's Hour* about the amusing messages you'd hear if you rang celebrities like Peter Cook and Miriam Margolyes. While I was in Zambia I went back down the mines and spoke to government ministers for a documentary about the copper industry for the BBC World Service. But, much to my surprise, the bulk of my income, such as it was, still derived from Radio London.

I was surprised because to me the station seemed to be on its last legs. There had been more crisis talks, but these had resulted only in programme re-scheduling tantamount to re-arranging deck chairs on the Titanic. *Look, Stop, Listen,* which we assumed was for the chop in 1979, staggered into the next decade. But it had little support. An article in the *Times Educational Supplement*[47] referred to Radio London's output as 'amateurish...naïve and superficial' and attacked Mike Sparrow personally for referring to Wordsworth as a Lakeside poet. Only Sarah Dunnant [*sic*] was complimented.

During my last months at Radio London I again behaved like a *prima donna*, regularly swanning off to participate in more glamorous projects. Nigel Finch's documentary *Climb Every Mountain Or Nothing Succeeds Like Failure* was my second and final shot at TV fame. It was a lightweight but amusingly quirky piece in which Stephen Pile and I met people who were even less successful than us. I spoke to Miriam Hargrave, who had failed

---

47   11th July, 1980

her driving test 39 times, and Jahn Teigen, who had scored nil points for his native Norway in the 1978 Eurovision Song Contest.

I also toured London theatres, predicting which shows would fail at the box office. Days after the programme was broadcast, on 2nd April, Harold Fielding, the producer of *On the Twentieth Century*, one of the shows I'd condemned, announced his intention to sue me. I was not unfamiliar with the British legal system. I had received my first summons (for failing to keep up the rental payments on my TV) in 1973 and I've been unable to keep out of court ever since. But Fielding *v* McGillivray promised to be my most high-profile case.

Climb Every Mountain kept me in the public eye for quite a few months. The BBC repeated the programme twice in 1980, but neither then nor ever again with my contentious references to *On the Twentieth Century*. The show closed on 9th August with estimated losses of £150,000 and Harold Fielding threatened, 'I'm doubly determined to see this action through.'[48] When he withdrew his claim in 1983, the story didn't make the papers, even though I'd sent out a press release. By that time I was once again a forgotten man.

My next project with Nigel pretty much ended our working relationship. It was *The Errand*, the film produced from my literally drug-addled brain. Godfrey Kirby and John Vilton, who, in case you have forgotten, introduced me to hardcore pornography in 1966, put up some of the budget. Godfrey wanted to shoot on another new format, super 16mm, which, when blown up, was indistinguishable from the higher-quality 35mm. I went to a demonstration, where a producer claimed that she'd sold one of her short films to a distributor for £30,000. I fed exaggerated figures such as this to Nigel, who was thereby convinced not only that he should direct but also that he should pay us £2,000 for the privilege.

The pre-production and two week shoot convinced me that I had found my true vocation as a conniving, two-timing bastard that everyone hates, i.e. a producer. At the top end of the scale I was able to negotiate with agents and get practically every actor I wanted, even former movie star Dorothy Alison, for peanuts. I blagged some impressive locations too, notably a building in North London that had fascinated me since childhood, the Stoke Newington pumping station. It was a Victorian folly built in 1855 but it had been abandoned since the War. At the other end of the scale I dyed army surplus uniforms in a dustbin in my back garden. I was so busy with administration that I barely set foot on the set, something other producers should consider if they want to be more popular.

---

48   *Daily Mail,* 8th August, 1980

Nigel saw several young actors for the leading part, a soldier in an unnamed military unit that has its own way of disposing of new recruits that don't come up to scratch. He dismissed them all when I introduced him to unassuming but sexy boy next door Eddie Kalinski. He'd been in the naked, gay sex scene at the beginning of *A Bigger Splash* and had then been stabbed in the face with a pitchfork in *Frightmare*. Rather than returning to London after filming in Milton Keynes, Nigel paid for a night in a B&B for his star and himself and remained uncharacteristically coy about what may or may not have developed.

Nigel never thought much of *The Errand*. He tried to salvage what he thought was a bad job by re-voicing three of the cast including Eddie. I had to tell Eddie that his new voice had been provided by Berwick Kaler, whose chequered career had included the sleazy films of Andy Milligan, often called the second worst film director in the world. Eddie wasn't pleased and arrived late at the preview, thereby missing all his dialogue scenes. The film was 'sold' to Columbia-EMI-Warner, latest incarnation of the company that had dumped *House of Mortal Sin*. 'Sold' is written like that because, after the distributor had deducted the cost of the 35mm blow-up and eighty prints from the receipts, no payment was ever made to us. *The Errand* played with a flop horror film called *Happy Birthday to Me,* after which we were informed that the negative and prints had been destroyed. (One print in fact survived. In 2007 it was screened at BFI Southbank to general indifference. None of the cast responded to my offer of free tickets.)

My work on *The Errand* resulted in the end of my work on Radio London. When I told Mike Sparrow I hadn't got time to interview film director Alan Parker, Mike blew his top, called me a fucking wanker, and warned me never to set foot in Radio London's office again. Accordingly I wasn't involved in the last edition of *Look, Stop, Listen,* which went out with a whimper on 25th July. Listeners told me the programme simply ended with Mike saying, 'Good night and goodbye.'

Mike soon forgave me. I stayed in touch with him almost until the end of his life although this was not always easy for me, particularly when Mike's mental condition deteriorated. We had meetings during which I could only nod, psychiatrist-like, as he accused me of being the ringleader of a plot to undermine his authority, or bragged of unlikely TV and film offers in the pipeline. None of them existed. Mike clung on to his job at Radio London, doing bits and pieces until the station went off the air for the last time in 1988. It may appear as though I have nothing good to say about Mike Sparrow. But the fault is mine for being unable to maintain a happy relationship with anyone who tells me what to do. I'm well aware, however, of Mike's importance in my life. He was very much an audio version of Pete Walker, someone who gave me an opportunity to which I had no right and then allowed me *carte blanche* for four years. Such people are few and far between.

Through Radio London I met more stars than there are in heaven. I interviewed such writers as Dennis Wheatley, Ben Travers, Harold Robbins and William Goldman and I have their signed books to prove it. Animator Chuck Jones drew me a picture of Bugs Bunny and captioned it, 'Ask not what is up. What is up is what David says it is.' It's above my desk and I marvel at it every day. Likewise the LP signed by violinist Stéphane Grappelli. I also met film directors Cavalcanti and Bertolucci, John Waters and Otto Preminger, Stanley Kramer and Julien Temple.

Where now are the recordings of the weekly mini-dramas, written and directed by Nigel Finch, in which Mike, Sarah and I played artists and models, critics and patrons, depending on what exhibition Nigel wanted to plug? Probably all wiped or binned. Where now is the half-empty glass of gin and tonic that Tennessee Williams brought into the Arts Office one morning and then left on a desk when he went to be interviewed? 'We've got to keep it!' we agreed. 'It'll be worth a fortune!' Did I really get chatting about porcelain to Gloria Swanson when she popped in to talk about her autobiography? And if so, why?

I sat on a couch with Klaus Kinski and was transfixed by the most piercing blue eyes that ever have bored into me. No wonder he had such a hypnotic appeal on screen. I also arranged meetings with two wonderful old ladies. I had tea at a home for old thesps with 86-year-old Mysie Monte, who had played the same part in *The Mousetrap* for more than a decade. 90-year-old Athene Seyler told me that she hadn't been made a Dame because for most of her life she lived with a man who wasn't her husband. She had recently broken her arm in a fall. 'Frank Muir told me I must keep away from roller discos,' she reported.

Another old lady provided me with a story on which I still dine out. I went to see Marika Rivera, daughter of artist Diego Rivera, in cabaret, a show which bored the pants off me. The next day she came in to Radio London to be interviewed by Mike. I gave him a crib sheet on which I wrote, 'Marika Rivera is an ageing tart, who looks like a man in drag. She tells badly-rehearsed stories of Montmartre without jokes or indeed endings.' Mike had these notes with him during the interview, which apparently went very well. Alas, nothing was recorded due to a technical glitch. Mike left the studio to find help. When he returned, Marika was reading my crib sheet. 'Vot ist *zis*?' she demanded. Mike mumbled some excuse and then was forced to interview the ageing tart again. 'This time it didn't go as well,' he told me. Happy days. Later in 1980 I joined Sarah Dunant at Capital Radio, one of London's first commercial stations. I lasted two years there. But it was never as much fun as Radio London.

VII

"I was stopped by two policemen disguised as human beings."
~ Quentin Crisp ~

Because of my tidy-mindedness, I fancied completing a trilogy of Farndale Avenue plays. This was the main reason for creating *The Farndale Avenue Housing Estate Townswomen's Guild Dramatic Society Murder Mystery*. Historically the play should have been the *Beverly Hills Cop III* of the series, the last failed attempt to re-work a successful formula. But strange to report, it was the most successful play that Walter Zerlin Jnr. and I ever wrote. The first to be published, it took the Farndale concept around the world and became an amateur dramatic society pot-boiler. From here on, the remainder of my theatrical writing career was mapped out.

The play also was a watershed in that it marked a parting of the ways. An early draft had a part for Herschel. He didn't like it. Walter and I wrote him out. Herschel began to re-think his life. Soon afterwards he got married (to my ex-flatmate Vernon's sister, actually) and then retired from acting. Hoping to tempt him back into the fold, Walter and I devised a play specifically for him. But at the first script meeting, held at his flat, Herschel thought Walter and I were making fun of him. He told us to get out and we did. The following day he pushed the keys of the company minibus through my letterbox; it was a symbolic farewell.

Walter could be quite ruthless when it came to his stock in trade, legal matters. In the ensuing months he made arrangements to buy Herschel out of the company. After our settlement I generally came across Herschel only by accident. Although I dignified my obsession with him as love, infatuation seems the more likely explanation in that, as soon as he was out of my sight, he was out of my mind. He had appeared in our plays under sufferance, but he never understood the camp sense of humour Walter and I shared and, in the end, he came to resent it. He may not have wanted to play Hamlet, but nor did he want to play Lady Macbeth, which is what we required of him. Herschel returned to his former business and became very successful. I'm encouraged that he implies on his website that Entertainment Machine's 1976 award was given to him alone. In order to bask in reflected glory, you must at least have some affection for its source.

If *The Farndale/Murder Mystery* works as low comedy, perhaps this is because it contains the essence of our parody of middle-class values and an element of truth. The earlier plays are fantasies, with material – like a back-to-front set in *Macbeth* – that never would be seen in a genuine am dram production. The later plays tend to parody genres – science-fiction and Gothic horror – that aren't popular with amateurs. The *Murder Mystery,* on the other hand, is a more realistic depiction of the malfunctions that almost every actor has suffered – the gun that doesn't fire, the door that doesn't open. It's also set in an archetypal English country house everyone recognises from Agatha Christie and Cluedo.

Like many of our plays, this one grew from a single concept, the accidental revelation in the first scene that the butler is the killer. The rest of the nonsensical plot is basically mine. Walter's head was too full of madcap ideas for him to bother about construction. But it's interspersed with Walter's flights of fancy that I think give the Farndale plays their individual character. There's a fashion show, and a quiz, and a song and dance number. (It's 'I Could Be Happy with You' from *The Boy Friend,* one of Walter's favourite musicals.)

The talented actresses we engaged – one of them trained at the Actors Studio – became increasingly concerned as they realised that the amateurishness they were dredging out of their souls to convey came very easily to the people employing them. They saw no virtue, for example, in our ability to save money by recycling sets and props from previous productions. They retained their apprehension all the way to Edinburgh, where the Farndale Ladies once again cast their incompetent magic over the city. In *The Scotsman* J.Y. Simpson was ecstatic ('This is a superb performance that absolutely must not be missed')[49] and after a few days we were the fourth most popular show on the Festival Fringe. Later, on the road, our fame preceded us. This was Entertainment Machine's most successful tour to date.

Remarkably this triumph wasn't our most popular show in Edinburgh in 1980. We took up a second production, Walter Zerlin Jnr.'s one man show, *Running Around the Stage Like a Lunatic,* which caused a *Macbeth*-style sensation and very nearly catapulted the tap dancing barrister into the big time. Walter had written the show himself and planned to play all fifteen parts in it by effecting quick costume and wig changes in the wings. I had no idea whether he could pull off this feat and, after a slapdash preview in our London rehearsal room, I was even less sure. But J.P. was one of those who saw potential in the comedy and, equally ambitious at this time, he eased himself into the director's chair.

The audience for the show grew steadily each day and, at the end of the first week, glowing reviews began to appear. Now writing for the *Sunday Times,* Stephen Pile made the plot sound irresistible: 'Walter organises a weekend orgy with himself, but comes back early and discovers himself at it.' Stephen's piece was headed, 'The new masterpiece.'[50] J.Y. Simpson in

---

49 23rd August, 1980
50 24th August, 1980

The Scotsman agreed. 'One of the finest productions of this type on this year's Fringe,' he declared.[51] The next development was inevitable: crowds turned away from every performance and then Entertainment Machine's second 'Fringe First' award.

In London, where the one-man farce played five times, the reviews were similarly enthusiastic. 'Those who catch this little show may well be able to boast one day that they were in at the birth of a new comedy star,' predicted John Barber in the *Daily Telegraph*.[52] The rest of the media pricked up its ears. Walter made a lot of radio and TV appearances, the most prestigious being *The Russell Harty Show* on BBC Two. 'If the right offers come along,' Walter told the *Evening Standard*'s Charles Spencer, 'I'd give up my present job like a shot.'[53]

Walter never had to make that big decision. Almost as quickly as it had been dangled in front of his nose, the carrot of fame was jerked away. He outstayed his welcome in London, where his last gig was poorly attended. Then he was removed from *Boom Boom, Out Go the Lights,* one of the first TV programmes to collect together some of the stars of the new alternative comedy circuit. This decision may in itself explain why the name Walter Zerlin Jnr. is not known today. Alongside Rik Mayall, Adrian Edmondson, Nigel Planer and others who were about to revolutionise comedy, Walter's old school knockabout looked like the kind of comedy that was about to be revolutionised. Walter worked like a Trojan to get back in the game. For the next twenty years he churned out scripts for stage, screen and radio. Not one was accepted. You only get one bite of the cherry.

My home life during this period was hardly conventional and J.P. was involved in some way in much of the unconventionality. When his relatives came down from Liverpool, they would share his bed, while J.P. and I would sleep together in mine. Or rather he slept and I lay there, trying to think of England. One evening, as if to prove that he had no notion of what was going on in my head, he brought home two women he'd picked up, one for him and one for me. Mine was a Latvian named Marga. After I'd eaten a piece of her Lebanese Red with my kebab, I was quite happy to have sex with her all night and, as is my wont, again the next morning. Later, after planting some bulbs and going to the theatre, I went round to see David, a Kiwi librarian I'd contacted through *Time Out,* for more sex and drugs. 'Never had sex with two people in the same day before,' I confirmed.

I just now mentioned bulbs because I spent a lot of time trying to landscape my enormous back garden. This is how I had my next run-in with

---

51   26th August, 1980
52   7th January, 1981
53   19th January, 1981

the law. At a loose end, Nigel Finch had begun building me a path out of paving stones abandoned on the street by council workmen. Too late one night, I went out with my wheelbarrow to collect another slab and was pulled up by two policemen in a Panda car, one of whom asked, 'What's the story here then?' I was then loaded, together with the evidence, into a paddy wagon and taken to West Hampstead police station.

I knew what was going to happen next when I was told to turn out my pockets and take off my belt. Although I've got up to a lot of mischief in my life, this was the only night I spent in a police cell. I was released at 5am, without charge, after the cops had got J.P. out of bed to corroborate my claim that the wheelbarrow was my own property. Never underestimate the amount of inconvenience you can be caused by young policemen with time on their hands.

Because I'd left Radio London, I was now undergoing financial hardship again. These were tough times. And not only did I have myself to worry about, I now had upwards of five mouths to feed. When Vernon moved from the house next door (he sold his flat, bought for £5,000, for £27,000, just one example of how the cost of living rose in the 1970s), he left behind a cat, which I took in. I'd always wanted a pet. Things hadn't worked out when I acquired a dog, Frazer (named after actor Frazer Hines), in 1976. We didn't like each other and he ran away. But the cat (Marjorie; I don't know where that came from) was a much better choice. She was very popular with the neighbourhood Toms, who would queue up to gang bang her. She produced two litters of kittens, which softened my granite heart and turned me into the kindly old pornographer I am today.

I've kept cats ever since Marjorie and her family joined my household. But they're not cheap to run. And nor, come to that, am I. At one point I found I had £13 to my name. I borrowed from everyone and once had to ask Alan Yentob to lend me a pound for the tube fare home. I weighed up my options and decided I had to join J.P. on the dole. Until the new Conservative government cracked down on scroungers such as myself, 'everyone' was on the dole. By 'everyone' I mean two million people, the highest number of unemployed since the Depression.

There is a reason for everything and the reason so many of us claimed unemployment benefit in the late 1970s is that it was so easy. There were no questions asked. It was simply a case of 'signing on' after which you received a cheque in the post. The only bugbear for many of us was getting time off work to pick up the money. Alan Jones was so busy in multiple jobs that he visited the dole office in a taxi. The most famous exploiters of this system were Boy George and his cronies, who used their dole pay-outs to fund their 'one look lasts a day' club wear. I didn't know George at the time. But I did encounter his mate, Marilyn, at a launch of luminous disco jewellery at The Embassy Club, a pioneer gay bar in Mayfair. I still have a tape of our radio interview in which he spat, 'Marilyn Monroe would never wear this shit.' His opinion of the product didn't stop him and his crew grabbing handfuls of it before making their getaway. They were...er...survivors.

The dole couldn't support the lifestyle to which I had become accustomed; and when J.P. went to Birmingham to appear in panto with Ken Dodd, I rented his room to a Nigerian named Simeon. (I never laid a finger on him.) Within a very short time, Simeon had run up a telephone bill of £300+. He wouldn't pay me and he wouldn't move out. With the help of J.P., now living/having sex with a Russell Harty researcher named Jill, I deposited Simeon's belongings on the street and changed the locks. This was, of course, illegal. I found myself back in court, charged with unlawful eviction. I paid the fine.

I was still in dire financial straits. It was J.P. who provided a lifeline. He told me about his friend Brian. He had entered into a marriage of convenience with a Polish woman, who wanted UK citizenship. She had a friend, who was interested in a similar arrangement. It's difficult today to accept that this is how I came to be married. But it's all laid out in my diary. J.P. brokered the deal. Mira, a well-padded blonde with a wry sense of humour, was willing to pay £650 for my hand. J.P. got the price up to £1,000. I was worried about being arrested. I consulted David Sweetman, who had married a Thai woman in a similar arrangement. (I didn't mention his widow in David's obituary.)[54] David advised me that marriages regarded by the authorities as suspicious were subject to random checks. Accordingly Mira replaced Simeon as my flatmate. 'She's an intelligent girl. She seems to quite like me,' I wrote. 'Maybe the marriage will be consummated.'

I was married on 28th May, 1981, at Euston Town Hall. The only witnesses were J.P. and a Greek called George. The two wedding snaps have faded so badly that the bride and groom are barely distinguishable. It's almost as if the ceremony never happened. But it did. I've got the divorce papers somewhere.

I never really fitted in at Capital Radio. Producer Mike Childs agreed to try me out as a favour to our friend Alan Jones, but didn't like my arty-farty BBC ways. My first assignment was a baptism of fire. I was sent to talk to Bow Wow Wow, impresario Malcolm McLaren's first major group following the break-up of The Sex Pistols. 'Come back with something provocative,' I was told. I'm warning you now that this is where some readers who have remained unshocked may fling their copy of this book to the floor. We are entering 'attitudes were different then' territory. McLaren liked schoolgirls and his campaign in favour of underage sex was part of Bow Wow Wow's

---

54   *The Guardian*, 12th April, 2002

publicity pack. The pop Svengali introduced me to his 14-year-old lead singer, Annabella, who started talking about sex. It seemed perfectly reasonable to ask her, 'Have you had sex yet?' Her (in all likelihood rehearsed) reply was, 'I'm waiting for the right man.' This was all considered acceptable for Sunday teatime listening.

Mike's presenter on the Capital arts show, *Sunday Supplement*, was Kerry Juby, a Mike Sparrow clone even down to his tardiness. But after I kicked up a fuss about being kept waiting for another two hours, Kerry got the message. He became very attentive and rather took me under his wing, suggesting all kinds of interesting arts features on which I had virtually free rein. I showed my appreciation by leaving Capital to produce a succession of appallingly bad shows for Entertainment Machine.

Ssshh... was another of our innovations, a comedy without dialogue. Its conceit was that the President of the Noise Abatement Society has left £50,000 in his will to the relative who can remain silent for a year. The reviews were kind, but used words like 'overlong' and 'overindulgent' that didn't bring in the crowds. It was a blockbuster, however, compared to Walter's late-night show, *Dolly Goes to Broadway,* a bottom-drawer script he'd re-vamped to incorporate the quick changes he'd introduced the previous year. It played to the smallest audiences – sometimes in single figures – we ever had in Edinburgh.

After that it was a case of goodbye, *Dolly*. But *Ssshh...* had been booked for a national tour and, despite its deficiencies, we had to prolong the misery. The cast hated me and, after a screaming row at the Sherman Theatre, Cardiff, the leading man, Ian Harvey, went off to telephone his agent to 'get me out of this thing.' The theatre manager was well aware of the friction, but he was a fan of the Farndale Ladies and, on that basis, he'd already booked Entertainment Machine to produce the theatre's 1981 Christmas show. This was to be *Snowbound in the Glitterdrome Hotel,* such garbage that it's remarkable in retrospect that I was ever allowed back into any theatre in the land.

The show was in trouble from day one because Walter didn't get on with David José, whom I'd brought in to enliven another old script that was unproduced for good reason. Walter and I were a dream team and we sparked off each other as comedy writing teams are supposed to do. But from the earliest days I'd asked outsiders to join us because I thought that the best comedy is written by committee. This never worked and the outsider always ended up outside. This was because I was influenced by friends who were funny only in 'real life.' You know the type. They come up with observations at parties that make everyone listening fall about with laughter. Unfortunately, when it comes to producing jokes to order, these people tend not to be able to do it. Comedy is a business like any other and you can't just be thrown into it without knowing the rules.

The story, 'such as it was',[55] concerned three cleaning ladies elevated to stardom by a fairy godmother. The fairy godmother walked out during rehearsals and we fired two more of the cast before arriving in Cardiff with a show that never had been properly rehearsed. Four performances were cancelled because of poor bookings. The audience, most of whom had been expecting a cabaret, were usually apathetic and sometimes downright hostile. I was playing the Demon King and at one point I had to say, 'I hereby strip these women of their talent!' Someone in the audience shouted, '*What* talent?'

The only woman in the cast with any real talent was our new Fairy Godmother. She never acted again. But ten years later she re-emerged as a TV director and is now highly respected. She's done *Doctor Who.* Her name is Sheree Folkson. As for Ian Harvey, who nearly walked out of *Ssshh...*, he later became my agent. But the play itself will never take the stage again. In the 1990s, after I'd learned British Sign Language, I thought *Ssshh...* might make a good entertainment for deaf audiences. I dug it out of my filing cabinet. I discovered that it was shit.

Touring unfunny shows around the UK came with a price to pay. I seem never to have been able to leave London without stocking up on something called Nobrium. Periodically I was also collapsing in screaming agony from kidney stones. After my first attack I knew that I could expect hours of torture that even the Spanish Inquisition would have difficulty matching. Doctors in A&E at that time wouldn't give me precious pethidine until they were absolutely sure I wasn't an addict desperate for my next fix. I'd like to meet the junkie who could have equalled my performance – writhing, weeping, pleading, vomiting – until I received the blessed needle. I snipped something from a newspaper which listed the Top Ten Agonies, as tested with a dolorimeter. (No, me neither.) Number one was my very own renal colic, which tied for pole position with a burning cigarette held against the skin. Number ten was piddling old toothache.

The next unfunny show I directed was for the Covent Garden Community Theatre, an outfit that had been performing right-on entertainments in London pubs, clubs and parks since 1975. They were just one of around 1,200 groups given seemingly limitless amounts of tax-payers' money by the Arts Council of Great Britain. Sometimes the CGCT set up their loud and lively shows in the very bars of pubs, something which did not endear the company to punters trying to have a quiet drink. I was well aware of their activities. One of their writers, Joe Lang, had helped Walter and me with the script of *Creepy Crawlies.* Young actors who got their Equity cards with the company included Keith Allen, Saskia Reeves and Julian Clary of whom there will be more very soon.

---

55 *The Guardian,* 21st December, 1981

Ironically, in view of the fact that I was still drawing the dole, *On Yer Bike* was about unemployment. The title was inspired by Employment Secretary Norman Tebbit's claim that, in the 1930s, his unemployed father had 'got on his bike and looked for work', a remark that was much ridiculed. When rehearsals began, only part of the script and none of the music had been written. I had to start scribbling and so the succession of puns and innuendos, about workers taking over their cardboard box factory, ended up resembling an unemployed man's Entertainment Machine production. In the cast was Janet Sate, a Northern lass who seemed to do sullen and feisty and nothing much in between. I took an instant dislike to her. But she became one of my closest friends and most trusted colleagues and I think the world of her. My first impressions of people are as reliable as a *Daily Express* weather forecast.

Chastened by our dismal failures in 1981, Walter and I decided to stick to what we did best, plays in which things went wrong. The fourth in the *Farndale Avenue* series, a French farce called *Chase Me Up Farndale Avenue, s'il vous plaît!,* was the one that made the critics turn against us. For them, the joke was over. But the public never tired of it. There was a night during the long run of the farce that I'll never forget. We were at the Uppingham Theatre in Rutland. The character of Minnie the wardrobe mistress had entangled the entire cast in her knitting wool, a classic Walter Zerlin Jnr. device. The audience was convulsed. They would not stop laughing. We stood on the stage, unable to speak, probably for thirty seconds, possibly even longer. That's a very long time. It was a comic apotheosis. It was what I'd always dreamed of. I wanted more. Who wouldn't?

There was plenty more of the same, I'm pleased to say, for the rest of the decade. I won't go into elaborate detail. But allow me to recount the whole story of the *Farndale* farce, if only to remind myself of the veracity of another of my adages: once you know that there is something wrong with a situation, it will never improve; it will either stay the same or it will get worse.

The first actress I cast in the play was Janet Sate because we had bonded over the awfulness of *On Yer Bike*. She was joined by another irresistibly acid-tongued Northerner, Erika Poole, who put us in mind of a younger, more splenetic Margaret Rutherford. She, too, remained part of my ensemble. But I was unable to cast the actresses I wanted for two older characters and unwisely settled for second best, Jacobi and Rita. They didn't want the jobs. And Rita really wasn't very good at all. Janet, who always has had a wonderful turn of phrase, described her acting as, 'We are in a cave.' (Picture a bad actor who, when told to imagine he's in a cave, raises his arms above his head in a gesture of awe and studies the ceiling.)

Even during rehearsals, everyone knew I had blundered. When I suggested Rita might change something, she glared at me through narrowed eyes.

Jacobi wouldn't look me in the eye at all. During the London run, I overheard them agreeing that they weren't going to invite any agents because the play was so dreadful. When I reported this to Janet, she told me that they both had to go. She suggested that I could play Rita's part as Gordon, a stage manager, while Jacobi's part, Mrs Reece, the chairman of the Dramatic Society, could be played in drag by her friend Julian Clary, another CGCT alumnus. We could engineer a situation whereby Jacobi and Rita would resign in Sudbury; we would then have a couple of days for rehearsal before the new cast opened on the Isle of Wight. I thought it was a ridiculous idea. I said yes. Janet and Erika were almost hysterical with glee.

I didn't know who Julian Clary was. I had a single memory of a lissom, blond creature wafting into the back of the rehearsal room while I was working on *On Yer Bike*. Throughout this period, I refer to Julian in my diary as a female impersonator. That's what he was. He was appearing on the new alternative comedy circuit as Gillian Pieface, an agony aunt. Secret rehearsals began. Before the opening in Sudbury I began to get cold feet. What if Jacobi and Rita shopped us to Equity? 'Grasp the rubber snake!' Janet demanded.

'Accordingly I ordered Jacobi and Rita on stage to test voice levels. Jacobi was immediately stroppy, announcing that she'd already done hers. I said that I wanted to hear her nevertheless. She complied with bad grace and afterwards a row developed during which she reiterated her offer to leave. The row continued in the dressing room. Jacobi and Rita both confirmed they weren't doing any further rehearsals. I said this wasn't good enough. "Re-cast!" they repeated.

'As soon as the curtain came down [after the second and final performance] the following night I wrote out two cheques and presented them to the ex-members of the cast. Jacobi accepted with hardly a flutter of her stupid false eyelashes. Rita was slightly taken aback. 'Are our services required for the Isle of Wight?' she asked. 'We'll manage,' I snapped and never spoke another word to them. They drove off without a goodbye. We took Chinese take-aways back to the digs. There were also many joints and home-made rhubarb wine. Julian, who had hidden in the lighting box to watch the show, reckons he's learned the whole of Act I.'

As he reveals in his own memoir,[56] Julian had done nothing of the sort. The performances in Ryde were nerve-wracking because none of us knew

---

[56]   *A Young Man's Passage* (London: Ebury Press, 2005)

what Mrs Reece would do or say next. But Julian was already a brilliant improviser:

'There were a lot of lines to learn and I was far from ready on my first night at the Prince Regent Theatre on the Isle of Wight. Instead of saying, "That was a narrow squeak," I came up with, "That was a short quack." I also had a large, explanatory speech to reel off in Act II, which was vital to the plot. My cue came from David, who was playing the part of Gordon. The time came and he said, "But what shall we do when we get to the bistro and Mr Barratt isn't there?"

"That's your problem," I said, and promptly left the stage.'

I don't know what became of Jacobi and Rita although Julian later reported that he'd seen Jacobi serving in a snack bar. Julian and I, on the other hand, are often seen in public together. He's amused when fans think we're partners. (I've never laid a finger on him.)

For a little while married life was much more conventional than it had been when I was a bachelor gay. Mira and I kept adding to our feline family. Some of the kittens had gone to other homes, but Marjorie and her son, Killer, were still with us. Then, while I was at the vet's, someone brought in a box of kittens to be put down and I couldn't resist adopting the liveliest, which we called Kicius (Polish for pussy cat). Three months later they were joined by Vincent, a ginger Tom, the friendliest cat I've ever owned.

I walked out of Capital Radio for the last time after I'd been kept waiting once too often. I flung my script at the receptionist and told her, 'Get someone else to read it.' But my life has been a succession of doors opening as others close. My friend Michael Darvell, to whom I'd chatted at press shows for years, was now the features editor of *What's On in London,* a very old listings magazine that was in a long drawn-out struggle with the racier *Time Out,* and he began employing me. I stayed with the magazine until 2006, the year before it finally it gave up the struggle.

It still pains me to write that a cloud hovered over almost the whole of 1982 and sometimes made it very difficult for me to concentrate on earning a living. Jean Salter, my former landlady and now the woman upstairs, had been diagnosed with breast cancer in 1980. In February, 1982, she told me it had spread to her liver. I had no idea that this type of cancer was almost invariably terminal, and I expected her to recover. Mira did, too. We were very shocked when Jean died on 24th May. She was 60, had just retired and was looking forward to travelling to South America.

I went to bed that night disconsolate. Mira came into my room and asked if she could sleep with me. I threw back the bedclothes. This was the only time we had sex in six and a half years of marriage. Mira was more spiritual than me, but we were both atheist. Nevertheless it seems to me that we were both driven by some primitive urge to express a power of life after death. I have no other explanation. It wasn't as if we were in love.

Jean bequeathed her flat to me and the three children of one of her oldest friends, whom I bought out. I had no money, but in those days it was easy to find an accountant willing to attest that the joint incomes of my wife and I were sufficient for us to be granted a loan. Most of the money (£26,000) came from my bank. The rest I got from my parents. After Mum had sent me a birthday present in 1980, I had taken her to dinner. Then I asked her and Dad to stump up the rest of the cash I needed. After what had happened in 1975, they hardly could refuse their flesh and blood a second time.

I bought Jean's flat because J.P. told me he was miserable and wanted to come home. A month after Jean's death he was back, but this time living upstairs. For the next twelve years I came to dread the late evenings. First I would hear J.P.'s front door open and footsteps. Then his voice and a female voice: 'Oh, this is nice!' Then the romantic music started. Then a wine bottle cork popped. Then two sets of footsteps went to and from the bathroom. Finally there was the rhythmical squeaking of the bed springs, growing in pace and volume, for about ten minutes. Then silence. Only then could I return to work. Prior to that I'd been floating in time and space, the saddest man in the world.

VIII

"I love you to death,
I love you to death,
I love you to death, oh, baby.
'Til you're out of breath,
I'll love you to death;
I need you."
~ Song by Village People, 1980 ~

On 15th November, 1982, I went to review *First Blood* for *Films and Filming*. I met a friend, Geoff Simm, there. He was reviewing this first *Rambo* film for a gay magazine called *Him*. Geoff had been the boom swinger on my film *The Errand*. He was one of Alan Jones' disco crowd, one of that generation of gay men for whom there were so many men, so little time. He mentioned that he'd read something about a female impersonator, who was under observation in a New York hospital because he'd come down with just about every disease going. Hepatitis. TB. Herpes. Plus a rare cancer.

The ominous significance of this conversation, which will be apparent to everyone reading this today, was lost on us during those last days of blissful ignorance. But the full horror of the situation was only weeks away. Terry Higgins was a barman at Heaven, London's biggest gay disco, who flew regularly to New York to buy new dance tracks. He had fallen ill in 1980 with the same mysterious immune deficiency as the New York drag queen, Brandy Alexander, and he was already dead. His obituary appeared in the 26th November, 1982, issue of *Capital Gay* together with the announcement that his friends were forming the Terry Higgins Trust. 'I knew that we had to educate people that this was coming,' Martyn Butler, one of the founders of the THT, told me in 2012.[57] 'I got some of the early leaflets from New York. We decided to take action and do it in Terry's name.'

Action came too late to save Geoff Simm, who died of AIDS on 11th June, 1990.

By the end of 1982 London was buzzing with rumours. 'A new form of virulent cancer is plaguing the gay community. It's transmitted sexually. Sounds terrifying,' I wrote on 6th December before noting that already I was only one degree of separation from this gay plague. 'Alan Jones says two of his friends have already died.' The response to the news from New York was incredulity. A disease that only killed gay men? That was impossible. There must be some mistake.

---

57   *QX,* 5th July, 2012

And in any case whatever was happening was happening a long way away. Initially almost nothing on the London gay scene changed. On the contrary, Subway, London's first answer to New York's Mine Shaft, only recently had opened, and men went there every night to have sex on the premises. The sex was always what would later be called 'unsafe.' Condoms were used at the time only to prevent unwanted pregnancies. One slight modification to gay behaviour was that clubbers tended not to have sex with Americans.

By 1983 everyone who travelled regularly to the U.S. knew the true extent of the threat. Alan Jones, who returned from California, reported that, in my words, 'The gay community is now scared stiff. Over a thousand people have died of the dreaded AIDS.' In 1984, when I toured the U.S. on a Greyhound bus (I'll come back to this), I found that life had changed irrevocably. Ross, a composer with whom I'd been having sex since he contacted me via *Films and Filming*, didn't like condoms. The only alternative as far as he was concerned was something I later learned was called intercrural sex. In San Francisco I found that the porn cinema where I saw a double bill of *Knockout!* and *Printer's Devils* had become a club at which I was required to sign a form absolving the proprietor of any responsibility for activity that may occur on the premises.

On 19th December, 1984, I went to give blood. I decided against it. 'Since I went in August, the AIDS scare has well and truly got a grip,' I wrote. 'Donors are asked to read a leaflet and are then on their honour to own up if they're in a "high risk group." No. 1 on the list used to be "male homosexuals who have sex with a number of partners." But this has now been crossed out and replaced with "all practising homosexuals."' Because of the 'health crisis' paramedics were being advised not to give the kiss of life to AIDS suspects, i.e. gay men. Gradually it was recognised that other groups appeared to be high risk: Africans and intravenous drug users.

On 11th December, 1985, Julian Clary told me that his partner, Christopher, had AIDS. I wrote, with a callousness for which Quentin Crisp was later castigated, 'This is the first person I've known to develop the fashionable killer disease.' I joked about AIDS because it scared me. I overheard someone at my gym say, 'They'll never find a cure.' The certain knowledge flashed through my mind that we were all going to die. We were living a scenario that only a science-fiction author should have been able to conceive: a new disease was capable of wiping out blacks, drug addicts and gay men, in other words most of the world's undesirables. But this wasn't science-fiction. It was science-fact and inescapable. By the end of 1986 the gossip was that AIDS was the new bubonic plague.

I wasn't the only one living in fear. Almost every week, throughout the 1980s, I would have an anguished tête-à-tête with someone similarly affected. Alan Jones told me that almost all his friends, including his Portuguese partner, Fernando, had been diagnosed HIV+; that he accepted that he must himself be infected; and that there was therefore no point in him going to the clinic to be given his death sentence. From 1986 the spectre of AIDS grew ever more tangible. Douglas Lambert was an American actor in London who declared Heaven open in 1979. I met him when he worked with Herschel in the play about Judy Garland. When he died on 16th December, 1986, he became the first victim of AIDS I'd known personally.

I moved one step closer to mortality the following year while I was having sex with a woman we'll call Veronica. By 1987 I'd been using condoms for four years. But then a Durex split and I became paranoid when Veronica told me that her ex-boyfriend was HIV+. He died in 1989. By that time the whole of the UK must have been paranoid. There had been commercials on TV and leaflets through every letterbox in the land warning us that there was a deadly new disease with no cure. I went to the pictures and before the main feature there was an AIDS awareness commercial with Bob Geldof, who held up a condom and demanded, 'Put one of these on your dick.'

By 1989 Geoff Simm was looking worryingly thin. He also had developed KS lesions. These had been eradicated and he was struggling on. But by 1990 he was in St Mary's hospital in Paddington, where I was to spend increasing amounts of my time. It was a place of enormous inspiration and despair, inspiration because the staff were angels, despair because my friends were near death. Alan Jones' partner, Fernando, was here, in great pain and wanting to die. On 11th June I went to see Geoff. On the way I picked up Alan and his friend Kjell. Kjell said to me with chilling candour, 'I'm in the queue.' He had been diagnosed HIV+ in 1982, and already had AIDS-related shingles, but he was convinced he wasn't going to die.

Geoff was now skeletal, his mouth agape, like a Belsen inmate. I didn't know what to do except to tell his mother that I'd like to write his obituary.[58] To my relief she was happy to talk about him. The next day I was on my way to St Mary's when I bumped into Alan, who told me that Geoff had just died, helped on his way with morphine. I burst into tears and then pulled myself together because we had to go to the hospital. Fernando, who knew Geoff, had been sedated, but the tranquilliser had made him find everything funny and his infectious laugh made the tragedy bearable. I met another Portuguese patient, António, who had just been diagnosed HIV+ at the age of 20. A Brazilian had been fucking him without condoms even though he knew he was infected. António had had two HIV tests that came back negative and a third that was positive. I was distraught. I told him I would do anything I could for him. 'Take this virus out of my body,' he replied. I heard that shortly afterwards he had tried to commit suicide. Later the same year I heard that Nigel Finch was ill.

---

58   *Variety,* 20th June, 1990

These were desperate times that altered our perception of reality. During 1991 I was having regular sex with a *Time Out* contact called Stephen. On one of our dates he told me with a serious face, 'I'm afraid I've got something to tell you.' Time stopped while I waited for him to add, 'I've got AIDS.' Instead he said, 'I've found someone else,' and it was as much as I could do to prevent myself from hugging him and crying, 'I'm so happy!' I was brought down to earth with the news of the deaths of so many friends: Peter Buckley, who had written most of the *Films and Filming* article that had got me fired from the British Film Institute; John Kobal, owner of the world's greatest photo archive; Julian Clary's partner Christopher. The disease was still able to kill like lightning. Two actors I worked with in Los Angeles and who seemed in fine fettle in 1991 were dead by 1993.

Poor Fernando went through the gamut of the opportunistic diseases that people with AIDS suffered at this time. His eyesight failed and then a silicone tube was attached to a heart valve. But he was a fighter. He was still fighting in 1994, when his family was called to his bedside. As with many families of the period, they learned at one fell swoop that their son was gay, had AIDS, and was about to die. Fernando died on 3rd September 1994. The worst wasn't over. I was to lose a lot more friends to AIDS: Nigel Finch, David Warbeck and Richard Warwick among them. As late as 1996 I was fairly sure that I was to be the next in Kjell's queue.

We know now that this cataclysm had a happy ending. In the mid-1990s new therapies gradually brought AIDS under control. The gay scene, pretty much decimated in the 1980s, rose from its ashes in the late 1990s. This was a new, proud gay scene. Instead of locked doors and blacked-out windows, gay bars now had neon signs and flew rainbow flags. By the turn of the 21st century every country in the west had decriminalised homosexuality.

I can also add a personal postscript to this appalling period, the worst for gay men since homosexuality was made a capital offence in the 13th century. In 2015, on a whim, I typed António's name into Google. In all honesty all I expected to find was the date of his death. After all, he had developed what was then called full-blown AIDS in 1994. I hadn't seen him since. My heart leaped when I found António on Facebook, very much alive. I told him, when I met him again on 7th March, 2015, that I was so very happy to see him. António, not unlike other gay men of his time, had taken his destiny into his own hands. He had done research, knew which combinations of drugs seemed to prolong the lives of people with AIDS, and demanded them from his doctor. By the time I met him António had become a landscape gardener. He is now looking forward to the next development in his life.

He is an inspiration to us all and his statue should be on the empty plinth in Trafalgar Square.

IX

"Censorship is a way to avoid change and make sure that society remains static.
It is a means of exerting power, preventing debate and discouraging challenge."
~ Peter Hall ~

Tim Webster's day job required him to don a Goofy costume and jump around in football stadiums. But he also directed one of Entertainment Machine's minor shows in Edinburgh (don't ask) and then, in 1983, he was put in charge of Gemini Theatre, a project designed to get unemployed young actors back to work. Although I was now 35, I just about qualified for the scheme. For six months I played a few juicy roles I might otherwise not have played including Ross, John Merrick's keeper in *The Elephant Man*. With very few exceptions there was a reason why the rest of the company was unemployed. They were abysmal. One of the exceptions was Saul Jephcott, who played Merrick and later went into *EastEnders*. He was a Muscle Mary with star quality he never realised.

There was a gym next to the rehearsal room and Saul asked me to train there with him. I agreed, initially because training included sharing a communal shower. But, after a few sessions, I realised that weight lifting was the way forward. I loved it when I could no longer button my shirt over my chest. I've pumped iron, normally three times a week, ever since. I've always maintained that this has been a keep fit regime. It's probable that today I'm in better shape than some other men of my age. But the driving force behind the tedious workouts to which I submit myself has been the desire to keep having sex. You may have heard that, in the gay world, nobody over the age of 28 has sex unless they're built like a brick shithouse. It's true. I may never have looked like Arnold Schwarzenegger. But nor have I looked like the Michelin Man. Some gerontophiles have been very grateful.

Despite being unemployed, I was by now a full-time entertainer, moving from project to project, sometimes with barely a day off, although I still never missed a party. Julian Clary was now working as a singing telegram for a company called Songbird, run by Kara Noble, daughter of Peter Noble and Marianne Stone. He would give lifts home in the back of the company van, full of balloons and a helium pump. We learned that, when inhaled, helium makes your voice sound like a Chipmunk's. Hours of amusement.

From Gemini Theatre I went straight back to Entertainment Machine, now sufficiently well-established for us to re-cycle old hits. The first show to have a make-over was *The Farndale/Macbeth*, which was increased from 70 minutes to nearly two hours. Among the additional material was a production number in which the Three Witches sang 'That Old Black Magic.' It was on this production that I began a fling with an actress who subsequently had a successful career and won't want to be reminded of youthful indiscretion. She once played a character called Marge and this is as good a name as any.

By 1984 Marge and I were going at it to such an extent that I ended one diary entry with, 'My God, is this a relationship?' In case you're wondering, yes, this happened while I was married *and* while I was having sex with men. My newest ploy for meeting blokes was to write personal replies to readers who sent suggestive letters to my column in *Films and Filming*. The first man I met through this process was Ross, the American composer mentioned in the previous chapter; and although the sex was gratifyingly carnal and drawn out for hours, this was also a meeting of minds. We were to have regular encounters, on two continents, for the next ten years.

Ever since *Running Around the Stage Like a Lunatic* hit the headlines in 1980, someone at the Adelaide Festival had been trying to bring the show, complete with Walter and myself, to Australia. In 1984 we were at last set to go, safe in the knowledge that the British Council was footing the bills. Something like a week before our departure, the British Council watched a tape of Walter's antics and promptly refused to pay our fares. I was so disappointed that I took off on a Greyhound bus from New York and travelled 5,500 miles through fifteen states, finishing up a month later in San Francisco. It was an uncomfortable but enlightening way to travel. Somewhere around El Paso I overheard a woman on the bus say to her companion, 'I'm gonna start reading the bible and getting my shit together. I hear the world's gonna end in the year 2000 and these big old locusts are gonna sting us.'

Although I'm partial to the occasional tourist attraction, and was able on this trip to tick off the Houston Astrodome, the Alamo, and the town of Baker ('Gateway to Death Valley'), this was no travel brochure tour. In New Orleans I chose the nearest hotel to the bus depot, which was Le Dale. When I got inside I found it was a doss house. I didn't have the courage to say I'd changed my mind. I shared a room with an itinerant manual worker. I'd seen enough films to know that, in this situation, I should sleep with my wallet under my pillow. (One decade on, I was astounded to see a photo of the hotel, completely unchanged, accompanying an article[59] that exposed Le Dale as the grimy, cockroach-ridden last known residence of Ylenia Carrisi, Tyrone Power's granddaughter, who disappeared without trace in 1994.)

Later during my trip, while I was having breakfast in a cafeteria in Indio, on the way to Las Vegas, I watched through the window with fascination a man on the sidewalk methodically dropping a piece of wire inside the window

---

59   *Sunday Times,* 17th April, 1994

of a parked car to disengage the lock. He then got into the car and drove away. Even my hosts, relatives of theatre people I'd worked with back in the UK, turned out to be felons. 'I was just preparing for bed when Russell knocked me for six by inviting me into the garden for a smoke. He'd been stoned all day. He's got two convictions for possession. I got a buzz and turned in.'

In California I stayed with my schoolmate, Jim Giddens, who was now directing TV commercials. I was invited to his daughter Jennifer's school to talk about my horror films. A boy asked if I knew his mother, who had had her eye gouged out in Andy Milligan's *Monstrosity*. I spent a day at Disneyland. As I approached its entrance, I had palpitations. You'll recall that, as a boy, I'd wanted to be one of Donald Duck's nephews. Thirty years on, I was in the Magic Kingdom. I loved every minute. I wished I were nine again. I also hung out with Michael Billington, who now wore a baseball cap and dark glasses and drove a Cadillac. He'd appeared in a couple of TV episodes, but had started trying to flog movie ideas to producers. He talked me into writing a treatment of one of them.

Despite his A list connections (for some time he'd been walking out with Barbara Broccoli, daughter of *James Bond* producer Cubby), Billington never got a movie off the ground. I, on the other hand, began directing my new comedy film shortly after my plane touched down in London. This is the film that was so bad it made my earlier train wreck, *Losing Track,* look like the work of Ernst Lubitsch. It came about at the fag end of the arts subsidy bonanza and indeed the fag end of the Greater London Council, which spent money like water before it was abolished in 1986. It splashed out £23,000+ for a film of a Covent Garden Community Theatre show, *Fair Cop*, a timely piece about police corruption and accountability.

Film making is like giving birth. After a couple of years you forget how painful it was. In this particular instance I also wanted to work again with Peter Leabourne and Alex Maguire, two amusing fellows who had been in *On Yer Bike*. We needed a leading man so I cast J.P. At one point there was also to have been a cameo for Paul Boateng, chairman of the GLC's Police Committee. I went to visit him at County Hall and found him very enthusiastic about making his acting debut. Then he read the script. That was the end of that. From then onwards the GLC wanted no involvement in the film and, after it was finished, they expressed no interest in seeing it.

Fair Cop was never released. Rumour persists that it had a solitary screening for a community group, few of whom were still in their seats by the end. Today only one VHS tape of the film is known to exist. Recently I watched it. Although my direction is incompetent and the plot is incoherent, one or two of Alex's surreal gags made me snigger. Alex Maguire was another writer I tried to drag into Entertainment Machine's orbit.

photo credit: Frank Manning

top: Poor man's Cleese. With Susanne Forster in *Snowbound in the Glitterdrome Hotel*, Cardiff, 1981.

above: How we laughed. Nigel Finch and Walter Zerlin Jnr. channelling Kristofferson and Streisand for a 1977 Entertainment Machine publicity shot.

left: That's your problem. With Julian Clary in *Chase Me Up Farndale Avenue, s'il vous plaît!*, tour, 1982.

top and above:
Paying homage at Hippie Central,
1984 and 2000.

left:
Former movie star reduced to working
for me for £7.50 a week. Lisa Daniely
with Emma Rogers in *Living Skills*,
London 1985.

above: Like a marriage. With Walter Zerlin Jnr., Wimbledon Theatre, London, 1988.

left: L to R: Me, Jennifer Lautrec, Janet Sate, Cindy Lee Wright, Dawn Toms and Chas Millward, the company of *They Came from Mars…* at John o' Groats, 1986.

below: A year later Erika Poole joined the cast.

above: With Mary Dreyer, Fiona Coyne and Mark Hoeben, who were in *The Farndale/Murder Mystery*, Cape Town, 1989.

below: Me, Hilary Cromie, Jennifer Scott-Malden and Amanda Symonds in *The Farndale/Macbeth*, Southwold, 1990.

photo credit: Laura Widener

top: Lisa Gates, Lisa Beezley, Carol Newell, Ceptembre Anthony, and me filming them for the Los Angeles production of *The Farndale/Murder Mystery*, 1991.

above: The 1st and as it turned out only issue of my anti-censorship magazine, 1994.

left: Film fans. Me and my schoolmate Jim Giddens, Los Angeles, 1991.

above: The class of 1959. Christopher Beale, John Keane, me, Kester Whitehead. Reunion at John Keane's, St Alban's, 1992.

below: The last time I saw Pete Walker. Manchester, 1992.

photo credit: Tony Edwards

above: Smut pedlars. With Stanley Long and Michael Armstrong at the launch of *Doing Rude Things*, Scala, London, 1992.

left: Date night. Harrison Marks and Pamela Green.

bottom left: Rough justice. In the film of *Doing Rude Things*, 1995.

below: It's all because of him. John Lawrence, one of my oldest friends, 1994.

top: Men in my life 1. John Pidgeon.
I worked with him from 1971 until his death in 2016.

above: Men in my life 2. Vincent Wang.
Named after my cat.

centre left: Men in my life 3. Nathan Schiff.
Words fail me.

left: Men in my life 4. Russell Churney.
So brilliant his memorial concert ran 3 hours
40 minutes.

For my 37th birthday J.P. organised a surprise party in my flat. It was no surprise to me because one of the guests spilled the beans beforehand. But I entered into the spirit of the occasion with such fervour that I was soon blotto. 'All back to my place!' I told Alex Maguire, Peter Leabourne and Jennifer Lautrec, who was playing Mrs Reece in *The Haunted Through Lounge and Recessed Dining Nook at Farndale Castle*. Jenny was what would now be called a MILF. In my bedroom I took off all my clothes and the others followed suit. When they found out about it, people found it hard to believe that I had group sex with this particular group. But it happened and I have witnesses, the other guests who walked in on us and caught us at it.

Our driver on *Fair Cop* was Mick Perrin, a cheerful Liverpudlian musician with the gift of the Scouse gab. He told me he could light Entertainment Machine's next production, a revival of *The Farndale/Murder Mystery,* and I hired him. He did perfectly well even though, as he later admitted, his previous lighting experience amounted to little more than changing a bulb. Mick is a fine example of my creed that bluffing is one of the essential keys to life's riches. From his first theatre job working for me Mick went on to become a comedy impresario of some magnitude and by that I mean producing tours with Eddie Izzard. Come to think of it, Mick Perrin owes me everything.

By the mid-1980s my life had been turned upside-down, chiefly by AIDS but also, admittedly to a much lesser extent, by the video revolution. I came surprisingly late to the world of home video. It was 1980 before I acquired my first VCR; but almost immediately I found myself part of an exciting underground community that traded illegal tapes. The healthiest currency was pornography. Many men went to cities like Amsterdam and then smuggled back into the UK porn films that were then passed hand-to-hand, copied and re-copied, until the images were little more than abstract patterns. It was these bootleg videotapes, also sold from under the counter in equally unauthorised sex shops, which provided another nail in the coffin of the soft porn industry from which I had once earned a living.

Those on both sides of the law knew where they stood with pornography, which was illegal in any form under the Obscene Publications Act. But then along came a sensational new genre, which threw everyone into confusion. The films in this genre were generally crude and violent. But they were also legal because they were released on videotape, which didn't have to be submitted to the British Board of Film Censors (or Classification as it became). The umbrella term for these problem pictures was 'video nasties' and the press began complaining about them in 1982. Once again it was the warden of our souls, Mary Whitehouse, who effected change. She encouraged Tory MP Graham Bright to introduce legislation, which was passed in 1984 as the Video Recordings Act, a version of which still requires every movie we buy or rent to have been classified by the BBFC.

There never was any understanding, much less an agreement, of what constituted a video nasty. The Director of Public Prosecutions published a list of films that featured something unpleasant, like a decapitation or a castration. But it was a pretty arbitrary list that included, for example, only one film by Andy Milligan even though his entire oeuvre was just as horrid. It also didn't seem to matter that many of the films, like *The Evil Dead*, already had been passed for cinema release by the BBFC. All that mattered was that we could now be prosecuted for selling or owning a film on the list. This was the fate that befell David Hamilton Grant, whose World of Video 2000 company distributed *Nightmares in a Damaged Brain*, an effective little psycho thriller with a bit of blood-letting. For this transgression he was jailed for eighteen months. His barrister, Geoffrey Robertson, has described Grant as 'the last victim of censorship in this country.'[60]

By the time the DPP list appeared in 1983, most young gore-hounds already had seen everything on it. But for me and others like me, middle-aged film fans losing touch with popular culture, it was a wake-up call. Here was a list of around seventy films, some of which we'd never heard of, but all of which *we had to see now!* I was fortunate to be introduced to a succession of blokes, with names like Jez and Chas, who were willing to lend me illegal tapes. The most important connection I made was with Marc Morris, who remained a friend long after the 'nasty' furore had been forgotten. Marc was one of a new hybrid, the geek-goth, whose ashen-faced descendants now swarm through horror festivals and conventions. He lived in a black-painted flat whose walls were lined from floor to ceiling with forbidden videotapes. He lived in dread fear of the official knock at the door, and whispered terrible tales of others in our secret society who had been carted away in dawn raids.

Marc was the first young man I met who knew more about movies than I did. We would gossip for hours in his den of iniquity and through him I saw an astounding amount of bad, banned films. I realised, after the first couple of dozen, that these films weren't dangerous, just silly. Indeed, halfway through one of the most notorious nasties, *The Driller Killer*, the drilling actually gave us the giggles. Today you can see far more realistic scenes of torture and dismemberment on TV. In the 1980s, however, I was so angered by the idea that we could be locked up for watching a maniac cannibal eating the entrails spilling out of his stomach (the film's called *Anthropophagus* if you'd like to make a note) that seeds were sown for my first major political statement. (Further ahead still Marc became a film distributor responsible for releasing *Between Your Legs*.)

---

60 *Video Nasties: Moral Panic, Censorship and Videotape* (Nucleus Films, 2010)

I was becoming an ex-film buff because, as far as I was now concerned, there was more to life than escaping from it into a celluloid fantasy. Back in the old days I thought nothing of seeing more than 300 films in one year. By 1985 this number had fallen to 66. This was because I had begun a lifelong mission. I was determined to try everything in the world except falconry and knife-throwing. I was also convinced that one could enjoy a new experience at any age. I was 37 when Marge taught me to swim, 38 when Mick taught me to drive (I passed my test at the third attempt in 1985). I was also on the road for most of the year and increasingly insinuating myself into the spotlight.

In readiness for the last leg of *The Farndale/Murder Mystery* tour I once again fired two actresses. I brought back Janet Sate to play one of the roles and played the other as the stage manager, Gordon, a character that was to become a staple in the Farndale canon. Although I say so myself, I was very good at being very bad and sometimes detected a frisson of appreciation from the audience each time I reappeared in my ill-fitting suit, gesturing to emphasise the wrong word, a device I learned from a Gemini Theatre actor. After much pressure from the rest of the cast, I then replaced the lead actor in Entertainment Machine's next production, *The Revenge of the Really Big Men.*

I wrote this play with Alex Maguire because Walter Zerlin Jnr. was busy writing a sitcom for Channel 4 that never materialised. The subject of the play was masculism, my riposte to feminism. It was inspired by what I felt were two inequalities. In a play my friend Bryony Lavery wrote it was proposed that, because men were utterly useless, they should be put in a rocket and blasted into space. Later Erika Poole told me that, if she were asked to mediate in a dispute between a man and a woman, she would side with the woman even if she were wrong. I was a feminist. I voted for a female prime minister. But I thought there was some injustice here.

I think I still have a script of our masculist comedy; but I don't want to read it because I think it may even be worse than *Ssshh...* There is a good chance that, in CGCT tradition, the message was all but lost in the panto-style treatment. The reviews suggest as much ('A crude inversion of the most easily caricatured features of the women's movement'[61]) and some of the more left-wing venues were aghast. The tour was rent apart by dissent. But I still have the fondest memories of our time in Edinburgh, where a crowd of us found hilarious solace together. Entertainment Machine was sharing a vicarage with Julian Clary (now accompanied by Fanny the Wonderdog) and a troupe of idiots called The Grand Theatre of Lemmings headed by yet another ex-CGCT performer Dave Danzig. We were all failures. Halfway through Danzig's show, he would escort his audience to the bar and then leave them there for the interval, quite

---

61   *The News Central South (Portsmouth),* 21st April, 1986

a good wheeze; but Danzig had to cut the interval when he found that half the audience wasn't returning for the second half. Meanwhile Julian, who had by now adopted his persona as The Joan Collins Fan Club, was playing the Southside Youth Centre, sometimes to two Japanese tourists. Earlier in the year he had made his TV debut; but his overnight success was still two years away.

The vicarage had lots of rooms and there were many visitors. The camaraderie was delightful. On a typical evening some performers would be preparing dinner, others would be rehearsing, and Julian would be having his hair dyed purple. Alex found a soulmate in Lyn Rees, a tubby Welsh comic actor with an acerbic sense of humour, who was a supporting player in Channel 4's *Comic Strip* films. At mealtimes I was happy to be the audience for their unofficial double act and would sometimes be incapacitated with laughter. Lyn was equally sardonic about himself and the cancer that was to kill him in 1987. He was 27.

Because Entertainment Machine was now internationally famous, we received a lot of scripts. We didn't like any of them apart from a one-act play called *Living Skills* by Jurgen Wolff. It was about a middle-aged woman well aware that life has passed her by. The first theatre to which I sent it, the King's Head, accepted it. One of London's first pub theatres, the King's Head was now one of the last theatres still producing lunchtime shows, a fad that had reached its peak in 1978, when there were more than twenty venues in London giving mid-day performances.

Living Skills was my first attempt at directing a straight drama. It was a good script so we got a good cast. Lisa Daniely had been a glamour girl in the 1950s and was now coming towards the end of her acting career. American actor Ed Bishop had starred in *UFO* with Michael Billington and was still a well-known TV face. Hardly anyone came to see us, but I was puffed up with prestige. The cast graciously accepted £30 each for four weeks' work, and Lisa Daniely became another of my surrogate mothers. I thought Jurgen Wolff would become the new Edward Albee; but instead he went on to teach people how to write sitcoms.

J.P. wanted to go home for Christmas and asked me to come with him. I drove him in my new car. We met up with his mates and went on a pub crawl. 'Out came the spliffs,' I wrote. 'From here on it was only the fact that I was totally pissed and stoned that got me through the evening.' We fetched up at a black community centre, where a Rasta toasted over a vile sound system, and I was warned not to wander off on my own. 'They'll roll you as soon as look at you,' J.P. advised me, 'and if someone's knifed, the police won't come in.' Back at J.P.'s mum's, I passed an awful night on a couch. On the way home the car broke down. The journey took more than eight hours. 'Given the opportunity I think I would rather have watched Andy Warhol's Empire State Building,' I moaned, 'but I also hope I never grow too old to say, "No, that's not for me."' So far, I don't think I have.

X

*"It's only fitting that the Farndale Ladies should go out
at the peak of their success, like Wham!"*
~ Diary entry, 1st August, 1987, aged 39 ~

After nearly six years on the dole, I signed off in 1986. The times were changing. Scroungers now had to provide substantial evidence of their unemployment and unsuitability for employment. The day before one interview at the DHSS I tried to dye my hair green to show that my services wouldn't be required by the average high street business. I could no longer spare the time to draw unemployment benefit because I was working so hard. Entertainment Machine wasn't exactly a cash cow; but the tours usually made profits, and provincial theatres were now paying us to mount their own productions of the *Farndale* plays. In 1985 there had been a rollickingly funny production of *The Farndale/Murder Mystery* at the Redgrave Theatre, Farnham. (Director Stephen Barry invented wonderful new comic business, which went into the revised version of the published script.)

The income ended up in my bank account and, because I was 'unemployed', I didn't declare it in my tax returns. I got my just deserts when the Inland Revenue investigated me with a rigour I assumed was reserved for the likes of Al Capone. In my own mind I had 'overlooked' only two or three thousand pounds; but my inadequate paperwork suggested a much greater sum. The shuffling of bank statements and cheque book stubs went on for months, and the eventual settlement took me six years to pay off. You might have thought this would teach me a lesson. It didn't.

The final years of Entertainment Machine were in some ways our most successful. The demand for our penultimate show, *They Came from Mars and Landed Outside the Farndale Avenue Church Hall in Time for the Townswomen's Guild's Coffee Morning,* was so persistent that the tour managed 112 performances, our longest ever run. Halfway through it, in order to keep everything fresh, the female members of the cast swapped parts. The male member of the cast was me in my signature role as Gordon.

It was the peak of my acting career. I loved honing my performance, experimenting each night, for example by waiting one second longer in order to raise a bigger laugh. The response made the effort worthwhile. 'The evening belongs to David McGillivray, whose bewildered, twitching, deadpan Rev. Allsopp becomes the focal point of the show,' declared *The Guardian.*[62]

---

[62]   16th September, 1986

'[He] is a natural clown with an inventive comic eye and a superb sense of timing.' Another accolade came from a less prestigious paper, the *Huddersfield Examiner*, but I'm still going to quote it: 'David's performance, in fact the entire show, is built on unerringly accurate observation. The delivery is skilled, polished to an awful degree. The result is hilariously funny.'[63]

The play, whose plot bore more than a passing resemblance to that of *Creepy Crawlies*, was inspired by a joyous evening spent at an Irish community centre in North London. The attraction was a blissfully tatty production of *Cinderella* in which the palace was represented by a cardboard box covered in tinsel and Christmas wrapping paper. And yet, when it came to the inevitable 'Haunted Bedroom' sequence, the kids shouted, 'He's behind you!', with as much fervour as if they had been at the London Palladium. It made me realise that we didn't need any of the equipment we'd been carting around the country for ten years. We began selling off the sets, lighting and costumes we'd been storing in an expensive garage. *They Came from Mars*, which had a budget of virtually nil, was written to be performed amidst junk we found backstage at each venue. It worked. Whatever we did, as long as it involved actors acting badly, worked.

What was intended to be the Farndale Ladies' swansong, *The Farndale/Christmas Carol* became something of a goldmine. It's still revived every holiday season, particularly in the U.S., where audiences are in dire need of a non-traditional version of the Dickens story. The published script, as always, contains genuine fluffs and blunders that occurred in rehearsals and on the road. In *A Christmas Carol* Jennifer Lautrec was back as Mrs Reece, this time giving her interpretation of Tiny Tim. Jenny was never very good at remembering her lines. She was supposed to refer to God, 'who made lame beggars walk and blind men see.' This came out as 'lame men blind and blind buggers walk.'

Jenny was our Mrs Reece for three years. She was still beautiful into her 90s; but in her voluptuous prime she had been a showgirl and performed with The Goons. She knew of my adoration of Spike Milligan and in 1986 invited me to take her to his Boxing Day party. At that time he was living in a castellated edifice with a baronial fireplace on the edge of Hadley Wood in Hertfordshire. 'The guests,' I wrote disparagingly, 'varied between old and extremely old.' (I'm now horribly aware that even the oldest were actually around the age I am now.) 'One of the youngest was Lynsey de Paul, who went on about what a bitch Clodagh Rodgers was.' Everyone sat around, politely trying to engage the attention of the host. Eventually Jenny succeeded. 'David's a writer as well,' she said of me. Came the glum reply, 'Being a writer is slightly preferable to having AIDS.' That was my comic hero speaking.

---

63   17th September, 1986

The Farndale Ladies were destined to make comeback after comeback in shows Walter and I wrote for other companies. But their begetter, Entertainment Machine, was phased out because Walter and I found other things to amuse us. After defending John Cleese for a parking offence, Walter was hired as a legal adviser on Cleese's film *A Fish Called Wanda*. Together Walter and I formed another company, this time to save the *British Alternative Theatre Directory*. Since 1979 this reference book had listed all the UK's Fringe companies and the theatres that booked them. But in 1986 its publisher went bankrupt.

We bought the title from the editor (she wanted £4,000; she got £1,000) and had 1,500 copies printed. They were snapped up by Fringe theatre companies, which needed the *BATD* as much as we did. Before it went to the typesetter, the entire 1987 edition was typed by me on my Olympia portable. I was aware of word processors. A friend had shown me his Amstrad in 1986. But I had no intention of ploughing my way through the doorstep-sized instruction manual. The typesetter, on the other hand, had no intention of producing the 1988 edition unless the information was provided on something called a floppy disk. He sold me an Amstrad word processor for £700 and then taught me how to use it. This was a giant leap forward for me. But bear in mind, kids, that the floppy disks still had to be put in envelopes and taken to the post office. We kept the *BATD* going until 1996, by which time we had email. But we no longer had alternative theatre.

Entertainment Machine also became too much of a handful because I'd started making regular appearances on television. I say television, but I mean cable television which, in its early years, was like BBC Radio London with pictures. Nobody was watching apart from a handful of guinea pigs in seemingly randomly selected communities throughout the UK. My agent had put me up for a presenter's job on Premiere, a pioneer movie channel funded by the *Daily Mirror* publisher Robert Maxwell. He had managed only to do deals with a couple of major distributors. Twice a week I had to get terribly enthusiastic about unknown films with unknown actors.

I needed a new shirt for every appearance and, until I got a clothes allowance, I borrowed from Julian Clary. My dressing room was the tape storage cupboard. The studio had such a low ceiling that, when there was a shot that required me to be standing, I was actually on my knees. No reputable director would work for Premiere, which is why a con artist called Terry came to be hired. When he wasn't directing *The Premiere Movie Club* he was renting the studio equipment to mates and pocketing the proceeds. He was sacked. The runner who shopped him was immediately promoted. He's now a BAFTA award-winning editor.

In addition to these exhilarating new developments, I was still answering readers' questions, and not just for the soon to be defunct *Films and Filming* but also *Film Review*. This was another of the movie magazines I devoured as a schoolboy. I particularly liked its column 'Can You Beat the Expert?' in which the 'walking encyclopaedia of the screen' had to answer questions pulled out of a hat at random by an independent person. The expert was Peter Noble, who had now become a friend. He sloughed off to me TV and radio jobs that were beneath him.

Peter was quite open about the fact that, in his *Film Review* days, there never had been a hat, nor an independent person, and that in order to find his answers he merely had consulted reference books. Sometimes not enough readers sent in questions and so Peter fabricated them. After he had been fired in 1964, he even wrote the letters demanding that Peter Noble be reinstated. Somehow I had contrived to become Peter Noble and, probably as a homage to my mentor, I adopted his *modus operandi*. As time went on more and more of my most interesting questions were written by me. Something tells me this practice may not be obsolete.

All this activity produced another show biz maelstrom. A typical day might find me rehearsing with the Farndale Ladies in Edinburgh in the morning, taking a plane to London, answering questions or correcting proofs on the flight, recording a week's TV shows on my knees, and then boarding another plane for a performance in Edinburgh the same day. I doubt whether I would have been able to sustain this workload had it not been for Alexander. The Alexander technique is basically airy-fairy bollocks, one step removed from homeopathy (I'll come back to this); but a succession of actors told me I needed it and I think they were right. My first Alexander teacher told me I was the tensest person he had ever met. After six years of Alexander training, however, I mellowed out, man, even to the extent that I could continue to function while the world, literally in the case of the Twin Towers, was collapsing around me.

It's impossible to explain Alexander to someone who has not experienced it. There is almost literally nothing to it. You lie down. Or you sit in a chair. You rise from a recumbent to a standing position. And yet somehow, by repeating these everyday motions without expending undue energy, you learn how to eradicate stress. 'Are you really as laid-back as you appear?' I was asked at an audition. Yes, it's not an act. There is nothing that can upset my equilibrium except the slow, inflexible grind of the English legal system (and I'll come back to this as well).

My policy of almost never saying no to anything also extended to my sex life, but this rarely provided any kind of fulfilment. Sex really should only be allowed between adults who have passed some kind of examination. It's all very well to say yes to skydiving; but, unless you land on top of someone else, you only run the risk of hurting yourself. Failure at sex runs the huge risk of wrecking two people's lives, or more if it's group sex. Today, even at my advanced age, there is no end of people with whom I'd like to have sex; but I've learned to say no because I'm no good at what we'll call aftercare. Even into my 40s, however, I was, to use an easily understood term, a heartbreaker. Except that that word implies some sort of sex god. The word that more accurately describes my former self is cunt.

On-and-off sex with Marge continued until 1987, when she crept into my room in Edinburgh at 4am and told me she loved me. I don't know what I was doing to initiate these declarations of love because I treated my partners with callous indifference. While I was behaving just like this with Marge, I was having stupid, drunken sexathons with Veronica, who I mentioned in the 'AIDS' chapter. I had met Veronica at Lisa Daniely's 1986 Christmas party. In days gone by, for fear of someone reading my diary, I would have described our steamy encounters with a brief, encrypted reference. By 1986, however, I had become devil-may-care.

'The thing was winding down around midnight. By this time Veronica was falling down drunk and making a play for me. I offered to drive her home. At her flat her knickers were off and she was pleading for it. I wasn't that keen because of (a) her condition, (b) the world's most uncomfortable bed, and (c) her surly flatmate, who shouted at her to keep her voice down.

'We returned to Kilburn. Within minutes she had grabbed my member and jammed it into herself. She made a lot of noise, which I found quite a turn-on, and so we kept whamming away practically until dawn. My back is scratched to blazes.'

And all the time I was putting myself about, I was still married.

The Mira era came to a predictable conclusion, but for unpredictable reasons. I first suspected that my wife was searching for something I couldn't provide when I came home and found her enacting a candle-lit ritual to expunge a terrible, unnameable sin. Then, in quick succession, she became vegetarian and celibate, and began meditating from 3.30am until breakfast. For a brief period she switched to astrology. Then she decided that vegetarian celibacy was the way and moved into a commune in Cricklewood with a group of like-minded enthusiasts. I received my decree nisi on 15th December, 1987. As with all my former partners, I never saw Mira again.

Christmas Day, 1987, was the first I'd spent with my family for sixteen years. My brother, Paul, hosted at his house on the outskirts of St Albans, where he'd worked as a French teacher since 1979. Conversation with Dad was impossible. 'He can talk about nothing except shopping, TV and the travelling times between two points,' I wrote. I proudly played videotapes of my appearances on Premiere; but nobody seemed very interested and at 7pm Paul went to bed. I was left watching TV with Mum and Dad. Something made Dad unstable his favourite hobby horse ('This country is a haven for immigrants'), which required me to feign a migraine and drive home. If it hadn't have been for Alexander, I may have opened a vein.

XI

"The American debut of this British spoof confirms the fact that nothing falls
flatter than imperfectly performed slapstick."
~ Variety, 1991 ~

I had no misgivings about closing down Entertainment Machine. Travelling around the country and showing off on stage was one thing, traipsing to the post office with parcels of posters and handbills was quite another; I'd had enough of it. Now I was free to work for other companies and just enjoy the showing-off. I directed and appeared in a couple of *Farndale* shows at the Southwold Summer Theatre, something of a legend among the actors who returned year after year to this fusty Edwardian resort. We didn't go for the artistic satisfaction (audiences required nothing more stimulating than a farce or a whodunit), we went for the *craic.* By springtime, if we hadn't had a better offer, we might as well spend the summer in Southwold for what amounted to a paid holiday.

The Summer Theatre was the self-contained domain of a former movie star called Jill Raymond, who had retired from acting after marrying the lugubrious jack-of-all-trades Clement Freud. Jill Freud was a female version of me with nicer vowels. Late in life, she had returned to the theatre as an actress-manager. There was no aspect of the summer season that she did not oversee. Clement, or Clay as we knew him, was considered impossibly snobbish and irritable by those who worked with him regularly, for example on the radio panel game *Just a Minute*; but during our occasional encounters, I found him the most enjoyable company. When I was first entertained by him in 1987, he was still shell-shocked by the loss of his seat as the Liberal member for Isle of Ely. 'I was expecting a life peerage,' he told me. Subsequently, whenever we met or even spoke on the phone, he would tell me a joke I hadn't heard before. We never once spoke of his grandfather.

The Southwold Summer Theatre company lived and rehearsed in Jill's delightful Tudor-style residence in the nearby village of Walberswick, where there was, shall we say, carousing every evening. On one occasion several of us were in the Grand Hall when part of one of its timber walls caught fire. I was the first to notice the incipient conflagration. I was so bladdered that I was able only to murmur, 'Is that meant to be happening?' This observation roused those more alert than I to fetch buckets of water. It transpired that the blaze had been caused by one of the Farndale frocks hung over a lamp. 'Once the smoke cleared,' I wrote, 'everybody laughed about it.' It was comical incidents such as this which forged more lifetime friendships.

Jill Freud's box set as well as actress Mary Roscoe re-appeared in a production of *The Farndale/Murder Mystery*, which by some quirk of fate I directed at the Swan Theatre in Stratford-upon-Avon in 1988. The Swan was and still is administered by the Royal Shakespeare Company, which seems originally to have had no clear booking policy for its new theatre. When it realised the blunder it had made in engaging us, it decided not to advertise the event, and our week as the guests of the UK's most prestigious theatre company passed almost without notice. For me, however, it was a momentous production because of what occurred during rehearsals.

Our rehearsal room in London was near a city farm, and each lunch hour I got to know its pigs. The upshot of this unexpected relationship is that I have not eaten pork from that day to this. I believe other actors who have worked with pigs have undergone a similar epiphany. I firmly believe that, in a parallel universe, we eat dogs and keep pigs as pets. The animals are equally intelligent, equally lovable. While on the subject of appealing yet edible animals, ducks can be quite amusing and I would rather not eat them either. I have flirted for decades with vegetarianism, but have never been able to keep the pledge for more than a few months. This is mostly to do with laziness. Perhaps if I could afford to hire Yotam Ottolenghi to cook all my meals, I wouldn't miss meat at all.

Offers also began to come in for me to direct *Farndale* shows abroad. The first caused me weeks of indecision because it came from the Nico Malan theatre in Cape Town. Apartheid was by now in its death throes in South Africa, but officially it was still in force. After the initial buzz of excitement, my first question was, 'Is your theatre integrated?' The manager assured me that it was and that, as a measure of their commitment, they had recently staged a production of *The Comedy of Errors* with black and white twins. I said I'd have to make some enquiries.

Equity told me that it didn't forbid members to work in South Africa because that would be illegal. It wasn't illegal, however, for the union to prevent British TV companies from selling programmes to South Africa. There was also a blacklist and I was told in a sinister fashion that I might find myself on it. My informant would say no more. When I contacted the Anti Apartheid Movement, which had been in the forefront of the international boycott of South Africa since 1959, I was informed that their position was unequivocal. There must be no trade of any kind with South African organisations, integrated or otherwise. The hardliner on the other end of the phone even objected to the anti-apartheid Market Theatre of Johannesburg appearing in London because its programme had included an advert for South African Airways. I was warned of another blacklist, this one operated by the United Nations. 'Those appearing on it may find it difficult to get work from British authorities that subscribe to the boycott,' I learned.

I didn't like the sound of these blacklists, which smacked a little too much of McCarthyism as far as I was concerned. My old dislike of being told what to do was hard to control. The last piece of advice I was given made up my mind. 'In cases like this you know what you're going to do,' my Alexander teacher told me. 'The time is spent in justifying the decision to yourself.' Fate stepped in to wave me on my way when it was announced that *The Premiere Movie Club* would come off the air a month before my planned departure to Cape Town.

Premiere was another contender for the best job I ever had. I could write and say almost anything I liked. The people at head office had little idea of what we were doing and, quite late in the day, I discovered that some of them didn't even know who I was. There was a fair amount of messing about and times when I was unable to speak because I was helpless with laughter. 'I got the giggles over my inability to pronounce "shrimp fishermen,"' I wrote in 1988. 'Cameraman Dave had to stand in a cupboard because I couldn't say the line with him looking at me.'

Towards the end of the year the cuts began. My programme began going out once weekly instead of twice. The only new films being screened were Canadian TV movies. 'I feel like the caretaker in a condemned building,' I wrote. Then, just before Christmas, Robert Maxwell pulled the plug on the entire channel. He went on to sell a lot more of his businesses and even embezzle his *Mirror* Group's pension fund in an effort to clear debts. Premiere's half a dozen subscribers were offered something called Sky and several of the Premiere staff were given jobs on this new satellite TV station, run by Maxwell's rival Rupert Murdoch. For my part I rescued as many tapes of *The Premiere Movie Club* as I could carry, and these may now be the only surviving records of the station's output.

I find that we can save ourselves a lot of time and anguish if we only regret the things we didn't do. I don't regret flouting international sanctions by working in South Africa. I was among the privileged few to witness the last gasp of an *ancien régime*, a unique throwback to the days of Empire. (Only five years in the future South Africa was to have its first black president.) In 1989 there were still visible remains of apartheid, fading signs on bridges and benches that said, 'Whites only. *Slegs blankes.*' But I didn't have to dig very deep to exhume more chilling evidence of the recent past. On the day I arrived I was taken to a charming restaurant overlooking crashing waves on the beach below. I couldn't help but notice that those in the vicinity were predominantly white. I was told in hushed tones that we were on the site of the notorious District Six, a thriving community of mostly black and coloured residents, which, during the darkest days of apartheid, had been forcibly removed to shanty towns like Nyanga and Khayelitsha. Their former homes had been bulldozed and District Six had been designated *slegs blankes.*

After a few days of mutual suspicion, my hosts decided I was a fellow traveller. The joints came out and guards were let down. I was relieved to find that most of the white people I met were a far cry from the drunken, bigoted expats I'd encountered in Zambia. They ranged from Geoff, a white businessman who was busy training black South Africans to take over the top jobs in his firm, to Laurie, activist boyfriend of *Farndale* actress Bo Petersen, who told me I shouldn't have come to South Africa. Bo, who went on to do bits in many international movies shot in Cape Town, made sure I visited the Nyanga township, where seven cold water taps served something like eight thousand families.

I was disoriented to go straight from Nyanga to Idols, a Cape Town disco which could have been in London, Paris or New York. It was here that Laurie informed me that the boycott of South Africa must be absolute. But then others countered that sanctions affected black South Africans more than anyone else. That night I wrote, 'Can you imagine what it was like going from a black township to a white yuppie disco? Even at the end of my third week here I still don't know how I'm going to describe my experience when I get home. The play is almost going to be an incidental.'

Although South Africa began my political education, the play turned out far from an incidental. I had a superb cast and the production was a success, so much so that, after I returned to the UK, it went on a provincial tour. The last date was Oudtshoorn, an ostrich breeding community in the Western Cape. When they discovered that its theatre maintained segregated audiences, my company refused to go. The theatre hastily revised its policy. Consequently the first play seen by an integrated audience in Oudtshoorn was *The Farndale/Murder Mystery*. In the unlikely event of somebody asking me what I've done to help society, I shall mention the part I played in the dismantling of apartheid.

By the time I got home, Julian Clary had become a star. His breakthrough had been two appearances on the second series of *Saturday Live*, Channel 4's stand-up and sketch show, in 1987. It was the show that brought us Ben Elton, Harry Enfield and others that were to become part of the comedy establishment. Of these, Julian was unique in that he was a camp turn with a performing dog. I maintained, in my history of cabaret,[64] that Julian Clary wasn't the first gay comedian on the 1980s cabaret circuit and that he was pipped to the post by Simon Fanshawe. 'I was the first funny gay comedian,' Julian retorted.

Unquestionably, however, Julian quickly became the UK's most famous gay comedian. His first star turn was as the co-host of a TV game show, *Trick Or Treat*, which went out on ITV on Saturday nights. I was astonished to look up at a billboard in London's Euston Road to see Julian's face, six metres tall, gazing

---

64 *QX*, 8th October-23rd December, 2010

down at me. The caption was 'BEYOND COMPERE.' The tabloids decided to be outraged that a homosexual (as opposed to Larry Grayson, who was just a bit effeminate) had been allowed on to prime time TV. The abuse began. It was still acceptable to call a gay man a poof and that's what Julian was called.

I suppose it was partly the shock of being thrust into such a cruel spotlight that made Julian stop returning our calls for a while. But at the time we thought that stardom had gone to his head. He didn't come back down to earth until the end of 1989, when Channel 4 gave him what he needed, a safe place and an adoring audience for his brand of gay comedy. The show was *Sticky Moments*. That's me in the audience for the episode that first went out on 14th November, 1990. Julian's parody game show was to have a profound impact on a generation of gay teenagers who thought that there was nobody else like them in the world. Two decades later, when I was in Australia with Julian, I had to gulp manfully when men came up to him in the street and gushed, 'You changed my life.'

Throughout 1989 and 1990 my front room was occupied by an angelic-looking posh boy of the Hugh Grant school. I needed somebody with ideas to sell advertising space in my theatre directory and Mark Goucher seemed to fit the bill. It was just as well there was somebody responsible at home while I was in Cape Town. Just before I left, my favourite cat, Vincent, disappeared. For four days Mark heard a faint mewing. He searched every nook and cranny and found nothing; but the sounds continued. Mark realised there was only one place Vincent could be and took up the floorboards. The cat leaped out, seemingly none the worse for wear. I remembered that a plumber had been fixing pipes underneath the floor. While Vincent had been exploring the foundations unnoticed, the plumber had sealed him in.

Mark set about selling thousands of pounds worth of advertising and even began employing his own staff. He used his sizeable commission to establish himself as a theatre producer. He started small with a one woman play above a pub in Camden Town; but within a few months he had put together two comedy shows for Edinburgh. The unknown comics in them were Steve Coogan and Will Durst, which suggested that Mark had some ability as a talent spotter. 'Impressionist Coogan is destined to be the Mike Yarwood of the 90s,' I predicted. For a while Mark promoted some very risky entertainments including Mark Ravenhill's *Shopping and Fucking*, which nosedived on Broadway. Nowadays he plays it safer, but he's still in business. He owes me everything.

While he was still struggling, Mark helped out with another of my failed schemes, a comedy night in London. By 1988 the only alternative enterprise that was dragging in the crowds was comedy, and I wanted a piece of the action. My partners were Jack Stew, who had appeared in *Revenge of the Really Big Men* and was now dabbling as a stand-up comic (before he switched permanently to dubbing noises on to film soundtracks), and the larger-than-life comedian Tony Allen, whom I credited[65] together with Alexei Sayle as the inventors of alternative comedy.

For a while it seemed as though we might move into the Elgin, the very pub in Ladbroke Grove where Allen and Sayle had introduced non-sexist, non-racist comedy in 1979. Eventually, however, Stew's Cabaret opened on 11th May, 1989, at the Pembury Tavern, a vast, old school boozer in Hackney Downs when Hackney was not cool. The opening bill – Jerry Sadowitz, John Hegley and Tony Allen himself – played to capacity with many punters turned away. Jack and I congratulated ourselves. But although the following week's bill was equally appealing, the audience never came back.

We cancelled more shows than we staged. Julian Clary, now managed by the profligate wide boy Addison Cresswell, declined an invitation to appear. But week after week, acts of the calibre of Lee Evans, Neil Mullarkey and Jack Dee turned up only for us to send them home. Mostly they were very nice about the situation and didn't even ask for their bus fare. 'What's this?' exclaimed Lee, arriving in a room empty apart from the staff, 'an encounter group?' I put the line in the next *Farndale* show. We couldn't wait to clear out of the Pembury Tavern, never to return.

I also found myself in a position to direct my first pop video. Jez, one of my video nasty suppliers, was a neighbour of Sean Cronin, a would-be wild man rock star, who was the vocalist with a Goth group called The Screaming Marionettes. Their first video was directed by Terry, the Premiere petty criminal, and I did some donkey work on it. I thought I could do better than Terry and put myself forward as the director of the video for the Marionettes' next single, 'Like Christabel.' Sean, who was under the impression that I'd directed *House of Whipcord* (I didn't disabuse him), agreed.

The video was thrown together in a day, mostly at the Marquee, a once venerated Soho rock club that had fallen on hard times in what was to be its last venue, the former cinema in Charing Cross Road where *White Cargo* had opened. (It was soon to become a pub.) Take it from me, anyone can direct a pop video and, if you screw up, the footage can usually be salvaged by a talented editor. I had one, Rodney Sims from Premiere, who worked miracles. Rumour has it that the video was seen on network TV once, on Channel 4's 'yoof' programme *The Word*, and only then because the programme considered the Marionettes to be the worst band in the world. It was to be years before I made my next music video, which, I'm happy to say, was rather more successful. In another of those unpredictable developments of which I'm so fond, Sean became a shaven-headed tough guy in gangster films.

---

65   *British Alternative Theatre Directory*, 1988

Still keen to tick off items on what now would be called a bucket list, I gave myself a new challenge, learning British Sign Language. This had fascinated me ever since I saw Alan Ladd's son signing in a 1958 Western called *The Proud Rebel*. Later, out of the corner of my eye, I would watch deaf people conversing in BSL on the tube or the street and wonder what they were saying. But the main reason I signed up for a course at the City Lit, the famous London college that teaches adults everything from basket weaving to Mandarin Chinese, is that I fancied Clive Mason, the presenter of *See Hear*, the BBC's programme for deaf people. We've never met so I've been unable to lay a finger on him.

BSL uses a fair amount of facial expression and mime. As an actor of sorts, I therefore had an advantage over the rest of the class, the usual ragbag of loners, introverts and women with dry, unmanageable hair. I was soon both teacher's pet and top of the class and I looked forward to every lesson. I remember that in my first exam, the assessor signed to me, 'What sports do you like?' and I showed off by signing back, 'I hate sports,' and went on to sign just about everything I wrote in Section 2 about school football until she signed, 'Thank you. That's OK.' I sailed through the exam and eagerly put my name down for the next level. I had every intention of becoming a BSL interpreter and appearing in a box in the bottom-right corner of the TV screen. But then, as is always the way, another challenge came along and I pursued that instead. I did, however, use BSL in several acting jobs. One of them was the worst play I've ever appeared in. I'll come back to this.

In case you're wondering, I indulged two of the main compulsions in my life, sex and parties, to the full during this time. 'Boring sex in the evening and what a long way to go for it,' is a typical diary entry towards the end of 1989. I have no idea to what and to whom remarks like this refer. But a dinner party a few weeks later was more significant. I was sat next to a dancer who proceeded to tell me about his blighted career. He was immensely boring and so, just as a game to help me get through the evening, I kept commenting on what he said and asking questions, wondering just how long it would be before he asked me something about myself.

He never did. When we parted company, he didn't even know my name, let alone who I was. You may have met similar people. There are a lot of them. I decided that in future I would never provide information about myself unless I was asked. This is still the way I roll and it has stood me in good stead. People tell me, 'You're such a good listener,' seemingly without realising that we have not been having a conversation, they have been delivering a lecture. This is how I continue to have an inordinate amount of sex. Men, who tend to be so much more shallow than women, actually think

I'm interested in them. I've had three long-term relationships with men who only have the vaguest idea of who I am or what I do. This is fine by me.

By the late 1980s the Farndale Ladies had become a village hall sensation. In the 1986-87 season *The Farndale/Murder Mystery* was the ninth most popular play among members of the Little Theatre Guild. By the following season McGillivray and Zerlin were the UK's eighth most popular playwrights. (We tied with Oscar Wilde. Noël Coward was number seven. Tennessee Williams came nowhere.) I was honoured to be invited to a production of *The Farndale/Murder Mystery* by my *alma mater* Trent Players. It was a terrible shock to find how low the society had sunk from its halcyon days twenty years earlier. It was now performing in one room of an arts centre in Edmonton to thirty people. The cast and the director had no ability and the audience sat in silent puzzlement. 'We're just going through a bad patch,' Eve, the indomitable, 85-year-old founder of the society told me. She admitted defeat six years later and Trent Players was no more. It has no presence online and therefore it is as if it never existed. (Eve was 95 when she died in 1997.)

Jonathan Banatvala, a keen-as-mustard Anglo-Indian, who ran a company called Moving Theatre, boosted my ego by telling me that, when he asked provincial theatres what sort of play they'd book without question, most nominated an Agatha Christie or a *Farndale*. Walter and I wrote him *We Found Love and an Exquisite Set of Porcelain Figurines Aboard the S.S. Farndale Avenue,* our version of a romantic comedy, modelled on Coward's *Private Lives.* We found that Banatvala's method of cutting corners was to use inexperienced students to do very important work, e.g. set design and stage management. This resulted in an opening night of cataclysmic turmoil and, later, a very good story for Rotary Club lunches and sundry Evenings with David McGillivray.

Two days before we were due to open in Brighton, the designer had not delivered the set, props or costumes. Practically everything that subsequently turned up was unusable. With the same kind of gung-ho spirit that saved England from the Spanish Armada, the cast proceeded to build a new set and to raid wardrobes and charity shops for costumes. With 24 hours to spare, I was obliged to stay up all night with Balaclava, as he was now known, constructing the S.S. Farndale Avenue's funnel and gangplank in my flat. In Brighton the next day there was no chance of any kind of technical or dress rehearsal because props had to be bought and the set had to be painted. Nevertheless we went up at 7.45pm as advertised.

Only in the movies does a débâcle of this magnitude produce a smash hit. The reality of our situation was that actors went on stage to do a highly technical comedy involving split-second timing in clothes they'd never worn, using props they'd never seen. It was nerve-wrackingly awful. Throughout the day the theatre crew had looked at us as if we were insane and afterwards the management tried to avoid paying the fee because the performances were in their view dress rehearsals. Weeks into the arduous run we still had a show that hadn't been finished. My name was mud. But the next *Farndale* show resulted in me being completely ostracised in parts of St Albans.

Walter and I had written *The Farndale Avenue Housing Estate Townswomen's Guild Operatic Society's Production of "The Mikado"* between 1985 and 1986 in the mistaken belief that angels would give Entertainment Machine tens of thousands of pounds to bring this spectacular production into London's West End. After it had been shelved, I went to St Albans to see an amateur production of *The Farndale/Murder Mystery* that was so good I invited the company there and then the opportunity to premiere *The Farndale/Mikado*. It came to pass in 1991. It was a production just as spectacular as Walter and I had envisaged, with a cast of 21 and a full orchestra.

I became over-ambitious, promising everyone that I would take them to Edinburgh the following year to take part in the grand comeback of the Farndale Ladies. We would hire an entire venue for a Farndale festival comprising a children's show, a bring-and-buy sale, a tea dance, a new production of *Chase Me Up Farndale Avenue* starring Julian Clary and, in a prime evening slot, *The Farndale/Mikado*. For a while it all seemed possible because Christopher Richardson, the flamboyant old showman who had opened The Pleasance, one of Edinburgh's first supervenues, was planning to expand into a nearby white elephant called the Roxburgh Rooms. This, he delighted in telling us, would become a veritable Farndale Avenue Experience complete with walkabout townswomen losing keys and forgetting how to operate the tea urn.

But the deal never went through. Instead he offered *The Farndale/Mikado* a teatime slot at The Pleasance, which sounded second-best at best. Then the St Albans amateurs began dropping out because they didn't want to pay for their transport and accommodation. While Walter and I were trying to reach a compromise, Christopher gave our teatime slot to some Russians. *The Farndale/Mikado* didn't make it to Edinburgh. Somehow the legend arose among am dram enthusiasts in St Albans that we had exploited them from the very beginning in order to have an unproducible play published[66] and make some money out of it. To this very day I cannot visit the Verulamium without wondering if the woman of a certain age standing next to me carries an umbrella with a poisoned ferrule.

In July, 1991, I was directing *The Farndale/Murder Mystery* in Milford Haven. Gordon was played by Barry Killerby, who should have become one of the great comic actors of our time. Instead he chose to be the unknown performer inside Mr Blobby. More to the point as far as this memoir is

---

66 *The Farndale/Mikado* (London: Samuel French, 1993)

concerned, it was on 10th July that I learned that Entertainment Machine had been wound up. I had been forewarned of this event and had planned a farewell party for 15th August. It was to be a harbinger of the parties that were to come, a 24 hour event beginning with breakfast and ending in the early hours of the next morning.

Apparently I began to flag after twelve hours. I attributed this to a delayed reaction to the official termination of my theatre company after fifteen years. Then I got my second wind and carried on until dawn like the madcap I am. I had no reason to be dejected. We had achieved a fair amount considering we started out as a bunch of amateurs. By 1981 we were so famous that Mike Nichols (*that* Mike Nichols, the man who directed *The Graduate*) invited Walter to his suite at the Savoy to discuss the transfer of *Running Around the Stage Like a Lunatic* to Broadway. Of course nothing came of the meeting. But that doesn't matter. At the party we had something to celebrate. It was fun to see again people who had been in our earliest productions. The most notable absentee was Herschel. He didn't even respond to my invitation. Probably I won't mention him again.

A month after the party I flew to Los Angeles to direct the American premiere of *The Farndale/Murder Mystery* at the Colony theatre. Although they worked like Trojans, my cast of struggling soap opera actors never in my view grasped the am dram concept. According to the terrible reviews, however, the play's failure was due to the flawed script and my flat misdirection. But for six weeks I couldn't believe I was being paid to live it up in L.A. I stayed in the pool house of Jim Giddens' latest mansion, a building so palatial that the theatre director, who drove me there, was surprised when I told her that Jim didn't deal coke. When I wasn't working I defied convention by driving Downtown, then a lawless Mexican ghetto, where cripples and panhandlers lined the sidewalks. I had no intention of missing the baroque Bradbury Building and triple bills at the majestic Los Angeles theatre. But I also behaved like a typical middle class Angelino by joining a gym. I was surprised to come across a Stairmaster, a machine that previously I assumed had been invented by Bret Easton Ellis for *American Psycho*, the novel that had made me feel sick on the flight from London. Another surprise, in the sauna this time, was a little Mexican named Alejandro. I was to grow quite fond of saunas.

The Farndale/Murder Mystery won an Outstanding Achievement Award from the only critic who liked it, Bruce Feld at *Drama-Logue*. I went to the Pasadena Playhouse to collect it. Towards the end of the evening, the presenter was required to read out the whole title of my play. I mounted the stage of the state theatre of California. 'It's been a long night and that title didn't help any,' I declared. 'It's a great surprise to be here because, according to the *L.A. Weekly*, my play was absolutely terrible.' This got a bigger laugh than any of the gags in the play.

On 9th December, 1991, Mum and Dad came to my flat to bring me their cassette recordings of a BBC radio series, *Second Unit Blues*, in which I talked about my career in exploitation movies. Following our disagreement, things had returned to the way they were before, when Dad seemed proud of my smutty achievements. The previous February he'd had a mild stroke. He recovered although Mum said he wasn't the same and seemed to be in a world of his own. But he was well enough to do odd jobs and recently he'd been painting my flat. He'd moved into the companionship stage of his long marriage to Mum. 'I don't know what I'd do without your mother,' he told me.

Mum and Dad left me to do some shopping. Later I picked up the telephone to hear a policeman on the other end of the line. The thought went through my head, 'What trouble am I in now?' But the policeman told me that Dad had collapsed and died. I drove over to Palmers Green and arrived at the same time as Paul, my brother. We learned that Mum and Dad had become separated in the Safeway supermarket and that Mum had gone home alone. In fact Dad had wandered out of the shop and fallen on to the pavement after suffering a heart attack. Later the coroner assured us in so many words that probably he was dead before he hit the ground.

Before the funeral took place the following week, Mum went to volunteer as an assistant at her local Oxfam shop. I went to the RSPCA and bought her a ginger kitten. She had always wanted a cat, but Dad wouldn't allow it. Mum's new life after Dad began with almost indecent haste and seems inescapably to have been an attempt at the life she might have had if she hadn't fallen for the flattery of a man with nice legs. Soon she was a new woman named Pat, who joined clubs and spoke in public and went to Disneyland. There's another message here that's not too hard to interpret. There were seven mourners at Dad's funeral and all the kindly old vicar had to say in Don's memory was that he liked to stay at home. 'That was it,' I wrote, 'rather a sad epitaph for 75 years on this Earth.'

A Farndale lady we'll call Frances was my entrée to a literally intoxicating new world because she spent most weekends taking loads of drugs at decadent clubs like Kinky Gerlinky. For years she'd been trying to persuade me to come with her to one of her favourite haunts, Whirl-Y-Gig (£15), and take ecstasy (£17). MDMA may have been synthesised about a hundred years earlier; but to all intents and purposes ecstasy was a new drug and, throughout the late 1980s, we'd heard about it driving the equally new dance culture on Ibiza. In 1988 ecstasy and dance music dubbed 'acid house' had created the second Summer of Love. I was intrigued. Who wouldn't want to take a drug that made you feel as though you were in love?

On New Year's Eve I met Frances and her cohorts at the crumbling Shoreditch Town Hall, which was heaving. There may have been a thousand people on the dance floor, 999 of whom were younger than me. But I wasn't given so much as a second glance. I learned down the years (and I was still going to dance clubs when I was over 60) that we are invisible to those who are not sexually attracted to us. I took my medication with much trepidation. 'It's a white pill,' I recorded with interest. Throughout the evening I was convinced that the pill had had no effect. Then I looked at my watch and realised that I had been dancing without a break for four hours. At chucking-out time, it seemed that every man and woman in the club wanted to hug and kiss me. And I wanted to hug and kiss them back. I decided I wanted some more of this.

XII

"This is what I get for liking a guy too much."
~ Edward G. Robinson in *Little Caesar* ~

The story of the book I never intended to write, *Doing Rude Things: The History of the British Sex Film 1957-1981,* goes back to 1976, when the British sex film was still alive and writhing. Soft porn was such a money-spinner in the mid-Seventies that journalist Sue Summers, with whom I was working on Peter Noble's trade paper, *CinemaTV Today,* suggested we write a book about it. The chapter we put together didn't find a publisher and the project was abandoned. The next person to tell me that I was the man to document the now moribund soft porn industry was my buddy Alan Jones in 1981. But unlike Sue he also had a prospective buyer, Alan Mackenzie, editor of *Cinema,* a new film magazine published by Marvel Comics.

Early in 1982 I managed to interview almost everyone who had played a major part in a quarter of a century of nudies, saucy comedies and sex education films. Many of these men never had talked before about the history of the business, which was generally regarded to have no social or cultural value. Pete Walker had been interviewed before, by me, but he was now wary of all journalists and didn't want to be interviewed again.

'When I asked him earlier this year about the female image he was trying to put across in his glamour films, he exploded, "Why are you going into all this? I know exactly the kind of article you're trying to get out of this and I really don't think I want to be involved in it honestly. I mean the whole thing's a put-down, isn't it?" I was not allowed to continue speaking to him until I switched my tape recorder off.'

Although I also described him as 'without doubt this country's most talented director of exploitation films,' Pete was displeased by my criticism of him in *Cinema,*[67] and this soured our relationship irrevocably for the rest of our lives. He has remained peevish with the press until the present day and, as recently as 2015, Walker threatened to sue the author of a book celebrating his career. The publisher took fright and withdrew it.[68]

I was convinced that nobody was reading my four-part series and, inspired by Peter Noble, I wrote letters to *Cinema* every month praising it. In case the editor smelled a rat, I also wrote letters castigating it. I was Malcolm Howden of Boreham Wood, Herts., who fumed, 'McGilvary [sic] has got no

---

67   No. 4, August, 1982
68   *Frightmares: The Exploitation Cinema of Pete Walker* by Steven Gerrard
      (Bristol: Hemlock Books, unpublished)

artistic criteria at all. All the films he writes about are *utter garbage.*[69] It turned out that nobody was reading the entire magazine, which folded the following year. By that time I was writing obituaries for Virgin Books, which expressed a modicum of interest in a book exploiting nostalgia for soft porn; but this waned and, as always, I moved on.

In 1991 I discovered that at least one person ('maybe a crank?' I surmised before I met him) had read me. I was relieved to find that Anthony Blampied was 'relatively normal.' He was a cataloguer who had used his Mum's money to set himself up as a publisher, Sun Tavern Fields, and was just about to bring out his first two books. He wanted an expanded and updated version of my *Cinema* series to be his third. I set to with a will. I never imagined I would write a book and I said as much in the first line: 'I am that very rare animal, someone who has worked in the film business for more than six months without writing a book about it.'[70]

Doing Rude Things was not only the first book that acknowledged the existence of a forgotten genre, it was also the book that made the genre a cult. Prior to 1992, when it was published, the films about which I was writing were largely unavailable. The book was responsible for everything that came afterwards: the video releases, the film seasons, the TV screenings, and the blogs and other books that continue to appear to this day, mostly written by young fans far more knowledgeable than I. I may have stumbled over the grave of the British sex film; but those who followed me exhumed it.

Researching the book was a joy. Anthony wanted the foreword to be written by Pamela Green, muse of the talentless smut merchant Harrison Marks and the most famous British nude model of the late 1950s and early 60s. I was a long time admirer (she featured prominently in the wank mags I found in my father's wardrobe) and I was only too willing to track down Pam to the Isle of Wight, where she was now a leading light of the Yarmouth Women's Institute. Happily *Doing Rude Things* also revived her own career. She spent the rest of her life attending conventions and selling sets of her photographs at £5 for five. I was also one of the first to reveal that, after 'languishing in a Turkish jail', David Hamilton Grant was dead, 'possibly by murder.'[71]

Just before publication, I had the great good fortune to meet, for the first time in 21 years, my former flatmate John Lawrence. As much of a porn aficionado as I, John was perplexed when he read in my manuscript the claim that sex cinemas in London had been banned in 1985. He took me to one in King's Cross that somehow had managed to survive every attempt to shut it down since 1969. Although I didn't mention it by name in the book,

---

69 *Cinema* No 6, October, 1982
70 *Doing Rude Things* (London: Sun Tavern Fields, 1992)
71 *ibid*

it was the Abcat Cine Club, a few minutes' walk from what would soon be my home in Keystone Crescent. When Anthony heard about our adventure, he wanted to visit the Abcat as well.

The cinema was in the basement of a former shop. There were illuminated exit signs and rows of tip-up seats. 'I've been in worse places,' I wrote in a reference to the Adonis in New York, where the toilets were under six inches of water. The Abcat only recently had switched from 8mm film projected on to a screen to video tape shown on a large screen TV. John, who didn't want them lost to posterity, had bought as many of the celluloid reels as he could. He still has them in storage. My evening with Anthony at the Abcat was brief but memorable. We got in for £3 instead of £5 because it was near closing time. As it approached, the manager swilled out the toilet with disinfectant, then turned up the house lights, revealing the discarded tissues, and announced to the handful of wankers still in situ, 'Right, that's your lot!' In 2013 the Abcat was threatened with closure for what was to be the last time. I went to a meeting of Islington's licensing committee to speak in its defence. 'I hope people are not making moral judgments about this venue, which adds to the variety and diversity of the area,' I deposed. This story made the local newspaper[72] in which I was described as 'David McGillivray, who writes gags for comedian Julian Clary.' Julian protested 'This is an outrage!' in an email, and the UK's oldest surviving sex cinema closed in 2014.

Only one venue was considered for the launch of *Doing Rude Things*. The Scala Cinema was a cavernous fleapit, once a 1920 picture palace, which now programmed trash, classics and trash classics, sometimes all night. The auditorium was the darkest in London and the condition of the seats and carpets was a matter of conjecture. 'High on atmosphere, low on comfort,' proposed manager Helen de Witt. The cinema attracted a wide variety of winos, students, punks, minor celebrities, tired businessmen, bikers, Goths and OAPs, some of whom had sex in the toilets at 3am. Little did we know that, only months after we commandeered it on 29th August, 1992, the Scala would be forced to close. 'Many people have talked about the manner in which they'd like to die,' I wrote in a tribute.[73] 'I regret that my wish, to peg out in the Scala during a Russ Meyer triple bill, can no longer be granted.' To my great relief, the building was not demolished. It became an ambisexual, indie dance club called Popstarz, very popular with my clientele after a toot or three at my place, over the road. I'll come back to that.

With Helen's co-operation, Anthony and I organised an all-day event at the Scala that included screenings of *utter garbage* and personal appearances

---

72 *Islington Tribune*, 22nd November, 2013
73 *What's On in London*, 16th-23rd June, 1993

by Ray Selfe, Michael Armstrong, Stanley Long and – together again after 25 years – Harrison Marks and Pamela Green. Pam also stayed over in my flat and, while I was out, cleaned up after one of my cats. I was aghast that the star of *Naked as Nature Intended* was now reduced to getting down on her knees to dispose of cat vomit. But Pam was a cat lover and every subsequent year she sent me a Christmas card from her own cat, Toffee.

The Scala's policy always had been to screen any piece of celluloid that possessed half a dozen intact sprocket-holes. On my big day it was business as usual. The tattered print of Michael Armstrong's magnum opus, *Eskimo Nell,* jammed and burned in the projector and, while this problem was being rectified, Michael himself stood up in the auditorium and explained that the reels also had been projected in the wrong order. I could not have been happier. In the depths of night, a party of us went along to King's Cross station to buy the first edition of *The Observer,*[74] in which Julie Welch commented on the fact that the narrator of *Nudes of the World* was Valerie Singleton of *Blue Peter* fame. (I had invited Val to the Scala. She declined.) The very next day I flew to the US to make a programme about ice cream for Radio 4. This was the life.

Doing Rude Things was reviewed everywhere from the *Daily Telegraph* to *Penthouse.* This publicity shifted the entire run of 2,000 copies and turned me into an overnight 'sexpert.' One junket I could have done without was a poorly-attended festival in Manchester, which had contrived to reunite me with Pete Walker for the first time in ten years. The devil made me late arriving for our onstage interview and Pete was noticeably cool as he shook my hand. The interviewer was incompetent, the questions from the fans were banal, Pete was pompous, and I was incoherent. I feared that the whole thing had been a bore, and afterwards Anthony confirmed my fear. That was the last time I saw Pete Walker.

My final years in Kilburn now appear to have been spent winding down and tidying up prior to upheaval of which I was as yet unaware. The chief architect of my new design for living, King's Cross resident John Lawrence, took me to places of interest in his manor: the flight of steps that inspired Arnold Bennett's novel *Riceyman Steps*; the railway bridge over which Alec Guinness wheeled the dead body of Danny Green in the Ealing comedy *The Ladykillers*; and a pretty little crescent with each of its houses looking almost exactly as it did when it was built in 1845. Historian Peter Ackroyd also knew the crescent and wrote about its 'sudden silence.'[75] It was indeed an oasis of calm in what was otherwise an urban hell-hole. One night, when I was

---

74   30th August, 1992
75   *London: The Biography* (London: Chatto & Windus, 2000)

driving slowly up Pentonville Road, looking for the new offices of *What's On in London,* I was stopped by the police on suspicion of kerb-crawling.

The actual countdown to my departure to King's Cross can be dated to 1992, when the man upstairs, J.P., lost his marbles, a crisis for which I hold myself responsible. I inspired many of my friends – Walter Zerlin Jnr., David José, Janet Sate – to start writing; but unlike the rest, J.P. had a modicum of success. In 1988 he'd got a foot into the door of BBC television when he wrote an episode of a drama series. There was talk of further commissions. At this point he decided to sue another BBC writer for plagiarism. This did not end happily. In 1997 a High Court judge dismissed J.P.'s claim because he had not been telling the truth. J.P. never worked for the BBC again.

Meanwhile I discovered that J.P. had persuaded a neighbour to pretend to be his landlord in order that he could claim £75 per week housing benefit. Camden Council had discovered the deception and he had been cautioned. Because I was J.P.'s real landlord, I was dragged into this scam, which rapidly became a tangled web of Kafkaesque proportions. (I no longer owned my two flats because I was being investigated again by the Inland Revenue and had signed over my property to my brother.) I was required to attend a hearing at which I could do little but claim ignorance; but J.P. was belligerent, demanding, 'Just pay my rent!' i.e. money to which he wasn't entitled because he'd tried to defraud the system. I had never seen him behave like this before and I was convinced that it was my love-crazed ill-treatment of him that had driven him mad. Somehow we extricated ourselves from this mess and J.P. received his ill-gotten housing benefit. But the damage had been done. I decided that it would be better if we lived apart.

The last major project I completed in Kilburn was *Scapegoat,* my anti-censorship magazine. I was driven to action initially by the book burnings, bombings and murders that followed the publication of Salman Rushdie's novel *The Satanic Verses* in 1988. There was another wave of ignorant stupidity closer to home in 1992, when British Trading Standards officials wrongly claimed to have discovered snuff movies changing hands at film fairs. When Marc Morris showed me the TV coverage of this poppycock, I was left open-mouthed. Commentaries fulminated against films with mutilation, cannibalism and 'real' murders, but were accompanied by visuals which showed only copies of such videos as *Blue Velvet, Wild at Heart* and – yes – *House of Whipcord.* The worst offender was Channel 4, whose experts linked horror film collectors to a mythical underground sex network and claimed that men who enjoyed porn soon moved on to sex with children and animals. If nobody else was going to introduce a voice of sanity to this scaremongering, I would have to do so myself.

I put the magazine together (there was only one issue) with help from people I'd met on the mythical underground sex network – Alan Jones,

Marc Morris, John Lawrence and so forth. There were articles by Tony Allen (should Holocaust denier David Irving be censored?); Mark Kermode (should the BBFC continue to cut films intended for adults?); and David Flint, whose piece on David Alton, an MP who had tried to make it illegal to show an inappropriate video to anyone under the age of 18, was censored. I was proud of the whole magazine but particularly of my international censorship survey, with contributions from 39 countries.

This was achieved by sending questionnaires around the world by post and the new-fangled fax machine. I first discovered this piece of equipment at Premiere in 1988. 'It's a technological miracle,' I enthused. 'You feed pages into what looks like a photocopier, dial a number, and moments later identical copies appear in Croydon. Wow!' I bought my own fax machine the following year. The Internet was so new there was an article in *Scapegoat* explaining it. The magazine was launched at Cyberia, 'a trendy new café, where the customers sit playing with computer terminals.' It was, in other words, London's first Internet café. It's an *haute cuisine* restaurant now.

In October, 1994, I began looking for a new home. I received a tip-off from John Lawrence that a house was for sale in Keystone Crescent. I was shown inside on 21st November. I put in an offer the next day. My life was about to be turned around. This is where the story really starts.

PART 5

OVEREXCITED
(1994-2002)

I

*"Keystone Crescent has the smallest radius of any crescent in Europe
and is unique in having a matching outer and inner circle."*
~ Sign posted at either end of the street ~

Noël Coward called his success in later life 'Dad's renaissance.' I experienced a similar experience in my own little world just before it was turned topsy-turvy by my move to King's Cross. My dual role as a sexpert and authority on censorship culminated in a film of my book *Doing Rude Things*. Producer Mark Forstater fought for years to get it made and finally succeeded with the BBC. Nigel Finch put in a word for me. I last spoke to Nigel in September, 1994, just before he went to New York to shoot what was to be his last film *Stonewall*. He died on 14th February, 1995. A month later I was one of the Radio London survivors who gathered to watch Nigel's best-known documentary, *Chelsea Hotel*, which the BBC screened as a tribute. So many joints were in circulation that, after a while, everyone lost interest and the TV was switched off. 'A sobering reminder of the transience of comradeship,' I wrote. 'One day I too will be switched off.'

Doing Rude Things the movie was presented by Angus Deayton, the perfect man for the job. Even in those days, long before the cocaine and prostitutes revelations, he was known as 'TV's Mr Sex.' He opened the programme by revealing that all the leading exponents of the British sex film had refused to participate. What had happened was that Pete Walker, now my arch-enemy, had warned Stanley Long and another hack, Derek Ford, that this was to be another stitch-up. But others who weren't that bothered about their reputations (Harrison Marks, Pamela Green, Bachoo Sen) said yes and there was enough skin to ensure a hit. When it was first broadcast in 1995 the programme was watched by 4.93 million viewers (BBC Two's highest viewing figure of the week). When it was repeated in 1996 it picked up a further 4.01 million voyeurs. I've since been in quite a few TV shows of this type. You would think there was nothing more to say about boobs and bums. But there always is.

It also seemed for a while as though the Farndale Ladies would regain their former prominence by way of a new production in California. The Ensemble

Theatre in Santa Barbara had had a big hit with *The Farndale/Christmas Carol*; and when I went to see a revival of the show at the end of 1994, I decided that this was the company to premiere a production Walter and I had dreamed of for years: the Farndale version of *Peter Pan,* which would open with Peter crashing through a window that hadn't been opened. Ensemble's artistic director was intrigued. Walter and I prepared a detailed synopsis. A typical Zerlin brainwave was to have the whole play done in the set and costumes of *The Sound of Music* (because Mrs Frobisher had ticked the wrong box). But after one look at the proposed Gestapo uniforms, the theatre took fright. *The Farndale/Peter Pan*, the last play Walter Zerlin Jnr. and I ever wrote, sat unfinished on the shelf for the next twenty years.

I underwent my change of life at the same time as Julian Clary. His was rather more cathartic than mine. At the 1993 British Comedy Awards he had cracked the fisting joke that allowed the tabloid press once again to deplore his filthy mouth. Julian found his TV career in abeyance. I offered my sympathy and he offered me the chance to write him some new material as opposed to occasional one-liners. It was just as filthy as the joke that got him into trouble; but live shows weren't front page fodder. My stuff was tried out at a corporate gig in Liverpool. I then wrote a chunk of Julian's Australian tour *My Boyfriend's Back*, the show that marked the debut of the joke, 'I began my career in the circus. I was the human cannonball. I used to shoot over the ringmaster's back.' In 1995, when the time was right for Julian to be eased back on to TV, I suggested a sitcom in which Julian was a prison governor solving the inmates' problems. This gradually morphed into *All Rise for Julian Clary*, since when Julian has been my main, and at times sole, employer. I have no idea why. He could have had Barry Cryer.

Months before I left Kilburn forever, my domestic arrangements were shattered as if by Enola Gay. A builder neighbour convinced me that, if I turned my two bedroom, one bathroom flat into a three bedroom, two bathroom flat, I would make more of a profit on its sale. I agreed to what turned out to be a two month conversion during which time the cats and I remained in situ. The cats reacted very badly. Marjorie and Killer ran away and were never seen again. Vincent began having fits that left him almost incapacitated. He didn't return from a trip to the vet. Only Kicius made the journey to King's Cross.

Coincidence or not, I suffered the worst and most prolonged period of renal colic of my life. After the first attack I was an object of intense interest for three days at the Royal Free hospital in Hampstead. Doctors couldn't understand why I had been forming kidney stones for twenty years. No sooner was I discharged than I was struck down again. I couldn't waste another three days in hospital. I had to supervise the builders and I was preparing to direct a play with Lisa

Daniely for Edinburgh. I decided to grit my teeth and ride out the pain, lying on my dusty bed in the wreckage of my home, while the stone made its impassive, leisurely way through my entrails.

'It turned out that I was in agony for six hours. Even writing this now I can't believe I lasted that long. At first I just shifted and stretched and suffered. Then I began to chant a mantra, both to myself and out loud – "You can beat it. This isn't happening." This got me quite light-headed. But I was still in excruciating pain. I went to the bathroom cabinet and took five Nurofen and something Veronica gave me. Would I overdose? I didn't care.

'The drugs made no difference. I dealt with the pain in a new way, first writhing like an anguished belly dancer, then sucking like a baby on a bottle of water while kicking and waving my legs. I came close to understanding the affinity between agony and ecstasy. I've often heard pain described as a friend and I knew what this meant too. As dawn came up I felt the pain approaching my groin and I knew the stone was about to leave my body. That gave me the strength to carry on.'

Nietzsche said, 'That which does not kill us makes us stronger.' Idiot.

By rights I never should have taken possession of 16, Keystone Crescent. In 1987 British Rail had announced plans to demolish 150 buildings in King's Cross, including half of Keystone Crescent and the Scala Cinema, in order to build the new Channel Tunnel terminus. The parliamentary bill necessary for this degree of reconstruction steamed through the House of Commons. But when it reached the Lords it hit the buffers. Keystone Crescent resident Randal Keynes, a relative of divers distinguished personages of that surname, was a highly organised activist, who had the ears of two influential Lords. When they spoke in the House, the bill died, and seventeen acres of King's Cross was spared. In 2007 the new Channel Tunnel terminus opened further west in St Pancras station.

British Rail had acquired all the property it intended to raze somewhat prematurely. Now it was obliged to put it back on the market. My house, which BR had bought for £190,000, was offered at £145,000. There were no takers. King's Cross was a dump. Eventually, after months of negotiations, number 16 was sold to me for £134,000, a price I could afford. I had sold my newly-refurbished basement for £82,000 and the flat upstairs to J.P. (or rather the woman with whom he was now living) for a knock-down £53,000. The move was one of the best things I ever did. Or, as Dorothy (Sheila Keith) said in *Frightmare*, 'I think I left all my headaches and problems behind at the other place. I closed the door very carefully when I left and I locked them all in.' Dorothy was also certified insane, but we'll let that pass.

The first house I ever owned had four storeys and five bedrooms. I moved my bed into the attic because I wanted to listen to the rain on the roof. Another bedroom on the ground floor became my study. The day after I moved in I was informed that English Heritage was offering grants for the restoration of houses in Keystone Crescent. The street was now part of a conservation area, of outstanding architectural interest, listed Grade II*. After council workmen had laid cobbles and erected Victorian-style lamp posts with yellow, gas-style lighting, film crews and tourist groups became commonplace. (Although I had left Marianne Stone behind in Kilburn, I learned that she had been born within walking distance of Keystone Crescent in Caledonian Road.)

During the first few months, when I did little other than rearrange the furniture, I lived alone for the only extended period of my life. But I decorated the guest bedroom first and a succession of friends came to stay. Some never returned because they were a bit alarmed by the neighbourhood. A lot of people also wanted to have a look at my new house. This is where that nice young man, Ricky, finally returns to the story. Ricky had been taking me to see the elderly actor Michael Ward, who now lived in a nursing home he hated. Michael drew my attention to the fact that he sat all day in his wheelchair looking through a window at a brick wall and barbed wire. There was one occasion when I left the building and started crying. I wanted to let Michael know that he wasn't forgotten and gave him a photo from Julian signed, 'You're an inspiration.'

Every so often Ricky would disappear. Then he turned up at my house with money he owed me. He told me he was now working for a theatrical agent and meeting a lot of famous people, one of whom, a Hollywood action hero, had asked him to get him some cocaine. Ricky had started dealing and wanted me to try his ecstasy, which he said was the best he'd ever had. I stored this information away. Although I wasn't aware, Ricky stored away the information that I was living in a house too big for one person.

When I returned to work I moved from job to job with no effort in a manner that's continued to the present day. A lot of the work was very dispiriting indeed. Lisa Daniely wanted to star in a play she'd written, *Snakes About Her Cradle*, about a heroine of the French Revolution. I helped her get it to Edinburgh, but she paid the bills and lost about £3,500. I was surprised to read in one of Lisa's obituaries[76] that this production was 'highly successful.' It was in fact three weeks of anguish that played to two men and a dog. Lisa never stopped arguing with

---

76   *The Guardian*, 24th February, 2014

her brainless stage management, who didn't want to be there, and she never learned her lines. The review in *The Scotsman* is too cruel to quote.[77]

Next I played a couple of parts in an equally uncommercial play, whose unqualified failure drove the younger members of the cast to light up at every spare minute. 'I've had fifteen joints tonight,' one actress told me as the last night party in Leicester wound down at 8am. We had played a variation of the Truth Game, which involved players voting for 'the person most likely.' When it came to the person whose name was most likely to end up in front page headlines, every single player voted for me. I wonder what made them do that? Although I was much older than they were, I bonded with young rebels like these on every subsequent engagement, and many of them went on to become regulars at my Friday night parties.

For its London showcase the play could manage only a Brixton cellar known to me as the home of a sex club called the Torture Garden. I haven't mentioned sex for a few pages so please indulge me. I was introduced to the TG by one of my protégés and his girlfriend, the latter of whom eventually was to take over from me as Friday night host. He can be Carl and she can be Miranda. We all frequented the TG when it still was a cutting-edge alternative to the commercial club scene, and before it became a fancy dress party for the Sunday drivers of the fetish world. Just before my first visit I told Carl I was excited as a teenager on his first date.

'The place was packed with fetishists of every type, age and colour. There were crazy extroverts, young clubbers, middle-aged couples, dirty old men. People were led around on dog leads, nerds licked Miranda's shoes, SM lovers tied each other to various contraptions, and whips cracked away.

'Carl and Miranda got zonked-out on E almost as soon as we arrived and then never moved from the chill-out zone. I wandered, captivated. The techno music was to my taste. It was so loud and the strobe lights so violent that I didn't need to pop my E. There was real sex going on in dark corners almost from the time I arrived. In one nook an enormously fat, naked woman was wanking young guys. A big, black bouncer came over and I thought, that's it, we're all going to get thrown out. But he'd just come to watch.

'American performance artist Ron Athey came on at ridiculous o'clock and I joined the throng to watch him. He announced a

---

77   23rd August, 1995

blood sacrifice. To my astonished eyes, he took a scalpel and carved an intricate design into an assistant's chest. No trick, this; the blood flowed. Then there was an orgy of mutilation and deafening music. Then another assistant had his prick stapled inside his ball bag. When I saw this, I began sweating profusely and knew I was going to faint.

'I pushed my way out of the crowd and sat down at the back of the room. I told Carl I was leaving. He thought I was a wuss. I'm still overwhelmed. This is life on the edge as we approach the Millennium. I'll be back – with others.'

Subsequently I derived mischievous enjoyment from taking the young and innocent (on one occasion a party from the Southwold Summer Theatre) to the Torture Garden. Soo Drouet, Banquo in *The Farndale/Macbeth*, was included. Soo was a game old bird and went on to become another of my great mates. But I will never forget the politely petrified look on the face of her companion as she listened to Graham the exhibitionist, who was talking to her about the terrible traffic outside. And masturbating at the same time.

By the end of 1995 I had been answering readers' questions for almost 25 years, half my life. Like Peter Noble before me, I had begun to make mistakes. I knew I had to stop pretending I knew anything about movies; I contrived to get myself fired from *Film Review* by instigating a row about money. My plan worked and I was told my services were no longer required. Secretly I hoped that the magazine would then fold. That's exactly what happened. Thirteen years later.

Although not everything I touched turned to gold, I was enjoying myself to such an extent by 1996 that I was able to write, 'This is undoubtedly the happiest and most exciting year I've had since the 1970s, when I was writing movies and being a hit in Edinburgh.' Julian Clary was involved in some way in much of the fun and games. For his new touring show, *Barefaced Cheek in a Lycra-Free Zone*, I suggested that he talk to men in the street outside the theatre via walkie-talkies. This stunt was something of a novelty, particularly when I saw the show in Tunbridge Wells. Julian's stage manager, Helen Jackson, found a man in a pub down the road. She brought him back to the theatre and he walked on stage, pint still in hand.

I also adored the concept of *In the Dark with Julian Clary*, a TV game show which was the first in the UK to exploit night vision cameras. The audience was able to see punters attempting to perform tasks in a pitch dark room. In the studio the blundering about and falling over was hysterically funny. But the humour didn't come over to the audience at home. The pilot was buried in a graveyard slot, which infuriated us because of the effort we had made to tailor Julian's humour to family viewing. (The producer, Lisa Clark, was convinced that we were trying to smuggle innuendos into Julian's script. We included a character named Mrs Fradgley. At a production meeting Lisa tried to veto the name. When we protested, she responded, 'Come on, you guys. What does it mean to fradge somebody?')

Simultaneously *All Rise for Julian Clary* put me within grovelling distance of shiny floor celebrities. Julian wanted a special guest to appear on the show every week and we compiled our wish list. Sadly most agents still regarded Julian as too much of a risk. Probably the biggest star to commit was Lionel Blair. But that didn't stop me trying. At the BBC Writers Party (where I also met the great Alan Simpson) I spotted Salman Rushdie. Fortified by champagne I interrupted his conversation with Alan Yentob and asked Rushdie if he liked Julian Clary. He said he did and so I asked him if he'd like to be a guest on Julian's show. To my amazement, he said he'd consider it and told me to 'get in touch' as though I knew how to find him. (Eight years after his death sentence, he was still in hiding, under 24 hour police protection.) We wrote a sketch in which Rushdie came to Julian's court with a problem that required Julian to advise Rushdie to lose weight 'in order to get rid of that unwanted fatwa.' Somehow this comic gem was communicated to the great man. He said no. I think we got Peter Stringfellow instead and made jokes about his hair.

My new political awareness also came to the fore during a script discussion for *All Rise* with Head of Comedy John Plowman, known at BBC Television Centre as Joan Plowright. We had heard that he was going to object to a case in which two flatmates, who happened to be gay, were arguing over who should have the larger bedroom. Plowman went through our script, came to the appropriate page, and then said, 'Well, this is the gay case and we're not having that.' *Au contraire*, it was me who wasn't having this homophobia. But Plowman was intransigent. 'I want Julian to appeal to a wide audience,' he argued. 'People might switch off if they infer the programme's not for them.' I countered that anyone who was going to be put off would be put off by the opening titles, which showed Julian cavorting with two semi-clad leather men. At this Plowman sheepishly backed down on the proviso that the flatmates' sexuality wasn't mentioned. The case went ahead. Here was the unschooled boy from Palmers Green telling the BBC's Head of Comedy what to do. As Mr Clary might have said, 'If this isn't the pinnacle of my career, I'll be very surprised.'

While high on hashish in Tangier, Joe Orton wrote with unwitting prescience about the perils of self-satisfaction: 'Kenneth [Halliwell] and I sat talking of how happy we both felt,' Orton confided to his diary on 25th May, 1967. 'We'd have to pay for it. Or we'd be struck down from afar by disaster because we were, perhaps, too happy. To be young, good-looking, healthy, famous, comparatively rich and happy is surely going against nature.'[78] Less than three months later, Halliwell murdered Orton and then took his own life. I pondered Orton's words on New Year's Eve because, in the midst of happiness, health and wealth, I too had been struck down by disaster and was dreading the first few days of 1997. They didn't bring death, but they pulled me up short and shook me rigid before I was allowed to proceed with the next phase of my life.

---

78 *Prick Up Your Ears* by John Lahr (Harmondsworth, Middlesex: Allen Lane, 1978)

II

"I have of late...lost all my mirth."
~ The Bard ~

During my last years in Kilburn I maintained an intensive gym regime because I was bullied into it by training partners. One of them was a cute Chinaman, who had come to the UK with no money and no English. After meeting my ginger cat, he began calling himself Vincent. As with so many of my civilian friends, he was intrigued by my glitzy showbiz milieu. I gave him some acting tips. Before I could turn round he was given a line in *Tomorrow Never Dies*. Vincent Wang is now a stuntman. He owes me everything.

Shortly after arriving in King's Cross I joined a local fitness centre known as The Cally. I became aware that its sauna was gay, not shrieking, popper-sniffing gay, but sufficiently gay for one of its straight users to ward off unwanted attention by singing 'There Is Nothing Like a Dame' when he was in the shower. The Cally sauna became my main pick-up place, three times a week, and I wouldn't be able to count the number of men I've met there with whom I've had sex. (Suffice it to say that eventually our activities made the national press.) I discovered in King's Cross that saunas suit my purpose because you can see what you're getting.

Previously, you'll recall, I'd had little or no success at getting what I wanted via *Time Out*. I can now reveal that the back pages of this magazine actually constituted my road to ruin. We'll deal in the final section with my nemesis, Naim, who is only alive today because I don't know any hit men. But let's now discuss a couple of sex pig partners named Alistair and Thomas. Thomas is an exotic furry animal, who leads the double life of a secret agent. His claim to be single and living alone was put to the test when a woman phoned Alistair and screamed, 'Keep away from my husband!' Thomas in fact lived with his wife and two children. His duplicity made it difficult, but our relationship lasted twenty years and included two foreign holidays together. He always maintained his wife never suspected. Of course she didn't.

Alistair was a bearded streak of libido with mirrors in his bedroom and a box of sex toys under his bed. My threesomes with him and Thomas were, apart from being of volcanic intensity, civilised. Afterwards Alistair served fine wine and a cold collation and we would discuss the arts. During one of these post-coital symposia I asked Alistair if he had had an AIDS test. He said he had. 'And?' I probed. 'It's OK,' he replied. Like Thomas, Alistair was economical with the truth. In 1995, about eighteen months after we'd met, he stopped returning my calls. I persevered and eventually heard his weak voice on the other end of the line. I asked him how he was. 'All right,' he said and then added in a matter-of-fact way, 'Living with AIDS.' I learned at his funeral that he already had announced to the congregation of his Catholic church that he was dying.

Alistair was given the last rites on 23rd April 1996. He became distressed and was pumped with the drugs that probably helped kill him shortly afterwards. At his funeral mass he was given Eucharist, a Catholic variety show with chalices, censers, sermons, hymns and 'The Peace' in which mourners shake hands with those near them, like the audience during a TV warm-up. It was bewildering for a non-believer; but I was relieved that the priest talked honestly about Alistair as a gay man with AIDS. After fifteen years of the health crisis, prejudice was beginning to fade, even in the church. During those fifteen years the disease had been gaining on me, growing ever nearer until now it was practically at my door: I had had sex with someone who had died of AIDS. Like so many others, I was petrified by the thought of taking the test and then being confronted by a doctor with a solemn face. But then I was overtaken by circumstance and could delay the visit to the clinic no longer.

At the end of 1996 I flew to Portland, Oregon, to see the opening of a production of *The Farndale/Christmas Carol*. The day after I arrived I was taken ill. I felt as though I might be in an early stage of 'flu; but I also felt drained of all energy. I then developed a most aggressive and relentless diarrhoea and spent several days soiling my clothes and the bedsheets, much to the alarm of my host. He gave me medicine that didn't work. When I dragged myself to the theatre, the cast commented on how terrible I looked. I began to panic. But by the time I was due to fly on to Los Angeles, I appeared to be in remission.

Back in the City of Angels, I found that another production of *The Farndale/Christmas Carol* had been cancelled. With unexpected time on my hands I met up with Julian, who was as miserable as I was, but because he was shooting an American version of *In the Dark* that turned out so inept it was never screened. Four days after I returned to London the diarrhoea returned. Every time a friend telephoned me, I found myself breaking down and weeping that I thought I had AIDS. Julian assured me that he'd gone through the same process – the diarrhoea, the panic and fear of AIDS – while Christopher was dying. But Julian tested negative. Soo Drouet was sympathetic but insisted I go for a test. 'Every time you get sick you're going to get into this state,' she advised me with a firmness I dared not disregard. On 18th December I made an appointment for 2nd January. No walk-in clinics in those days. But how was I going to go on as normal, working every day, for the next two weeks? As is so often the case, my diary provides the answer: 'I keep telling myself that Spike Milligan wrote *The Goon Show* while he was having a nervous breakdown. If he could do it, so can I.'

I continued working while my mind and body both fell to pieces. When I awoke in the middle of the night, I found myself covered in sweat, another symptom of AIDS. Alan Jones came round to see me. He too had tested negative. He dismissed my anxiety in a typically blunt way, quoting an Italian saying, 'When you have nothing to worry about, you worry about nothing,' which helped somewhat. In the cold light of day I did wonder if I was turning into one of my worst nightmares, the imaginary invalid. But at night the terrors returned and probably I exasperated my friends by appearing hypochondriac. Soo, who part-timed as a 'buddy' (a carer for AIDS patients), knew about symptoms and asked if I had a cough. 24 hours later I developed one. Veronica, who also knew what she was talking about, told me very sternly, 'You have *not* got AIDS,' which shocked me into temporary good health.

At Julian's New Year's Eve party his mystic friends Penny and Barb demanded that we all write down what we wanted from 1997 and then go into the garden to burn the papers. If I'd been asked to do this the previous year I would have made some shallow request for more fame, more fortune. But now I bargained only for life itself. Two days into the New Year, still plagued by the trots, I met the steadfast Soo and she accompanied me to what in those now far-off days before the pandemic would have been called a clap clinic:

'We went in to see Simon for counselling. He asked me why I was there and I told him my fears. On the strength of what I told him he felt it was "unlikely" I was positive. In another room someone else took my blood. My fantasy up until then was that, before the needle went in, I would say, "I've changed my mind." But the doctor was chatting amiably and, before I knew what was happening, I was putting on my jacket and there was no turning back.

'We had to wait eight hours for the results. Soo took me to Patisserie Valerie for breakfast and we talked about everything except why we were really spending the day together. There were three films we fancied and I chose *Matilda* because I thought a comedy might be a good idea. Towards the end I got very restless and was on the verge of walking out.

'Soo suggested walking back to the clinic. It was like the long walk down Death Row to the electric chair. As we entered, my brain helped me out by clicking into neutral. We passed Simon. Could I interpret the expression on his face? We waited in reception. I held Soo's hand and she kept talking to me. Basically she is Superwoman and no one could have got me through the day better than her.

Another patient came in. He seemed very calm. He told us it was his third visit. 'Just like the dentist,' he joked.

'My name was called. Now I was almost numb. Simon asked me my name and date of birth and then said, "I'm happy to tell you you're negative," at which point my tear ducts opened and they let me get on with it. I pulled myself together and we exchanged pleasantries. Soo and I left. I couldn't believe what I'd been told. We passed a pub and I felt I needed a double brandy.'

Back at home the telephone rang a lot, and I told my inner circle the same story again and again. My friends had formed such a tower of strength during my hour of need that I resolved to become a much better friend to all of them, even the brutally outspoken Alan Jones. (Once, when we were getting dressed up for the Torture Garden, I attempted to follow fashion by tying a scarf around my now bald head. I asked Alan, 'What do I look like?' and, without missing a beat, he replied, 'Like Gracie Fields in *Sing as We Go*.') Within a year I was to become, in my own peculiar way, a very reliable friend to almost everyone I knew and many more I came to know. By general consensus I was the best drug dealer they ever had met.

My strange illness was never diagnosed and it looks to me today as if my body was more determined than ever to get me to lie down in order to deal with stress, in this case caused by the AIDS monster. It reduced not just me but almost every gay man I knew into a fearful creature of the night, afraid of every sneeze, every new skin blemish. Early 1997 brought the development we had longed for – not a cure, but at least a life-saver. First with the news as always, Alan Jones told me about new drug combination therapies that could reduce the 'viral load' (a new phrase to me) to nil. It was antiretroviral drugs that were now prolonging the lives of American basketball player Magic Johnson (who at first claimed that he had been cured by God) and Alan's friend Kjell (who is currently one of the longest-surviving people with AIDS in the UK).

Anyone with experience of hypochondria may expect me to admit that, as soon as I was told I wasn't ill, my symptoms disappeared. But they didn't; they got worse. The cough and the diarrhoea returned. I couldn't climb the stairs to the attic and had to sleep in the guest bedroom on the ground floor. 'This is Hell,' I wrote. 'Hell could not provide anything more diabolical than an illness that prolongs itself with old and new symptoms. I am currently in a woeful state, far worse than anything I experienced in Portland.' I was willing to try anything for relief, which is why I agreed to visit Erika Poole's homeopath. She cured me. I find it as difficult as the next man to accept that a homeopathic remedy contains anything curative. But I was cured. It was a long process.

The first remedy didn't work. The second remedy made me feel different but not better. The third remedy acted like a magic wand. I don't expect you to believe me. After all, I think that everything we do is predestined and I've tried to contact the dead.

Quackery or not, I was able because of it to sit happily once again at the light entertainment conveyer belt, churning out trash as before but disseminating it for the first time via email, which I had first come across at the British Film Institute in 1994. Getting me online was another long process, achieved eventually by Beth Porter, actress turned computer nerd, and I think one of the first women in this field. After months of fiddling, I sent my first email on 8th March, 1997. By this time I had collected a grand total of twenty email addresses, almost all of them in the US. Exactly three months later Beth introduced me to the Internet and I discovered that already David McGillivray was all over it. The 'front page headline' prediction had come to pass. Sort of.

My first project to come to grief because of computer technology was *Let's Go London*, a screenplay I wrote with punk novelist Stewart Home. We were put together by a producer with a peculiar sense of humour. Stewart talked a lot about philosophy, occultism and romantic classicism. The first time I met him, I told him several times, 'You've lost me,' but it made no difference. Whatever we wrote together was also lost – on a corrupted disk. If you're wondering what the authors of *I'm Not Feeling Myself Tonight!* and *Cunt* produced together, forget it. (But later I took the script's basic premise – going off with a stranger at an airport who holds up a card bearing someone else's name – for my film *Mrs Davenport's Throat*.)

Knowing that Julian Clary was considering fathering a baby with his lesbian stage manager, Helen Jackson, I persuaded him that this should be the theme of his next touring show. 'We'd had a lot of wine and a bit to smoke and the ideas came tumbling out.' What eventually emerged was *Special Delivery*, another big hit, put together while Julian was shooting the second series of his TV show *All Rise for Julian Clary*. The original producer had been fired and replaced with Lisa Clark from *In the Dark with Julian Clary*. Lisa still didn't get Julian's humour. I had written a joke about a 'tenner', which anyone familiar with Julian probably would know referred to penis size. 'We can't do jokes about ten-year-olds,' Lisa decreed. The show failed even more miserably against the second series of Lisa's *Shooting Stars*.

While my equilibrium was being restored by homeopathy, my beloved mentor Peter Noble was coping with heart disease for which there was no cure, alternative or otherwise. Peter and Marianne had been required to quit their celebrated residence in Abbey Road. Somehow they had contrived to move to Winchmore Hill, where I was schooled. I telephoned Peter to welcome him to his new home and was distressed to hear his slurred voice. 'I've gone into a decline,' he told me. I visited him and learned that I was one of the many making the pilgrimage to this North London outpost. Farley Granger and his boyfriend had been the day before; Sylvia Syms and Herbert Lom were due tomorrow. While Peter and I chatted about the old days, the Nobles' housekeeper, Norma, who once lived next door to me in Kilburn, served Peter his regulation gin and tonic. It was about 11am. Respect, Pete.

Peter Noble died on 17th August, 1997. To my astonishment, his daughters, Kara and Katina, asked me to officiate at Peter's funeral. Although it shouldn't have been me, how could I refuse? 'I think that what I did today,' I wrote on the day of the funeral, 'was the most important day of my life.' The honour has not been surpassed to this day. The chapel was thronged, quite rightly, with show biz elite, and I found myself reading messages from Sean Connery, Roger Moore and Shelley Winters. I introduced Sylvia Syms, who told funny stories about chemical toilets in North Africa, and then I said uncertainly, 'And now here's Bob Monkhouse?' because I wasn't sure he was present. He was and he delivered a typically polished set. Afterwards we all went back to Winchmore Hill and I was overawed to be able to chat to TV and radio star Barbara Kelly, still smoking despite being diagnosed with cancer. The resilient Barbara hung on for another ten years. I remained friends with Marianne Stone until her death two years later in 2009.

Despite an earlier clean-up operation, King's Cross was still a place of ill-repute. A teen hoodlum, who stabbed headmaster Philip Lawrence in 1995, had met fellow gang members outside King's Cross station and, after leaving Lawrence to die, played in an amusement arcade opposite. In 1996 a New York-style 'zero tolerance' attitude to King's Cross crime was announced but, as I could see from my window, it wasn't working. By 1997 King's Cross still meant sex, drugs and worse. The canal, minutes from my house, was the repository of rape and murder victims. There is a chance that this human jungle influenced Ricky when he was considering where he should live next. In September he asked me if he could move into my guest room on the ground floor. After two years on my own, I knew I didn't like it, and anyway I was determined to be true to my new vow. (Always say yes.) I said yes. Without this little word, you would not be reading this book.

In one of his many autobiographies[79] Stephen Fry wrote, 'It seemed to me from the late 1980s through the naughty 1990s and into the opening years of the 21st century inconceivable that there was anyone in London not doing coke.' Stephen's cocaine habit began in 1986, much earlier than mine, and because he did most of his deals in the privileged surroundings of Soho's Groucho club, our paths didn't really cross. But his consumption was the stuff

---

79 *More Fool Me* (London: Michael Joseph, 2014)

of legend. In 1993 Julian's pianist, Russell Churney, told me that, during a Stonewall charity concert at the London Palladium, he'd opened a dressing room door and found Stephen on his hands and knees snorting gak off the lino. Many of our experiences were the same and consequently Stephen's name will crop up here and there from now on.

For starters it's certainly true that television was one of the many places in the 1990s where cocaine was impossible to avoid. Almost everyone for whom I wrote used it. One comedian had a policeman boyfriend who shared out the spoils that cops had confiscated from dealers. But television was nursery slopes compared to the cocaine Winter Olympics that the music industry had become. I accompanied Julian to a music awards show at Alexandra Palace, where the pre-show party was awash with white powder. When I tell you that the guests included East 17, Shaun Ryder and Michael Hutchence, you'll appreciate that I need add little more. At showtime practically everyone was incoherent, and some were unable to locate the Autocue, let alone read it.

Because I worked in television, my friends assumed I could score for them. What I said before about friendship still applied; but, as Stephen Fry observes, drug deals are an enormously time-consuming business when you're on the receiving end. Nothing had changed since the 1960s, when Lou Reed sang about waiting for his man. Because Ricky's source had dried up, we found ourselves hanging around a club in Soho because the promoter (the boyfriend of the actress who smoked fifteen joints in Leicester) was able to get hold of the best gear. Eventually. He was always trolleyed and promising that his contact would arrive soon. Hours would pass and often we would go home empty-handed. But when we collected, we would go off to sample the goods and snog and talk into the early hours about going into business ourselves and providing a much better service. I thought it was just cocaine talk.

Before I go on to describe how fantasy became reality, allow me to bring the Naim story up to date. This is as good a place as any because at the end of 1997 I went with the wretched good-for-nothing to Havana and this was to prove a momentous holiday. Naim was one of the last lame dogs I adopted as a result of seeing an advertisement in *Time Out*. (During our first date in 1993 I should have heeded the warning signal that his previous boyfriend had dumped him with no explanation.) Naim comes from Pakistan where, in case you didn't know, sex between men is more prevalent than in the back room of a leather bar in San Francisco. He has the sexual appetite of a rabbit, all the more surprising in that he looks like a henpecked Asian chartered accountant.

Sex with Naim was like sex with a blow-up doll, but less passionate. He just needed constant buggering and I referred to our trysts as 'doing my duty.' I would have dumped him like his man who got away, but Naim had a secret, unlawful job copying gay porn videotapes and selling them via coded classified ads in newspapers. VCR machines whirred away in his house 24 hours a day, but this still wasn't enough to cope with demand, and Naim farmed some of the work out to me. In 1996 he was raided by Customs and Excise officers, whose department had intercepted a mucky tape sent from the Netherlands. When the officers found one of Naim's price lists, they confiscated his stock and marched him to the nick. The next day I agreed to rent a storage unit in my name in order to hide hundreds more of Naim's tapes. Naturally I found such cloak-and-dagger activity a bit of a buzz. But this was soon to become a thing of the past. Naim and my *Scapegoat* contributor David Flint were two of the last people charged under laws which became obsolete in 2000, when pornography was legalised in the UK. (This, as we'll discover, was largely because of me.)

Naim was a sex tourist. He regularly asked me to accompany him to the world's hot spots, I think mainly because he was worried about being mugged by one of his rent boys. I agreed to Havana because there is nothing I like more than faded grandeur. Habana Vieja consisted of little else and I adored Galeano Street, once the Bond Street of Havana, whose fancy stores were now occupied by squatters selling junk, and the shell of the Capitolio theatre, where men sold bicycles in the back of the stalls. It became clear soon after we arrived that Naim had returned in order to have more sex with a hot-blooded and insatiable student and part-time prostitute he'd picked up in La Rampa, Havana's main cruising area. He'll be known from now on as Bernardo.

It was Bernardo's friend, Luis, who showed me Havana and taught me the Spanish words of the chorus of 'Macarena', still one of my party pieces. On a couple of occasions the four of us went to Joker, a gay disco, which opened at midnight and which by 12.30am was a heaving throng of sweaty bodies rubbing up against each other, an experience I found electrifying. 'I struggled off the floor to the bog,' I wrote, 'and never have I had my bum squeezed by so many men in such a short period of time.' One night the atmosphere became so charged that a couple were ejected for having sex on the dance floor.

Cuban nightlife, throbbing with that infectious salsa beat, completely captivated me although I was well aware that most of its joyous participants were living in slums on rations. I was more than happy to contribute to the Cuban economy and returned to London weighed down by cigars, rum and tourist trinkets. Shortly afterwards I learned that both our hosts had escaped to a better life. Luis made it to Mexico. After many adventures, Bernardo ended up in my house in King's Cross, where he became a kind of mascot, a little bit of Caribbean sunshine at my Friday night parties. I rescued him from Naim's clutches. But Bernardo doesn't owe me anything. Still hot-blooded and insatiable, he's repaid me many times.

Gradually The Cally became my main source for – to use an Alan Jones term – 'maintenance sex'. I no longer wished to shove it up Naim, and he relieved me of the responsibility. But we remained friends. It was Naim who called me at 9am on 31st August, 1997 to tell me that Princess Diana was dead. For some years Naim, John Lawrence, Anthony Blampied and I also travelled all over London to watch Hindi movies. John and Anthony had the hots for a Bollywood actress named Tabu, and we all loved the musical numbers, which sometimes involved hundreds of dancers. Because the films had no subtitles, Naim gave us a running commentary. 'I feel as though I've dreamed the whole evening,' Anthony told me after our first outing. He and John never asked how Naim and I met. But I think they suspected it wasn't at the rugby club.

III

"It seems Friday night is the time people are in the mood."
~ Diary entry, 19th June, 1998, aged 50 ~

The phrase that explains why I became a drug dealer in 1998 is *fin de siècle*. When we look back to the end of the 19th century we think perhaps first and foremost of toffs drinking champagne out of chorus girls' slippers while back at home their wives are draining laudanum bottles. Perhaps because of fear of the unknown 20th century ahead, everyone was going a little bit crazy. It's now possible to look back to the end of the 20th century and see that we were behaving in a similar fashion.

The attitude to mind-expanding substances had become vastly different from 1971 when, as a result of the hedonism of the 1960s, the Misuse of Drugs Act was passed by the Conservative government to general approval. By 1998, however, the news that young bucks such as Prince Harry and the Home Secretary Jack Straw's son, William, smoked weed was greeted with amusement. The biggest backlash against Conservative drugs policy came as a result of Shadow Home Secretary Ann Widdecombe's announcement at the Conservative Party Conference in 2000 that Tories intended to adopt a 'zero tolerance' approach to cannabis and fine everyone £100 for possession.

First Peter Williams, national secretary of the Police Superintendents' Association, responded, 'We would not support this proposal.'[80] Then the press ridiculed Widdecombe. 'The proposal is flat-out absurd,' scoffed a *Guardian* editorial.[81] Tory leader William Hague buried the policy after seven shadow cabinet members admitted smoking dope in their youth. A MORI poll in *The Mail on Sunday* suggested that six out of ten thought that the personal use of cannabis should no longer be a criminal offence.[82] Twelve years later, Widdecombe, by then a TV entertainer, admitted that her zero tolerance intolerance was 'the biggest hash I've made out of something.'[83] Cocaine was never treated as light-heartedly as weed; but only the tabloid press thought that it conferred 'shame' on its user. For the first time in history public figures – two from the Parker Bowles family alone – were not at all ashamed to admit that they liked it. And Stephen Fry was not the only person to notice that cocaine was terribly popular. 'On some evenings, going from bar to club to party, it seems like everyone's

---

80   *Evening Standard,* 4th September, 2000
81   5th September, 2000
82   15th October, 2000
83   *Time Out,* 23-29th February, 2012

doing it,' wrote Toby Young.[84] 'I used to think drug users exaggerated how widespread the scale of abuse was to make themselves feel less guilty about the abuse they were inflicting upon themselves. But no. Everyone *is* doing it.' Young was certainly doing it and was banned from the Groucho club because of it. Columnist Julie Burchill's remark that she had 'put enough toot up my admittedly sizeable snout to stun the entire Colombian armed forces'[85] was widely quoted. There was more sympathy than reproach for celebrities encouraged to deal cocaine by the notorious *News of the World* reporter Mazher Mahmood. A jury told Judge Timothy Pontius that the law should have allowed them to acquit the 10th Earl of Hardwicke, victim of a sting in 1999. Jailing TV actor John Alford for nine months the same year, Judge Stephen Robbins stated that the sentence would have been longer had it not been for the newspaper's entrapment. (Later the unscrupulous and deceitful Mahmood tried and failed to entrap one of my clients.) Today, when it comes to shame and disgrace, it's not a couple of cokeheads that come to mind but the *News of the World* and Mahmood himself.

It was this *Zeitgeist* – and I mean not just the prevailing mood but the fact that, for the first time in my life, I had made contact with a big potential market – that convinced me to set up shop. Surveys at the time suggested I wasn't alone. More than a third of the readers who responded to a *Time Out* investigation[86] claimed to have dealt drugs. A survey conducted by *The Observer* found that 'close to ten per cent of the UK adult population (over 4 million adults) could be classified as drug dealers.'[87] When I wrote about my new profession (under a pseudonym), I said, 'Everyone's at it now. There's no "them and us" any more. It's the right time to be doing this game.'[88] (The features editor, who commissioned this interview, was another of my clients.)

And so we descend from here onwards into the murky world of pseudonyms and disguised identifying features that will be our milieu for the remainder of this section. Except that I never once found the world murky. 'I love the exciting illegality,' I wrote early on. I also loved the glamour, the introductions to jet setters, the invitations to high society functions. But most of all I loved the parties, which we never planned, but which became major events in our social calendar. As the trend began to develop, I referred to these get-togethers as salons because they were spent discussing the arts, religion and politics into the early hours. I saw myself in the tradition of Lady Ottoline Morrell with a bit of Elsa Maxwell and Alma Cogan thrown in.

---

84   *The Modern Review,* August-September, 1994
85   *The Guardian,* 6th June, 2000
86   12th-19th April, 2000
87   21st April, 2002
88   *Scene,* Christmas, 1999

I was once again in my element, the leader of the gang, although I preferred barrister Daniel's description, 'the paterfamilias of a very happy family'.

Although later I used other sources for acid, speed and ketamine, my main supplier for almost the whole time I was in business was the sullen and unfulfilled Casey. We found him through his brother, a drinking pal of Ricky's. Casey had a failed marriage behind him and was in the process of failing to make anything of his legitimate career. I'm fairly sure that, to compensate, he had his snout in the trough a little too often; at any rate, eventually he lost most of his teeth. This is par for the course for the serious cocaine addict as DJ Fat Tony will confirm.

Initially we never socialised with Casey. It was always strictly business, with few pleasantries, and most of the time in Casey's flat was spent waiting while he counted our cash. In ten years he had had only one brush with the law. The police turned up with a search warrant, but not for drugs, and so the stash went undetected. But Casey didn't want any more of that mallarkey and became angry if buyers didn't adhere to his code words on the telephone. If we wanted to know if he had cocaine in stock, we had to ask if the wedding photos had come back. My recollection is that this derived from the Billy Idol song 'White Wedding'. Geddit? One of the first things Casey told me was that he was reliable. And he was. This, as we've established, was an extreme rarity in our line of business. So I stuck with the devil I knew. Gradually I got used to Casey's grumpy old drug dealer ways and he came to trust me. In the 21st century we were to embark on a very different business together, one that I can't elaborate on. For now.

Casey's first batch of coke was tried out at my Radio London friend Zena's dinner party. There were some other Radio London cronies present. They weren't used to such quality. The evening was a wild success; I was recommended left, right and centre; and this is why I was soon virtually By Appointment at Broadcasting House. But to begin at the beginning: Friday, 13th February was a relatively quiet night that gave no hint of what was to come. Kevin, a new friend who was later to become a lively and informative broadcaster, came round to pick up supplies for a dance party and then invited me to it. It was held in a place I knew well, the former pumping station we'd used for my film *The Errand*.

I wasn't to have another Friday to myself for the next five years.

Back in my youth the tag-line of the TV pop show, *Ready, Steady, Go!* broadcast on Friday evening, was 'the weekend starts here'. Published nearly forty years later, a series in the *Evening Standard* entitled 'Drugs in London' brought that catch-phrase back to me. Describing a smartly-dressed drug dealer with a psychology degree from the University of London, the writer went on to reveal that 'Friday evening is peak trade time, when his young, professional clientele call to buy the relatively cheap but high quality [drugs] they need to keep them going through the night.'[89]

By the end of 1999 I had been introduced to almost all the colourful characters who would form the hub of my new social circle. Ricky's barrister friend Daniel brought others from the legal profession and, because many lawyers are frustrated actors, they became the glitterball around which my Friday night parties cavorted. The genuine theatricals – actors, producers, directors, designers – had to struggle to compete. Others in the arty corner of the room included my radio crowd plus journalists, painters, dancers and a clown. There was also a large medical section; several manual labourers including electricians, carpenters, decorators and plumbers; an astro-physicist; teachers, magistrates and social workers. People came from all over the world, but there was a particularly large South American contingent. And of course the sex trade was represented. I had several male escorts among my regulars and they sent their clients along too. I didn't count the guests in and out. 'More than three hundred' is an estimate. Generally, regardless of our individual backgrounds or interests, the marching powder made us one. There were perhaps a dozen individuals I didn't like. They happened to be my fair-weather friends as well. When I stopped dealing, they stopped contacting me. The vast majority of my guests are still my friends today. Or at least they were before I wrote this book.

Early on in 1998, before the parties got going, Ken the clown brought round his friend Helen, a psychiatrist. I nearly turned straight for her. This is because she is irresistible – attractive, intelligent, witty, warm-hearted. She arrived in my life with a bottle of wine. There was music. I had just acquired my first CD player. We talked late into the night. I'll explain later why nothing was consummated. But because it wasn't, Helen embarked on a succession of flings with fellow partygoers. The first was Daniel, feckless but charming. The second was Grant, an arrogant Kiwi who certainly would be part of my Dirty Dozen. After a particularly long night listening to Grant talking, talking, talking, I nearly said, 'What are you on?' but realised I knew what he was on because I'd sold it to him. Helen soon realised she'd backed another loser, but then upped and married Grant's mate Jason, her worst choice to date.

Miranda, who I met at the Torture Garden, was a black-garbed beatnik with all the artistic pretension, existential angst, and taste for narcotics that one associates with Greenwich Village in the 1950s. She was the kind of alien creature I cultivated and I found her fearfully exciting. I remember that she

---

89   10th April, 2001

once drawled to me, 'Ninety per cent of your clients seem to be gay and even the ten per cent who aren't are.' The nail had been hit squarely on the head. For a gay man such as myself, interested in instant gratification, the pool was sizeable. By mutual consent some of my clients climbed the additional flights to my bedroom. I have the fondest memories of them. When I first knew him, solicitor Joe looked as eager and bright-eyed as the new office boy. I couldn't wait to help him out of his perfectly tailored suit. After a brush with death I'll detail later, Joe reinvented himself as a barrel-chested muscleman, who won sashes for looking good in a harness. As David Dan Joe he's naked and wearing a cock ring in *Age of Consent,* a documentary about one of his favourite leather bars.

The nearest I came to a relationship was with stage manager Burt, who looked like a teddy bear and was just as lovable, even though, as Burt was quick to point out, love was not on the cards. 'Burt felt it necessary to tell me he didn't love me,' I wrote. 'I told him this didn't bother me in the slightest. Then we had sex.' In 2002 Burt took me to his favourite holiday resort on Gran Canaria and introduced me to the Yumbo Centre, an imbroglio of drinking dens, drag shows and sticky-floor sex bars that I dubbed Dante's Gay Inferno.

At first Ricky was in charge of what we called The Factory – the weighing and wrapping of coke; the counting of pills; the carving with a hot knife of the cannabis resin – but, as business increased, he had to teach me the tricks of the trade. We tried to develop our own code words. But there was no cohesion and everything became hopelessly confused. One code was inspired by animals. According to this system cocaine = camels, grass = giraffes, acid = antelopes, and so forth. But often when I answered the telephone I was so incapacitated that I couldn't remember which animal was which. Eventually I told callers to ask, 'Is the zoo open?' If the answer was yes, they would have to pop round and hope that what they wanted was in stock.

Simultaneously a quite separate code developed because Miranda and her friends were in a trade that preferred colour co-ordination whereby cocaine = white, grass = green and pills for some reason = yellow. The confusion didn't end there. Julian Clary and his pals referred to cocaine as 'executive'; Casey's circle called grass 'reggae'; and a cadre of West End Wendys called everything 'the loveliness.' (Stephen Fry remembers references to coffee at 60p a jar.) This druggy game-playing developed from the fear that 'someone' tapped phones. It didn't occur to us that anyone tapping my phone on a Friday evening and listening to our insane conversations about antelopes and green T-shirts would have been round to my house like Usain Bolt.

Ricky was also able to look after the store, either when I went off to strange places – Alabama, Nebraska, Malta – to see Farndale Avenue productions, or to participate in Fringe shows. As regards the latter, there were a couple of real stinkers in 1998. The first was a stage adaptation of Michael Armstrong's unproduced horror film *The Curse of Tittikhamon* in which I played the narrator. It was meant to be funny, but very few people found it so, and the critics were vicious. '*The Curse of Tittikhamon* must go down as one of the most ineptly executed, ill-conceived, visually hideous efforts at entertainment in the history of human endeavour,' wrote Robert Lloyd Parry in the *Hampstead and Highgate Express*.[90] But I liked Michael and the company and, after I'd started inserting ad-libs, I quite enjoyed myself.

I can't say the same for my next stage appearance, the most miserable of my life. Because I was able to use British Sign Language I was cast in an impenetrable bi-lingual mess called *A Minute of Silence*. I knew this play was in trouble during rehearsals when actors began rolling in hours late or not turning up at all. Two walked out before the opening and I wish I had too. From then onwards we played to handfuls of friends and relatives and every Friday I deeply resented having to tear myself away from the best party in town in order to work on a piece of junk that even the cast – let alone the audiences – hated.

Every night I would drive to the theatre praying that it had been hit by a comet. On one occasion I arrived to find the rest of the company coming out of the auditorium waving and smiling at me. 'We don't have to do it!' they exclaimed with glee. The performance had been cancelled because of poor bookings and we went into the pub downstairs to celebrate. I pondered this ridiculous situation. Here I was dreading doing the work I loved. (But within months I was back on stage in a very interesting adaptation of a Philip K. Dick novel and the agony of *A Minute of Silence* was instantly forgotten. Show biz is like that.)

Because Ricky had been first good company, then a perfect flatmate, and finally a popular party host ('Peter flirted outrageously with Ricky,' I recorded, 'but then everybody loves him'), I was very sorry when I had to ask him to pack his bags. He had begun to take what I considered the piss. As far as his sexuality was concerned, he made a decisive choice when he went to his favourite gay club, Heaven, and brought home a woman. Fair enough. But within days and without a word to me he invited her to share his room, which I thought was a bit of a cheek. Then, when the merchandise began disappearing, I gave him his marching orders. He accepted them with equanimity and moved with his girlfriend (later to be his wife) into a flat in nearby Pentonville Road. But for some months afterwards we continued to co-host the parties.

I had been toying with the idea of a second flatmate; but now, because of Ricky's imminent departure, there was the possibility, as long they were both sympathetic to my alternative lifestyle, of having not one but two new tenants. Kevin seemed interested in one room, but changed his mind 'because of a fear of wild animals.' He recommended and I accepted his friend Paula, whose Pam Ayres appearance belied her party girl alter ego. She had similarly wild friends and before long we were clubbing together. When I gave the second room to Helen's friend Trev, a psychiatric nurse, I never could have imagined how much fat I was adding to the fire. Trev was a rubber-legged soulboy speed freak with a hard-as-nails girlfriend and a sexual imagination that put him in Kenneth Tynan's league. I've always regretted that a journalist has never asked me, 'Where's the most unusual place you've had sex?' because I would be able to reply, 'Driving through Camden Town while Trev, wearing Paula's knickers, gave me a blow job.'

Here are some more made-up names that will figure prominently in the remaining chapters. I think the appropriate phrase is: 'You know who you are.' Daniel's colleague, Toby, the most flamboyant of the legal eagles, was an imposing presence who often argued and over-indulged until he had to be carried home. He was heading, alas, for a succession of the breakdowns that go hand-in-hand with being the life and soul of the party. Brett is a sinewy American writer I met many years ago in the British Film Institute library, whose caustic wit brings to mind a gay, male Dorothy Parker; but instead of the Algonquin hotel, Brett's milieu was the same fetish club frequented by David Dan Joe. Brett once returned after a Friday party to collect a 'disgusting, smelly jacket' he had forgotten. 'My sex life depends on it,' he declared.

Tadzio is a highly erudite and distinguished-looking East European, who worked for the BBC World Service and was my main source for the 'editor's razor blades with a protective bar on top,'[91] which Stephen Fry used to steal from sound studios. Like Brett, Tadzio enjoyed a hair-raising sex life that involved slings and dildos; but you never would have guessed, etc. Duncan is a similarly intelligent, multi-talented Glaswegian drop-out, stick-thin because of the ravages of AIDS, but absolutely indomitable. Tadzio interviewed me for the World Service and I interviewed Duncan about his previous careers, which included porn shop manager and

---

91   *More Fool Me* (London: Michael Joseph, 2014)

dominatrix's assistant. (By the turn of the century almost all my legitimate work was connected in some way with people to whom I sold drugs. Cocaine opened up a whole new world of work opportunities.)

There were also several examples of spirited, sociable women with pleasant enough but stolid husbands, not an unusual combination in a predominantly gay environment. Helen's friend, Caroline, was an immensely upbeat Midlands lass married to pensive Australian Shane. Helen, Caroline and Miranda (the latter needed chemical enhancement to help her over her split with Carl) would often be seen locked in earnest feminist conversation. They called themselves, with post-modern irony, Charlie's Angels. Former Farndale lady Frances was by now hitched to Tunde, an attractive but unambitious Nigerian handyman, useful because he could fix the stereo and always brought a supply of McDonald's drinking straws, cf Fry, page 99. The most interesting couple by far was Tom and Betsy, who were in the process of establishing themselves in the new digital art scene of which they are now leading lights. I didn't know what she saw in him; but I expect he was hot stuff in the sack.

By the summer of 1998 Friday was the busiest day of my week; or, as some of my older radio chums put it, Friday night was music night. I had to be up at the crack to drive to Sainsbury's for crates of beer and wine and bags of nuts and crisps (I earned my reputation as the perfect host); then I had to whip around the living room with the Hoover and a damp Spontex because sometimes the first guest arrived at 11am. Ricky and I began putting in bigger and bigger orders with Casey; but occasionally we would still run dry, and then there was panic in The Factory, followed by an onslaught of visitors. Ricky decided that the business had expanded sufficiently for us to acquire mobile phones.

These devices were not new. I remember making my first call to a cellular phone in 1987. I called Nigel Finch's cameraman Mike Southon, who informed me that he was on the beach. He had bought his phone for £1,450. In 1998 I rented mine for £25 per month and was allowed free calls on weekday evenings. From then onwards my services were available seven days a week. I could make deliveries at all hours of the day and night and let callers know when I would be at home for visitors. 'It's just as well my writing career is over,' I wrote in August. 'Every minute now seems to be taken up with running the new business.'

Utterly fearless, I drove around the West End with a Cuban cigar box, stuffed with plain, sealed envelopes, on the passenger seat. A typical evening might begin at Broadcasting House, where I would be ushered into a studio and complete the transaction while the DJ was spinning a disc. Then I might head to Shaftesbury Avenue, first to a swanky bar called Teatro, teeming with West End producers to whom I would register my presence and then wait for them to join me in the toilet. After a swift tour of stage doors in the vicinity, I would often end up at L'Odeon, a smart new restaurant in Regent Street, where I had several clients including Ginny, a glamorous young Kiwi, who tried all kinds of jobs before becoming prominent in the literary trade. My dealings at this high-class joint required the kind of subterfuge we associate with espionage. I'll describe them in full in a later chapter because in 2000 they were re-enacted for a TV documentary.

My clientele grew ever more celebrated; but it would be pointless to dwell on this because there is so little I can say. My first famous client was an Italian movie actress I thought I might be able to name. But I have scoured the Internet and, although there are references to her 'openness toward drug use', nowhere does she admit to buying the stuff. Therefore her secret is safe with me. In *More Fool Me* Mr Fry talks about 'SWSRN' (Someone Who Shall Remain Nameless), who had a white substance visible in his nostrils while he was appearing with Stephen on the radio programme *Loose Ends*. Stephen's description of the man matches that of another of my celebrity clients, the show's presenter Ned Sherrin. I can write about him because he's dead. I always enjoyed going to meet Ned. He was one of my most senior clients, well over 60, but, when he opened the door to me, his lovely smile lit up his whole face and he was always amusingly indiscreet about his latest Latino rent boy, who would either be sprawled on the sofa or who would arrive just after me.

My first client who turned out to be famous was Alexander McQueen. I had no idea who he was. To me he was just a geezer who seemed to live quite well. He too was a charmer. After I'd discovered that he was the head designer at Givenchy, Lee (that's how I knew him) invited me to a warehouse in Victoria to see his Spring/Summer 1999 collection. This was the show in which a model in a white dress stood between two robotic arms, which rose and twisted menacingly and then sprayed the dress with colour. It was a *coup de théâtre*. Lee took a bow with two of his dogs. He never seemed depressed when I knew him; but subsequently this became a problem. In 2010 I had to write his obituary.[92] I did not mention our connection.

Although, as you may be able to tell, I was completely caught up in the excitement of the business, I was well aware that it had a seamier side. Every so often an outsider would witness the unedifying inner workings of my trade and be appalled. Jonathan Rigby, author of *English Gothic*, a book to which I contributed, happened to deliver my copy of it on a Friday and surveyed the activity with great disapproval. Maurizio, an Italian-Australian, who stayed with me quite regularly, also didn't like the comings and goings. I was once performing oral sex on him in the kitchen when the door bell rang. He's one of the many men who could now be Mrs McGillivray if I hadn't been a drug pedlar. On one occasion he returned to Australia, but called me from Bangkok to tell me he was coming back to London because I was the one for him. Maurizio was a little fireball and I was very happy to see him again. But after three weeks of Friday nights he decided he was mistaken and left for good with the words, 'I don't like the zoo.'

The crunch came at Erika Poole's party at the end of the year, by which time my new career was the talk of the town. I developed a migraine and lay down in a bedroom, where I was visited by a succession of friends – Julian, Janet, Marge, and others – who warned me of the terrible consequences of what I was doing and told me that I must stop at once. Julian went so far as to say that he wouldn't work with me again unless I did. He then locked himself in the toilet to snort the Charlie I'd just sold him. When I called him a hypocrite he accepted my criticism but maintained that in becoming a dealer I had crossed the line.

'I made no commitment to anyone but knew what I intended to do in future: to carry on but keep it much more secret. I don't want to lose the friendship of people I've known for so long and I appreciate their concern. It must appear as though I'm going into a downward spiral, etc. But equally I've had a marvellous year and I love all my new friends. I really resent the proper jobs that keep me away from the new business'

An actor who had played Gordon in *Farndale Avenue* plays asked if I had space in my house for a friend, an Irish musician named Brendan. He had the look of a leprechaun, even down to the ginger whiskers, and the first time I met him he said, 'Top of the morning to you!' How could I resist? (I should have done; but that's a story for the next chapter.) I cleared out another room and Brendan became my third tenant. My house was becoming very lively indeed, the nerve centre of an increasingly profitable cottage industry. The build-up to the holiday season was manic and resulted in the biggest turnover of the year. By 30th December I was cleaned out and took a night off to attend Shane and Caroline's New Year's Eve party.

'A limitless supply of drugs was passed around all night. I had my first taste of absinth, recently available in this country after being banned for eighty years. I noticed it on sale in King's Cross recently at £5 a shot. Apparently a few glasses cause hallucinations. Kisses at midnight. Caroline almost went out of her head on her E so I thought I'd better have only half of mine. I made my excuses at 3am.'

'When I got home Trev was slumped in front of the TV, sound asleep with an empty whiskey bottle in his hand. I couldn't rouse him. I took a valium and passed out. An incredible, unpredictable year. I can't imagine what 1999 might bring.'

I doubt if anyone could have imagined the extent of the unruliness that would occur during the countdown to Millennium Eve.

IV

"There was a void in the centre of her own life,
which she filled with these friends and it made her feel complete."
~ Rachel Johnson on Ottoline Morrell ~

1999 was a year of Fridays, hitherto unprecedented and never to be repeated. The descriptions of them in my diary, written while they were happening, now appear to me to be so vivid that paraphrase would lessen their impact. Therefore I now present many of these entries almost unedited. This, the most intense period of my entire life, began in December, 1998.

Thursday, 3rd December Helen came round to report that she's now knobbing Grant's friend Jason, much more suitable for her purposes, she says. She's off to Bristol with him tomorrow. Really, she's worse than me.

Friday, 11th December Helen phoned to tell me she's engaged to Jason. He proposed on Tuesday and she accepted immediately. She may chuck in everything and go with him to NZ in the New Year. What can one say to something like this? They've only known each other three and a half weeks.

Sunday, 20th December Helen brought Jason round to meet me. He told me he has no money, no work and no prospects because he's alienated everyone with whom he's worked. I know Helen has a self-destructive streak; but this is ridiculous.

Monday, 4th January I went very uncertainly to my first massage lesson at Islington College. We were given some literature to read, then it was down to business. The tables were brought out and tutor Carlyn demonstrated six basics of Swedish massage on a female student who's been here since last year. She stripped above the waist although there was a lot of 'towel technique', essential for preserving modesty and 'professionalism'. We'll learn this next week. When Carlyn had finished, we had to divide into couples and massage each other's backs, using the six Swedish strokes. It was remarkable how everyone got their kit off without a murmur. I suppose, however, that those enrolling on this kind of course must realise the implications. Enjoyed myself. Looking forward to next week. If I do well, I'll move on to the next level in April.

Friday, 8th January Drove to Southwark Register Office for Helen and Jason's wedding. There was a turnout of maybe ten, mostly Antipodean men.

Helen had hired a red velvet dress and fur stole; but some of the blokes came in work clothes. The ceremony was brief. We took pics and threw confetti. We drove to Helen's flat, where we had champagne. The bonhomie was forced. Cards on the table: I'm afraid this isn't going to work out. I had to leave to host the usual evening. When I arrived Brendan was entertaining Daniel. Trev flew in and out before Miranda arrived. They've been having a fling and this isn't working out either. Casey's friend, Giovanna, arrived with her badly-behaved 7-year-old, Gervaise. She played a tape of songs she's recorded. They're quite unremarkable and I told her I loved them. Giovanna's a casebook flaky rock chick. Miranda sat stunned while Gervaise ran riot. They left not a moment too soon.

Friday, 15th January I got home at 3pm and the Friday thing got going. Daniel came, then Toby, then we had to cool it while the phone engineer did his stuff. Ricky took Brendan off somewhere to get him drunk. At the end of the night only Trev and Miranda were left. They started getting on very well again and, not wanting to be a gooseberry, I beat a retreat.

Friday, 22nd January People were in and out quite sharpish, but then began to stay. Helen told me all the things about Jason that irritate her. They're mostly to do with his indolence. She claims that the fact she's remaining calm about this means that she's giving the relationship a better chance. Ginny came round with two friends, Manuel and Nasreen. He's a barman, she's an economist, and they're both darkly beautiful, like Brazilian *novela* actors. We got on well and suddenly it was nearly 3am again.

Friday, 29th January Last night I went to bed, leaving Ginny and Daniel at it. I heard the front door slam at 4.30am. Today Toby phoned me early, wondering what had happened here. Daniel didn't go into work today and someone had to cover for him. Tonight Toby came round and we discussed Daniel. He's taken two days off work this week and people are beginning to suspect. Miranda was here next and she re-dyed Trev's hair blond. Naim came round with a French essay he wants me to type out. He stayed a little while, very perplexed by the company. Miranda and Trev went off to bed. I turned in at 2.30.

Friday, 5th February I quickly bought booze and snacks and hurried home for a momentous evening. Visitors came in two waves and included [well-known film star] and his new boyfriend. They seemed a bit alarmed by the festivity and didn't stay long. During the early hours of the morning, Trev kept going to bed and then reappearing. I didn't think anything of it. Then, when I was bedding down around 3.30am, he came into my room and said, 'I'd really like to suck your cock.' Despite the psychic powers I've developed in this house,

I was not prepared for that one. He claims he's never kissed a man before, let alone had sex. *Considering that* (emphasis mine), he's very good at giving a BJ. He also wanted me to come in his mouth, but I said no. (I haven't done that since 1983.) But I shot a load over his chest. He has a very nice body; but I don't fancy him at all. At 5.30am he got on his bike and rode into the night.

Sunday, 7th February Trev returned. I wondered how he would behave regarding Friday. Never in a million years would I have predicted that he'd get into Paula's room *through the window*, steal her clothes, dress up in them and then ask me to treat him as my slave before fucking him. Where is all this coming from? The drag was a complete turn-off. I suggested he strip so I could give him a massage. I then gave him what he wanted, using my entire repertoire of positions. During this noisy business, I heard the other tenants leaving the house one by one. I'm not sure whether I should draw any significance from this.

Monday, 8th February Alan Jones came round and made an outrageous play for Brendan. Considering he keeps telling everyone he's straight, Brendan was very receptive. 'I think that's in the bag,' Alan confided as he left. This house is incredible!

Tuesday, 9th February When I got up at 6.30am Kicius was obviously unwell and didn't want to eat. But he was still able to totter around and stagger up the stairs. Later he had a piss on the bathroom floor. I made plans to take him back to the vet tomorrow morning. But when I got home tonight, I found him hiding under my desk, twitching. I knew the end had come. I phoned an emergency veterinary service. I lifted Kicius into the pet carrier and he made his last sound, a pitiful mew. He never liked this box and I wish I'd taken him to his death in something else. It was a long drive to Finchley and all the way I could hear Kicius having fits. As soon as the vet saw him, she said, 'He's dying.' I cried quite a lot because 19 years is a long time. I stayed with him while the vet stuck in the needle. He went very quickly. I drove home alone. I hoped somebody would be up so I could talk. But they'd all gone to bed. I quickly got rid of the feeding bowls and then had three glasses of Cinzano.

Friday, 12th February I set up shop for Ricky, holding the fort tonight while I attended a meeting of a group that goes down abandoned tube stations. Present were about a hundred men, all looking like child molesters, and two women. When I got home, Ricky said it had been a quiet evening. It certainly livened up. At 2.30am I'd had enough; but the party was still in full swing and there must have been a dozen still at it.

Friday, 19th February Trev slunk into my room early this morning and got down to it again. He was wearing more of Paula's underwear. I told him this can't go on. She's going to find out. The sex put me somewhat behind for the rest of the day. I'd just tidied the living room when Genevieve came round with a light lunch. She's preparing herself for the death of her mother, who seems to be in a similar state to Kicius, even down to pissing on the floor. While she was here, Alan and Brett arrived. I had to clear everyone out in order to rush to Sainsbury's for supplies. As soon as I returned there was a steady stream of guests. At about 11pm Giovanna arrived in a terrible state. I had warned the others what she was like; but this is the worst I've seen her. She was drunk, slurring her words, singing her songs. She has a concert next month. We're almost tempted to go. It could be quite an experience. Finally Ginny came at midnight with a sad story about getting mugged at knifepoint by two junkies near Hatton Garden. She gave them £60 and a packet of fags.

Thursday, 25th February Trev was acting strangely and I knew what he was after. I suggested a scenario I thought he'd like. It was all about forcing him to do everything. He played along very well. I've never done anything like this before, but I could easily get into it. It's like acting in a porn film, something I think I'd have been very good at. Trev was so excited, he stayed in my bed all night for the first time.

Friday, 26th February I bought two CDs, 'Carnival of the Animals' and 'Let Me Show You' by Camisra, which is basically two notes, repeated for three minutes. I know of no one else with such catholic musical taste. When I got home Ricky said he'd hosted a busy evening. The visitors had included Grant, who'd described Helen's husband Jason as 'a psychopath from way back.' The partygoers were very wired by the time I joined them.

Sunday, 7th March Several of us went to the King's Head in Fulham, where Giovanna was performing with her band. The support was Love Spuds, young punks who sang, 'Shave Your Muff.' Then on came Giovanna, looking sexy in satin and a feather boa. She was exactly the same as she is in my living room, acting up the rock vamp. Her music is hard to categorise, but I'd call it ambient crap. Every so often it seemed as though a tune might emerge. I think it did in their last number, something about 'When you left me, I went crazy.' The audience responded with little more than curiosity. I escaped at 11.30pm assuring everyone that I'd had a great evening.

Friday, 12th March Ricky arrived at lunchtime and we got the assembly line going in the nick of time before the onslaught began. After everyone had gone, Trev came home, had a shower, and then asked me, 'Do you want your cock sucked?' We had a twenty minute session before Miranda arrived. They sat downstairs, canoodling in the candlelight, while I got my new minidisc player working.

Friday, 19th March Ricky was here early to arrange his take-over of tonight's salon. Alan arrived at 11.30 for our trip to the Bradford Film Festival. I told him I was going to dress up and insisted that he did too. He said, 'It's only Bradford,' but I said he couldn't go on stage in jeans. In Bradford we got dragged up as I required and then walked to the Priestley Centre, very full for the all-night horror show. Alan and I went into a dressing room and snorted a couple of lines to get us hyped up for our interview. Our chat got a few laughs. I checked the presentation of *Frightmare*. It was being shown on a VHS tape obtained that afternoon from HMV. It really didn't look very good. Afterwards, when a couple of fans came up to me, Alan seized his opportunity to pounce on a 20-year-old blond he'd spotted earlier. Within minutes he'd got a phone number and an email address. 'I just like sex,' he protested as we left the theatre around 1.30am.

Saturday, 20th March We got back to the house at around 12.30pm. Going down to the basement was like descending into the Underworld. The curtains were still drawn; the room was devastated. Trev, Miranda and Brendan looked terrible, sallow with sunken eyes. They hadn't been to bed. Last night's affair was riotous with a crowd of celebs going wild until 7am. Brendan said it was the best yet. He'd met [Radio 1 DJ], [character actor often on TV] and [TV presenter]. I'll have to get further details from Ricky. Even my study was wrecked, with tell-tale signs on every flat surface and the clock missing.

Friday, 26th March Before the hordes descended I asked Trev to dye my hair. I permed it in 1978, but it's never been dyed successfully. I thought it might be now or never because very soon I won't have any hair left to dye. Trev covered my scalp in peroxide paste and then put a plastic shopping bag over my head for fifteen minutes. The bag came off and, when I looked in the mirror, it was a great surprise to see myself blond. We shampooed and dried it. I liked the look very much. It didn't make me look like a pathetic old queen as I thought it might. The first guests to arrive were two of the Chileans – Max and Aquiles – who didn't notice that my hair was a different colour.

Wednesday, 14th April First day of the new massage course. Tutor Carlyn gave a long talk on cells. It was quite interesting, but I sensed that most people were bored. They don't know they're born. If I'd had a teacher like Carlyn when

I was at school, I'd certainly have learned more. She's like a stand-up comic on speed. We paired off. I was with a nice black lady, Lydia. She was most impressed with my massage, as well she might be. I'm way ahead of the rest of the class and hope to remain so. Before next Tuesday we have to perform four back massages and write them up.

Friday, 16th April Helen sent a letter from New Zealand ('I still feel like his girlfriend...I'm gobsmacked by how one can be talked at!!') Brendan has got three friends staying here, a bit of a liberty as he hasn't paid rent since January. One of them took his first E, then asked to borrow my porn catalogues and disappeared to have a wank. By the time Ginny got here, he was hot to trot and ended up leaving with her.

Thursday, 22nd April Errol, an actor with whom I had a one afternoon stand in 1980, is now a restaurateur. I noticed him on an episode of Channel 4's *Electric Avenue,* trying to open a new eaterie. His wife was seen quite a lot and they were said to be celebrating their 25th wedding anniversary. Well, well. Then Trev got all fired up watching a football match and demanded sex. Eventually I said yes; but I think I'm being used.

Friday, 30th April The Friday callers began arriving very early. Brett tells me he's lost his acid connection. Police have made several arrests. Trev came home and hung around until sozzled. [Theatre producer] brought a Kiwi friend, Nicki, who wanted a massage immediately so I took her upstairs and gave her one. Naim phoned to say he had been in Old Compton Street ten minutes before a bomb exploded at the Admiral Duncan. We switched on the TV and for the rest of the evening we watched the developing situation. The Brixton and Brick Lane bombs were shocking, but this was Soho, an area I know like the back of my hand. There were a lot of phone calls from people wanting to check that I hadn't been in Soho and was the party still happening? The number of injured and two [later three] deaths make this the worst outrage yet. Which community will be hit next? Golders Green? Chinatown? Late arrivals included [film producer] and [production designer] who had been in Soho and heard the explosion. The area had been cordoned off immediately by police, and they had only just managed to escape. I believe the last guest was solicitor Winston. Trev started chatting him up. I bid my farewells at midnight. I think I heard the door slam for the last time around 4am and assumed everyone had gone. On the contrary Winston was in bed with Trev. At 5.30am Winston came into my room. He grumbled that Trev was too small and he wanted a bigger cock. I said no. Winston was very insistent and suggested getting Trev out of bed to watch. I still said no.

Saturday, 1st May I was cleaning up when Trev appeared, apparently mortified. Then Winston appeared and claimed he couldn't remember anything that happened last night. I found that hard to believe, but then again I can remember hardly anything about My Night with Nigel. I went to the Adelphi to deliver to [two of the cast of *Chicago*]. Then I went to look at Soho. Londoners had reverted to Blitz mode. They were determined a bomb wasn't going to make any difference to their Saturday night out. I stood at the Dean Street/Old Compton Street junction and saw the top of the Admiral Duncan beyond a blue tarpaulin that had been strung across the road. A big crowd had gathered here. Many were laying flowers against the police barricade. I very much agreed with the sentiments expressed by one mourner: 'Incidents such as this serve only to make people more sympathetic to the struggle of minority groups, turning the perpetrators into a minority themselves.' The atmosphere was very solemn and respectful and a shouty old drunk was told to shut up. Back here Nasreen and Manuel called round. Then Giovanna, drunk again, joined us mercifully briefly. Brendan says he's moving back to Dublin. It hasn't worked out here. The poor lad is going through a confused stage. He's not having any luck with women and can't deny the thoughts he's had about men. After two bottles of wine and three lines, he seemed up for anything. As if he sensed this, Trev came prowling around. But I advised Brendan that he wasn't ready for Trev.

Friday, 7th May By the time [theatrical agent] had left, the cupboard was virtually bare. I thought I'd have time to go to Casey's and get back before the evening rush; but the Friday night traffic was terrible and by the time I got home there was a queue outside the door. The crowd included Ned Sherrin. How embarrassing for a man of his position. Paula says she's leaving next week. This is not a surprise. She's never liked Trev. Disturbingly, however, she claims she's also had things stolen from her room. Who's the thief?

Friday, 21st May Five massages in one day! But now I can cope very well. I did them all extremely well and, because I've learned the correct stance, I didn't feel exhausted at all. First client was Giovanna, who was late, so her session had to be curtailed when Naim arrived. No sooner was he dressed than Kjell arrived, followed by Daniel and Toby. While I was in the massage parlour [my bedroom], the phone rang off the hook. As soon as I'd returned the calls, the guests began to arrive. Frances and Tunde brought Dafydd. How long is it since I've seen him? The Whirl-Y-Gig? I didn't recognise him. He's put on an enormous amount of weight. Trev disappeared to go dancing in Derby and, when she found out he wasn't here, Miranda decided not to come. Just as I was clearing up, Paula arrived with Mr and Mrs Ricky in tow. I believe they're having a tète-à-tète downstairs right now. I decided many months ago that I'd start giving my profits to charity and today I made my first small donation, £100 to the Terrence Higgins Trust.

Saturday, 22ⁿᵈ May I heard Paula packing up this morning. She said she'd also lost a £200 watch. I didn't know what to say. Later I heard her driving off. I have a feeling I won't see her again. I phoned Ricky. It's even worse than I thought. She actually caught Trev in her room once. He made some feeble excuse. But I can't believe he's a thief. We reckon Brendan's friends took her CDs and jewellery. Naim brought Bernardo here. He managed to escape from Cuba and went to Spain, where he worked illegally until he was advised to come here and claim political asylum. He's moved in with Naim, who is supporting him. What a mess.

Friday 18ᵗʰ June An action-packed day. After discussions with Ricky, I paid Paula £500 hush money, a justifiable business expense, I feel. Helen phoned from Melbourne, where she's staying with Caroline and Shane. She escaped from Jason by putting together essentials secretly, hiding them in the garden, and then zooming off in a car. During this past week she's been very frightened by the possibility of violence. Jason is, as Grant maintained, a psychopath and he's been getting worse. Helen likened her experience to *Sleeping with the Enemy*. She should be back in London soon. I had to deliver to Zena. Lots of other Radio London folk there. I stayed on to indulge and Zena said we were the people she'd want with her on her last night on Earth. Touching. I got home at 2am to find [actor] on my doorstep. He's opened in this high-profile, druggy play at [theatre] and he's been getting a lot of coverage.

Sunday, 20ᵗʰ June I'm in shock. Brendan came round. He says he was drinking with a policeman friend, who said that he's been keeping an eye on a house in Keystone Crescent. Brendan asked, 'Which one?' and the cop replied 'Number 16.' It all sounded like a joke and yet all too plausible. Council workers have been at work in the Crescent, erecting a huge pole on which CCTV cameras will be mounted. Action had to be taken and I left a message on Ricky's machine.

Monday, 21ˢᵗ June I met Ricky. He wants out. I said perhaps we shouldn't panic. Firstly Brendan is a stereotypical Irish drunk and was even pissed yesterday when he was dropping his bombshell. Secondly we could cool it with the Friday nights for a while and I could deliver seven days a week. Ricky wouldn't hear of it. I had to devote the rest of the evening to Helen. She's had a very traumatic experience. A lot of what she said was very disturbing.

above: The boys are back in town.
With Jim Giddens, Los Angeles, 2011.

right: House of mortal sin.
Me and *Driller Killer* T-shirt, 1995.

below: His last hurrah.
Walter Zerlin Jnr. in Barcelona for the
Spanish premiere of *The Farndale/
Murder Mystery*, 1995.

left:
That's another story.
With David Warbeck at Britfest,
London, 1995.

below:
I've still got that shirt.
With Julian Clary on the roof of the
BBC's rehearsal rooms in Acton,
west London, 1996.

bottom left:
We called them Huntley and Palmer.
With Michael Bukowski (L) and
Peter Sernling (R) in *All Rise for
Julian Clary*, 1996.

bottom right:
Irreplaceable.
June Whitfield (1925-2018).

above: Deadly silence. With Paula Garfield and Ilan Dwek in *A Minute of Silence*, London, 1998.

below: Millennium night. This is how it started, around 4pm.

bottom left: It's one of yours! Whoever shot this picture for a 2000 *Guardian* feature on the drug trade used one of my wraps.

lower right: Son of Blondie. 1999 on Victorian streets later swept away for the St Pancras station development.

photo credit: Suzanne Grala

above: As Jaques (here and on the cover in Michael Ward's hat) with Stephen Glover as Amiens in *As You Like It*, London, 2004.

left: The stories she told me!
Anna Wing in *Wednesday*, 2005.

below: Another djinn, darling? L to R: Keith Claxton (director), me, Sam Hardy (cameraman), Ian Brown (make-up artist) in Marrakech for *In the Place of the Dead*, 2005.

top: Just ignore him.
Harry Fowler (L), Denis Norden (R) and me at
a typical Marianne Stone garden party, 2006.

centre right: Bit player 1. As the undertaker in
Tincture of Vervain, 2006.

bottom right: Double Oscar winner Luise Rainer
(1910-2014) wants nothing to do with me.

below: Bit player 2. My old mate Godfrey Kirby fixes
my radio mike for *In the Place of the Dead*, 2005.

Luise Rainer Knittel, London SW1W 9BE

*Thank you for sending your script.
Unfortunately did of no interest
to me.
Good luck to you!
LR*

top left: Freudian clip.
L to R: Clement and Jill Freud,
Charles Davies and Keith
Claxton in Southwold for
Tincture of Vervain, 2006.

top right: That yellow shirt again.
With Sarah Dunant at my 60th
birthday party, 2007.

above: I don't know him really.
With Paul O'Grady for a radio
programme, *Come to the
Cabaret,* 2010.

left: Tony's Hemp Corner was a
King's Cross institution. When
it closed, 2011, renovations
revealed a much older façade.

top:
Godfrey Kirby (1947-2017) worked on almost all my films. With Janet Sate, *A Kiss from Grandma*, 2011.

above:
Bad boys, two generations. Peter de Rome and Julian Clary in *Peter de Rome: Grandfather of Gay Porn*, 2012.

right:
It's all because of her. With Beth Porter, 2013.

below:
I may have had something to do with this.
L to R: Boy George, Julian Clary, Sarah Travis,
Philip Herbert at London's St James Theatre, 2014.

right:
It was all worth it. At BFI Southbank, 2014.

bottom:
Maybe I dreamed it all? The roof of the Scala from
my bedroom window in Keystone Crescent. Magic.

She knew on the wedding day something was wrong. The registry office bill hadn't been paid and Jason never bought her a ring. In fact he never spent a cent all the time they were in NZ. She cooked, she cleaned. He got angrier and more remote. She learned gradually about his mental state from friends. It sounds terrifying and it could have got a lot worse if she hadn't escaped.

Thursday, 24ᵗʰ June I met Ricky in the Ruby Lounge, He doesn't want to come to the house any more. I paid him off. I'm now in business on my own. I've told everyone that in future I'll come to them.

Friday, 25ᵗʰ June The first day of the new system. I did have one visitor, but it was Naim trying to foist Bernardo on to me. I went on my travels, first meeting Toby and the rest of the legal eagles at their favourite Soho bar The Box. Then I covered the rest of the West End. Every time I heard a police siren, my blood ran cold. When I got home I knew what would happen and I was right. Now we have the house to ourselves, Trev is becoming more demanding. Tonight he'd invented another elaborate fantasy but, as usual, it involved punishment. He told me he's convinced the workmen digging up our road are installing gear to tap our phone. Thank you, Trev. That's all I needed.

Friday, 2ⁿᵈ July I had to go back on the production line, but it's a lot of work for one person. I got bored and eventually gave up. I drove out to [theatrical agent's] pad in Leytonstone, an hour's journey in hot, sticky weather, which I'm afraid I can't repeat. Then on to David Dan Joe's place in Stoke Newington, another deadly drive due to a road accident in Finsbury Park. Then to Casey's. His girlfriend gave me vodka and tonic and smoked salmon, which perked me up somewhat. I was able to go on to Jackie in West Hampstead and Cameron, apparently 'entertaining' an older gentleman in Kilburn. Back here Ricky brought round a friend to upgrade my computer. He was anxious and plainly didn't want to be here. Toby didn't help matters by disobeying instructions and turning up just as Ricky was leaving.

Friday, 9ᵗʰ July Ricky and his friend came back to continue upgrading my computer. Ricky was grumpy, anxious to get away the whole time he was here. He's decided that he can't be in this house after 8pm. Afterwards I went to the Ruby Lounge to meet Peter, weirdo to whom I was introduced at [film director's] party. He's the only man I know who's admitted to fucking a Thai ladyboy. Unwisely I invited him back here to do the business. He began rambling on about being arrested this morning and then claimed he's the victim of a Masonic conspiracy. Suddenly he rushed to the toilet and vomited. I had to drive him home.

Friday 16th July Went to see [play] at [theatre]. It's terrific, the best I've seen this year. Afterwards [producer] took a selected few including myself to a dressing room for 'shampoo' as the luvvies now call it. Because I'm now supplying most of the cast and crew, I was the star attraction. When I extricated myself I had a lot of messages on my mobile. I wouldn't have been able to conduct the rest of my evening without this invention. As I neared home, around 2am, two vans full of police roared past me and pulled up at the end of Keystone Crescent. My heart skipped a beat. But then I saw a scuffle between cops and perhaps two guys. Later there was a rumour of another stabbing.

Friday, 30th July How interesting. I went back to that flat in Kilburn. It's not Cameron's. It belongs to the older gentleman, Dirk or Brad ('I have several names.') He had a different young man with him, Chris, who said he used to be the assistant editor of *Empire* magazine. What's going on here?

Friday, 6th August Janet Burgis of the BBFC booked me to talk to the examiners in September. No, I can't believe it myself. If only they knew. Out to cater to countless clients. Alberto, Camillo, Winston and [actor] came round here later because I can't be everywhere at once.

Sunday, 15th August 10.30am Peter was here again, trashed beyond belief. He claimed to have been partying for two nights without sleep. He made no sense whatever. I then closed the shop, parcelled up the stock and took it round to Frances and Tunde's, who are going to look after it while I'm in San Francisco. I don't want to spend two weeks in another country worrying about Trev and Peter using my house for coke-crazed drag balls.

Saturday, 4th September Did last-minute revision and then set off for my 10am massage exam. When I turned over my paper, I stared at it stunned for several minutes. It seemed I knew none of the answers. Eventually I answered everything.

Wednesday, 15th September Went to the BBFC to give my lecture to the examiners. Margaret Ford is still there; but everybody else is now younger than me. I told them what was going on in the world of porn. There wasn't a question I couldn't answer. I quoted an American academic, 'Censorship is belief that one's obscenity is the obscenity of all,' and afterwards an examiner asked me for it again because he wanted to write it down. I think the BBFC is changing and that there is a big development just around the corner. I came out feeling very cocky. Telling the censors what their job should be is for me the equivalent of the backwoods boy becoming president. I went to John Lewis and bought out the store. I want to get the house nice for visitors again. I'm seriously thinking of reviving the Friday salons. In a modest way. I miss them.

Friday, 17ᵗʰ September Ginny and her volatile friend, Jane arrived. We chatted over a bottle of wine and a gram just like old times. Then I had to go out for a drive. Trying to meet [producer] I got hopelessly snarled up in midnight Soho traffic. I must never drive into Soho on a Friday again.

Friday, 1ˢᵗ October Got up at 6.30am to get on the production line because I knew it was going to be a big day. Went to meet Chris, the guy I found at Dirk's flat in Kilburn. He's an editor of *Scene,* a fashion and lifestyle mag, and he wants to pay me £250 to write 800 words on zoo-keeping. He agreed to all my precautionary demands. Later [Radio 3 producer] rang, inviting me to talk about porn on *Nightwaves.* Yes, two jobs in one day and both from zoo visitors. I met Ricky at the Ruby Lounge and told him I'm going back to my old ways. It's been about four months since Brendan's revelation, which I now reckon was complete fantasy. 'I think you're right,' said Ricky. Back at the house people came round and stayed just like the old days. I hadn't got enough wine in. I'll make up for it on future Fridays.

Saturday, 9th October Kjell came for a massage. [Actress] phoned wanting supplies for a party to bid farewell to Chita Rivera, who's leaving *Chicago.* I said yes. Kjell asked for a lift because he wanted to see the Ferris wheel [the London Eye], which is being raised on the Embankment. We drove off and then I ran out of petrol outside Charing Cross police station of all places! I put a note on the dashboard then popped into the stage door of the Adelphi before Kjell and I walked south. The wheel is hovering at a spectacular 30° angle over the Thames. I filled my petrol can at a garage near Vauxhall Bridge; but when we got back to the cop shop, I was furious that I'd picked up a ticket. I got the desk sergeant to write me a note confirming I'd broken down. It was only after we'd driven off again that I realised I'd been going in and out of a police station with my pockets stuffed with coke and weed.

Friday, 15ᵗʰ October Rushed to Sainsbury's to stock up for tonight. The first visitors began arriving at 3pm. Daniel was first and didn't want to leave; he's getting counselling for his addiction. I think Tom was next, but it all blurs. [Actor] has been working on an indie movie with improvised dialogue. He plays a drug dealer and told me he slipped in a reference to 'Charlie lite.' My influence is spreading. Early evening there was a major invasion: Mr and Mrs Ricky; Chris the editor, who brought a friend, Rachel, high on absinth; Tadzio and his friend, Chris, who's into fisting; [theatrical agent] and her girlfriend; I think Shane was the last around midnight. At 1am I was wilting under the strain and bowed out. The others were at it until 7.30am. There's something about this house that prevents people from going home.

Monday, 25ᵗʰ October Geoff Dyer put me in touch with Sue Jones, who's producing *Secrets and Lines,* a dramadoc for Channel 4's *Cocaine Night* in January. Tonight her researcher, Rachel, recorded me for two hours. My contribution will be used as background for actors playing dealers.

Friday, 29ᵗʰ October I got a letter telling me I'd passed my massage exam. I got 70% for the theory and a whopping 86% for the practical, enough for a credit. The visitors started arriving at 12.30pm and, by the end of the evening, I think virtually the entire Inner Circle had been here. Helen, telling tales of terror, was the star guest. The party produced the biggest turnover on record.

Friday, 19ᵗʰ November There were dribs and drabs throughout the day and I thought Friday was never going to get started. The Miramax guy came round and asked if I'd got any screenplays. Ken's Portuguese friend, Nuno, was here to talk about taking one or other of the spare rooms. He's studying at St Martin's [School of Art], has one blue eyebrow and a ring through his septum, like a bull. He should fit in perfectly. Then it all kicked off. Tunde was supposed to have gone home at midnight, but couldn't leave. By this time I was high and happy and didn't care.

Friday, 26ᵗʰ November Toby and his boyfriend, Anthony, have had a terrible holiday in homophobic Jamaica. Toby counselled Trev on his sexual confusion. I left them at it and apparently they continued until 3.30am.

Saturday, 4ᵗʰ December Caroline and Shane took me to Hay-on-Wye, where Helen is now living in a farmhouse outside the town. Daniel was already there and served chilli con carne. Shane rattled me by something he said: 'There are too many people coming round to your house. The neighbours are going to get suspicious.' Toby said the same thing last night when the door bell was still going at 3am. I know warning signs when I get them and I'd got them. I made the pronouncement that I was giving up the business. I shall wind it down after my grand Millennium party, which will end two years of life-changing fun and excitement. Surprisingly there were general grunts of approval.

Friday, 17ᵗʰ December Tunde came and helped me decorate the tree. He rolled Trev one of his demon spliffs, and the poor lad staggered up to bed, never to be seen again. The phone rang constantly and I knew it would be another busy Friday. It was, probably the busiest ever. I gave everybody their Christmas presents, solid silver straws, inspired by a Tiffany original. Late evening there was a very loud knock on the basement door, which stopped us all in our tracks. I peered through the curtains and didn't recognise the people outside. They turned out to be friends of Aquiles', who hadn't told me they were coming. They all trooped in, but I think they could tell they weren't welcome and they left pretty sharpish. It's another sign.

Friday, 24th December I'd just finished breakfast when Tadzio came. Then there was a steady stream, all stocking up for the holidays. Toby says the Inner Circle is planning a Christmas surprise for me. At midnight [TV actor] arrived with his friend, Scott, and the two of them spent about 45 minutes talking to boyfriends on their mobiles. Some people just do not know how to behave in other people's houses. After they'd gone, I thought I'd settle down to an appropriate film, *The Wind in the Willows*. But Nuno wanted to watch porn so I called it a day. The big event of the first week of the New Year will be the screening on Channel 4 of *Secrets and Lines*. I think I'll move the Friday salon to Thursday, 6th January in honour of the occasion.

Friday, 31st December An absolutely wonderful stupid childish day a properly excessive celebration of the end of one thousand years and the best New Year's Eve in memory and remarkably it was spent almost entirely in the company of friends I've met during the past two years I didn't expect any of them to come for breakfast but Helen Caroline Shane and Trev were here so I made them smoked salmon and scrambled eggs and then Tadzio came as well and then Trev disappeared up north until next week of course he and Toby never went to that gay sauna which was supposed to settle whether or not Trev really gets off on male flesh and now instead Trev's anguished about his latest girlfriend dumping him anyway from lunchtime onwards the phone and the door bell went constantly and it was even busier than yesterday when we had the return of Paula although I don't know why because I feel she's now part of my past and how about the new additions to my medical team Neil is incredibly good-looking like a doctor on *Casualty* and Abdul seems to divide his time between A&E and the gym so it's hard not to stare at those biceps which seems to be what he wants because he's always wearing a tight T-shirt although when I told him Nuno was interested Abdul politely declined because he's straight but anyway I made soup for lunch and Tom and Betsy were here for that and then outsiders Jack and Teresa who had to be shielded from the truth and then Ken with his lovely new baby before Zena came with the kids and then Caroline and Shane arrived with a big crowd of people I spent last New Year's Eve with who came as aliens in silver suits and face paint and the kids had fun playing with their ray guns and then there was Ed who somehow holds down a teaching post at Harrow but Helen finds him so obnoxious that she went and had a bath but he stayed so long that she had to emerge and be sociable over dinner for which I served spaghetti in tuna sauce an old favourite but few partook because the appetite suppressants were freely circulating I can't remember who else was in and out but the lovely Chileans were definitely here and [Radio 1 DJ] too which was a bit of a surprise although Chris Evans said half the BBC are on drugs and then we watched the fireworks in Sydney just a phenomenal display around the Harbour that made us quite emotional and we couldn't imagine that London would come anywhere near equalling it but Ed and his long-suffering girlfriend Sally left to watch the display on the Thames and then Miranda was here with her new man Stuart of whom everyone approved although he's a surprising choice being a cross-dresser with two feminine alter egos one nice and one nasty and he's been celibate for years but there was now a core group and some wanted to go down to the River for midnight but the TV suggested there may be five million people there and then Ed phoned to say they'd been unable to get anywhere near the Embankment and that they were coming back at which point somebody suggested going up the road to watch the fireworks from the roof of Toby's penthouse and that made sense so at 11.30pm we set off in a convoy of cars to Toby's where he was having problems with his ex-boyfriend Anthony who's come back but Philippe was there with a big crowd of French and Belgian friends plus [up-and-coming leading man soon to be a Hollywood star] and at midnight we went up to the roof with champagne party poppers cameras and mobile phones although we weren't sure what we'd see because it was now very cold and damp but although it was probably nothing like the experience on the Thames the fireworks were everywhere 360° and they went on and on until most of us returned downstairs around 12.30 and now everyone was on something and I had an E that made me wobbly for five to ten minutes but then eased to provide a nice gentle buzz until about 4am and Stuart gave head massages and I remember looking across the table at Miranda who was no longer on this planet but then Daniel got restless and wanted to go back to mine for more of the same so the convoy set off again very slowly because none of us should have been on the road but it was empty thank God and then when we got here more stuff was consumed although by now I couldn't even look at a glass of wine but I remember Ed continued to annoy Helen and then Manuel and Nasreen came round at 6.30am because their boiler had broken down and they wanted to take showers and that gave Shane the idea and he had one too but others were falling asleep and I packed it in at 8.15 marvellous.

V

"There are three levels of drug addiction.
The first one is fun. The second is fun with problems. And the third is problems.
I definitely got to the problem stage."
~ Dennis Quaid ~

I couldn't possibly know it at the time but Millennium Eve was the highpoint of my career as a drug dealer. As we know, the cracks already had begun to appear in my pleasure-dome; but for close on 24 hours on 31ˢᵗ December it was possible for me to forget about them and surrender to unalloyed delight in the company of the dearest friends for whom anyone could wish. Although it was never quite the same again, the party continued well into the 21ˢᵗ century. Much of the merrymaking came about because of the huge amount of money I was making. Up until now I have merely alluded to my income and for obvious reasons I can't reveal exact figures. Suffice it to say that, by the end of the century, I was accumulating such an obscene amount of wealth that I decided that I would have to start giving most of it away. 'Tell that to the judge,' Geoff Dyer once told me. But it's not a defence, only a fact. From 2000 onwards I donated tens of thousands of pounds to charity.

After making modest donations to the April 1999 Bombings Appeal and the Terrence Higgins Trust, I asked friends which charities I should support big time, then accepted their recommendations: The National Canine Defence League, The Cats Protection League, Arthritis Care, The Alzheimer's Disease Society, SOS Children's Villages UK. In February 2000 I went to visit my friend David Sweetman. He and his partner, Vatch, had opened a new Thai restaurant in Maida Vale. During the course of an excessively drunken evening I learned that David was unwell (he had an illness that doctors hadn't yet diagnosed) and that he and Vatch had launched their own charity. From then onwards I pumped money into the UK/Thailand Children's Fund, which helped Thai children orphaned by AIDS.

The main beneficiary of my largesse, however, was the AIDS charity Crusaid. I have to confess that the main reason it benefited was that its office was around the corner from my house. After the Friday party I would put £1,000 in an envelope and stick it through their letterbox. The Chief Executive was effusive in his gratitude and his response graduated from typewritten acknowledgments to hand-written notes to invitations to red carpet events. I was at the premiere of *The Next Best Thing*, featuring one of my clients, and then I went on to the afterparty at Home House, and later I was listed in Crusaid's Annual Review as a benefactor. My name came after Lulu's.

I attended a wine and canapé party and was incredulous when the Chairman was brought to meet me. 'When I was completely blotto,' I wrote, 'I stuffed some more money into somebody's inside pocket and left.' In the summer I was at Crusaid's pool party, which degenerated into an orgy. 'The beautiful people's lives are so empty, so pretentious, so bourgeois,' I wrote. 'More, please.'

The spectres at the feast were Fear and Paranoia (we've dealt with both of those) plus Addiction. This affected roughly three per cent of my clientele, but of course it was still three per cent too many. One of the most tragic victims was Helen, a good part of whose life was wasted. When she returned from her voyage of doom Down Under we had a couple of heart-to-hearts. The man for whom she was searching unsuccessfully was the father of her children. We were a near perfect match and we both knew it. But I also knew that, quite apart from being gay, I was now too old. Shortly after our discussions, Helen chose to return to the arms of fellow addict Daniel. During her weekend with him at the Cardiff Hilton, Daniel got wasted, disappeared until 4am each morning, and then left Helen to pay the £800 bill. I wasn't the only person to tell her she was mad.

Early in 2000 Daniel seemed to me to be out of control. There was a particularly stupid evening when, because of the post-holiday drought, he went out, scored some crack from the street traders on the Caledonian/Pentonville Road junction, and then appeared to be all too knowledgeable as he adapted a Coca Cola can in order to smoke it. After disappearing for two months he turned up on my doorstep, bruised and bleeding and asking to be hugged. When I tried to get him into a taxi, he wandered off to chat up a blonde tart, and they went off in the taxi together. Daniel was back at my house hours later with more bruises and his jacket slashed. He claimed that he had been set up by the woman and attacked by her pimp, who robbed him of everything.

I saw myself as the equivalent of the publican who doesn't give a drunk another drink. I told Daniel I couldn't go on supplying him. I said the same thing to Peter (the weirdo) when he turned up incoherent and stinking to high heaven. Peter's tragedy is that he didn't start out as a weirdo. He had a wife, a home and a good job at Film 4. Then, bit by bit, he lost everything. 'Among my friends,' I wrote, 'he's the number one candidate for ending up destitute.' I wasn't far wrong. Years after we parted company, I found him busking in King's Cross station. There were other casualties; but we'll come to them later.

On 6th January the Inner Circle met as arranged to watch Secrets and Lines, Channel 4's dramadoc 'about the chain of people working as cocaine dealers in this country.' Quite a bit of the programme went by before I recognised myself. Most of the actors were portraying various species of low-life; but then it became apparent that I was 'Andrew H', portrayed by a very distinguished young man seen driving a nice car and eating in a posh restaurant. The latter represented L'Odeon and 'I' described how I would be served an excellent meal and then ask for the bill. It arrived in a folder; but inside was not the bill but a wad of cash, which I would transfer to my pocket. Instead of payment, I would deposit the required number of wraps into the folder and leave. 'It makes me feel like James Bond,' I said. We all had a good laugh, I opened the remainder of the New Year champagne, Manuel sent out for Chinese, and everything ended on a riotous note. Next day I wrote anonymously to George Asprey, the actor who had played me, and congratulated him on his performance.

But this lifestyle could not continue. Its danger was compounded by the death of Jill Dando the previous April. The TV personality had been shot dead in what appeared to be a hit and subsequently many theories were advanced as to the motive. Tadzio's gave me food for thought: according to him the rumour at the BBC was that she was a dealer and had fallen out with big-time criminals because she wanted to retire. But I was torn. Pragmatically there was the matter of the growing amount of legitimate job offers that were developing out of the drug trade. I began working for a well-known magazine. I was involved in, of all things, a programme of contemporary dance in which another of my clients, a loose-limbed Sri Lankan, bared his body and soul on the stage of London's ICA. But the most substantial project, which filled a lot of my time in 2000, was ghosting an autobiography.

Casey had told me about his father, who had been a small-time entrepreneur in Soho in the swinging Sixties, when he crossed swords with Paul Raymond, the Krays and the Maltese Mafia. While in prison on a trumped-up charge, he had hand-written his memoirs, which had been smuggled out of the nick page by page. The story of a one-man crusade against archaic censorship, corrupt police and dangerous rivals, set in the Soho I remembered as a teenager, was one I very much wanted to share with the world. I grilled the author for details he had omitted and, after scouring the archives, I verified almost all his claims. The book was published in 2005 and it's another of my proudest achievements.

I am also proud that I did my bit when it came to the liberalisation of film censorship in the UK. Following my lecture to the BBFC I was the only anti-censorship representative to address a so-called Citizens' Jury, which met at the Hilton hotel in Portsmouth in February, 2000, to study censorship methods. The ordinary folk on the panel comprised a good cross-section of the public; but none of them showed any particular interest in being protected from depictions of real life. There was general agreement that the 'pig fucker' song from *South Park*; wanking in *There's Something About Mary*; and coke-snorting in *Trees Lounge* were all suitable for 15-year-olds. On 15th May a judicial review found that the BBFC was breaking the law by continuing to ban films simply because they contained unsimulated sex. Pornography was legalised and, because it was openly available for the first time in history, the British public exercised its prerogative by refusing to buy it. You won't make much money nowadays from making porn movies.

My proposed winding down of the drug dealership was a very protracted business indeed. Back in the swing of things after my change of heart in Hay-on-Wye, I just couldn't bring myself to curtail the Friday parties. We were having too much fun. In February there was a particularly excessive evening that I doubt anyone present will ever forget. I served the guests a cocktail called Liquid Heroin, based on a recipe given to me by Brendan. (It consists of Jägermeister, Goldschläger and crème de menthe.) We all had one shot each and couldn't detect any effect. Miranda arrived with news of my Christmas surprise, a hand-made waistcoat lined with leftover material from Mick Jagger's jacket. We all had another shot. At this point Daniel fell off his chair and remained lying on the floor. I meant to mention this to someone; but then Nuno brought down some of his artwork, disturbing images of humanoids having sex, and we discussed it over further shots. I looked around to find that Daniel had disappeared; but when I went upstairs to answer the door bell I found him lying in the hall. By the early hours we were sufficiently *non compos mentis* for me to suggest that I sell the business to Miranda and for her to accept.

It was business as usual for some months, however, because everyone involved in the change-over went on holiday. My destination was Rio de Janeiro for the Carnaval to end all Carnavals, the one that celebrated the 500th anniversary of the city. From the top of the Sugar Loaf mountain I looked down on the very bay where the Portuguese first docked in 1500. I also took the funicular up the Corcovado to experience the Cristo Redentor, and it seemed to me that Christ was stretching out his hands in a shrug of resignation as he contemplated one of the world's most thrillingly heathen cities. The all-night parades through the Sambadrome, during which floats dripping with sequins, feathers and half-naked lovelies entertained a screaming, sweat-drenched crowd of 150,000, provided a spectacular piece of theatre. But the street parties, which went on for weeks, were impromptu and unadulterated versions of the main event and were in many ways more exciting.

By the golden sands of Ipanema I joined a crowd of people, singing and dancing as they followed a truck. I was tightly packed, as I like it, between shirtless men with perfect pecs and rococo drag queens in showgirl head-dresses. On another evening, following the sound of music, I encountered hundreds and hundreds, possibly thousands and thousands, of people shuffling along, old and young; black, brown and white; in masks and costumes; babes in arms and people in wheelchairs: all singing an old song about how great it was to be a Carioca. Then it was off to Le Boy, a gay bar in a former cinema in Copacabana, where Peter Mandelson met his Brazilian boyfriend Reinaldo, and where, behind the old cinema screen, there was a dark room that, around 4am, became a Boschian mass of damp flesh.

Time and time again I found myself in Rua Farme de Amoedo, Rio's Old Compton Street, thronging with boys, and drummers, and tourists. On one occasion I caught sight of a concert taking place in a nearby square and went to watch. While groups of little girls got on stage to dance to well-known samba tunes, I met Eder from São Paulo. I knew this was going to happen and this is why I went to the square. Eder was a dark-haired, sensitive-looking young executive type. We cruised each other until he felt confident enough to greet me. Suddenly we were promenading together, finding out about each other (he was married with two children, but in the throes of divorce after realising he was gay), and in the next instant we were swept up in yet another street party, carried along by thousands more revellers, until we broke free and under darkening skies wandered down to the beach, where we pledged over beers to stay in touch. There was nothing more we could do that night. Eder was about to catch a bus back to his home town. I felt as though I had experienced my first true romance and, not this alone, but a proper, old-fashioned romance, the type that begins with courtship rather than mutual masturbation. I returned to London full of the joys of Brazil. 'The Rio Carnaval makes the Edinburgh Festival look like a vicarage fête,' I raved to anyone who would listen, 'and there's no bloody pretentious theatre to put up with.'

'I really resented having to return to The Factory. It seemed so mundane,' I wrote on 24th March. 'But then Friday got going and I thought, "I still really enjoy this."' Having moved into Paula's room, Bernardo was blooded the same evening and held my guests enthralled with his stories of high drama in the Gulf of Mexico. His first attempt to escape from Cuba had involved drifting for two days in a boat with a broken motor, in shark-infested sea, before being picked up and jailed by Cuban police. His new bid for freedom was altogether more successful. By June he had a job and by July he was granted permanent residency in the UK. (He's now a British citizen.) Throughout the process Naim, who claimed that Bernardo had used him and owed him money, behaved venomously, finally attempting to have Bernardo deported. In letters and faxes to me he used the language of a woman scorned – 'monster!', 'BETRAYED!', 'BRUTAL!' – which seemed somewhat *de trop*. But seven years later, when he turned against me, he used the same language.

Being a social animal, I found that the people I met through the drug trade impossible to abandon. These were people I never would have met in my former life. It was an honour to meet the very well connected. I delivered to people who had Christmas cards from Tony and Cherie Blair on their pianos. But as a born rebel I was more intrigued by the outsiders. Imagine my delight when I discovered that the mature gentleman, Dirk, who I had assumed hired rent boys, was himself a prostitute and that the young hunks I met at his flat were his clients. He advertised his services in *QX* ('Daddy wants to control your hole') and I interviewed him for the same magazine.[93] Another rent boy, Stuart, was pimped out by one of Lord Boothby's ex-lovers. His house, bequeathed to him by the Tory peer, was used by Stuart for assignations. Meanwhile, back at my own home, Trev, increasingly speed-driven, was an endlessly inventive lover. It meant nothing to him to crawl under my bedclothes, his anus smeared in honey. In June, driven wild by amphetamine and England's triumph over Germany, he left clues all over the house that directed me to Nuno's empty room (Nuno was working in Mozambique), which Trev had re-designed as a brothel with himself as its only working girl.

Meanwhile Eder telephoned me constantly and in one call he told me that he loved me and wanted me to visit him in São Paulo.

On 12th May I recorded 'the last Friday as we know it?' I had sold the business to Miranda. The deal constituted a compromise. The Fridays I loved would continue at my house, but I was no longer the supplier. I had introduced Miranda to Casey and from now on she would do all the leg work. My clients were unsure about the new arrangement. 'Toby thinks disaster looms,' I wrote. 'Miranda will get totally neurotic and consume half the stuff herself.' For my part all I wanted was that she kept going until the New Year, when I envisaged another 24 hour party. The early days of the new regime worked relatively well. Friday, 9th June was a fairly typical evening.

'Miranda and I talked about setting opening time at 5pm. She has a day job and can't keep getting time off. The hot topic of the evening was the shocking picture of Daniela Westbrook with no septum. Some thought that the photo was doctored and that cocaine couldn't have such a devastating effect. But Dr Abdul confirmed that it could. Miranda clung to him all night and behaved very girlishly.

'Kevin showed me his boring websites. He kissed all the men and talked about moisturiser so it can only be weeks before he comes out. Dirk stayed for the first time and talked shop with Ginny. He's got a legit job in the book trade. Nuno made a move on Duncan.

'Dr Camillo is the latest of our friends to get into big trouble. He's been caught raiding the pharmacy and now it seems he'll have to resign before he's dismissed. Miranda said she was definitely leaving at midnight but didn't because she couldn't stand up'

---

93   21st April, 2004

Two notable newcomers joined the party in 2000. One, a fluffy, black cat who arrived with one of my guests, was very friendly, and didn't want to leave. At the end of the evening I put it out; but it was back the next day. I advertised its presence on nearby lamp posts but nobody claimed it. I allowed it to stay. We named it Charlie. The other arrival first struck terror into my heart and then captured it for all time. I now think the story of how I met my best friend is quite wonderful. I was at London's National Film Theatre for a three hour documentary about Marcello Mastroianni. During the interval I was approached by a man who introduced himself as Alex, my next door neighbour. Without beating around the bush, he told me that he and his housemates had been discussing what might be going on in my house on Friday evenings. They'd all come to the conclusion that I was a drug dealer. Shane's words of warning echoed in my head. But Alex, who guessed from my stunned reaction that he had scored a bullseye, asked if he could pop in on the following Friday. Something made me say yes.

I warned Miranda of what to expect and we nervously anticipated Alex's arrival. He came as arranged, bought some gear, had a chat, and left. 'He looks like a policeman,' said Miranda. He did indeed. Alex is a big, imposing man with a gaze that dares you to tell a lie. But this comes not from his days in the interrogation room but as a journalist. Soon he was one of the gang; and when Bernardo moved out of the house in a short-lived attempt to share a flat with a boyfriend, Alex took his room. From the day we met he talked about a girlfriend; but one Friday he brought up the subject of the gay porn director Jean-Daniel Cadinot and I said in genuine surprise, 'How do you know about him?'

Alex's own admission is that he is 'forty per cent gay.' My own estimation is that he's gay practically every time he gets drunk. It was on one of these occasions that he took my fuck buddy Winston to bed. But then on another occasion, when Bernardo made an advance, Alex threw a glass of wine over him. Not knowing whether or not Alex is in gay mode has certainly kept our relationship lively. He is as likely in my experience to introduce me to a new female lover as he is to demand that we go to a drag bar. But the real reason we have been friends since the turn of the century is that we are *simpatico*. We have the same interests, the same politics, the same sense of humour. Alex is the latest in a long line of people I have loved because they make me laugh. Noticing our compatibility, people have assumed that we're partners. Of course we should be. I think that probably we were made for each other. But I've never laid a finger on him. I am now a fervent believer in Gore Vidal's maxim that you should only have sex with acquaintances. If you have sex with a friend, you lose the friendship. I wouldn't want there ever to be a time when Alex and I aren't friends. Plus Winston tells me he's rubbish in bed.

VI

"The thrill has gone,
To linger on
Would spoil it anyhow;
Let's creep away
From the day,
For the party's over now."
~ Song by Noël Coward, 1932 ~

From 2000 the hours I used to spend toiling in The Factory could be spent on more enjoyable pursuits. For a while I was a professional masseur. This new career lasted until I was required to give regular treatment to a nut case racist, who gave me his unsolicited opinions about 'darkies.' I decided I didn't like massaging people I didn't like. Ever since then I've used massage as I originally intended, as a treat for sex partners. In the early years of the 21st century, sex remained a highlight of my week. Usually my heart was pounding as I pushed open the door of The Cally sauna. I never knew exactly what to expect. One perfect Saturday I ended up alone with a thick-set brickie and we got down to business, aroused by the knowledge that at any minute the door could be opened by a member of staff. The brickie discharged on to the floor, said, 'Thanks, mate,' walked out and I never saw him again. Ideal.

For quite a while the weekly Friday night party remained a unique assembly, part social experiment, part drug-fucked bacchanalia. There have been similar meetings of minds going back as far as you care to research; but whether the venue was a coffee house, a country house or a coffee bar, it was almost invariably exclusive to one particular class. In my living room, however, the waiter could talk to the architect, the public school teacher to the plumber. Our lives were enriched by learning more about those we may not otherwise have met.

'Abdul told a story about a man who had been admitted to his hospital. He had fallen from a window, hit his head on something on the way down, and then impaled himself on two railings. He was brought in with his skull caved in and the railings still sticking out of him, like a horror film. He was still technically alive, but didn't last long. We were incredulous that Abdul could attend something so horrible only hours ago and then come here for a drink and a line.'

No matter what our background, we were most of us gossip-mongers, intent on

286

discussing the tittle-tattle of the day. At any one time we all would be reading the latest best-seller; we all would have seen the big new film or play; we all would know which upcoming art exhibition was the one to book for. We loved popular culture and in the summer of 2000 we became hooked on the new TV reality show *Big Brother*. We had our favourites, our theories, our predictions, and each Friday we would tune in to see who had been evicted. 'The show says a lot more about the viewer than the participants,' I declared. The only subject that divided us was popular music. I would put on Backstreet Boys and there would be demands for it to be taken off. There was general acceptance of Eminem.

It was cocaine that made all this possible and cocaine that made it impossible for us to continue. As we philosophised and prattled into the night there was always the knowledge at the back of our minds that one or two of our number were falling by the wayside. Daniel, who had been thrown out by his girlfriend, had disappeared. I bumped into another absentee, David Dan Joe, making his way slowly along Caledonian Road with a walking stick, and barely recognised him. He was gaunt with a scrawny neck and could speak only with effort. We had heard stories about his state of health, but what on earth could be wrong? The subject of other rumours, Camillo had, as we feared, lost his job. He was never able to practice medicine again; but he still couldn't control his addiction and he had to be added to the list of those we couldn't supply. The next person to cause concern was none other than our new hostess, Miranda, who, as Toby had predicted, was the last person who should have been put in charge of a stock of class A drugs.

The first sign that all was not well was when Miranda began turning up late at my house. Sometimes there was a crowd of people waiting for her. She claimed that she was ill and certainly appeared to have a perpetual cold. Suddenly, at the end of the summer, she announced that she didn't want to keep making the journey to my house and that in future the Friday party would be held at her flat in the rather more inaccessible suburb of Muswell Hill. Again I found this acceptable. The parties would continue but from now on far away from the prying security cameras in King's Cross. For the next few weeks members of the Inner Circle would meet at my house and I would drive them to Miranda's.

Initially the old wine seemed to taste just as good from a new bottle; but very rapidly the numbers began to thin. Miranda couldn't throw a party. She was often under the weather and sometimes everything would be over by 10.30pm. One evening we were alone together. She claimed that she would carry on indefinitely. I wasn't convinced. She appeared to be wilting under the strain. I came home to watch an all too regular client playing a cameo in an episode of a sitcom. 'Oh, dear,' I wrote. 'He didn't seem to know where he was or what he was doing. I wonder why?'

Purists had been claiming that 1ˢᵗ January, 2001, marked the true beginning of the new millennium. Few believed that the euphoria of twelve months earlier could be repeated, but I wasn't one of those pessimists. I set out determined to recreate my previous New Year's Eve. Fate cannot of course be manipulated. I was to be disappointed. Nobody came for breakfast. Later the day was nothing at all like it had been a year earlier, when kids and aliens had chased each other around the room. This time a few people popped in and out and Abdul had some soup. Miranda became ill again and went home, leaving me in charge. Once again I chauffeured people to Toby's penthouse before midnight. Once again we went up on the roof; but there were only a few fireworks somewhere in the distance, and we quickly came downstairs. A speaker blew and the sound system packed up.

Around 2am Ginny said that a few people wanted to go back to my place and the cars set off. When we got home, we just lay around. There was a lot of chatter, but I didn't say anything because I was feeling queasy. I turned in at about 5.30am. I didn't want to take a zopiclone because I thought I might choke on my vomit. 'There was no sense of excitement,' I complained to my diary on New Year's Day.

On the first Friday of the New Year I took Helen to lunch because it was time for a talk about her former colleague, Trev, who had been a nymphomaniac on speed in my house for nearly three years. I confessed that the sex was still wildly and unpredictably exciting. The most recent session had developed after I had received a phone call in the living room from Trev in my bedroom, which he had managed to transform into a pitch-black maze with himself at the end. The charade was even more enjoyable than usual because it was performed while Chris de Souza presented a classical concert on Radio 3. But Trev also was becoming more reckless. He would masturbate all over the house and never bother about drawing curtains. When she heard this, Helen gave me a grave, professional look. 'I don't want to sound alarmist,' she said, 'but can you lock your bedroom door?'

Back at my house, we waited for some more of the Inner Circle and then drove off to Miranda's. She was grumpy because we had interrupted her take-away Thai. We didn't stay long. From then onwards I didn't visit unless I had booked in advance. Occasionally, for example when her mother came to stay with her, Miranda would ask me to host Friday night myself. Somehow, with almost no advance warning, everything would be back the way it was. 'Busiest Friday in months. Crates of beer and wine consumed,' I wrote of the party on 9ᵗʰ March. 'It probably always could have been like this if I'd stuck with it. But what's done is done. I could *never* do this again full-time. It's a full day's work.' Famous last words.

No longer required to remain on duty, I took some leave. Sarah Dunant's flat in Florence was available and I took artists Tom and Betsy, the perfect companions for the cultural capital of Europe. Helen was supposed to join us but I think she dropped out at the last minute because we would have had to share a bed, and probably we would have had sex, and things would have become far too complicated at a time when Helen was on the verge of finding true romance. (She was to meet her future husband, as near as dammit to a sane human being, later in the year.) But we did hook up with Caroline and Shane on the Ponte Vecchio and later drove with them to Siena. We then continued to Orvieto, stopping on the way to luxuriate in the hot springs at Montemerano, which we called God's jacuzzi. We had another quasi-religious experience when we saw Orvieto crowning a hill in the distance and looking celestial in the late afternoon sunlight. It was as though we were ascending to heaven and it gave Betsy an idea for a mural.

My next trip was instigated by Eder, my boy from Brazil. He had a five hour stopover in London before he flew on to the U.A.E. and we spent the time together. We hadn't talked much in the past about his career; but he had an ammunition case in his carry-on and it transpired that he was an arms dealer. He also said with great seriousness that he wanted us to grow old together and that he had bought a new double bed for my visit to São Paulo. I didn't know what to make of all this until our first physical contact, a passionate snog in a lift that lasted all of seven seconds, after which I was on the telephone to Varig.

My time in São Paulo and the nearby seaport of Santos (where the planters all say, no, no, no) was everything I had hoped it would be. The visit to the munitions factory was not without interest because Eder taught English at evening classes there and some of his colleagues found it curious to meet a real, live Englishman. But the main source of my enjoyment was the sex, which I had been anticipating for a year. There was a lot of it, and Eder even set the alarm for 5am to allow for additional congress before he went to work. Just for a few months afterwards, I seriously contemplated not only the hitherto inconceivable possibility of a long-term partnership but also how I was going to tell everybody that my boyfriend was helping to prolong the war in the Middle East. Fortunately I never had to.

When I was in London, Friday became the day I spent answering telephone calls from Miranda's disgruntled clients. Sometimes she wouldn't answer her own phone for days, or she wouldn't be at home when people called. She announced that *in addition to being coked out of her skull* (my emphasis because she never admitted what we suspected) she was now on Prozac. 'I sense the beginnings of disintegration. Everyone's on edge,' I wrote. 'Maybe we all need a break?' Pining for the parties I loved, I compensated by keeping every available room in my house occupied. As soon as Nuno gained his BA (Hons) and moved back to Lisbon, I replaced him with Werner, a droll German studying mime in London with Ken. When Manuel broke up with Nasreen and asked if I had a spare room, I moved my study into my bedroom and squeezed him into the vacant space.

My most consciousness-raising, emotionally-draining and libido-satisfying excursion was to Thailand to observe the work that my drug money had helped to fund. An important point to establish is that the administrators of the UK/Thailand Children's Fund, David Sweetman and his partner Vatcharin Bhumichitr, were men who moved in a social circle far above mine. Vatch came from very good stock and was connected in some way to both the Thai royal family and government. David, who was my intellectual superior as Plato is to Pluto, was also the only man I ever have met who more sex-crazed than Naim. This meant that during our time in Bangkok and Chiang Mai we were (a) treated like lords and driven in private cars to the most exclusive night spots and (b) pampered in Thailand's most luxurious sex spas before we moved on to the orphanages I was supporting.

Before we left for Thailand, David had been diagnosed with a rare wasting disease named multiple systems atrophy. He walked with a stick, and was visibly slowed down, but he had not surrendered to his illness. On our first day in Bangkok, David's banker friend drove us to a 'restaurant' with a gym full of muscular young men who weren't using its equipment. 'They're all just sitting there,' I observed before it became clear that the banker had paid for us all to pick a boy of our choice and take him to a private room. My choice (remind me to show you his photo) put all thoughts of jet lag out of my head; but what remains more prominently in my memory is the *après sex* meeting at which, David, in reality only months from death, was as serene as Mother Teresa as he murmured of his rented companion, 'He was very attentive.' The next night we were at a notorious live sex show whose performers were all for sale after the curtain fell; and the next night the outing was to the Thai version of a San Francisco bath house, but one as if designed by Richard Rodgers. 'Many Thais here are interested in mature Europeans,' our guide explained; and as I fought off young admirers, I realised this was an understatement.

In Chiang Mai we were snapped back to reality as we visited projects that were attempting to cope with the havoc still being wreaked by AIDS in Thailand. The life-saving drugs still were not available in this part of the world. Young men and women were dying and leaving orphaned children; babies were born with the virus in their systems. A nine-year-old boy ravaged by the illness, his body covered in sores, tried to give us the traditional Thai greeting, palms pressed together, and I bowed my head only so that he couldn't see my tears. A group of women, all with AIDS, made handicrafts so beautiful that I bought all my Christmas presents here. David behaved like the man I could only aspire to be, an insatiable libertine who lovingly pressed handfuls of bahts into stricken relatives' hands. As I proclaimed in his obituary, 'Rarely was a man so brilliant, playful and compassionate.'[94] Our story was by no means at an end.

Just before he went back to Portugal, Nuno introduced me to his friend, Eduardo, who was at his wits' end trying to find an actor for his play *The Crime of Father Amaro* at a pub theatre in Greenwich. I read for the part of the corrupt Canon Díaz and got it. I would have got it if I had been one half of conjoined twins with halitosis. The play was due to open a week later. More to the point, however, it was a quality production through which I rediscovered my acting mojo and which consolidated my association with crazy Portuguese artists that has continued to this day. I'll return to this subject if I may.

On the first Friday after the run had ended I recorded that I was at very low ebb. The play had taken my mind off the inexorable decline of the parties, and now my life seemed empty. People still made enquiries about the zoo but, instead of giving them Miranda's number, I put them on to Darius, a former client who had set up his own business. He was also an actor, with a usefully ethnic look, and he was beginning to get important parts. That Friday I went to see a play about drug dealers hanging around phone booths in King's Cross. Although it was new, the play already had dated badly. Practically all the phone booths in King's Cross had been removed long ago. Now the latest and most rigorous clean-up operation, instigated in readiness for the opening of St Pancras International, was having an effect. The prostitutes, the street drinkers, and the dealers that stood on the corner of Pentonville and Caledonian Roads had all disappeared earlier in the year. Apparently they had moved up the road to Euston. King's Cross was changing. 'There is too much happening,' wrote one of those property pundits,[95] 'for it to be anything but appealing. I give it two years, then bang.'

Things had not changed to such a degree by 2001 that it was possible, as it is today, to be alerted by mobile telephone to incidents happening at the same moment across the globe. On 11th September I was busy in London's West End for most of the day. I reviewed a Spanish *tapas* bar for *What's On in London* and then went on to the British Film Institute library to research an obituary. When I got home I found a message on my answering machine from Eder about an awful event I knew nothing about. Downstairs Manuel was watching the destruction of the World Trade Center on TV. I could not take in the magnitude of the disaster. 'But...hundreds must be dead,' I stammered.

---

94 *The Guardian*, 12th April, 2002
95 *The Guardian*, 13th February, 1998

'Thousands,' Manuel responded. I tried to telephone New York, but it was impossible to get through. Alex came home and we all watched the unfolding horror in disbelief for the rest of the evening. 'This is the worst catastrophe that has occurred in my lifetime,' I wrote. 'Before I was born, such an act would have precipitated a world war. Today...?'

Over the next few days, as the personal stories of the passengers on the doomed planes were reported, it was difficult to concentrate on such trivia as a restaurant review. But gradually, as it always does, the trivia took over from the earth-shattering cataclysm. Miranda made the announcement that we had all been expecting. She was giving up because she wanted her Fridays back. Ginny cajoled her into a farewell soirée. Miranda acceded but added that she didn't want anything to do with its organisation. I set to, sending out an irresistible invitation ('All stock must go. Many popular lines available.') I didn't want a repetition of Miranda's recent, sparsely-attended birthday party, which may not have helped her current malaise. That evening had ended with caterer Dafydd throwing almost all the food he had prepared into a bin liner. The party was held at my house on Saturday, 13th October.

'At 2.30pm I began preparations. Brett came round. He had a scar on his forehead, the souvenir of a sex session in the disabled loo of a leather club last weekend. I had a shower and waited. There were no others. This was what I had been dreading: a handful of us making the best of it. I didn't want it to end like this. But then Tadzio arrived and there was a steady stream until well after midnight. There were a few absentees, but otherwise almost the whole of the Inner Circle celebrated the end of an era in style.

'Early birds got champagne cocktails. Those happy boys, Mario and Alain, brought a Barbie Birthday cake, and Caroline and Shane brought seven-week-old Jesse, very cute. It was a pleasure to see David Dan Joe, sexy in leather and almost back to normal. The silly kid had let himself get really ill before going to his doctor, who put him on the combination therapy immediately.

'Later Ginny was in tears because of her imminent departure. She's had enough of London and is going to Australia. Others are moving on, too. Mr and Mrs Ricky have already gone to Yorkshire. Miranda was in a good mood, but I don't think she ever budged from her chair, where she held court. I went to bed at 3.30am, when there were still a dozen here, all having a good time. Glad we did it; wish we could do it again, but we can't.'

The book should end here but, as you'll have noticed, it doesn't. An era had ended but my career as a drug dealer hadn't. Although he never knew anything about it, David Sweetman was to blame. After our trip to Thailand, David's condition worsened. I took on some of the administration of the charity. David was sufficiently impressed with my efforts to retire as Secretary and appoint me in his place. In September there was a meeting at which he described exactly what my duties would entail. It was hard to understand him because he was losing the power of speech. He now moved with the aid of a Zimmer frame. After the business had been concluded, David whispered to me that he wanted to die and asked me if I could help.

In October I attended a committee meeting of the UK/Thailand Children's Fund. The directors co-opted me and, in my new role as Secretary, I began taking minutes. Fund-raising was on the agenda. The charity was in desperate need of cash and the Elton John AIDS Foundation still hadn't confirmed another grant. I said nothing. But I thought, 'This is silly.' These friends of mine were scrabbling around, begging for an amount of money which, in my former life, I could have cleared in just over a month.

The next day I made my decision.

VII

"One, holding his book like a rice bowl
So his eyes can pick out words, steady
While the other impersonates age and infirmity."
~ David Sweetman, *Looking Into the Deep End* ~

The circumstances surrounding my return to big-time crime were hardly propitious. The good times were over. I was very unhappy indeed, not because my own life was less than it might have been, but because my friends were suffering. Ray Selfe, the man to whom I owed my film career and so much more besides, had been ill for a long time, the wages of too many fry-ups and too much smoking. On 3rd September he collapsed and, like my father, went out like a light. The funeral, conducted by two spiritualist lunatics, who mispronounced Ray's name and reminded us that he was now with his loved ones (Ray was a devout atheist), caused me untold distress. Weeks later Walter Zerlin Jnr. was dead as well.

Walter was my best friend and for a quarter of a century our writing partnership was like a marriage. I think that, until the end of my life, I shall continue to think, 'That's a good joke. I must tell Walter,' and then realise that I can't. 2001 had got off to the worst start imaginable when Walter told me that he had cancer of the oesophagus and was undergoing chemotherapy. By August the cancer had spread to his lungs and liver and I knew that I should prepare myself for the inevitable. I struggled to complete the script of *The Farndale/Peter Pan* so that I could at least show it to him. I failed. I couldn't do it alone. Instead I wrote his obituary.[96]

Just before he died Walter began refusing all visitors. But at midnight on 4th November his wife, Pat, telephoned me to tell me that he wanted to see me. I went to the Royal Marsden Hospital the next day. It was a terrible shock to see a man with such a dynamic life force almost spent. He could no longer laugh and without laughter he wasn't Walter. 'I've had a tough time,' he said plaintively in a little falsetto voice. Pat had found a cranky cancer treatment, apricot kernels, on the Net and she fed them to him on a spoon. 'It's my last hope,' he whispered. I told him we'd achieved quite a lot, hadn't we, and he agreed.

Walter died at home five days later. At the Orthodox Jewish funeral there were only prayers, no eulogies, no tribute to the man Walter was. I was again heartbroken. Pat came up to me in the chapel and asked me to say something at

---

96   *The Guardian*, 14th December 2001

the wake. I tried to make amends. I wanted people to laugh and my memory is that they did. When *The Farndale/Murder Mystery* was reprinted, I dedicated the new edition to 'Walter Zerlin Jnr., the funniest man I have ever met.'[97]

And now David Sweetman wanted me to kill him.

My diary becomes very Ortonesque at this period because I was going direct from funerals and wakes to meetings necessary to re-establish myself as a drug dealer. Casey was as hard-headed as always and refused to advance me any merchandise until I coughed up the entire purchase price, an amount I didn't have because I'd given it all away. There was nothing for it but to ask my clientele for loans. The generous junkies came round to my house with bundles of banknotes. It took only a few days to amass the capital required. Any doubts I had that business might not recover were dispelled equally quickly. The clients I asked for cash told others what was happening and then it was as if a bush telegraph were in operation. I warned everyone that the Friday parties couldn't possibly resume. But within weeks Friday night was again music night. It was just that the music was now a little discordant.

I also turned to my clientele for help with David Sweetman's dilemma. Everyone was sympathetic. Some of us were approaching the age where the subject of euthanasia had to be taken seriously. Toby warned me that David had to commit suicide alone. Anyone who aided and abetted could be prosecuted. Helen advised me that I needed Nembutal and how much of it would constitute a fatal dose. She also recommended that anti-emetics be added to the mix. Abdul said that he might be able to skim small amounts of drugs off patients' prescriptions. But this may take some time. Then Dafydd told me that he was going to India, where almost anything could be obtained over the counter. I now had enough information to make a promise to David.

I met him ostensibly to sign papers for the charity. He seemed barely able to lift his pen. He was by now in a wheelchair and had had an operation to have a permanent catheter fitted. One by one, his functions were shutting down. When we were alone, I told him that everything was prepared. He told me that we must make arrangements before he was incapable of feeding himself. He then sank back into his chair, incredulous but relieved. He had been pleading with every doctor he knew to give him what he wanted and all had refused. I left David watching TV. My wish was for him to change his mind, but if this didn't happen, I was determined to help him. That night I wrote, 'I hope that, if it comes to it, someone will do the same for me.'

When I swung back into fund-raising action, I was able to offer the same range of products and more. I had a very good relationship with my GP,

---

[97]   London: Samuel French, 2007

who was happy to prescribe any amount of the sleeping pill zopiclone (very popular with the late night crowd) and Viagra. The miracle aphrodisiac had first turned up in Soho in 1998 priced £40 a tablet. I was able to undercut the sex shops quite considerably. But these wonder drugs made it all the more likely that party animals were going to come round to see me on Friday to stock up for the weekend.

Right from the off I saw the way that things were going to go. Another client was teetering on the edge of the abyss and I think he caused us more concern than anyone else. Toby started to worry us when he was admitted to hospital with pneumonia, and claimed that he had an hereditary degenerative disease and very little time to live. After he was discharged, he would visit me drunk at 7.45am. When he hugged me, I could feel his bones through his suit. He spent several days in my house, watching TV and sleeping on the sofa. He stopped working and said he was in therapy. On the evening of Walter's funeral he went berserk in my living room. In the early hours of the morning Alex and I were fighting with him in the street. He was trying to get into his car and we failed to restrain him.

Whether Toby really had the life-threatening illness he claimed I'm not sure although I doubt it. For one thing, he's still very much with us. For another, Toby on drugs cannot distinguish fantasy from reality. He once telephoned me because two gay male pop stars were having sex with young boys in his penthouse and he wanted me to contact the press. The next day he blamed that episode on one of the new designer drugs. Toby is a loose cannon who never should be allowed near anything stronger than a Trebor mint. But he is also one of the kindest and sincerest of my friends and it was his stimulating company that enlivened my parties for four years. I remember that the discussion about art, inspired by the 2001 Turner Prize going to someone who turned the lights on and off, was particularly lively.

It was druggy Toby who was also responsible for breaking up my whirlwind love affair; but I can't even hold this against him because afterwards I was consoled by caring Toby. Early in 2002 Eder arrived back in London for a somewhat longer stopover, which we planned to make the most of. It went horribly wrong on the second night at my house when Toby dropped in and brought out the drugs. Eder was not happy and took himself and his toothbrush back to his hotel. The next day he told me it was all over. We shook hands and I never saw him again. When I phoned Toby to tell him the news, he came round in a trice and soothed me with wise words about the importance of honesty in a relationship. I could have pretended that I was as pure as the driven snow; but sooner or later Eder would have learned the truth and the ending would have been the same. While on the subject of honesty, I have to say that Eder was a bit boring. Nevertheless I couldn't watch any Brazilian films for the rest of the year.

As if Toby wasn't causing us enough worry, Trev chose this very time to lose the last shreds of his self-esteem. After drug-related misbehaviour at work, he was informed that his career as a nurse was at an end. He took to lying around the house in a stupor and then stole money from me. At this point I asked him to leave. It was a case of all change at King's Cross. Manuel moved into Trev's old room; Bernardo returned to take Manuel's old room; and when Werner went back to Hamburg, he was replaced by a friend of Manuel's, a croupier named Bruce. Previously Bruce had spent Christmas Day with us and had appeared bright, inoffensive and convivial, all of which he was. But he was also a full-time stoner, who used skunk because he lacked self-confidence. He told me he hadn't had sex for two years; and it was his lack of success with women that ultimately led to one of the worst outcomes of my drug days.

One Friday we heard that police had found Neil, the best-looking of our medical team, asleep in his car, searched it, and found three wraps of my coke. Another career down the drain. Around 11.30 that night, the mirror, on which a thousand lines had been chopped, broke. The omens would not leave me alone. 'Right now,' I wrote, 'I never want to see another line of cocaine in my life.' But it was not easy to extricate myself from My Drug Shame now that I had pledged myself to dying children in Thailand.

The wheel turned full circle around this time when once again my legitimate career proved more fulfilling than the drug-driven phase through which I had been going. A chocoholic from childhood, when I was weaned on the boxes of Black Magic on the sideboard, I was now revelling in my job as the world's first chocolate correspondent. Each week in *What's On in London* I would review the new arrival on the sweetshop shelf or interview a celebrity about his or her favourite chocolate treat. I worked my way through nearly a hundred chocolebrities, a selection box that included many of my clients along with Denis Norden, Holly Johnson, Fenella Fielding and of course Julian Clary. Julian and I had drifted apart because of my lifestyle choice. The interregnum had not been particularly beneficial for either of us. While I was working as the world's worst drug counsellor, Julian had suffered the ignominy of presenting a game show that was taken off the air halfway through its run. He then postured on a beach in Majorca for a programme that may have been available on some Sky channel.

We got back together again after I appeared as a talking head in one of Channel 4's cheapjack list shows, *Top Ten Camp Icons*. Julian made it to number three behind his customary rivals Graham Norton and Paul O'Grady. Shortly afterwards Julian asked me for ideas for his next touring show and I suggested a history of homosexuality that eventually became part of his 2003 tour *Natural Born Mincer*. A rapprochement had been achieved.

I was summoned with my fellow conspirators, Helen and Dafydd, to David Sweetman's. David wanted to be sure that his departure from this world would go according to plan. It was difficult to talk because Vatch was hanging around. But then he left the room and Helen assured David that we had amassed enough drugs to do the job. Days later I accompanied David and Vatch under the Channel to France, where David transferred his house in the village of Pittefaux, outside Boulogne, to his nephew. David had written some of his books in this retreat, the former gatehouse of a château. Many friends and family had gathered for the ceremony. My job was to substitute for Vatch, who was flagging under the strain of caring for an increasingly tetchy invalid. David and I conversed in hushed tones while I changed his bag and made sure that there was no muck around his mouth and nose. He remained fastidious until the end, which pleased me. I had seen much younger and less infirm people lose more of their dignity.

After the property had been transferred, there was a celebratory meal during which David ordered wine and cognac and grew steadily drunker until we could not understand what he was saying. He refused to go to bed and several of us carried him upstairs, which seemed to amuse him. At the top of the stairs he fell silent, his eyes closed and the same thought flashed between his friends and me. But no, he was asleep. We got his clothes off, put him to bed, and then sat downstairs for a while, stunned by the gravity of the situation. I didn't know while we were in France that David already had decided the date of his death.

A week after our return to London, David summoned me again, this time to a hospice. I learned that he had chosen this location for his death so that Vatch wouldn't be put through the ordeal of discovering his corpse. What was more, he wanted to die the day after tomorrow. After I had recovered my composure I asked him whether he was certain that this was what he wanted. He was utterly pragmatic. He was worried that, if he waited any longer, the word would get around that he wished to die and that he would be put on suicide watch. He assured me that his only other worry was that he would botch his suicide and survive. I told David that he could rely on me to ensure his death. I came home and placed the lethal cocktail we had obtained into my 'herb grinder.' Then I was quite unable to do anything else.

Sunday, 7th April was much like any other day. Manuel wanted a massage and I complied. I went to a lunch party at Jenny Lautrec's; but I was more determined than usual to get sloshed because my next destination was the hospice.

'I was a bit late. There was still absolutely no doubt in David's mind. As soon as his tea was served, we got started. He had planned everything down to the last detail and was calm. He told me what to tell Vatch. It is a cliché, but the fact remains that there were tears streaming down my face. David was implacable. 'Don't let them see you crying,' he instructed me.

'I brought out the drugs, put them into a dish and then mixed them with yoghurt. I don't know where it came from but I said, 'See you later,' and his last words were, 'See you later, alligator.' I tried to walk out of the hospice with a blank face, but I was crying all the way to the tube station and on the train I fancy that the woman opposite looked at me askance.

'At home I got rid of all the evidence. I watched TV, and waited for the phone call. Oh, God, what would happen if the staff found David and revived him? But at 12.30am Vatch called and told me that David had died at 11pm. I made all the right noises including what David had instructed me, that he wanted Vatch to find someone else.

'Manuel came home. I was in such a state that I had to tell him. He was a great help. He's a lovely feller, says he's happy to be here, and I'm certainly happy to have him.'

The worst was over, but the fat lady had not sung. The next day I returned to the hospice. Thai men were everywhere. Vatch was ushering people into a darkened room to view David's corpse. I declined the invitation. The general consensus was that David had planned his death. He had spent the past week saying goodbye and Vatch suspected that he had acquired 'special medicine.' I was alarmed when a doctor informed me that the death should not have occurred. I made my excuses and went to the Cally sauna, where 'a nice guy gave me a thorough seeing to.' Later I was relieved to hear that David had been cremated. But questions were still asked.

The launch later in April of Vatch's latest book, *Thai Street Food*, was extraordinary in that its true writer, David Sweetman, who was in both senses of the word a ghost, was very much in evidence. His obituaries were on display and *The Times*[98] made it reasonably clear who actually had written Vatch's cook books. Vatch wanted to speak to me alone and my heart went out to him.

---

[98]   15th April, 2002

He regretted growing impatient with David in his hour of need. I could not help but be struck by another Lesson in Life.

Life as I had come to know it continued. In some ways it became even more decadent. On Friday nights Manuel served cocktails or Bernardo served Cuban street food. But I could not deny the sense of desperation in the air.

In May there was a succession of memorials to David Sweetman. At one of them Sarah Dunant suggested that there should be an Annual Memorial David Sweetman Dinner. There was general approval. But the Annual Memorial David Sweetman Dinner survived for only one more year before people lost interest.

By that time I knew that all the *fin de siècle* nonsense to which I had been a party was over.

PART 6

OVER
(2002-2015)

I

"Magnus ab integro saeclorum nascitur ordo."
~ Virgil ~

Here's a major confession. I continued in some way as a drug dealer until 2011. How could I stop? I had major commitments. But the life I had known, the life that had cast me as the host of one of London's most à la mode parties, ended in 2002. It seems now that in that year I was all too aware of the decline. As early as Friday 5th July, 2002, I wrote, 'I was alone, feeling miserable, hoping that at least one of the old Friday crowd would pop in to cheer me up. But not a peep. I think those days are over.'

The repercussions of the business venture I began at the end of the 20th century have continued to the present day. What I am now is what I was then. My friendships are almost entirely those I made while I was a drug dealer or those I have made subsequently. My previous life barely exists. I think there is a tribal mentality at work here. When I form a close new relationship it turns out almost invariably that the other person has had a similar background. Usually this will have involved both agony and ecstasy, comedy and tragedy. I find as I embrace old age that I cannot be doing with anyone who doesn't know what's going on in the world; hasn't snogged someone of the same sex; and isn't broad-minded about recreational stimulants. I don't feel I'm missing out by restricting myself in this way even though there are increasingly few interesting people who tick all three boxes.

Toby was one of the many new friends who drifted off in the early years of the 21st century. Generally my former clients moved out of London or out of the country; but Toby's disappearance, we learned, was accounted for by his spells in rehab. He later referred to his time hunched over a mirror and gabbling as his wilderness years. But he made sure he left me with something to remember him by. At the beginning of 2002 he insisted I exploit the collateral of my lovely home by purchasing a buy-to-let flat. I did as I was told and the contract for a two bedroom property opposite Pentonville prison was signed in the summer. The first tenants, a couple of friends of Manuel's, very rarely remembered to pay the rent and I had similar trouble with everybody else who lived there. The nadir of my dismal career as a property tycoon came in 2012, when a tenant trashed the place and did a runner. I had to hire a private eye to locate the dirty swine. I sold the flat to a neighbour shortly afterwards.

My inability as a landlord was compounded one thousand-fold by the catastrophic affair in Morocco, which also began in 2002. Naim had been to Marrakech on around thirty occasions before I first accompanied him. It was apparent on our first day what drew him to this ancient city and it wasn't the Jardin Majorelle. The boys lined up for inspection on the main cruising strip, the Avenue Mohammed V, and stood around fondling their crotches even in the grounds of the Koutoubia mosque. I was in the foyer of our five star hotel when I was beckoned into the newsagent by its beefy salesman. He pulled out his cock while tourists thumbed through *Paris Match*.

Naim always booked an expensive hotel for the rare occasions when he needed some sleep and rented a run-down apartment for his assignations, which took up most of each day and night. This was the first time I had seen Naim in full-on sex tourist mode and he was a sight for sore eyes. The apartment was sometimes filled with languid youths waiting to be summoned into the bedroom. My job was to ensure they didn't make off with anything valuable. I cannot deny that occasionally I took my own pick and I have a fond memory of Karim, a photographer from Fes, who was making a few extra dirhams while on holiday. Remind me to show you his photo. But Naim, more possessed than a dervish, thought nothing of hiring up to eight boys a day. 'I don't think I want to go to this apartment again,' I wrote on 19th July. 'It's all going to end in tears.' This was one of the reasons I suggested, on only our second trip to Marrakech the following year, that we buy an apartment together. Eventually we bought two apartments. And everything disintegrated to such a degree that I considered killing myself.

In October there was another fact-finding mission to Thailand. The facts I found in Chiang Mai weren't greatly to my liking. Antiretroviral drugs finally were getting through to the children; but the Thai administrator was withholding them from kids who weren't doing well at school. This was a 'cultural thing' I found very difficult to accept. A harassed doctor from a hospital in London, undeniably dedicated but lacking David Sweetman's theatrical flair, worried away at the messy accounts and tried to impose Western ways on the unwilling Thais. He wormed out of me the truth of David's death and told me we were extremely lucky that nobody had demanded a post mortem.

On this trip there was a large party of European observers, some of whom used the all-night Kathin festival at Mae Jem, where women spin cotton to make monks' robes, to avail themselves of the local hookers.

Not that I am criticising this of course. Back in Bangkok I tried more than one 'health club' although I also spent some time in Lumphini Park writing songs for Julian Clary. In one of them I was very proud of rhyming Winston Churchill with Julie Burchill.

At the end of the year I took two clients, Dafydd and Bruce, to the South of France, where the wife of another client owned a holiday home. We very nearly failed to get out of Luton Airport, where Bruce looked so nervous that he was given a thorough frisking by security officials. They didn't find the stash without which Bruce never travelled. On the Riviera we found most of the places Peter Noble used to write about during the Cannes Film Festival. One morning I said, 'Let's go to Italy,' which just seemed such a romantic notion. The trip took us through the old town of Menton, high on the rocks, where we picked oranges off a tree and I said, 'I want to make a film here,' never thinking that one day I would. I was back on the Riviera the following June, although this time accompanied only by Dafydd. We couldn't take another week of Bruce drooling over unattainable Oriental women.

My life has remained a parade; but from 2003 it has been the tail-end of the parade, with the dustcarts and the street sweepers and the onlookers who perhaps wished they could have been dancing on the floats, but have to be content to listen to the stories of those who actually were. The merest excuse for a party has always been indulged. I hope that in the fullness of time I'll drop dead at one of them and that, like the actress Betty Marsden, I'll be granted two precious seconds before I snuff it so that I can place my gin and tonic safely on the bar. But from 2003, although I continued to work part-time as a philanthropist, I was once again primarily a full-time hack, journeyman and luvvy, involved in sundry forgettable activities. I shall remind you of some of them as we go along.

My housemates came and went as the fancy took them. Manuel, who moved out in the mistaken belief that he and Nasreen were going to reunite, was replaced by Bruce's friend, Stuart, slender, bald and moody as if he were Vin Diesel's younger brother. He did the ironing with his shirt off, asked me if I could get him into porn, and then, not exactly out of the blue, admitted to being bisexual. This was an opportune admission because I happened to be writing about BiCon, 'a festival for bisexual people and their allies,' for *What's On in London.* I interviewed Stuart. He told me about the time he was working on a cruise ship and went to a party. He was kissing a girl, who was kissing another guy and, at one point, he realised that 'the hands on me weren't hers. It was him. I let him carry on.'[99] Soon Stuart was back on the cruise ships and Manuel had reclaimed his old room.

---

[99] 6th-13th August, 2003

Casey had begun his inexorable fade into the background and, because I needed to keep up the payments to the Thai charity, I replaced him with a succession of dealers. The best contact for weed was the owner of a King's Cross deli somewhat brazenly called Tony's Hemp Corner. What went on in the corners of this corner shop was an open secret among the locals; but nothing was officially confirmed until 2001, when a piece appeared in the *Evening Standard*: 'The shop has been selling cannabis for several years to more than 250 people.'[100] No charges were brought. 'The times they are a-changing,' I wrote. When actor Darius was cast in a major TV series, he attempted to retire from the coke trade and introduced me to his dealer, David, who ran a thriving business with his mother and a shady partner from a ground floor flat in Queen's Park.

One of the last social engagements I had with my mother happened around Mother's Day in 2003. Always intent on making my chocolate column in *What's On in London* topical, I quizzed the mothers of the *What's On* staff about their favourite confectionery. After interviewing my own mother,[101] our conversation turned to the arguments we used to have when I was living with the McGillivray family in Palmers Green. I had always assumed that I had been the cause. My mother's reply took me aback. 'It was because of your father,' she said with the candour of the elderly. 'He was very highly sexed and half the time I wasn't interested.' I was tickled pink and all childhood traumas were instantly forgotten. I loved the idea that my father was a stallion and wondered excitedly if this explained my own sex drive, still undiminished at the age of 55. It was also in 2003, at the gay rendezvous that is The Cally, that I met the black sex machine who has remained my fuck buddy to the present day. He calls himself Jordan and, because this is almost certainly not his real name, I presume that it is OK to use it.

Jordan fascinates me because, like my other fuck buddy, Thomas, he is a straight man who becomes a rampant, unashamed homosexual in my bedroom. He has a specific need that I am required to fulfil. I play the plantation owner who forces him, in his own role as my slave, to submit to my will. After we had enacted this scenario for the first time, I was a little disturbed. 'That was just a game, right?' I asked him. He was evasive. Years later, we were still playing the game. It was very important to him, all or nothing, which I think is a shame. But I may have spent all of five minutes trying to analyse it. It was as clear as day that it was I who was Jordan's slave, more than willing to cancel any engagement at the moment he texted his availability. OMG! Was this a relationship? (No, of course it wasn't.)

---

100 22nd June, 2001
101 26th March-2nd April, 2003

The first and as it turned out only David Sweetman Memorial Dinner took place at the flagship of the Thai Square restaurant chain on Trafalgar Square just over a year after David's death. There were a lot of absentees and too many long speeches. I tried to keep mine brief. When I quoted David as saying, 'I like the Sombrero because you know where you are. If a man fondles your bottom, you can be sure it's not a woman in a false beard,' I saw the harassed London doctor move away in despair. The sly old dog later married a Thai woman. The charity had become an arduous undertaking, a battle to rouse support among those who had lost interest.

The day after the party I received a phone call from a friend of a friend who, aware of my interest in British sex films, wanted to know if I had heard the rumour that a man calling himself David Hamilton Grant had turned up alive and well in Greece. Rumours have persisted that Grant faked his death; but of late the rumours have circulated only on some of the more *outré* sites. Like many of his films, this story has no ending.

End of the Night was a new spin on the country house mystery, performed somewhat incongruously in a sweatbox at the back of a blokey pub in Kennington. Like *White Cargo* and *Chase Me Up Farndale Avenue, s'il vous plaît!* it is one of those projects whose insignificance in the great scheme of things is out of all proportion to the importance it played in my life. Its begetter was actor Jonathan Rigby, who wanted a play with a stonking great part for himself. He hired a *Doctor Who* script editor to write him one. I was cast, in what must have been some kind of sardonic joke, as the host of a party who appears to drug his guests with lysergic acid. As is usual with this kind of tinpot production, hardly any critics bothered to review it; but a couple who did found it quite entertaining. It was instantly forgotten, but not by me.

I developed an immediate rapport with Jerome, the exuberant and very funny actor who played the juve lead. Our bromance began on the night I took him to a *What's On in London* dinner at which the fawning proprietor poured us three bottles of Dom Perignon. Jerome may well have hoped that this was a typical night out for me. In quick succession he became one of my housemates and one of my closest friends. Because he is a responsible husband and father, who also behaves occasionally like a teenage wildcat, I have found myself responding by playing both the helpless infant, unable to perform the simplest .mpeg2 file transfer, and the wise old counsel, tut-tutting the follies of youth. I can assure those dreading old age that this role play is one of its most unexpected delights. It was also on *End of the Night* that I met a young man with a steely intensity whom I described variously as garrulous, facetious and drunken. He was Keith Claxton, who was indeed all three of the above, but also a clever director with delightfully perverse ideas, and a wickedly funny twister of words. I was to make nine short films with him until the inevitable arguments led to a parting of the ways.

Throughout 2003 there were vestiges of the parties I had so enjoyed and some of them were crazier than anything that had happened during my halcyon days. One Friday in June I was having quiche in Marianne Stone's garden and talking to her daughter, Kara, about the way her life had been turned around. Few will now remember that in 1999, she sold a topless photo of Prince Edward's fiancée, Sophie Rhys-Jones, to *The Sun*. Even fewer will remember that it was just one of about twenty pictures intended to illustrate an article about Kara's days on Capital Radio. But as a result of her supposed treachery, she was called the most hated woman in Britain. The fall-out from this indiscretion was considerable; by 2003 Kara was living mainly abroad and it was in her Nice apartment Dafydd and I had stayed earlier in the year.

It was Dafydd who on that June Friday summoned me back to my house, where a hare-brained, drug-inspired scheme was getting out of hand. Bernardo's friend Osvaldo was visiting from Cuba and didn't want to go home. Bernardo had convinced Alex's friend Deirdre to marry him. 'The wine continued to flow and it was quite like the Fridays of old,' I wrote, 'even down to me leaving them to it and going to bed at 2am.' The next day Deirdre telephoned me in morning-after tears, worried that she actually may have set the date of the wedding.

Perhaps the most radical sign of the times occurred when Bruce tried to take over my mantle as party host and I objected. Admittedly this was because his weekday parties went on all night, keeping the rest of the house awake. One morning I found booze poured all over the remote control devices, making it impossible for me to switch on the television, a cardinal sin. Bruce's first reprimand followed.

Eighteen months after his departure, the prodigal Trev was back and it was as if he'd never been gone:

'He phoned and said he was in the area. He'd been to a soul night in Finsbury Park and was on his way to see me. We chatted over breakfast. He and Sue are on the point of breaking up. He claims to have been off the Charlie for a year.

'Suddenly – and this was a big surprise – he said he'd come for sex. I had no objection. Immediately he disappeared to prepare. It was the usual scenario. He'd put on stockings and suspenders and wanted me to treat him like the slut he was. But unusually he began to get hard almost straight away and eventually he came twice. He went for his train mid-afternoon promising to pay me the rent he owes'

Later a friend told me about his cousin; the trouble he'd had being Jewish and gay in Glasgow in the 1940s and 50s; and how he'd surmounted his early difficulties to become a successful songwriter in New York named Richard Kayne. His was another story I liked and I interviewed him. He was 76 and when he grinned he became much younger, little more it seemed than the dashingly romantic teenager in the photographs he showed me. Almost predictably his early career had been advanced by Peter Noble and Marianne Stone, whom he remembered fondly. (Later I took Richard to meet Marianne.) Richard gave great copy. 'I was sucked off on the stairs of the St James' theatre. You can put that in because it's gone now.'[102]

I sold the article to the first magazine to which I offered it. *QX* was a weekly, free gay magazine, picked up in London bars along with your next shag. The magazine was an odd mix because its back pages had photos of naked prostitutes advertising their unfeasibly large penises, while its front pages had serious articles written by the likes of the Chief Executive of the Stonewall charity and at least three of my clients. Timing has always played an important part in my career, but my telephone call to *QX* was unusually propitious. A new editor had only just been appointed and he wanted new writers with new ideas. Cliff Joannou gave me some of the most interesting assignments of my journalistic career and I stayed with *QX* for the next ten years. Cliff is a Greek Cypriot so sexually attractive that he makes the Greek Cypriots with whom I went to school look like garden gnomes. I never laid a finger on him. But as far as another member of the editorial staff is concerned, my integrity let me down.

---

[102] *QX*, 26th November, 2003

II

"Today marked the 40th anniversary of my entry into show biz.
I feel like a veteran who still hasn't quite got started."
~ Diary entry, 7th September, 2004, aged 57 ~

People came to and went from my house in King's Cross in great numbers throughout the first decade of the 21st century. The traffic was such that I went to Selfridges and commissioned a sign, 'Liberty Hall.' I never hung it because I thought that it would be stolen; but I still have it and one day I might consider making it a permanent memorial. By 2004 the haphazard administration of the Thai charity was causing me grief; the harassed doctor found another Secretary. But, because of my unusual personal involvement, I was determined to keep David Sweetman's name alive. I remained in business as a drug dealer in order to make payments to my new pet charity, The Food Chain, which delivered hot meals and other services to people housebound by HIV and AIDS. Although I became increasingly involved in projects that took me out of the capital, my diary suggests that mobile phone technology allowed clients to descend on me whenever I was in London.

There was always a queue of friends waiting for vacant rooms in my house. When Alex bought his own flat, he was replaced by Jerome; but although Jerome was rollicking good company, I missed Alex's intellectual stimulation. This was replaced within months when Manuel moved on again, making his room available to a friend of whom I had been growing increasingly fond. I shall call him, in honour of his Russian heritage, Yuri. Yuri is brilliant, compassionate and affable, a combination that draws people to him like moths to a flame. Within days of moving into my house, he was its alpha male. Hero worship was involved, certainly on my part. Like others before him, he moved a girlfriend into his room. I uttered the merest squeak of indignation and then maintained a respectful silence. I don't like rows but especially I didn't want a row with Yuri. He was too much of an asset to the house.

Yuri's chief contribution was the introduction of a more mature kind of party in keeping with the new era. He regularly cooked Sunday roasts, which were followed by quizzes and increasingly elaborate party games, which he also hosted. Sunday became the new Friday and this tradition continued for nearly ten years. There was a particularly dissolute Sunday, part of which was spent at Soho Pride. We settled outside a bar in Frith Street and Yuri demanded we knock back shots of absinth. For the first but not the last time in my life I awoke on the living room sofa with no memory of how I came to be there.

Within months of my suggestion to Naim that we should buy property in Marrakech, we were the owners of two apartments in the Ville Nouvelle. One was in a luxurious new development, the other, which needed refurbishment, was in an older but still attractive block. The cost to me, *de toute l'affaire*, from the bricks and mortar to the corkscrews in the kitchen drawers, was £179,000, raised with the aid of an unscrupulous financial adviser (they were ten a penny in those days), who swore that my income was twice what it really was. Naim and I agreed that we should rent out the apartments when we weren't using them. I commissioned a website, Apartments Marrakech, and wrote copy aimed at a market more aware of the sex than the souks ('Strictly between you and us, you can get almost anything you want in Marrakech, as long as you're discreet and take care not to offend local traditions.') The approach found its target audience like an Exocet. Even before the website went 'live', gay men throughout Europe were making enquiries. Regrettably we made promises to prospective clients that we rarely fulfilled. Our reliable agents forgot to collect holidaymakers from the airport, and our attentive concierges knocked at the doors of the apartments at midnight asking for tips. I had ventured into alien territory without proper research and was soon to pay the price. Just over a year after the formation of Apartments Marrakech, Naim and I had our first row.

Marrakech will remain burned on my memory until the day I die, not only because of the intense sensual pleasures and the suicidal misery it engendered, but also because it was on one of my business trips, spent signing agreements, buying sofas and fucking Abdullah, that my mother died. She hadn't been particularly unwell. Right up until 2003 she had been encircling the globe as her alter ego, the merry widow Pat, who got to her feet at community luncheons and talked about her life in Palmers Green, evidently to great acclaim. She had achieved late in life what I am fairly sure she had wanted as a young woman. I could not have been more delighted.

Then, in 2004, she had a relatively brief spell in hospital. Something was wrong but nobody was quite sure of its nature. I visited Mum and, although she seemed dazed, she led me to believe she was going to be discharged. A month later, while I was in Marrakech, I heard from my brother, Paul, that Mum was 'poorly', his euphemism for 'at death's door.' She died on 9th June at the age of 88. At her funeral I attempted to speak without notes and forgot my words. Somewhat magnanimously Paul claimed that this failure had its own eloquence.

Mum left behind a modest bequest – I shall return to this – and a cat called Sheba, a poor substitute for the ginger kitten I had bought her after Dad died. Mum had named this cat Leo. It was the love of her life. 'I don't like to say this,' she confessed to me, 'but I think more of him than your father.'

When it died of a heart attack in 1998, Mum was never quite the same again. Sheba, who arrived in 1999, was not house trained. Whenever I visited Mum's flat, I could smell cat piss. But I wanted to give Sheba a home. I had been without a cat since 2001 when Charlie's owner had seen it coming out of my house and demanded that I hand it over. 'This is a loved cat,' I was told. The fact that it had chosen to live in my house for a year was not addressed. Unfortunately Sheba never learned how to become part of polite society. We spent a year dousing the sofa cushions in bleach, and then handed the culprit to the cats' home. The remaining connection to my parents was severed.

On the rare occasions that I was not digging a hole for myself in Marrakech, I was engaged in a succession of artistic endeavours, all interlinked, all connected in some way with the life I had had at the turn of the century. Eduardo, one of my many mad Portuguese contacts, wanted me to appear in a mad Portuguese play called *All for Nothing*. I read the script and couldn't make head nor tail of it. But my role, as a Greek professor, had a lengthy and impressive speech right at the end of the play, which I thought I could hack. I said yes. The play was the opening attraction at South London's Menier Chocolate Factory, later to become a major Fringe venue. The opening attraction, however, was not a success. Somebody worked out that we played to two paying customers per night and the reviews were, shall we say, mixed. 'Jorge Guimaraes, the author of this play, is apparently Portugal's most prolific living playwright,' noted *The Guardian*.[103] 'He may be quick, but on the evidence of this effort he is also very bad.'

An associate of Eduardo's, Maria, then recommended me for a production of *As You Like It*. This is worthy of mention only because it is indicative of what a *klutz* of an actor can achieve if he has the *chutzpah*. The production was clumsy and amateurish, the work of a couple of teachers who had all the academic knowledge and none of the stagecraft. It was done in a derelict stable, shortly to become a Nando's. But none of this matters because I got to play Jaques, said, 'All the world's a stage,' and was commended for it. 'David McGillivray's Jaques was a surprise,' declared the *Times Literary Supplement*.[104] 'The overwhelming ennui that he injected in the Seven Ages speech was a wonderful performance.' This is one of the more respectable reasons that I can die happy.

Keith Claxton was sufficiently impressed with my performance in the play *End of the Night* to cast me as the Angel of Death in his film *After Image*. It was another non-event, never shown to anyone other than the cast and crew, but it had repercussions. Because I liked the way Keith had handled

---

103 14th April, 2004
104 22nd November, 2004

things, I asked him if he'd be interested in directing a film I'd written based on a piece I'd seen at a graduation show at Ken's mime school. He was. This became *Child Number Four,* shot over a weekend in a field in Hertfordshire. This too amounted to very little. But it suggested to me that Keith and I could continue working together. On the way to the Hertfordshire location I told him about our next film which, because Mum had left me £10,000, would be shot in Portugal.

Back at my house clients now tended to make a purchase and leave. A select few stayed for a free optional extra, a massage. There are many people around today who will confirm that I have magic fingers. They rose pain-free from my table. Manuel was a big fan. So was his actor friend, Darius. Yes, here I was handling a naked TV star in my living room. We had heard rumours that Darius had narrowly escaped the attentions of the *News of the World.* The rumours were true. At least one snitch had told investigative journalist Mazher Mahmood that Darius had an illegal sideline. Posing as a movie producer, Mahmood had tried to coax Darius into his customary lair, a hotel room rigged with cameras and microphones; but a couple of days before the appointment, Darius was warned by a friend that he ought not to keep it. He didn't. He was very lucky. Others – those I have already mentioned as well as Lawrence Dallaglio, Brian Harvey, Johnnie Walker and Neil Montgomery, who advised a House of Lords select committee on drug use – were less fortunate.

One of the major influences in my life, Mike Sparrow, died of kidney failure on 11th January, 2005. He was 56. I had seen him last at the David Sweetman Memorial Dinner, when at first I didn't recognise him. He had developed the jowls of a much older man. Subsequently I participated in two contrasting celebrations of his life. At his funeral I said what his family and former colleagues wanted to hear, that he had a talent for bringing the right people together, and that he packed all his achievements into a few short years. This was true enough. But a few days later at Mike's local, the North Star in the Finchley Road, a very different group of people shared a different truth. These were the drunks he had gathered around him in the last years of his life; those that knew he polished off half a bottle of vodka every day before propping up the bar until closing time. They idolised him. An Irish labourer blubbed into his beer that Mike had been his first male lover and that they had been inseparable almost until the end. I could easily imagine Mike being drawn into this convivial coterie, holding forth on past glories to a new but no less appreciative audience. Probably it was a lovely way to go.

In March I took Keith Claxton and the rest of my crew to Portugal to make my next film, *Mrs Davenport's Throat,* an old idea shoehorned into a striking location. When Nuno, my artist in residence, had invited me to visit him in Lisbon, I found that he was squatting in an abandoned veterinary hospital.

I loved its monolithic marble slabs on which animals had been operated. A mad but talented Portuguese soap opera actor, Luis Castro, ended up on one of these slabs and had his throat cut with a Stanley knife by Celia Williams from *All for Nothing.* I loved Keith's kinky climax, which intercut the bloodbath with Celia sucking one of Luis' fingers so that she could remove the ring she coveted. A tough critic, Alan Jones, was similarly impressed and, later in the year, accepted the film for his horror festival, FrightFest, which took place at a cinema in Leicester Square. We celebrated my return after a quarter of a century to London's West End by getting word-slurringly drunk. Sadly both the hospital and the cinema are no more.

As soon as I returned to London I got stuck into Julian Clary's latest TV show, *Come and Have a Go,* a complex, interactive game designed to promote the National Lottery. It went out live on a Saturday night and was consequently immensely exciting. Minutes before transmission Julian would throw things at me like, 'Think of a joke about a sea lion.' The producers were also on tenterhooks, worrying that their unpredictable star would slip banned words, such as 'bullocks' and 'cochlea', back into the script. The ratings were very good; but we heard that Camelot, the all-seeing eye of the Lottery, wanted something simpler. Or, in other words, Eamonn Holmes.

I was now free to make another film. I had the bit between my teeth. *Wednesday* was the script I wrote for Marianne Stone. But wild horses couldn't have dragged her back in front of a camera. She had retired in 1989 after an estimated 224 film appearances (at that time a record for an actress) and had resisted every attempt to lure her into making a comeback. 'I don't want to be Marianne Stone, the actress,' she told me. 'I want to be Mary Noble, the widow of Peter Noble.' I thought I could change her mind. I had read many stories of producers wearing down actors' resistance with gifts of flowers and chocolates. I tried the same ploy. But I failed. All I succeeded in doing was getting her to make her last public appearance at a *Carry On* convention at Pinewood studios in the autumn of 2004. 'No one will know who I am,' she protested. I knew this wouldn't be the case and, sure enough, there was a long queue for her autograph. But she was distressed by her more obsessive fans and I never got her out of the house again.

Marianne's part in *Wednesday* was taken by 92-year-old Anna Wing. It was hers after she asked us at her audition, 'Do you want me to take my clothes off?' I arranged to meet Keith in Soho to discuss script changes. But neither of us could keep the appointment because the date was 7th July.

'I left the house before 10am. But at King's Cross traffic was gridlocked and literally thousands of people were milling around Pentonville Road. A woman told me a bomb had gone off and that

312

she had seen bloodied people. There was no public transport out of the area; cordons everywhere. I tried to walk to my meeting with Keith and eventually found a way down Gray's Inn Road.

'At Holborn lots of emergency vehicles screamed down the streets. Holborn underground was closed. At Covent Garden an official said the entire tube network was shut down. In Leicester Square people were gathered around a van, which had its radio on. That was the first I knew that there had been four bombs, one on a bus, the rest on tubes. Twenty reported dead.

'Keith phoned and said he couldn't make the meeting. There was by now no public transport throughout London. There was nothing to do but to walk home. The streets were strangely empty, like an apocalyptic movie. But in Tottenham Court Road people were gathered around shop windows, watching TVs. King's Cross was on all the screens.

'At Euston I found another cordon. I couldn't get home. I had to walk north, almost to Camden Town, then south down Caledonian Road. By now my phone was bleeping constantly: texts from friends asking if I was OK. Yuri called from Spain. He's running with the bulls in Pamplona.

'I got in and collapsed in front of the TV. The death toll had doubled [eventually there were 52 victims and more than 700 people injured]. Stirring speeches from Blair and Livingstone. Suddenly there was Emily Maitlis, from *Come and Have a Go*, the first commentator to say that this attack was inevitable after the Madrid bombings last year. Clients began arriving and, just like 11th September, 2001, we couldn't tear ourselves from the TV.

'At 11pm Caledonian Road was still closed to traffic and a fleet of TV vans was parked there. The eyes of the world are on us!'

III

"Progress does have a reverse gear."
~ Alex Main ~

For a man in his late Fifties, who under normal circumstances should have been planning his retirement, life remained full of incident. And not just incident but high-flying, soul-searing incident to which by rights only the very prominent or the very august should be privy. 15th October, 2005, was particularly notable: 'Today,' I wrote, 'I attended a memorial, a wedding and a birthday party, i.e. birth, marriage and death, but in the wrong order, which appealed to my liking for the inverse.' My clients were involved in some way in each event.

At my house residents continued to come and go. When Bruce went on holiday, I went into his room to close the window and was appalled by the filth in which he was living, although 'living' is the wrong word. The room was by any standard other than Quentin Crisp's uninhabitable. Evidently he had spent the last three years sitting in one position on the end of his bed to smoke his joints. Fag ash was piled up on the carpet like an ant hill. Shortly afterwards Bruce achieved what should have been his heart's desire. He began a relationship with a Japanese woman named Keiko. Like many girlfriends before her, she moved in, but Keiko was also accompanied by what appeared to be the entire contents of her previous flat. We had to negotiate our way around cardboard boxes piled in the living room. My patience was at an end and I told Bruce he had to leave. Bernardo and I spent a dreadful weekend cleaning the room and emptying bucket after bucket of black grime down the toilet.

Bruce was replaced by Bradley, whom Yuri had known at college and who now had a dull but well-paid job as an account manager. Bradley was the epitome of a relatively new phenomenon, the metrosexual. He was as straight as a die, but in his smoulderingly good-looking youth he had been one of those who took off his shirt to indulge in anything going at a thumpingly popular gay dance club called Trade. Bradley's old habits weren't about to die. He, Yuri, Jerome and their friends over-indulged their metrosexual fancies (watching footie, thrashing PlayStation, and driving Bernardo wild with desire) pretty much every evening in my living room. I struggled to satisfy their drug intake. My dealer, David, was in turmoil after he had caught his shady partner stealing from him. I replaced him with a couple of misfits who were to be my final drug connections. Warren was a younger, more paranoid carbon copy of Casey; instead of sitting in front of his TV, he sat in front of his computer, playing online poker. Isaac was an old-school smuggler, who had spent time in at least four jails, one in Algeria, and periodically returned from foreign parts with a stomach full of cocaine-filled condoms. They both rather scared me. Drug dealing wasn't what it was.

Every few weeks, it seems, I was either in Marrakech or trying to sort out problems in Marrakech. The electricity was cut off; the TV aerial was blown off the roof; doors were locked and keys were lost and the emails from customers who were not getting the service they expected mounted up. Like many before him, Naim discovered that he couldn't work with me. After our first row, things deteriorated very rapidly. During one of his solo trips to the pink city, he bombarded me with angry texts. 'Naim said he was over there doing all the work,' I wrote. 'I very nearly replied saying you're over there getting cock up your arse. But I controlled myself.' A year later the partnership was over and Naim was making plans to buy me out of it.

The Moroccan affair dragged on for six torturous years during which time I began scouring the Internet for Nembutal. But even as the black dog was at my door, I remember telling friends that I didn't want my miserable experience to sour my attitude to Marrakech, a city I had grown to love. Once, at sunset, I was sitting on my balcony with two Friday night pals and a bottle of wine and I told them, 'I've imagined doing this for decades and now I'm doing it.' Even more substantially, I produced one of my most admired films in Marrakech. *In the Place of the Dead* stars Anthony Wise, my friend from *The Crime of Father Amaro,* who goes in search of rent boys (mostly played by Naim's rent boys) but succeeds only in conjuring up a djinn. The film was accepted by the London Lesbian & Gay Film Festival after which it played internationally and won two awards in the US. I then sold it to MTV's gay channel Logo.

The last time I stayed in our properties in Marrakech was early in 2006. Naim and I were required to sit around while workmen repaired everything that had been broken. Actually, however, Naim spent the time hustling boys in and out of bedrooms in a manner that put me in mind of a French farce. I wrote the screenplay of my next film, inspired by Kara Noble's adjoining apartments in Nice (what's going on in the mysterious flat next door?) and the picturesque beauty of nearby Menton. It was called *We're Ready for You Now.* Four days after we arrived on location, I looked at my mobile and read the text, 'Bruce has committed suicide.'

The circumstances of Bruce's death were horrific. His on/off relationship with Keiko was apparently off, and he was sharing a flat with a stoner mate, another of my former clients. On the night of his death, he had begun cutting himself in the living room, continued in the bathroom, and finished in his bedroom with his throat and wrists slashed. The official cause of death, however, was suffocation. He also had a plastic bag over his head. This was no cry for help. He began killing himself when he knew there was no chance of being interrupted. He didn't leave a note.

I endured another religious funeral which included almost no reference to the deceased. Everything was said afterwards: perhaps Bruce had unresolved issues with his father. Perhaps the co-worker with whom Bruce was smitten rejected his advance and this was one rejection too many. But this was all conjecture as was the worry that Bruce wouldn't have taken his life if he hadn't been high as a kite. Bruce's mother seemed to know more than she said when she observed that, 'He was too intelligent to cope with the life that he endured.' We nodded as if we understood. At the wake Keiko was passed, sobbing uncontrollably, from mourner to mourner, none of whom could tell her anything approaching the truth. It was extremely distressing and we couldn't wait to get home and get wasted.

Simultaneously we were coping with the terminal illness of Russell Churney. He had been part of our lives since we met him in Edinburgh in 1987. Russell had become Julian Clary's pianist; Erika Poole and I were Farndale Ladies; and Erika and Russell hit it off immediately. Later Russell was a Friday night regular and, every time we met, I wished so much that we could make some kind of radio programme together. His audience knew him as a brilliant musician; but his wit had not been exploited. After he was struck down by pancreatic cancer, I spent much of the early part of 2006 driving him to and from hospital for chemotherapy. But I wanted to do something that might take his mind off illness and devised a programme, *Table Hopping*, in which Russell and I visited restaurants and talked over dinner. Guests such as Julian Clary, Victor Spinetti and Barb Jungr joined us for dessert. Regrettably the series was broadcast on Resonance, a community station apparently operated by whoever happened to be passing the building at the time. I had my head in my hands as I listened to my lovingly prepared programmes stopping, re-starting and jumping forward, these glitches all interspersed by the broadcaster's *bête noire*, dead air. I hoped to God nobody, but especially Russell, was listening. Nine months after the final broadcast he was dead. He was only 42.

Julian Clary himself appeared to be in the process of settling down. He had bought a house in Kent previously owned by Noël Coward and was establishing himself as a novelist. But he was not above the occasional trip to London to appear in TV trash that paid for a new roof or the refurbishment of Marlene Dietrich's bathroom. Far and away the finest example of the depths to which he was prepared to sink was his role as a judge on *The All Star Talent Show* in which 'celebrities', so far down the pecking order that the alphabet is not extensive enough to categorise them, performed what amounted to their party pieces. Thus Andy Scott-Lee, who may have been in a reality show, did a magic trick, and joke MP Lembit Öpik played the harmonica.

I loved the show because I was surrounded by people with no talent and because it was live. Therefore I was required to write jokes while we were on air and slip them to my employer during the commercial breaks. This was the TV equivalent of cocaine. *Apropos,* several of my former clients were involved in this débâcle and one of them was very obviously popping back to her dressing room every time we went to ads. I felt there was a good chance that the show was so bad that it could become a Friday night cult. But I was wrong. Even *The Sun,* which probably represented its target audience, called *The All Star Talent Show* 'a TV disaster of such epic proportions Oliver Stone's interested in securing the film rights.'[105] After the final programme Julian emailed me, 'Having finished the series I feel slightly grubby.' It was not recommissioned.

I missed one of the live shows because I was in Southwold shooting *Tincture of Vervain,* intended to be the last of my horror movies with Keith Claxton. This project was, I felt, a cracking wheeze, a film shot in Jill Freud's house and garden while the Southwold Summer Theatre was in full swing. Its actors, who had nothing to do during the day, provided our cast. It was boosted by none other than Fenella Fielding, playing the Queen of the Witches, a part Keith had written for 96-year-old Luise Rainer, the first woman to win two Oscars. Alas, Frau Rainer sent me a curt message: 'This is of no interest to me.' Her loss. The time has come to reveal that, when we shot *Tincture of Vervain,* I had run out of cash. The film was quite elaborate and Fenella didn't come cheap. Therefore it had to be financed with drug money. Well, get over it. So was *Deep Throat.* And that's a classic.

Jerome decided that the time had come to move on from my house. I asked him what he would miss most as he ventured out into the world and he replied, 'The sense of belonging.' Mission accomplished. Jerome donated his room to his friend, Doug, who took up residence at the end of 2006. Doug seemed like the perfect addition to our family. He had been part of the metrosexual confederacy for some time and was so sympathetic to its ideals that he had nearly died of AIDS. But now he had bounced back from intensive care, appeared to have a steady job as a designer, and, although he was in what might be called denial, we felt very warmly towards him. I was encouraged to make him an offer he couldn't refuse.

At the end of 2006 I wrote a fateful email. In a deduction worthy of Sherlock Holmes' Smarter Brother, Naim held me responsible for the theft of his suitcase from an apartment I did not own. Perhaps due to the hangover I was suffering from the previous night's party, I told him never to contact me again and, with tautology I rarely employed, to fuck off. I set in motion thereby a train of events that was heading nowhere but derailment.

---

105   29th September, 2006

Perhaps it was a death wish. If it was, I very nearly achieved my aim. But I have to say, all these years later, that I believe that everything was meant to be. I came through a term of trial and I think I learned something from it. Could it be humility? You have another couple of chapters to decide.

2007 was the year in which my life was turned around, not by any spiritual awakening but, more in keeping with my chosen lifestyle, by a meeting with an 83-year-old pornographer. I shall be very surprised if its repercussions don't continue for the rest of my life. Then again, life being what it is, 2007 was the year in which everything stayed the same. It was the year of my 60th birthday and I was encouraged to throw an appropriately ostentatious party. I hired a bar built on the site of one of Soho's first strip clubs and about 140 of my friends accepted my invitation. Apparently the toilet cubicles were fully occupied throughout the evening.

I vaguely remember singing Justin Timberlake's 'Sexyback', but I clearly remember unwrapping one of my birthday presents. His name was Nick. He was one of those who made the journey from my mirror of dreams to my massage table and ultimately to my bedroom. He was a lithe and sensuous young man and I was a very lucky pensioner. The next day Alan Jones devoted the whole of his FrightFest blog[106] to his report on the party, which had me spluttering with incredulous laughter. 'Clearly David had gone through his address book and if they weren't dead, they were invited,' Alan recounted. 'Some of the guests were "clients" from his most unusual career turn away from showbiz, one not to be sniffed at.'

By this time I had decided yet again to get out of the drug trade, which had become a matter of going through the motions. It bore no resemblance to the money-spinning fiesta I had begun ten years earlier. I also felt more strongly than ever that I was about to have my collar felt. Word reached me that my latest dealer, Warren, had been busted. It turned out he wasn't paranoid after all. They really were after him. He was quite a catch. The police confiscated his stash and £26,000 in cash. For all I knew they had his mobile phone records as well. It was time to retire again. This time I sold the business to our new housemate, Doug. He seemed the perfect choice to carry on my bad work: intelligent, well-adjusted, and he had his own sources. Alas, within two weeks of taking over, he seemed to go to pieces. I would answer the door to clients and then be unable to get Doug to come out of his room. The next I knew he'd lost his regular job. Friends told me Doug was sticking most of his merchandise up his nose, and I had the most depressing sense of *déja vu*.

Our other housemate, Yuri, decided to go on a voyage of discovery, a six month tour of the world, before he decided what he wanted to do with

---

106   11th September, 2007

the rest of his life. In his absence his room was occupied by Eli, a sweet little stand-up comic, soon to top bills around the world, which is why I can't say anything else about him. I was fortunate enough to live in very congenial company (people with foibles but that was fine with me) and this is what got me through my trials. Naim's first claim against me was for £5,000 for monies owed and 'personal injury.' He wasn't satisfied with the outcome of this case, which did not go in his favour, and he sued me again, this time for £18,000, his estimation of the income that had been lost because I had mismanaged our properties. By the time we settled in 2011, his grievances against me had been heard by approximately fifteen judges and cost me a sum I have never dared calculate but which is probably in the region of half a million pounds. There was also, as I have indicated, a point at which I wanted to take David Sweetman's way out. But let us not dwell on this right now. Let us turn instead to the pornographer who helped me re-invent myself in such a positive way.

When I was working for *Films and Filming* in the 1970s I became aware of the work of a New York film maker named Peter de Rome. His pornography, impossible to see in the UK, was nevertheless covered extensively in my magazine and, in one issue,[107] a photo spread of *The Erotic Films of Peter de Rome* was placed opposite my own column, the one in which I answered readers' questions. It made me feel later that I was destined to work with Peter de Rome and, when the time was right, this is what happened. I went to BFI Southbank for a special event, which comprised a screening of some of Peter's films (being shown in the UK for the first time) and an interview with the man himself. The films were in all honesty variable; but he appeared to have introduced in the late 1960s and early 1970s stylistic devices that became the norm for the gay porn industry that developed subsequently. He also appeared to have lived the colourful life (hobnobber with the rich and famous, gay rights pioneer, civil rights campaigner) that appealed to me as a journalist. I wanted to interview him.

After meeting Peter and writing a piece[108] in which I described him as 'one of the most important gay film makers of all time', I became convinced that we should work together. Wearing once again my film producer's hat, I put together a package that I felt couldn't fail: a film starring Peter de Rome and directed by Nathan Schiff, who had an underground reputation for the amateur slashers he had made in New York as a teenager. Marc Morris showed them to me in 1993. They were crude, excessive and derivative, but one of them, *The Long Island Cannibal Massacre*, had some reasonably proficient special effects for what was little more than a home movie. I interviewed Nathan the

---

107   August, 1974
108   *QX Men,* August, 2007

following year and gave him a pretty easy ride although I did admit that the sex and violence in one of his films 'makes one fear for their creator's sanity.'[109] There's many a true word spoken in jest.

When *In the Place of the Dead* was shown in New York in November, 2007, I went to see it, had (unplanned) sex with a festival administrator, and tracked down Nathan Schiff. He hadn't made a film, or done anything in particular, for seventeen years, and was now a 50-year-old man living with his mother. His bedroom was filled with plastic monsters built from self-assembly kits. The alarm bells would have deafened even the world's most incompetent producer. But still I forged ahead. My rationale was that Nathan's films recently had been released on DVD and he was picking up new fans.

Abracadaver!, about the horror that befalls a man who answers an advertisement for a magician's assistant, was rushed into production in order to qualify for the following year's London Lesbian & Gay Film Festival. Peter wasn't able to come to London and Nathan wouldn't fly anywhere and so, in another fit of quixotic idiocy, I chose to shoot the picture in New York, where I had no contacts. Nor did Nathan, who contributed zilch to my panic-stricken pre-production. On the first day of shooting it was obvious that Nathan was still an amateur film maker. Sometimes he had to be reminded to call 'action.' If I had adhered to my own tenet, I would have fired him on the spot; but I let him hang around for the remainder of the hellish schedule, which was largely directed by my cameraman.

There are two versions of this film and they're both dross. I wouldn't give you tuppence for either of them. Nathan's cut, which features miles of extra footage, including an interpretative dance, is completely incomprehensible. My version doesn't make much sense either because important scenes were never shot; but it's a lot closer to the gay horror movie I had intended. Just to prove, however, that there is no accounting for taste, Nathan's *Abracadaver!* won the Best Short prize at a New York film festival, while my *Abracadaver!* was included as an extra on the BFI's DVD of *The Erotic Films of Peter de Rome*.

That BFI DVD also included *Fragments*, a short documentary I made about some of Peter's unfinished films and unrealised projects. It inspired me to make a much longer film about his remarkable life, *Peter de Rome: Grandfather of Gay Porn*, which went on to become the most critically acclaimed film of my entire career, the only one to receive a four star review in *The Guardian*.[110] One day, because there is no accounting for taste, I trust that people will look at *I'm Not Feeling Myself Tonight!* and see all the indications of a great film maker. You know I'm joking.

---

109   *The Dark Side,* October/November 1994
110   9th June, 2014

IV

"Be ye never so high, the law is above you."
~ Thomas Fuller ~

Tallulah Bankhead, whose opinion of diarists I have already quoted, is also supposed to have said, 'Cocaine isn't habit-forming and I know because I've been taking it for years.'[111] The perceived joke here isn't a joke to me because I, too, took cocaine for years, but kicked the habit. Beginning with the two years that Doug was in my house, running my business into the ground, the thought of coke rarely crossed my mind. The rarity of sampling Doug's product, usually done when my visitors were clawing the walls for any kind of stimulant, warranted a note in my diary. The product wasn't good. As police seizures went up in the first decade of the 21st century, the quality of cocaine went down. 80% pure in my day, gak was now rumoured to be only 20% the real thing. New dealers like Doug had to contend with dissatisfied customers, another reason for him to stay in his room.

Warren, the dealer in an even worse predicament than Doug, came to me with the news that he had been told by his solicitor (who was also, I need hardly add, one of my former clients) to expect a maximum four year sentence. Warren wanted from me a deposition, which he dictated. I found myself assuring the court that Warren intended to give up his wicked ways in favour of an engineering course. In reality this course was news to me. Several other upstanding citizens wrote similar pieces of fiction. In his summing-up the Crown Court judge said that he had taken into account Warren's hard life, depression and agoraphobia, and had been favourably impressed by the depositions he had read.

He gave Warren a twelve month sentence suspended for two years. As far as I am aware, Warren resumed dealing as soon as he switched his mobile phone back on. He sold first-rate skunk and sometimes he could acquire a rare and very popular type of resin called pollen. I continued buying from Warren for the next three years. I never really liked him but I had to admire how he played the system. Doug, on the other hand, had turned out to be another of those who couldn't handle temptation. I told him that the time had come for him to move on. His departure freed up a room for Eli to become a permanent fixture.

Back from his Grand Tour, Yuri had realised that his future lay in law. Even while he was studying, the support he gave me in my courtroom battle with Naim was inestimable. I wish I could use Yuri's real name in this

---

111 *Pentimento: A Book of Portraits* by Lillian Hellman (New York: Little, Brown, 1973)

acknowledgment of his kindness; but he keeps a low profile and an association with this tawdry memoir is the last thing he would want. It's probable that, during the first two years of my litigation, I entered another of my smug periods. One of Naim's claims was a 130 page stream of consciousness WITH LOTS OF WORDS IN CAPITAL LETTERS. Even after Naim had been directed to reduce the claim to ten pages, it remained unintelligible. On two occasions the recorder told Naim he was wasting the court's time. In his impotent fury Naim informed my local council that I should be investigated for an environmental infringement. I only found out about this when the letter from the council, stating that it was taking no action against me, was accidentally sent to my own address. I thought that Naim was not far off a mental breakdown. I was wrong. He was preparing to marshal his troops and strike back with all the self-righteous vigour and brutality of the Duke of Cumberland at Culloden. Another McGillivray would fall in battle.

Bernardo left my house because, like Alex before him, he had amassed so much money while he had been paying my peppercorn rent that he could afford a deposit for his own flat. We gave him a farewell party. 'Yuri made a "Goodbye, Bernardo" banner and blew up balloons,' I wrote. 'We knocked back a lot of wine and then Yuri sourced some Charlie. It wasn't very good. We pushed back the furniture and had a bop. The farewell fuck I had planned with Bernardo was perfect. He was sitting on my cock and came with no hands like a model in a Kristen Bjorn movie. I felt very sad about his departure.' (Have no regrets on our behalf. Bernardo and I were to stay in touch.)

At the time of writing this book it appears that my long career as a horror icon (I didn't invent that term, Alan Jones did) may be over. I fell out with Keith Claxton because he didn't approve of the way in which I tried to join together the seven short films we made together to produce a feature film called *Worst Fears*. Unwisely we attempted to make one more short subject together. It was a failure and it remains unfinished. It is unlikely ever to be removed from the cutting room shelf.

I have continued, however, as a backroom boy in the world of comedy. The first big hit on which I collaborated with Julian Clary was *Lord of the Mince*. The show was built around my suggestion that Julian should claim he had psychic powers. We worked with a conjuror who taught Julian a trick not dissimilar to one used by Derren Brown. While we were in Edinburgh the reviews were poisonous. But the tour that developed was a huge success, extended for months, both in the UK and Australia, and then filmed for a DVD release. I suppose that, assuming I can still come up with the ideas, I may have a job for life. Then again, I wouldn't put money on it.

The last dealings I had with Marianne Stone, the woman who had been part of my life, one way or another, since I had seen her in *The Good*

Companions in 1957, were in the summer of 2009. A friend at the British Film Institute told me that its archive held a copy of *Escape Dangerous*, a 1947 film in which Marianne played her first and only leading role opposite her future husband Peter Noble. Something told me she would want to see it. I was mistaken. The one-off screening at the BFI's office went ahead for the benefit of me, Marianne's daughters and a few friends. Marianne died four months later on 21ˢᵗ December. I officiated at her funeral and introduced the song 'You and I' by Michael Feinstein, which also had been played at Peter's service. Earlier there had been a discussion as to whether this song was too slushy. In the event it reduced everyone to floods of tears, an unforgettable memorial to one of the great ladies of British cinema.

My outlaw life went on in that I was still in touch with my former clients. 'Tadzio arrived with Mozartkügeln,' I recorded. 'After being disappointed by Doug, he took up with Boy George's dealer, an old fool who entrusted his ill-gotten gains to a pre-op transsexual. The two of them went to the US, where he/she absconded with all of the old fool's cash. He returned to the UK £70,000 lighter and has now disappeared.' There was also a party reminiscent of the old days: 'It was a surprising mix. Eli appeared briefly with a strange girl. Yuri and Bradley were both here. They had been ordered out of the pub next door for being aggressive. Manuel arrived and announced he hasn't had sex for a year. Later Manuel, Bradley and I discussed the Bruce tragedy. He would have done it anyway, we decided.

'The biggest surprise guest was [pornographer] Dominic Ford. He had told me he was in London and I had invited him, never thinking he would come. By the time he arrived, we were utterly smashed. We got out the 3D specs and looked at his stereoscopic porn in *QX Men*. Big fun. Dominic missed the last tube and I got him a minicab. More people arrived at 1am. Dancing ensued and a *QX* journalist did the entire Bananarama routine for "Venus." I think I packed it in around 3am, but I could hear the party continuing long after that.

At this time I was still up for sex. I ask you to believe that I wasn't on the prowl for it. It came to me. Alex invited me to a party at which I was approached by Mansoor: 'I suggested dinner,' I wrote, 'and Mansoor took me to a very basic Pakistani restaurant in Euston. I was obviously being auditioned and I failed on every count. He's a textbook, guilt-ridden, gay Muslim, who thinks he's going to Hell. His sisters in Pakistan have arranged for him to be married next year. He's met his bride-to-be. "She's not very pretty," he said. He asked me a lot of questions: "Do you believe in God?" The more honest I was, the more despondent he became. It was clearly all over before the bill came.'

As far as dating was concerned, I felt much more at home at The Cally sauna; but my bolt-hole came under threat when briefly it became the subject of national scandal. The front page headline of the *Islington Gazette* on 24th June, 2010, was 'POOL IS GAY CRUISING HOTSPOT', a story sufficiently spicy to be picked up the following day by the *Daily Telegraph*. 'FAMILIES' ANGER AT GAY RATING FOR POOL' was the paper's take on this tosh. I picked it apart in the August issue of *QX Men*. 'Gay men have fumble in sauna', isn't a story, I pointed out. The angle here was that the sauna had been awarded four stars out of a five on a gay cruising website. The news reports, which implied that gay men were having sex in full view of small children rather than in a locked room to which families had no access, were disgracefully homophobic; but they frightened the local council into making the rule that swimwear must be worn in the sauna at all times. For a long time I remained a regular at The Cally because the swimwear rule boosted the sexual excitement to an even greater degree. Erections could now be tucked out of sight the moment before a member of staff poked his head around the door.

Naim changed the rules of our legal thrusting and parrying when he turned up to court with a barrister, a genial old bumbler who assured yet another frustrated judge that a new and succinct claim would be presented. It arrived at my house a couple of weeks later and it took me all my courage to rip open the envelope. Inside was basically the same list of complaints, minus the more preposterous ones, re-phrased in legal language. The claim had been reduced from £18,000 to £11,230. 'Offer £10,000,' advised Yuri. 'I'm unwilling to do that,' I wrote, 'because I'm stubborn and I won't let him get the better of me.' This was to be the most expensive decision of my life.

When we returned to court, Judge Number Twelve, the sternest to date, made a list of directions including the appointment of an expert witness to testify as to the state of the Moroccan property market. 'This is getting out of hand,' I thought. All I could think of to say was that I intended to seek legal representation. I sought advice at *QX* because the magazine's lawyers were Mishcon de Reya, a firm whose very name was enough to instil terror in an adversary. Even though a warning letter headed by this outfit's insignia might cost £1,000, it was worth every penny. But I allowed myself to be talked into instructing a considerably less prestigious solicitor. He was an addle-brained scene queen, who was periodically photographed, wearing a leather vest and embracing half-naked twinks, in *QX* itself. I shall call him, in honour of Charles Dickens' 'attorney of no good repute', Sampson Brass.

Brass convinced me that I must not settle because, after a settlement, Naim could continue to harass me through a third party. While I wrote him the first of what were to be many four-figure cheques, Brass assured me that we would hammer the opposition. He recommended that I hire, for a further £3,000 + VAT, a 'very tough' counsel, who would 'make the application to strike for abuse of process at the outset.' The counsel was a rotund,

Rumpole-like windbag who, like everyone else appointed to adjudicate this revenge drama, had only a passing acquaintance with its details. He failed to have the claim struck out because there was indeed a case to answer. I had not provided Naim with adequate financial records. In an instant the tables had been turned. I now faced the prospect of a two-day trial, the costs of which could reduce me to penury.

It was while I was trying to make arrangements to sell my house to pay the legal bills that I foresaw appearing in my inbox until the end of my days that I was struck by that awful, incontrovertible truth that must have occurred to Bruce: life is not worth living. In my case I knew as a certainty that I did not want to sell my house of pleasure and give the proceeds to people I despised. No other considerations existed when I wrote in my diary, 'For the first time I am thinking of putting my affairs in order before taking my life. I am near breaking point. I can fully understand why Mary Millington took the easy way out.'

Among the many things I had in common with the sex goddess Millington were *I'm Not Feeling Myself Tonight*, cocaine, a hatred of censorship, and innumeracy. She stated in one of the suicide notes she left in 1979 that the tax man was hounding her for £200,000. She also stated, 'I have never liked people, only animals.'[112] This is where we differed. I was fortunate enough to have friends I liked very much indeed. It was because of these friends that I am still here. Julian Clary told me I would not be homeless because I could stay in his house in Kent; Alex took me on holiday to Istanbul; and Yuri informed me that in future he would accompany me on all my visits to Sampson Brass. By the end of 2010 I was on Prozac, whose effects were immediate. I was suddenly aware of considerations other than self-destruction, notably that suicide is a heartless slap in the face to those left behind. Brass asked the court for an adjournment, planning to use the extra time to negotiate the settlement he previously had repudiated. He blamed me for the course the case had taken. 'Never mind Naim and me, it's now Brass and me who are in opposition,' I wrote. 'I wonder whether I could cope with this if it weren't for Prozac?'

Even drug-numbed despair could not staunch my creativity. When I realised that I had three weeks with nothing to do, I knew immediately how I must fill them, by completing *The Farndale/Peter Pan*, left unfinished nearly ten years earlier. I gave myself the impetus to complete the task in the allotted time by announcing my intention on a newish social media network called Facebook. The positive response encouraged me and I continued writing, almost without a break, until the play was finished just over two weeks later. It seemed as though the time was right for the Farndale Ladies to make their comeback. But it transpired that the very opposite was true.

---

112   *Come Play with Me* by Simon Sheridan (Guildford, Surrey: FAB Press, 1999)

In 2013 a young company premiered *The Play That Goes Wrong*, a country house murder mystery as performed by incompetent amateurs. It was a box office sensation, hailed by critics as an entirely new form of comedy, and later it won a Best 'New' Comedy award, thus ensuring that the Farndale Ladies never will make their comeback and that their production of *Peter Pan* never will be staged. Forgive me for writing the word 'new' thus. I owe it to the dear departed Walter Zerlin Jnr. to state for the record that he and I are the onlie begetters of this style of comedy of errors. Yes, all right. Before us there was Shakespeare, whose rude mechanicals got it wrong in *A Midsummer Night's Dream*. How I resented the authors of *The Play That Goes Wrong* for throwing this in my face when we met. It sounded such a rehearsed defence. But now I have matured to such an extent that I wish them well. Walter and I had a good innings.

Toby, the most lawless lawyer of the Friday night parties, suggested in 2010 that I should have a reunion on my birthday. At this time I was in a very bad way indeed and I thought a party wouldn't do me any harm. I decided to make an event of it and created installations. Two easels bore montages of photos. For many of my clients it came as a revelation that my camera had been clicking throughout the years of craziness. I also covered the walls of my living room with the pages from my diary that recorded each and every salon.

A lot of people were conspicuous by their absence. They had moved on and wanted no reminder of their former indiscretions. Miranda had cleaned up her act and severed all connections to her past. She didn't even respond to my invitation. Ricky had become a successful author, remarkable in that the piece he submitted to *Scapegoat* was by and large illiterate. After reinventing himself as a muscleman, David Dan Joe had gone bananas on crystal meth, but was now clean and sober. Daniel, on the other hand, didn't come because he was still a coke addict and I was no longer a coke dealer. The party was none the less a night to remember and a proper act of closure. Those who did come – my good friends Dafydd, Tadzio, Alex and so many people I can't name – had a delightful evening reminiscing about the salons that had held us in their thrall a decade earlier. Come on, we were younger! We came through it! We're still here! Let's celebrate!

Human nature being what it is, the call went up for supplies. I'm not sure where they came from, but probably the newer housemates, like Yuri and Bradley, were responsible. The sniffage was in circulation until about 4am. It was really nothing like the old days. But the old days were such fun that we so wanted to believe they had returned.

OVER

V

"I'm a b-a-a-a-d boy."
~ Lou Costello ~

On 13th April, 2011, when he delivered my latest order of weed, Warren told me that he was retiring from the drug trade. On 20th May, when he bought an eighth from me, a *QX* colleague became my last ever client. This time there would be no second thoughts, no backsliding; it really was the end. I had been dealing for thirteen years. Was I going to continue until I was jailed, or toothless, or the worst possible option, a figure of fun, the oldest dealer in town? The answer to all these questions would in all honesty be yes if there had been no other demands on my time. But there were.

Throughout 2011, and through no one's fault but my own, I was committed to driving my petty quarrel with Naim to its bitter, dismal, utterly demoralising conclusion. There were meetings lasting hours and hours and hours, which netted tens of thousands of pounds for Brass and Rumpole, but precisely nil for Yuri, who got me through them. On one particularly distressing day, he suggested we cheer ourselves up by playing Lingo Bingo, which required us to make a list of legal clichés and then tick them off as my advocates spouted them. If it were not for Yuri and Prozac, I would not be here today.

My accounts proved to be in such debatable disarray that it was not a matter of whether we would have to settle, it was a matter of how much we would settle for. By the summer Naim and I had become pawns in the game. Our lawyers bluffed and counterbluffed each other in a game of chicken. Who would be the first to concede? What fascinated me was the way in which a claim that originally had required me to account for every last dirham spent on a table napkin ended in a completely arbitrary bargain, which bore no relation whatever to the alleged losses Naim had suffered.

Naim's lawyer demanded a very precise £18,423.23. Mine offered a nice, round £10,000. Naim's countered with £15,423.23. We raised our offer to £12,500 including a £5k down payment. And so the game was played for the rest of the year until Naim accepted £13,250. After five years it was over. But please bear in mind that, if you go to court in a dispute over monies owed, the legal process might well end like mine: a settlement plucked out of the air that gives satisfaction to neither party, followed by the *coup de grâce*, an astronomical legal bill out of all proportion to the original claim. I have no idea what Naim paid in order to secure his pound of flesh, but I doubt it brought him any pleasure. There was a time during our dispute when I wanted Naim to die. Today I feel guilty about that. A really bad accident would have been quite sufficient.

Because I was no longer a drug dealer, I could not fork out £13,250. I asked Julian Clary to lend the money to me and it was in my bank within days. It is a little-known fact that I am basically Julian's skivvy. I will do anything for him and this includes running to the shop to buy him twenty Benson & Hedges. This is because the man has a heart of gold and he has extricated me not from one jam but many. He has been called a camp old anachronism, but I will not brook any criticism of him. He saved me from the gutter that has been beckoning me since I was born.

I cannot begin to describe the fun that Julian and I have had in recent years. In 2012 we devised a show, *Position Vacant, Apply Within,* which was as near to comic genius as makes no odds. The conceit was that Julian was looking for a 'husband', civil partnerships having been recognised in the UK since 2005. In each town to which the show toured, Julian brought men out of the audience and then, via *Sticky Moments*-style games, eliminated them until he was left with a finalist, whom he married. It just so happened that rehearsals for this show were interrupted by another game show, *Celebrity Big Brother,* for which Julian had agreed to participate. He was the last man standing and this did the bookings for *Position Vacant* no harm. The show toured until 2014 and included a sold-out London gig for which Julian demanded six dancing boys in Latex shorts. I sat there in the palatial Palace theatre thinking that life doesn't get much better than this.

Position Vacant introduced a song, 'Cool to be Queer,' which addressed the difficulties faced by LGBT people in countries that do not consider them to be people. Fans wanted to know how they could access the song and, before someone could say, 'Wait a minute, David McGillivray cannot direct a film to save his life,' I was shooting another pop video. Unlike my earlier attempts, it was a modest success and it continues to rack up hits on YouTube. The song is now part of Julian's repertoire. It is hard for a gay man of my age, for whom discrimination and death seems like only yesterday, to believe that we have had to change its lyrics. 'We're legal now and *almost* fit to wed' has become '*even* fit to wed.' In 1971 same sex marriage seemed such an unlikely prospect that nobody in the Gay Liberation Front thought that it was worth including in the group's list of equality demands.

I have remained a film maker because of my association with another gay icon, Peter de Rome. When the British Film Institute was planning to release some of Peter's short films on a DVD, the BFI's Brian Robinson asked me if I'd like to write some accompanying notes. I told him that I would prefer to make a film. This was set up the way I like it, very quickly. Within two months I was in New York making *Fragments.* I wanted my best mate, Alex, to direct it; but by this time he had become a hot shot TV documentarist and was flitting from one international trouble spot to another. I gave the director credit to my cameraman; but I directed every inch of *Fragments,* and Alex was the éminence grise throughout post-production. Brian Robinson loved it and wanted us to make it longer. He immediately programmed it for the 2012 London Lesbian & Gay Film Festival and BFI members snapped up every seat before tickets went on general sale.

While I was shooting *Fragments* I knew that I was going to make another film with Peter, one that established him as the earliest known pioneer of gay porn, bravely at work from the 1960s, when both pornography and homosexuality were illegal almost throughout the world. *Peter de Rome: Grandfather of Gay Porn* was shot here, there and everywhere, throughout 2012 and into 2013, while Peter was suffering all kinds of debilitating illnesses. But he, too, wanted his story to be told. No matter what suggestion I made to him ('Do you want to go to Barcelona to meet Kristen Bjorn?'), he would just say, 'Sure.'

Alex sent the film to the 2014 Sheffield Doc/Fest, one of the world's most prestigious showcases for new documentaries. I thought, well, fat chance. But it was accepted. Peter flew to the UK for what should have been the first in a string of international premieres at which he would have been fêted and lionised. But shortly after his arrival, he collapsed in the street and was taken to hospital. He had leukaemia. We telephoned Peter from Sheffield to tell him that the film had had a good reception. He died a fortnight later, one week short of his 90th birthday. I became Peter's proxy at film festivals, telling audiences, 'Peter is not just a part of gay porn history, or gay history, he is a part of history.' He has inspired me to carry on making movies. I have loved them since I was four and a half, and it's hardly likely I'm going to fall out of love with them now, even the ones with lots of explosions, aimed at 14-year-olds.

I could continue to write about my life up until the present day, but I feel that I'm not sufficiently distanced from it. Perhaps I'll tell you about that later. Suffice it to say that I have been allowed to continue making an exhibition of myself throughout my errant youth, middle age and incipient dotage. What are we to make of this harum-scarum, beer-and-skittles, skin-of-my-teeth life? Naturally I know what I make of it. It has been a rich, full life, I wouldn't change any of it, and that includes the drugs. Well, actually, not so much the drugs, which of course are not good for you, but the drug culture, which from my teenage years offered me the world behind the curtain, a thrilling alternative to the norm. Unfortunately you can't have one without the other.

I have no contrition. I'm not alone here. Even former substance abuser Robert Downey Jnr., by comparison to whom I am a bumbling amateur, an absolute beginner, has no regrets, even about his rehab and 36 month jail sentence. He looks back to when he was out of his mind on mushrooms and rolling around in his friend's yard in Topanga and all he says, in his adorable American way, is 'Yeah, man!'[113] I look back on similar evenings, but in a terraced house in King's Cross, and my only regret is that we don't do them any more. I still miss them.

Does this make me a bad person? I do hope so. I genuinely believe that I'm not rotten to the core. Don't make me bring up the tireless charity work again, please. I hold my hands up to being sarcastic, bloody-minded and occasionally hurtful, and Yuri, who gave me hour upon hour of his wisdom and got precious little in return, thinks I'm selfish. But I was at my most popular when I was a drug dealer. I was very good at the job and everyone loved me. What we were doing was harmful in that we (and several million others) were links in a chain that reached back to the third world, where the drug trade most certainly damages and indeed ends lives. But the situation wouldn't exist if drugs were legal. This argument is unlikely to be settled in our lifetime. But if same sex marriage can be legalised in Texas, truly anything is possible.

Where the reader is concerned, I hope that he or she will look indulgently upon a disordered life lived as a result of taking 'the road less traveled' and, in particular, gain something from the stories about a subculture that flourished briefly and reasonably secretly while the Millennium Dome represented everything fine and decent about the end of a thousand years. That was my main incentive when I first sat down at the keyboard. But now, as I type the final words, I am all too aware that the truth of the stories is of course only the truth as I see it, the 137,000 words I chose to distil from the countless millions in my diaries. Of course I am intrigued by the idea that an editor could, after reading them all, interpret a completely different truth from the events, the places and the people I chose *not* to mention. Perhaps, as when a novel is adapted into a film, there can only be a sense here of the original, but I think it is still recognisable as my story. As opposed, say, to Martin Luther King's.

Let's not agonise over this. When all is said and done, my life has not mattered. I did not start a war, cure a disease, or (particularly significant in my case) inspire anyone to do anything they would not otherwise have considered. If what you have read has displeased you, I can assure you that you will soon forget all about it, and that life will go on.

"Do you think I can listen all day to such stuff?
Be off, or I'll kick you downstairs!"
~ Lewis Carroll ~

INDEX

Page references in **bold** refer exclusively to illustrations.

INDEX

INDEX

INDEX

INDEX

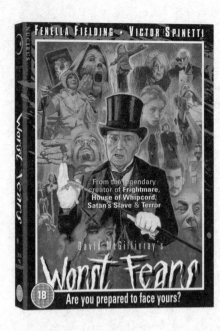

WORST FEARS

Director: Keith Claxton

Producer: David McGillivray

Country: GB

Year: 2015

Running Time: 97 minutes + Extras

DVD Format: PAL

Region: All

Seven nightmarish tales from legendary British horror film writer and producer **David McGillivray**: collaborator with Pete Walker and Norman J. Warren, and the fiendish screenwriter behind 1970s hits *House of Whipcord*, *Frightmare*, *House of Mortal Sin*, *Schizo*, *Satan's Slave* and *Terror*.

For the first time on DVD and featuring all-new material, *Worst Fears* is in the blood-soaked tradition of classic Hammer and Amicus anthologies, with a dash of BBC *Ghost Stories* and *Tales of the Unexpected*. Includes the award-winning *In the Place of the Dead*.

Filmed on location in Marrakech, Lisbon, Nice and London, the remarkable cast includes **Rebecca Santos** (*Seed of Chucky*), **Fenella Fielding** (*Carry On Screaming!*), **Rosie Alvarez** (*Casualty*), **Victor Spinetti** (*Help!*, *The Krays*), **Holly de Jong** (*The Last Horror Film*, *Electric Dreams*), **Sir Clement Freud** (*Chunky Meat*), **Anna Wing** (*Xtro*, *The Blood on Satan's Claw*, *EastEnders*), **Ben Pullen** (*Dark Knight*) – and **McGillivray** himself.

"The worst fears are those which you absolutely know will be borne out, but nobody else recognises – so you are alone with them."
– Consultant Psychiatrist

EXTRA FEATURES:

Horror Icon, the never-before-seen documentary edited and completed by Nucleus Films!

Facing His Fears – A new interview with producer and writer David McGillivray, talking candidly about the ideas behind the stories and their journey from page to screen.

Trailer, Bloopers, Deleted Scenes, Gallery, Booklet.

For more information or to order online visit Nucleus Films: **www.nucleusfilms.com**

SCALA CINEMA 1978-1993

Author: Jane Giles

Foreword: Stephen Woolley

Size: 375mm x 300mm

Binding: Hardback

Extent: 424 pages, illustrated throughout in colour

RRP: GB £75.00 / US $100.00

ISBN: 978-1-903254-98-1

Market: Cinema

SCALA CINEMA 1978-1993 is a gorgeous, oversized, extremely weighty and very entertaining illustrated book about the Scala Cinema, based on its iconic programmes. The most infamous and influential of all UK cinemas, the Scala's monthly programmes tell their own story about culture and society between 1978-1993, a post-punk/pre-internet period of significant change.

The Scala rose from the ashes of a defunct socialist collective on the site of an ancient concert hall and theatre in Fitzrovia. Pushed out of its premises by the arrival of Channel 4 television in 1981, the Scala moved to the Primatarium, a former picture palace and one-time rock venue within spitting distance of King's Cross station.

An atmospheric repertory cinema with its mysteriously rumbling auditorium and resident cats, people travelled to the Scala from all over the country to have their minds blown by its alchemical mix of Hollywood classics and cult movies, horror, Kung Fu, LGBT+, animation, silent comedy, Psychotronic and unclassifiable films, combined with live gigs and music club nights. Over a million people went through the doors of the Scala, and its reputation spread far and wide. A lone operator, the Scala closed down in 1993 following a perfect storm of lease expiry, the ravages of the recession… and a devastating court case.

Scala Cinema 1978-1993 features the complete collection of all 178 monthly programmes plus rare photographs and ephemera. It is also an in-depth and often outrageous time-travelling history uncovering deep roots and taking the reader behind the scenes of the Scala. This book is a must-have for fans of the legendary cinema, with appeal to anyone interested in film or the story of London in the 1980s.

For more information or to order visit the FAB Press web store: **www.fabpress.com**

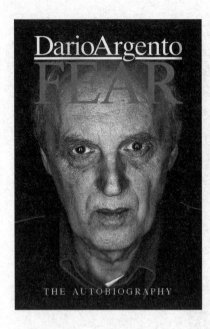

FEAR
The Autobiography of Dario Argento

Author: Dario Argento

Size: 234mm x 156mm

Binding: Hardback

Extent: 288 pages, including 32 pages of rare illustrations

RRP: GB £20.00 / US $30.00

ISBN: 978-1-913051-05-1

Market: Cinema / Autobiography

Dario Argento. To his legion of admirers he's a horror legend of the first magnitude. And to a host of his genre contemporaries – from **John Carpenter** and **Quentin Tarantino** to **John Landis** and **Luca Guadagnino** – he's a major inspiration and an icon.

For many years his name-above-the-title shockers like *Four Flies on Grey Velvet*, *Deep Red*, *Suspiria*, *Tenebrae* and *Opera* meant pure box-office gold to worldwide cinema audiences. Now the maverick auteur reveals all about his fascinating life, his grim obsessions, his talented family, his perverse dreams and his star-crossed work.

Fear lifts the lid on the trials and tribulations of Argento's glittering career during the Golden Era of Cinecittà. From his childhood mixing with glamorous Italian movie stars thanks to his well-connected entertainment industry family to his start in the fledgling field of cinema criticism, Argento divulges never-before-told anecdotes about growing up in La Dolce Vita Rome. Put on the popular cinema map when he co-wrote Spaghetti Western maestro Sergio Leone's masterpiece *Once Upon a Time in the West*, Argento suffered setbacks and humiliation making his debut feature *The Bird with the Crystal Plumage*. But when it turned into a monster global hit, Argento went from strength to strength, able to coast every controversy thrown at him as this scintillating memoir discloses with honesty and insight.

Adapted from the Italian translation, edited and annotated by Argento expert **Alan Jones**, a good friend of his for over 30 years, and illustrated with numerous never-before-seen photographs from his personal collection, the award-winning and critically acclaimed Master of Terror tells all. So put on your black leather gloves and start turning the pages of *Fear* for the answer to every question you've ever wanted to ask about the weird and wonderful world of Dario Argento.

For more information or to order visit the FAB Press web store: **www.fabpress.com**